Images of American Society

A History of the United States

Images of American Society

A History of the United States

VOLUME II

G. D. LILLIBRIDGE
California State University, Chico

HOUGHTON MIFFLIN COMPANY/BOSTON

Atlanta   Dallas   Geneva, Ill.   Hopewell, N.J.   Palo Alto   London

Acknowledgment is made for permission to reprint the following materials, alphabetically listed by authors:

From Nannie T. Alderson and Helena Huntington Smith, on pp. 101–102, *A Bride Goes West.* Copyright © 1942 by Farrar & Rinehart, Inc. Reprinted by permission of International Creative Management.

From Rupert Brooke, on p. 189, "The Soldier," from *The Collected Poems of Rupert Brooke.* Reprinted by permission of Dodd, Mead & Company.

From Ernest Hemingway, on p. 212, *A Farewell to Arms.* Reprinted by permission of Charles Scribner's Sons.

From Eric Lambert, on p. 264, *The Twenty Thousand Thieves.* Reprinted by permission of Frederick Muller Ltd.

From Barrie Pitt, on p. 190, *1918—The Last Act.* Reprinted by permission of Cassell and Company, Ltd.

From Bertrand Russell, on p. 206, *Mysticism and Logic.* Reprinted by permission of George Allen & Unwin Ltd.

From Siegfried Sassoon, on p. 191, "Suicide in the Trenches," from *Collected Poems* by Siegfried Sassoon. Copyright 1918 by E. P. Dutton and Co., copyright renewed 1946 by Siegfried Sassoon. All rights reserved. Reprinted by permission of the Viking Press, Inc. Reprinted also by permission of G. T. Sassoon.

Cover photo by George Malave/Stock, Boston

Printed in the U.S.A.

Library of Congress Catalog Card Number: 75–31017

ISBN: 0-395-21874-8

For Flo

Contents

Maps

Preface

Professor William McNeill remarked not long ago that an introductory course in history should be designed for citizens not professional historians. That seemed to me an eminently practical approach for an introductory American history. What I have attempted in this book, therefore, is to examine those major experiences, forces, and institutions that have occupied the time, energy, and lives of the American people and that *seem to me* to have most influenced us as a society, to have made us the kind of people we are today. I have sought to suggest a sense of humanity, a recognition that from the beginning this country has been made up of human beings who in terms of their own times and circumstances have suffered, agonized, exalted, loved, erred, lived, and died as human beings do in every age and time.

My concern has been with such powerful experiences as democracy, the frontier, war, and the city; with such forces as science, technology, and industry; with such institutions as the family and the church; with such interests as the arts, entertainment, and recreation; with such diverse fates as those of the immigrants, the blacks, and the Indians. I have tried to note the impact of all these upon the lives of Americans, and how their lives have been changed as a consequence. It has been my experience that this approach not only greatly appeals to students but also offers them a broad perspective enabling them to understand better the society in which they live.

As I have painfully discovered, it is not easy to organize such material so that one gets a sense of progression and time. The book is divided into four broad time periods that roughly cover (1) the seventeenth and eighteenth centuries, (2) the early life of the new Republic up to the Civil War, (3) developments from the Civil War to World War I, and (4) the period from 1920 to the present. Each chapter is preceded by a Spirit of the Times and followed by a Profile. I have used the Spirit of the Times to illuminate the chapter by focusing on a particular aspect of life during the period. I have deliberately avoided any set pattern to these, and they vary widely in approach. In each Profile I have chosen an individual, most of them well known but some unknown to the reader, and have provided a brief biographical sketch. The purpose of the Profile has been to use the life of one person to suggest the topic of the chapter and at the same time to remind the reader of the fact that American history is in the last analysis the story of individual human beings—the great and the obscure alike.

This is a personal book in some respects. It reflects, for example, my general optimism about the course of American affairs—no mean feat in these times. I become gloomy on many occasions as I look at the record of the past and the chronicle of the present, but in the long haul I see much to be hopeful about in the history of this country and the character of its people, and I have what may be an old-fashioned if wavering confidence that things will get better. At the same time, however, I have every conviction that we will always be plagued by problems and cursed with troubles that arise from the frailty of human beings. There may be those who believe that by genetic or legislative engineering, or by revolutionary revisions, we will eventually remove all the ills that flesh is heir to, but I am not one of those people. Being any kind of optimist at all about the human prospect, to say nothing of the American one, thus leads one to emphasize the good that lies in human achievement. Because as Americans we have certain marks on our record—and I try to point these out—is no reason for failing to take pride in our achievements.

While it is impossible for us to avoid passing judgments on the Americans of the past, we should recognize that these judgments are not based on any superior moral wisdom, but rather upon the accumulation of experience and knowledge that we have access to but that of course was not available to those in the past. What I am suggesting is that we can at least try to understand the men and women of the past in terms of the circumstances in which they found themselves—circumstances which did not include the gift of viewing themselves from the vantage point of the twentieth century. I am not, for example, inclined to regard myself as morally superior to Thomas Jefferson because he thought blacks unequal to whites and I do not. I am more inclined to praise people for their accomplishments than to condemn them for their failures, though the latter should not be ignored. Hence my general optimism.

This book is a personal one also because it reflects my long interest in the image other peoples have held of America and the impact this country has had on other societies throughout the world. I think our understanding of ourselves is greatly enhanced by knowing what others think of us, even though their views may not coincide with the facts as we see them. Throughout this book, therefore, I have tried to use this theme to advantage.

Then, too, this book is a personal one in that here and there I have relied on experiences and associations special to me. Thus in the Spirit of the Times for the chapter on immigration, the words of Stephen Yakich on why he came to America were drawn from a taped interview I made with him, a man who had wandered and worked his way across America, married relatively late in life, and had a son who eventually married one of my daughters. The Profile of Phillip Mizel in the same chapter is also on a man I knew most of my life—the father of my oldest and closest friend. The Profile of Fred Burton in the chapter on World War II deals with a close friend of my youth whose diary and letters to me and to his family I have used.

This raises a point about the Profiles. Most of these discuss well-known people whose influence in American life was considerable. But a number are of Americans not generally known, yet whose lives exemplify certain experiences. Not many of us are familiar with Eliza Pinckney or Nannie Alderson, for example, and only friends and relatives know of Phillip Mizel or Fred Burton, but all in their own way were important Americans. And recognition of their importance enhances our realization of the importance of all Americans in the history of this country.

* * *

A number of colleagues in other institutions read all or part of the manuscript. I am very grateful to them for their criticisms, some of which were sharp and relentless, all of which were justified and productive. I have tried to respond to these to the best of my ability, and the book is, in my view, enormously improved as a consequence. My gratitude is therefore extended to: Gerald Danzer, the University of Illinois; Emil B. Jones, American River College; Robert McColley, the University of Illinois; Allan R. Millett, Ohio State University; J. Carroll Moody, Northern Illinois University; Stephen B. Oates, the University of Massachusetts; and J. V. Reese, Texas Tech University. I owe a special debt of gratitude to a number of my colleagues at California State University, Chico. During a period when I fell behind in my work because of the terminal illness of my mother, my dear friend Carl Hein did the basic draft for the chapters on Reconstruction and the black American. Lois Christensen did the Instructor's Manual, tested material on her students, and gave me frequent advice. Some of my colleagues read extensive parts of the manuscript and offered fruitful suggestions for improvement. Carl Hein read much of the manuscript and I benefited by his broader world view of America. William Hutchinson and Clarence McIntosh read the chapter on the last frontiers and made numerous suggestions of value to which I tried to respond. I am also especially grateful to two old and dear friends who read large portions of the manuscript on their own time, and encouraged me to persist in spite of their criticisms: Merle Curti, Frederick Jackson Turner Professor of History Emeritus at the University of Wisconsin; and the late Bert James Loewenberg, Professor of History Emeritus at Sarah Lawrence College.

In all instances, however, I bear sole responsibility for errors of fact, incautious judgments, slippery interpretations, and dangling participles.

Finally, I must note that any claims to originality must rest on the general approach I have taken (following Professor McNeill's suggestion) and on my utilization of such devices as The Spirit of the Times and the Profile. For, like most who attempt to cover so much ground, I have had to rely on the work of others. The Selected Reading at the end of the book includes most of the major sources from which I culled material in the development of my interpretation.

G. D. LILLIBRIDGE
California State University, Chico

Images of American Society

A History of the United States

Part One

THE MARCH INTO MODERN TIMES

1865–1918

1865	Thirteenth Amendment
1867	Alaska purchased; Reconstruction Acts passed; Grange organized
1868	Impeachment of Andrew Johnson failed; fourteenth amendment
1869	Knights of Labor organized; Transcontinental railroad completed
1870	Fifteenth Amendment
1873	Panic and depression
1876	Telephone invented
1879	Standard Oil Trust organized
1881	Chinese Exclusion Act passed; President Garfield assassinated
1886	American Federation of Labor founded; Haymarket Affair
1887	Interstate Commerce Act to regulate interstate carriers
1890	Populist party organized; Sherman Antitrust Act
1893	Panic and depression
1894	Pullman Strike
1896	*Plessy* v. *Ferguson* upheld separate but equal doctrine
1898	Hawaii annexed; war with Spain; Philippines acquired
1900	United States Steel Corporation formed
1901	McKinley assassinated; Theodore Roosevelt became President
1902	National Reclamation Act to provide irrigation and conservation
1903	Panama Canal begun; Ford began to manufacture automobiles; Wright brothers' flight at Kitty Hawk, North Carolina
1906	Hepburn Act to fix railroad rates; Pure Food and Drug Act; Meat Inspection Act
1912	Progressive campaign; Wilson elected
1913	Department of Labor established; Federal Reserve System established; Sixteenth and Seventeenth Amendments
1914	Underwood Tariff; Clayton Antitrust Act; Federal Trade Commission Act; Ford began "continuous flow production"
1917–1918	United States in World War I

Chapter 1
THE CRISIS OF RECONSTRUCTION

The Spirit of the Times
MYTH VERSUS REALITY

The era of Reconstruction after the Civil War has long loomed in the public mind, North as well as South, as a tragedy of horrors. Certainly no one would look upon this period as a pleasant romp of jovial reconciliation between victors and vanquished. And the experience did indeed leave lasting scars in American society. But it is also true that in the long record of rebellions fought and lost, the treatment of the losers has often been marked by a ferocity of oppression and punishment not found in the aftermath of the American Civil War.

Punishment for those Confederates involved in the war, the rank-and-file as well as the leadership, was mild or nonexistent. Ordinary soldiers and supporters of the Confederacy achieved full pardon by simply taking an oath of allegiance. Furthermore, no military officers were ever arrested or brought to trial for treason. A few public officials were arrested—including Jefferson Davis, the Confederate President—but none were brought to trial and all except Davis, who remained in prison for almost two years, were shortly released. By the 1870s, in fact, Congress had issued a blanket pardon for all but a few, and former Confederate leaders were shortly holding local, state, and national offices again—not exactly a scene of stern retribution.

Brutal punishment of the losers was not an element in Reconstruction. Nor was destructive exploitation of a defeated and helpless people. It used to be argued that the South, placed under military occupation, was turned over to Northern carpetbaggers, Southern scalawags, and freed blacks now possessed of political rights under the Fourteenth and Fifteenth Amendments who all embarked upon an orgy of corruption and greed for their own enrichment. No one would deny that mistakes were made in the administration of the Reconstruction governments, that corruption was present, that self-serving operators took advantage of the economic confusion of the times.

But corruption was a fact of national political life in the years after the Civil War, and total corruption in the South was minor compared to the large-scale corruption going on elsewhere in the country. The Tweed Ring drained more from

Reconstruction. *The Christian ideal as envisioned by Horatio Bateman was never realized.*

the public till in New York City than filled the pockets of all malefactors in the South. Moreover, although blacks held office, their influence was never dominant except for a brief period in two Southern states. And of those blacks who served the majority were able men who displayed no evidence of vindictiveness toward whites. Far from ruining social and political life, the Reconstruction governments initiated important reforms and began many projects of improvement. Social services were expanded and public education was greatly extended. Although economic development was slow, especially in comparison to national growth, the Southern economy began to recover. Agriculture began its march back toward prewar levels of productivity. Railroad construction totaled seven thousand miles of track, and manufacturing and mining gains in tobacco, textiles, coal, and iron were made. By the official end of Reconstruction rule in 1877, conditions had greatly improved rather than deteriorated. The South, of course, remained behind the rest of the nation in economic growth, but this had been true in the prewar era as well.

Finally, it should be noted that military occupation itself was relatively mild and certainly did not result in violent suppression of the white population. In fact, the violence that occurred under Reconstruction came primarily from those whites who most resented the political role thrust upon blacks. Secret societies arose, the best-known of which was the Ku Klux Klan, which sought by terrorist tactics to drive blacks out of politics. Blacks were threatened and terrified by mysterious hooded nightriders, they were beaten and whipped, and hundreds were brutally murdered. Federal troops were used to help the federal government break up the Klan. But this force was of a completely different nature than that used by the Klan to force blacks from political life in the South.

Reconstruction can indeed be called a tragedy. No myth here. But the tragedy lay not in any presumed repression of the South or punishment for those who fought in the war or supported the Confederacy. Nor did it lie in the brutal exploitation of the vanquished by the victors. Its tragedy lay in the failure to achieve some kind of social, economic, and political integration of blacks into the life of the South—and indeed the nation—on terms acceptable to both blacks and whites, North and South alike. This failure was the tragic reality of the Reconstruction era, and responsibility for it lay with all Americans. If the majority of Americans by the 1870s had given up on the implementation of those rights granted blacks by the Fourteenth and Fifteenth Amendments, at least these protections were now in the law of the land for subsequent generations to draw upon.

The Reconstruction Period

The Confederate vision of an Athenian democracy, Southern-style, resting on white citizenship and black slavery, vanished at Appomattox Courthouse on April 9, 1865. Although slavery died, for American blacks the century to come was to be a long winter of disappointment, frustration, and despair. Yet at its beginning was a period of hope, the dozen turbulent years known as the Reconstruction. This era briefly held out the possibility that a genuine political and social revolution might be imposed upon the South, one that would alter the terms and conditions of livelihood and therefore the status of the black population. But Reconstruction proved to be a revolution that failed to ignite. After a generation, the status of the blacks was gradually reaffirmed at a level only somewhat short of actual legal slavery. White attitudes toward the blacks did not change. The national view of the place of the black in society became indistinguishable from the Southern view; and there was a successful counter-revolution in race relations.

The plight of the South after Appomattox was grievous for both its white and its black populations. Everywhere roads, wharves, machinery, buildings, and even land were destroyed or run down through neglect. Specie and loans were almost impossible to secure. Organized authority vanished in many areas and banditry was rife. Hundreds of thousands of blacks quit their rooted existence on farms and plantations and in cities and towns. Confederate veterans straggled home from the remnants of their armies and from Northern prisons, and picked up as best they could their former lives. Demoralization of the white ruling class accompanied its loss of political power. Southern society had apparently gone with the wind. What forces would move into the political and economic vacuum of the South?

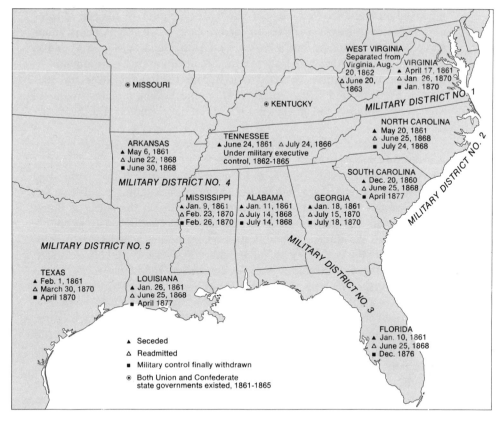

MISSOURI

WEST VIRGINIA
Separated from
Virginia, Aug.
20, 1862
△ June 20,
1863

VIRGINIA
▲ April 17, 1861
△ Jan. 26, 1870
■ Jan. 1870

MILITARY DISTRICT NO. 1

KENTUCKY

NORTH CAROLINA
▲ May 20, 1861
△ June 25, 1868
■ July 24, 1868

ARKANSAS
▲ May 6, 1861
△ June 22, 1868
■ June 30, 1868

TENNESSEE
▲ June 24, 1861   △ July 24, 1866
Under military executive
control, 1862-1865

MILITARY DISTRICT NO. 2

SOUTH CAROLINA
▲ Dec. 20, 1860
△ June 25, 1868
■ April 1877

MILITARY DISTRICT NO. 4

MISSISSIPPI
▲ Jan. 9, 1861
△ Feb. 23, 1870
■ Feb. 26, 1870

ALABAMA
▲ Jan. 11, 1861
△ July 14, 1868
■ July 14, 1868

GEORGIA
▲ Jan. 18, 1861
△ July 15, 1870
■ July 18, 1870

MILITARY DISTRICT NO. 3

MILITARY DISTRICT NO. 5

TEXAS
▲ Feb. 1, 1861
△ March 30, 1870
■ April 1870

LOUISIANA
▲ Jan. 26, 1861
△ June 25, 1868
■ April 1877

FLORIDA
▲ Jan. 10, 1861
△ June 25, 1868
■ Dec. 1876

▲ Seceded
△ Readmitted
■ Military control finally withdrawn
⊛ Both Union and Confederate
state governments existed, 1861-1865

RECONSTRUCTION, 1865–1877

Lincoln's plans for the South unfolded after his Emancipation Proclamation of January 1, 1863. He later won Congressional approval for the Thirteenth Amendment and universal emancipation, but he did not ask that blacks be given citizenship and equal rights. Rather, in December 1863 he put forth his Ten-Percent Plan, issued as an executive proclamation of amnesty and Reconstruction. This plan required that if a minimum of ten percent of the qualified voters of 1860 would take an oath of allegiance to the Union, their state might set up a state government, the President would recognize it, and readmission of the state to the Union would follow. Lincoln's announced policy was one of rapid reconciliation with the Southern states. But he had no opportunity to put it into effect. His assassination immediately after the war has left only speculation about how Lincoln would have adjusted the renewed Union with the subsequent demands for black equality.

Johnson versus the Radical Republicans After Lincoln's assassination, President Andrew Johnson took over the Ten-Percent Plan in slightly modified form and enacted it by executive proclamation. By the end of 1865, new state governments had been formed in every state except Texas. Johnson proclaimed amnesty for the bulk of ex-Confederates in May 1865, and as a result, former Confederate leaders took over the new state governments. In December 1865 Johnson declared that Reconstruction was over and that elected Senators and Representatives from the Southern states—many of them former officers and officials in the Confederacy—should take their seats in Congress.

But the Radical Republicans—a hard-line anti-Confederate persuasion—had entirely different ideas about how the South should be treated. During 1865 they had fumed helplessly as Johnson put through his program; now they simply refused to seat any Southern Congressmen on grounds that the states had not been legally reconstructed. Thus began the battle of Presidential Reconstruction versus Congressional or Radical Reconstruction.

Who were the Radical Republicans? Many of them had been foes of slavery before the war. They included Salmon P. Chase in Lincoln's cabinet, Charles Sumner and Benjamin Wade in the Senate, Thaddeus Stevens in the House of Representatives. Generally favorable to business interests, they had nonetheless diverse views among themselves on tariffs, money, banking, and internal improvements. They were united on advancing black rights, ultimately to the point of granting complete political and legal equality; and they favored excluding ex-Confederates and the former ruling class from political influence in the postwar South. The popular sentiment of the North after the war was understandably vindictive, and the Radicals sought to exploit this sentiment to advance black rights, an issue in which most Northern citizens had little or no interest. In the main, it would be accurate to say that what distinguished the Radical Republicans was their insistence on advancing the blacks to equality and their effort to create a political and social structure in the South that would guarantee that equality. The Radicals were the dynamic political and moral element in Reconstruction. During the war, they had dominated the Joint Committee on the Conduct of the War, a powerful agency in their hands. By the end of the war they had moved into open opposition to Lincoln's program for Reconstruction.

President Johnson revered Lincoln and followed the general lines of Lincoln's program, though without flexibility or tact. A man with definite views, he was fully determined to use his office to enforce them. His personal limitations were real enough; he unquestionably treated political opponents rudely and dealt unfairly with his critics, even those trying to help him. But the leniency of his program is sufficient explanation for his devastating collision with the Radical Republicans.

Johnson believed that the planter class, by promoting secession, had irresponsibly brought on the war and manipulated the Southern small farmer into supporting it. He reasoned that with peace the small farmers would come to recognize the full depth of their betrayal by the planters, would refuse to follow their leadership, and would ally themselves with their free-farmer counterparts in the North and West. Johnson's political ideal was to unite moderate and conservative Republicans with Union Democrats in a new national coalition, one in which the preponderant white farmer class would feel secure. With the classes roughly in balance, social harmony would prevail throughout the nation. America would return to the principles of the early republic.

Johnson maintained that the blacks, like everyone else, could work out their destiny without special favors and within an economic system governed by the laws regulating capital and labor. He strongly supported the Thirteenth Amendment and universal emancipation: free labor would not only undermine the power of the planter class but would establish a more efficient set of labor relations. The Southern economic situation would improve as white inventive and productive talents were released; and black economic fortunes would rise with those of the region. Politically, socially, and legally, the blacks would remain under white tutelage. Class and racial relationships would remain fixed. Johnson said nothing about changing the lot of the blacks in any special or positive sense. They would remain an unskilled, uneducated, and propertyless laboring class, and the South itself a white man's country.

The moderate and conservative Republicans, apostles of the waxing capitalist interests, were willing to work with Johnson, finding his propositions about the economic order acceptable enough as a place to start. But they envisaged a far larger role for their interest in the new order than Johnson would have found tolerable. And he would have been staggered, for example, by the vision of Secretary of State William H. Seward of a future mighty industrial America and of an American empire. But Johnson's program shattered on the conscience and power of the Radicals.

In the tangled history of Reconstruction, it is still possible to assert that the subservient place President Johnson assigned to the blacks in the Southern social order was the central issue that made any compromise with the Radicals impossible. More than anyone else, he turned Reconstruction into an issue of moral principle. Already in 1865, while Johnson proceeded confidently with Reconstruction by executive proclamation, the Freedmen's Bureau and the Black Codes illustrated the opposing forces that were to divide Presidential and Congressional Reconstruction.

The Freedmen's Bureau   Congress set up the Freedman's Bureau within the War Department just before the end of the war. Under General Oliver O. Howard, a high-minded philanthropist, the Bureau cut a wide humanitarian swath throughout the South. It also aroused white Southern anxieties. The Bureau was given "control of all subjects relating to refugees and freedmen," an elastic mandate in itself, which Howard and his fellow commissioners interpreted liberally. The situation indeed called for quick measures and considerable initiative and ability to improvise. As the war came to an end, hundreds of thousands of blacks took to the road. Many simply wanted to indulge their sense of adventure, muted so long on the plantation. Others set off to look for kin and friends separated from them during slavery. Footloose blacks roamed the countryside, picking up rations from the Union army or

A freedmen's camp on the outskirts of the city of Richmond.

living by theft. Eventually, most of them fell into dire need, as did a great many Southern whites as well. The Freedmen's Bureau gave help zealously and effectively. Thanks to its issue of food, clothing, and medicine, it saved untold numbers of lives and tempered much misery. The Bureau lent legal and moral support to blacks by acting as a court of law, assuring blacks the right to choose their own employers, and arranging fair labor contracts for them. Its widespread intervention in labor relationships struck a particularly delicate Southern nerve, and Southern whites resented the publicity the Bureau gave to many instances of mistreatment of blacks.

The initial successes of the Bureau in protecting blacks turned it into a lever that pried open the South to idealistic Northerners. Thousands of schoolteachers, ministers, and enthusiastic young people followed in the wake of the Bureau, working with it and augmenting its projects. Free public schools were set up on a wide scale, open to blacks and whites alike. Countless charities were established, supported by donations from benevolent societies in the North. Many white Southerners came to hate and fear the Bureau for such educational and charitable activities and were anxious lest they be perpetuated. The activities of the Bureau exposed the blacks to ideas and influences that stimulated black self-respect and that were in every way at odds with the picture of the world and of themselves that Southern paternalistic ideology had impressed upon the blacks in the past.

The Black Codes   The Black Codes were the immediate Southern answer to the emancipation of the slaves and particularly to the difficulties of securing the services of the black labor force. The Codes were enacted by the Johnson state legislatures in 1865. They remained until struck down in April 1866 by the Civil Rights Act—passed by Congress over Johnson's veto—

which guaranteed equal civil rights to blacks. The Codes varied throughout the Southern states. Although most Codes recognized certain legal rights for blacks, they also restricted their freedom. Generally they forced labor contracts upon the blacks in one form or other; for example, by arresting them for vagrancy and then as punishment putting them to work. The Codes were in fact not enforced unless agents of the Freedmen's bureau acquiesced. The Bureau, its own resources frequently stretched thin, often found in the Codes a convenient device to hold down black migrancy. But the Codes did enforce conditions on blacks so closely resembling those of slavery that many thoughtful Southern leaders became alarmed, particularly since they could perceive the Radical Republican reaction building up in the Congress.

Debate over Reconstruction   The Radicals in Congress were willing to believe the worst about the South in any event. Reports by the end of 1865 seemed to them conclusive evidence that Johnson's Reconstruction really meant the restoration of the antebellum South in all important essentials. In early 1866, the Joint Committee on Reconstruction held hearings. Witnesses attested to the degrading treatment of blacks under the Black Codes, and letters from Southern Unionists added to the complaints. The highly respected Carl Schurz toured the South and made a straightforward and particularly impressive report to the Joint Committee. Schurz stressed that the South was resigned to its military defeat, but that the blacks in general were being badly treated and required federal protection. And a former large slaveholder, R. W. Flournoy of Mississippi, told Thaddeus Stevens: "To leave the negro to be dealt with by those whose prejudices are of the most bitter character against him, will be barbarous."

Such evidence enabled the Radicals to criticize more effectively the return of ex-Confederates to leadership in the new state governments in the South. And Johnson's expectation that the Southern farmers would disavow their former leadership proved utterly mistaken. This fact added enormously to Johnson's political difficulties and was of persistent importance during Reconstruction and beyond.

The Radicals Reign   Radical Reconstruction was forced through by a determined minority. Its leader in the House of Representatives was Thaddeus Stevens, representative from Pennsylvania and Chairman of the important House Committee on Reconstruction. Charles Sumner of Massachusetts led the Radicals in the Senate. Outside the Congress, men like Wendell Phillips, Boston patrician and former abolitionist, and E. L. Godkin, editor of the New York *Nation,* channeled powerful moral sentiments from the larger community into the Congress. These sentiments were well received by the Radicals.

The Radicals were united above all on the question of human equality. Many got their primary convictions from the Declaration of Independence with its principle of universal human equality; others rooted their views in

Charles Sumner. The powerfully outspoken Republican leader steadfastly pursued his consuming goal, that of "absolute human equality, secured, assured, and invulnerable." It was through Sumner's tenacious effort that seceded states had to provide equal suffrage in order to be readmitted to the Union. But in his pursuit of his goal of equality for all Sumner's vision became increasingly limited and his intolerance of those who disagreed with him grew out of proportion to the disagreement. His last years in the Senate were spent in vehement denunciation of those he considered his enemies.

Christianity. In many Radicals, of course, these views fell into easy combination. Such articles of faith protected the Radicals against the prevalent folklore that was spread rather evenly amongst Northern and Southern whites concerning the natural inferiority of blacks.

Thaddeus Stevens was the clearest head amongst the Radicals in Congress. He had a tough-minded estimate of social forces, a program, a realistic awareness of the strength of the obstacles blocking its attainment, and a practical vision of what the reunited and democratized American Republic might be like. No dreamer, and equipped with balanced qualities of moral fervor, political adroitness and tenacity, he possessed also the decisiveness and audacity to act.

Radical Reconstruction was really an attempt to achieve a political and social revolution from the top, to be carried through by the Congress. It aimed at nothing less than modernizing the American republic which, after all, still largely conformed to the pattern of a simpler age of agrarianism and commercial capitalism. The Republican party was to supply the propelling force. The national government would be strengthened at the expense of the states; Northern farmers, workers, commercial, financial, and industrial interests would find allies among the freed blacks and, following destruction of the planter interest, ultimately with Southern white farmers as well. Native Southern capital and resources, no longer sidetracked into human chattels and plantation mortgages, would join in a swelling mainstream of capitalist industry and finance, to expand with them in a truly national market. Although the Radicals were not marked by unanimity of opinion on economic matters, nevertheless they shared the general view that the new society would be economically dynamic and prosperous, politically stable and free.

Those moderate and conservative Republicans who were representative of the new capitalist forces accepted the Radical economic suppositions, which in principle were much the same as President Johnson's in stressing an unregulated capitalism. All Republicans knew clearly that the "party of the Union" had come into being as a sectional party and still had not put down deep national roots. Under Radical urging, there was Republican concurrence that the party must be moved into the South; that therefore the blacks must be made voting citizens with such help as was needed to make their votes effective—that is, Republican. For the Radicals, to see a return of the Southern Democrats to the Congress in strength, to have to compromise again with them continually, was an intolerable thought. The Congressional elections of 1866, it was recognized, would be decisive. The Radicals flung all their resources into the campaign.

The campaign was marked by bitterness and invective. President Johnson attacked Radical leaders individually, and added name-calling for good measure. The Radicals replied in kind, reminding Northerners that in the late war Southern bullets had been fired mostly by Democrats, that the white South was unrepentant, and that matters of conscience could not be put aside regarding treatment of the blacks in the South. Economic issues got little attention in the campaign; all guns were turned on Johnsonian Reconstruction. The campaign showed that Johnson's program commanded at best a wide indifference. The Radicals were rewarded with a large Congressional majority that would enable them to override Johnson's vetoes with ease.

Radical Policies   Radical Reconstruction called for breaking the power of the planter class. Radicals were agreed that the blacks must be enfranchised and their civil rights guaranteed. The Congress put through the First Reconstruction Act (1867) over Johnson's veto, and this was subsequently reinforced by three other acts. The South was placed under military rule backed by the full force of the national government. Ten states were divided into five military districts. The Supreme Court, aware of the force behind the Radicals, chose not to sit on cases involving the Reconstruction Acts. Constitutional conventions set up new state governments in the South, replacing those established by Johnson. Blacks could vote in all these proceedings, but former Confederate leaders could not.

On constitutional guarantees of black rights, three famous amendments were enacted in the early Reconstruction years. The Thirteenth Amendment (1865) freed the slaves. No land was given to the freedmen, nor compensation paid to their former owners. The Americans thus confiscated private property on a scale unknown in the West in modern times until the Russian Revolution of 1917. The former slaveholders, still politically disorganized, and accepting emancipation as the likely limit of change, did not protest strongly. The Fourteenth Amendment (1868), opposed by Johnson, made the blacks citizens. The Fifteenth Amendment (1870) gave black males the vote.

The importance of these amendments cannot be overrated. Even though for practical purposes they were ignored in the decades to come, they remained the law of the land. In the changed circumstances of our time their existence came to represent a realizable ideal, putting on the defensive those who resisted their fulfillment. In the Reconstruction era itself, their importance was enormously magnified by the failure to give the blacks a stake in society through land ownership.

Land Reform   To the Radicals, land reform as a matter of course meant confiscation of the plantations. A division of land among the blacks, and including the poorer whites as well, would undermine the economic base for the political leadership of the planter class. Guaranteed the possession of a freehold farm, the blacks would be freed from the necessity of letting their labor on unfavorable terms to the landowner through sharecropping and tenantry, a system already fastening itself on the Southern landscape in the 1860s.

In spite of the considerable obstacles the more militant Radicals, with Stevens as usual at their head, were willing to make a try and to employ such precedents as were near at hand.

During the war, the Union armies had liberated thousands of slaves in their advance into the Southern states. In South Carolina the Sea Islands had been occupied in 1861 by Union forces. The plantations there were divided among black families, the blacks managed their local affairs successfully, and the community prospered. At Davis Bend, Mississippi, in 1864–1865 following their liberation by the Union army, blacks with government help undertook a cooperative agricultural venture that turned a handy profit. The Sea Islands experiment outlasted Reconstruction, but after the war President Johnson returned the land of the Davis Bend plantations to its former white owners. Though limited in the numbers of freedmen involved, both these experiments suggested success for more widespread application. Stevens did not fail to point to the liberation of the serfs, and the assignment of land to them, carried out in the Russian Empire from 1861 to 1866. The analogy with the American experience was weak, but Stevens affirmed that the Russian tsar had correctly recognized that freedom was severely limited unless economic security accompanied it.

Land reform had been discussed periodically by Northerners since the last years of the war. It was Stevens again who made the greatest issue of it, since he attempted to get it included in the First Reconstruction Act of 1867. Stevens used government statistics to work out the elements of a plan that would at first confiscate about 400 million acres of land held by five percent of Southern white families, the "chief rebels," as Stevens put it; some seventy thousand planters each holding more than two hundred acres would lose their land. The confiscated land would be distributed to freedmen's families in forty-acre parcels; the remainder would be sold to help pay the public debt and provide veterans' pensions as well as compensation to Southern Unionists who had lost property during the war. The blacks thus established as small freehold farmers would get long-term guidance from the Republicans in Congress till they could master the responsibilities of managing their farms. Land and the vote would guarantee their freedom while they made the difficult transition into self-respecting citizenship; and the "party of the Union" would acquire a firm base in the South.

Stevens and the Congressional hardcore Radicals tried to get the forty-acre plan written into the First Reconstruction Act of 1867. It received only slight support in the House, and the debate fizzled out by the end of the sixties. Land reform was the most revolutionary change asked by the Radicals, and its failure left Southern blacks helpless to control their economic destinies. Public opinion was unable to accept such a proposal.

E. L. Godkin's *Nation*, normally a Radical supporter, warned that "A division of rich men's land amongst the landless . . . would give a shock to our whole social and political system from which it would hardly recover without the loss of liberty." Northerners who had bought up Southern plantations after the war resisted the idea of confiscation as a matter of course. Even Northern workmen took a dim view of confiscation, since it seemed to be setting blacks up in business. Those in the factories, themselves with little or no property, could not understand why blacks should be given a special advantage. Individual skill, initiative, and the notion of making it on one's own were the virtues esteemed by the Americans. Most of the support Stevens got for his forty-acre plan came from those who saw in confiscation and land sales a way of reducing the public debt and hence taxes. But the general verdict was that with emancipation the blacks would be free to sell their labor wherever they could, at what price they could get, just like anyone else. Beyond that the nation would not go.

The Impeachment of Johnson   The progress of Reconstruction as designed by the Congress was marked by a series of confrontations between the Radicals and President Johnson—of bills vetoed and vetoes overridden, of Johnson's lack of restraint in dealing with those with whom he disagreed, and of an emotionally intense Congressional reaction to Johnson's behavior. Radical fury against his opposition to the Congressional program of Reconstruction climaxed in the attempt to remove him from office. The Republican argument was that Johnson had failed to fulfill his constitutional duty to enforce the laws of the land, but this was an unfounded argument. His real "crime" was political disagreement with the Radicals over Reconstruction. The issue on which the case hinged was the Tenure of Office Act of 1867, which forbade the President to remove any official appointed with the consent of the Senate without first securing the approval of the Senate.

Johnson in February 1868 dismissed his Secretary of War, Edwin M. Stanton, an avowed supporter of the Radicals. This precipitated Johnson's impeachment and trial, which the Radicals were convinced they had the votes to win. But the dubious nature of the charges, the malice apparent in the prosecutor's handling of the case contrasted with the dignity of the defense conducted by Johnson's lawyers, the dislike some senators had of

The Sergeant-at-Arms of the Senate serves the summons of impeachment on President Johnson.

Benjamin Wade, the president of the Senate who would assume the Presidency if Johnson were removed, and the realization that Johnson's effectiveness was nil and he would shortly be out of office anyway, all combined to convince seven Republican senators to vote against conviction. Johnson won acquittal by one vote.

The Grant Administration—Incompetence and Corruption With Johnson unacceptable to anyone, Republican or Democrat, the Republicans happily turned in 1868 to war hero General Ulysses S. Grant. Grant's presidential victory in 1868 over Horatio Seymour was overwhelming in the Electoral College, but his narrow popular majority was clearly attributable to black voters enfranchised in Republican-dominated Southern states under Reconstruction rule. Ironically, Grant's majority would have been much larger had not various Northern states rejected constitutional moves to permit blacks to vote in those states.

Grant was willing to permit Congress to assume control of Reconstruction. Brilliant on the battlefield, he was completely ineffective in the White House and his political naiveté was exploited not only by the Congress, which was also increasingly disturbed by his ineptitude, but by his friends and associates as well. His administration was marked by one of the worst periods of corruption in American political history, even though Grant personally was not involved. The Whiskey Ring scandal, which involved cheating the government of millions in tax revenue, involved Grant's private secretary. His Secretary of War took bribes in connection with the management of Indian affairs. Other scandals involved officials in the Navy and Treasury departments. To compound the problem, Grant out of a misguided sense of loyalty

This cartoon mocked Grant's failure to recognize corruption in his friends or take any action against it once discovered. General William W. Belknap, Grant's Secretary of War, received a kickback of nearly $25,000 as a result of an appointment he made to Fort Sills.

protected those who had betrayed him. Although the infamous Credit Mobilier scandal occurred before Grant became President, it broke during his second administration and he was forced to assume part of the blame. The scandal involved the bribing of key members of Congress with Credit Mobilier stock in order to cover up the granting of fraudulent contracts by the Credit Mobilier, a construction company involved in the building of the Union Pacific. A congressional investigation of the matter after Grant took office revealed that a number of prominent officials had been involved, including the man who had become Grant's Vice President.

Grant's inability to govern effectively allowed Congress considerable opportunity to increase its power and consequently institute significant change with the development of its Reconstruction programs.

The Impact of Reconstruction

The South remained under military rule until 1877. A variety of Northerners moved South. Some wanted to settle there in the fashion of "going West," others went to work with the Freedmen's Bureau to help blacks and poor whites, swelling the migration of such idealists begun earlier. The Union League, an arm of the Republican Party, penetrated into the South to organize the black vote. Most of the Northern immigrants supported the Republicans; Southerners labelled them all "carpetbaggers," attributing somewhat indiscriminately a get-rich-quick-and-leave motive to all the newcomers.

The Republicans also found allies among white Southerners themselves: former Southern Unionists, some Southern businessmen, some Southern humanitarians, and various Southern opportunists.

Southern resentment of Reconstruction governments is reflected in this cartoon of the "Solid South" shackled and burdened with "carpetbag and bayonet rule." An army of occupation was stationed in each of the military districts to enforce what at times was a flagrant disregard of civil rights. In some Southern states any commemoration of the Confederacy was outlawed, government officials were removed, and courts were replaced by military tribunals when they failed to punish violence against blacks.

The Radicals and their Southern adherents wrought considerable transformation in the South. Democratic state constitutions were set up, and a free public school system was established that drew in uneducated whites as well as blacks. Women's rights were expanded, taxes were made more equitable, and there were better facilities for the care of the physically and mentally handicapped and of the poor. Penal codes were reformed, punishments for minor crimes were made less harsh, and the number of crimes punishable by death was reduced. The blacks participated in making these changes. Black legislators sat in all the Southern state legislatures, but in only two, Mississippi and South Carolina, did they become the majority. No blacks became governors. On the whole, except for staunchly maintaining political and legal guarantees, the blacks were remarkably conservative, not even using their influence in the state governments to urge land reform strongly.

It was in personal human terms that Reconstruction had the greatest impact on the South. The coercion of black labor was relieved by the Radical influence. Blacks rushed eagerly into the free schools. They were able to develop a family life more nearly approximating that of the country at large. The simple fact of emancipation did away with the worst aspect of slavery, the fear of arbitrary separation from relatives and friends. Beatings, threats of beatings, and worse punishments were outlawed. Blacks continued to work very hard, but they could keep something of what they earned; consequently they ate better as well. Reconstruction generally made a genuine break with the black past and launched a serious program to incorporate blacks as equals into American life.

The Failure of Reconstruction   What failed to change during the Reconstruction years were white thoughts and attitudes towards the blacks. Changes in attitudes towards people as a class or race require changes in status within wider social relationships. Reconstruction supplied the political conditions for a change of status by making the black a voting citizen. Resistant Southern whites accepted Reconstruction at the time only because it was less painful to do so than not. But when the authority of the national government no longer enforced it, the white South fell back upon its conventional attitudes.

Why did Reconstruction finally fail? Purely political considerations within Republican ranks explain much. The Republican Party had risen as a sectional political force in the 1850s, dedicated to preserving the Union and the national market and augmenting federal power to these ends. The "party of the Union" had achieved astonishing success. Nationalist and patriotic feeling, greatly intensified by the war experience, and the increasing market for their goods in the East and in Europe, bound the Western farmers to Republicanism. As the Republicans won the West, the Southern blacks became politically expendable. Under these circumstances, the Republicans felt far less urge to push for the establishment of a party base in the South. The idealism of the Radicals, expressed originally in human terms of helping the blacks to citizenship, shaded off into the less dramatic goals of civil service and other reform as age overtook the Radicals and their energies declined.

A series of growing economic problems related to the stock market, the tariff, industrial expansion, and the shortage of money that climaxed in the Panic of 1873 increasingly commanded the attention of the voters throughout the country and correspondingly reduced their interest in the fate of the blacks of the South and the problems of Reconstruction.

With waning support from their own party, the Radicals gradually lost their zeal. Pressing changes upon an unwilling people is not inherently pleasant work. The South quickly developed techniques of resistance, first subtly, then more openly. White Southerners, as during the war itself, were fighting on their own ground and within a society that they knew well. The carpetbaggers, the Northern idealists, and others working in the South were far from home, living in a society that they did not fully understand and that did not want them. Northerners who provoked Southern resentment, whether with justification or not, came to feel isolated in the region.

In the South, opposition to Reconstruction was accompanied as time went on by a good deal of terror in the fashion of the counter-revolution following the radical phase of the French Revolution. A host of vigilante and secret societies blossomed in the late 1860s, of which the Ku Klux Klan was merely the earliest and best known. In the early 1870s, the military governors, aided by Congressional enactments, dealt with these successfully by force; but the appearance of these lawless elements sent a shudder throughout the black communities in the South.

Disappointment with President Grant as well as confirmation of a waning Republican interest in Reconstruction were clearly evident when the Democrats won control of the House of Representatives in the election of 1874. In

The Regulators. *White extremists turned to terrorism and violence in their reactions to Reconstruction.*

the following year Grant, who had earlier been willing to use federal troops to protect black voters from intimidation in the South, refused to send troops to Mississippi in response to an appeal from its Republican carpetbag governor, declaring that "The whole public are tired out with these annual autumnal outbreaks in the South, and the great majority are now ready to condémn any interference on the part on the govenment."

Thus Grant, who had originally represented the hope of the Radical Republicans in the reconstruction of the South, ended up presiding over its final failure.

The presidential election of 1876 confirmed the end of Reconstruction. The Republicans nominated Governor Rutherford B. Hayes of Ohio, the Democrats chose Governor Samuel J. Tilden of New York. Tilden apparently won the election, possessing a popular majority. But his claim to victory rested upon the votes of the last three Southern states—Florida, South Carolina, and Louisiana—which still remained in Republican hands. In the long and complicated dispute over who was to be awarded the electoral votes from these three states, it seems clear that both sides were guilty of fraud and corruption. Less than a month before inauguration day in 1877, the Electoral Commission created by Congress awarded the disputed votes to Hayes, thus insuring him election by one electoral vote. While Northern Democrats were furious and even talked of a military march on Washington to put their man in the White House, Southern Democrats had other things on their mind. Many Southern Democrats believed they were more likely to get federal economic aid for their section from a Republican administration interested in economic growth. More importantly, many Southern Democrats wanted to be left alone to run the South as they saw fit, and if Republicans could assure them that Hayes would go along with this point of view, they were willing to accept his victory.

Whether deals were actually made in this regard is still in doubt. What is clear is that Reconstruction had run its course, the entire country wanted to put the issue behind it, interest in providing special protections and privileges to blacks had long since disappeared in the minds of most Americans, and sectional harmony was eagerly sought by most. At any rate, after he became President, Hayes removed the last of federal troops stationed in the South, and the era of Reconstruction formally ended. A new era began, an era of national neglect of the black in American society that was not to be reversed until the second half of the twentieth century.

Profile: THADDEUS STEVENS

Few men of influence in American history have ever been so reviled as Thaddeus Stevens. And some would say few deserved it more. After his death on August 11, 1868, he was referred to by the New York <u>Times</u> as "the Evil Genius of the Republican Party." James Gordon Bennett of the New York <u>Herald</u> called him "malevolent, even malignant," and the New York <u>World</u> declared that Stevens was "the author of more evil and mischief than any other inhabitant of the globe since the end of the civil war." In the South, where for years he had been detested by whites, his death prompted one paper to exalt that "The prayers of the righteous have at last removed the Congressional curse."

Yet his achievements were of great significance. He served in the Pennsylvania House of Representatives from 1833 to 1842, and then in Congress from 1849 to 1852 and from 1858 until his death. He was uncompromisingly opposed to slavery before the war—he denounced any extension of slavery into the territories, prophetically declared the Compromise of 1850 would be "the fruitful mother of future rebellion," defended fugitive slaves without fee, and was opposed to the Supreme Court's decision in the Dred Scott case. His profound concern for the fate of blacks led him to play a key role in securing the Thirteenth and Fourteenth Amendments and in laying the groundwork for the Fifteenth, which he did not live to see enacted. He helped greatly to make American nationalism a political reality by his work to consolidate federal power both during and after the war. He was also a life-long supporter of free public education. In a powerful and eloquent speech in the Pennsylvania legislature in 1835 he carried the day for a free school law about which, over thirty years later as he lay on his deathbed, he said: "That was the proudest effort of my life."

The source of controversy over Stevens as a powerful political leader in Congress and the nation arose in essence out of his own character. He was a man of considerable wit, but seemed impelled to use it to the discomfiture of others. On one occasion he asked a legislator who had voted against a bill Stevens supported if his opponent was a married man with children. When his opponent replied yes, Stevens said, "I am sorry to hear that. I was in hopes, sir, that you were the last of your race." But there were larger flaws than this. He had a streak of vindictiveness that drove him to seek punishment for those he considered guilty of wrongdoing. And he possessed a fanatical commitment to principle that made him turn against all who did not see the truth as he did. Early in his political career he had proudly declared that "I would sooner lose every friend on earth than violate the glorious dictates of my own conscience." If this was his ambition, he came very close to attaining it. He would not admit of the possibility of his being badly advised by his conscience—the truth was his and his alone. This vindictiveness and his fanaticism about principle gave him a pathological conviction that if things did not go the way he thought they should the country was doomed to ruin and destruction. As he lay dying, he remarked, "My life has been a failure. . . . I see little hope for the Republic."

His unforgiving nature was apparent in his hatred of the "bloated aristocrats" of the South whose property, he believed, should be confiscated by the government. And opposing speedy and conciliatory reunion of the states, he believed rebellion justified the view that the Southern states should be treated as conquered territories not as errant sons to be welcomed home with open arms. But his vindictive streak was most apparent in his insistence on the impeachment and trial of President Andrew Johnson. It was Stevens who forced this matter to its sorry pass, even though he knew that the real issue was the political clash between Johnson and the Radical Republicans, not the indictable offenses under the Constitution of treason, bribery, or other high crimes and misdemeanors. So great was his hatred of Johnson that when the President was acquitted on May 16, 1868 by one vote, Stevens (though a dying man) doggedly but futilely tried to keep the issue alive by concocting new articles of impeachment.

Thaddeus Stevens was an enormously complex man, his life full of inner conflicts and personal contradictions, and as such he was not only hard to understand but difficult to appreciate. He took an essentially Calvinist view of human nature, believing humanity inherently evil, but at the same time he held the utopian belief that it was possible to legislate total equality overnight. He could be unsparing in his attacks on those who he believed stood in the way of progress, and yet he had a profound commitment to human rights. The social and economic revolution he wished to impose on the South was unacceptable to his contemporaries, but his work for the Fourteenth and Fifteenth Amendments was of crucial political importance for the advancement of civil rights in twentieth century America. His fear that his life had been wasted and useless was born of his innate pessimism, but was unwarranted by the long-range impact of his achievements. In the last analysis, his virtues outweighed his flaws.

Chapter 2
THE BLACK AMERICAN

The Spirit of the Times
BECOMING "AMERICAN"

Black comedian Godfrey Cambridge once told a white audience: "Let's face it. We've got to live together. You ain't goin' back to Europe and we're not goin' back to Africa. We both got too much invested here." He also remarked in regard to a trip he had taken to Europe that it was nice to go abroad and be hated solely because you were an American. The laughter that greeted these observations did not conceal the fundamental truth that lay behind them, that the black American is in fact an American: repressed, neglected, denied, but within the context of American culture. Restricted as the participation of blacks in American society has been, their very repression and neglect have been a denial of full or equal involvement in the American culture which by necessity became the only one they had.

The story of the black American is therefore the story of Americans struggling to share equally with other Americans in the benefits and opportunities of American life. It is not the story of Africans struggling to maintain their cultural identity in an alien society. The tragedy lies not in the fact that African culture was not transmitted to and preserved in America, but that full participation in American society and culture was so fraught with obstacles and peril destructive of dignity, achievement, talent, and often of life itself.

Any recounting, therefore, of the history of the black American is a recital in essence of American history. Black labor supported the economic development of a significant part of colonial society. Blacks served in all American wars ranging from a few thousand in the Revolution to the 1,154,000 in World War II. Black Americans were involved in the conquest of the West: there were black miners in the West; over six thousand black cowboys roamed the cattle frontier after the Civil War; and there were blacks on the farming frontier. In the twentieth century black labor helped forward the industrial achievements of the nation, albeit in the most menial tasks much of the time. Nor can the history of the city in modern America be written without including the story of its black population.

George Washington Carver at work in his laboratory. Born a slave in Missouri, Carver was abducted as a child and ransomed for $300 by a German farmer. After working his way through school and obtaining a degree in agriculture from Iowa State College, Carver contributed his talents and research to Tuskegee Institute, where he taught from 1896.

Nothing illustrates more clearly the black as American than black contributions to American cultural life. In music there are worksongs, spirituals, ragtime, and that unique contribution, jazz. Black musicians as well as popular, concert, and operatic singers have enriched the American musical tradition from the late nineteenth century to the present. In literature the record is equally impressive, especially in the twentieth century, although the first black writer, Phillis Wheatley, took up her pen two hundred years ago. From the explosion of the Harlem Renaissance in the 1920s to the present day, black poets, novelists, and playwrights have broadened the range of American artistic awareness. American scholarship in history, political science, and sociology as well as in the sciences has benefited greatly from the work of black scholars. The work of George Washington Carver, for example, in the synthesizing of hundreds of products from peanuts and sweet potatoes was a major contribution, as was the pioneer work of Dr. Louis Wright and Dr. Charles Drew in cancer research and blood plasma. Cultural and intellectual contributions were of especial importance because they continually gave the lie to arguments about black inferiority.

In the half-century or so after the Civil War, the changing configuration of American society and the course of events increasingly swept black Americans into more and more areas that had been closed to them under slavery, although rarely on terms of equality with others. These decades were also marked by a rising black concern about the terms of their involvement in American life and by an exploration of ways to alter those terms. But it was to take another half-century before this concern embraced any significant section of white America.

TENANT FARMING

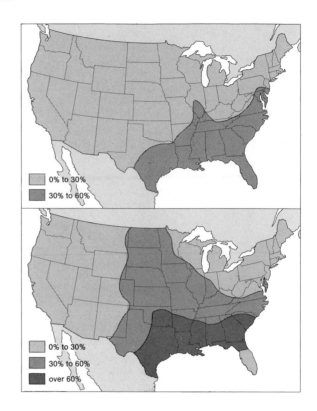

Repression and Segregation

In 1884, seven years after the end of Reconstruction, the distinguished Southern journalist, George W. Cable, wrote that man would land on the moon before equality was achieved in America between blacks and whites. What Cable could not predict was that the race would not even be close. After federal troops left the South in 1877, control over black destinies was returned to the hands of the whites. By the end of the nineteenth century a new system of labor relations to replace slavery had been worked out for the blacks; the vote had been taken from them except in scattered pockets where it lingered on for a time; a pattern of segregation in social relations had been established; and somewhat new justifications for discrimination had been advanced. It is useful to look at each of these developments in turn.

Economic Discrimination   After the Civil War, landowners would have preferred working the cotton lands in the old style, in labor gangs under the direction of an overseer. The blacks would no longer accept this kind of unrelenting discipline and the labor-gang system was in effect destroyed.

Sharecroppers in South Carolina head out to work the fields.

Accordingly, the landowners settled upon tenancy and sharecropping to get the land worked and the cotton planted, weeded, and harvested.

Under this system more than ninety percent of the tenants were share-croppers, and some eighty percent of the sharecroppers were blacks. In general, sharecropping was the typical device for using the labor of blacks and many poor whites, and for exerting ironclad economic controls over the Southern black population.

The black sharecropper, having little or no resources in money or credit, was thus usually "furnished" by the landowner with seed, implements, animals, and a small sum of cash or credit to meet immediate living expenses for food and clothing. The sharecropper family worked as an economic unit, and the size of the family typically determined the amount of land to be let. For a man and wife alone, this might run from fifteen to twenty acres, with perhaps five acres added for each child. Children beyond the tender years were, of course, an economic asset, since they could work in the fields and do chores. Local school boards were far from insistent that black children be in school during seasonal periods when crops needed attention. An indifferent education thus helped to build a cycle of poverty.

The sharecropper's dwelling was commonly a shack, or a house in an advanced state of dilapidation. The owner had no reason to keep it up, nor did the black tenants, since they were seldom compensated for improve-ments, and only patched it enough to give the barest protection against the elements. In return for the "furnishing," the sharecropper gave the landlord about half of his cotton crop directly, and the landlord sold the other half for him. The sharecropper got a small sum of money for food, or credit, or coupons redeemable at a store, frequently located on the plantation and owned by the landlord himself. Such stores were not noted for competitive prices. In December, after the cotton crop was sold, a settlement took place. The landlord maintained all the records; the sharecropper typically received neither statements of the value of his "furnishing" nor of store purchases. The landlord merely told the sharecropper whether he had broken even, made a small profit, or was in debt. Most blacks were afraid to ask for statements, even if they knew they were being cheated. They could not insist on honesty from the landlord; the judge in the local court was likely to be the landlord's friend or acquaintance and in any event understood the rules of the labor game from the white point of view. If the sharecropper was fortunate enough to escape debt and the obligation to work it off the next year, the best he could do was to move at the end of the season and hope to do better with another landlord.

Landlords were themselves hard-pressed in a market that, in the late nineteenth century, was characterized by agricultural depression. Competition from Egyptian cotton and from new cotton lands in western Texas and California drove prices down and encouraged landlords to bear down on their tenants. The storekeeper, or storekeeper-landlord, operating in a capital-poor region, also was obliged to borrow and at high interest rates set ultimately by Northern banks. In these circumstances, questions of economic fair play inevitably got pushed into the background. The way landlords treated their tenants was not a fashionable question in their circles and was an entirely personal matter. The tendency was for blacks to succumb to debt and thus to slip into peonage.

Political Disenfranchisement   By 1877 and the end of Reconstruction, the black vote in the South had been largely nullified. Blacks continued to vote in declining numbers into the 1890s, and even to hold office. In 1888, there were seven blacks in the Mississippi legislature and eight in the Virginia General Assembly; and as late as 1900 black representatives from the South sat in Congress. But once the white South determined to exclude blacks from political life, it required little ingenuity to find the means of doing so.

The Fifteenth Amendment (1870) granted blacks the right to vote but only in the sense that it outlawed race as a test for voting; the states remained free to restrict the vote on the basis of other requirements. The Mississippi Constitutional Convention of 1890 led the way by establishing a poll tax of two dollars a year along with other technical requirements that were soon copied elsewhere throughout the South. Voters might be required to read and interpret a clause from a state constitution. "Grandfather clauses" were applied: one could vote, in effect, if his grandfather had voted. The white primary, born in the 1890s, proved to be particularly effective. Party primaries, it was maintained, were private elections; it was therefore permissible to exclude blacks from them. With the establishment of the Democratic Solid South, a candidate who won the primary election in the Democratic Party almost automatically won the general election. Republican Senator Henry Cabot Lodge introduced a Force Bill into Congress in 1890, which would have used federal power to enforce black voting rights in the South. But it was killed in the Senate and was in any event a last, faint flutter of Reconstruction. The means of disenfranchisement became so formidable that blacks simply gave up trying to vote.

Populist successes in the South played an important part in pushing the blacks out of Southern politics. The Populists were Western and Southern farmers dissatisfied with an economic and political system that they felt discriminated against the nation's agricultural interests, particularly those of the small farmer. In the West they established their own political party and worked not only for economic reforms, but political reforms as well. Southern populists worked through the Democratic Party and in the 1890s captured all the Southern state governments except Alabama. Blacks ran into the color line from the beginning and were obliged to form their own National Colored Farmers' Alliance to participate in the populist movement. White Southern farmers, mainstay of the movement, feared the possible exploitation of the black vote by the monied interests that they opposed. Cooperation between white and black farmers thus faltered from the beginning; to white populists it was politically more comfortable to exclude blacks from the vote altogether.

By 1900 there was no significant organization or political power in either North or South willing to support the blacks in retaining the vote in the Southern states, and disenfranchisement was virtually complete.

Segregation   Segregation in social life joined with political discrimination to complete the isolation of blacks within Southern society. Down to the 1890s there had been considerable intermingling of whites and blacks in public services and entertainment. Then came a flood of discriminatory legislation—the "Jim Crow laws." In 1896, the Supreme Court accepted a Jim Crow law separating blacks from whites on railways if accommodations were equal (*Plessy* v. *Ferguson*); and the famous "separate but equal" principle was established. In 1899 it was applied to public education (*Cumming* v. *County Board of Education*).

The extreme inconvenience and expense of maintaining double facilities in public services seemed so absurd at first that in 1898 the conservative Charleston *News and Courier*, after criticizing the Jim Crow laws on railroads, declared in biting sarcasm:

> If there must be Jim Crow cars on railroads, there should be Jim Crow cars on street railways. . . . There should be Jim Crow sections of the jury box, and a separate Jim Crow dock and witness stand in every court—and a Jim Crow Bible for colored witnesses to kiss. It would be advisable also to have a Jim Crow section in county auditors' and treasurers' offices. . . . The two races are dreadfully mixed in these offices for weeks every year, especially about Christmas . . .

What was meant as satire all came to pass. After 1900 the principle in *Plessy* v. *Ferguson* was extended from railways to theaters, restaurants,

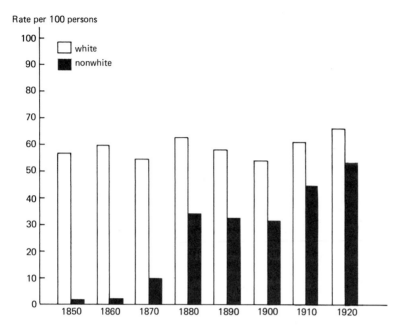

Rate per 100 persons

SCHOOL ENROLLMENT RATES

churches, hotels, and schools; to housing, employment, prisons, mental institutions and hospitals, even to the Bible. The result was a degree of separation between the races unmatched even under slavery. In little more than a
generation the transition was made from a slave to a caste society.

The degradation of the blacks during this period was accompanied by
rationalizations both old and new. Human beings have a strong urge to see
the world whole, to fit apparent contradictions into a picture that makes
sense. Under slavery, it had been difficult but possible to rationalize sectional
slavery as a "peculiar institution," based upon an assumed moral, intellectual, and biological inferiority of the blacks. This still remained the fundamental assumption for American whites. The experience of the Civil War,
which brought emancipation, and of Reconstruction with the Thirteenth,
Fourteenth, and Fifteenth Amendments, would if taken seriously have required a new conception of the blacks as a people. Nothing like this happened, because black status did not change, and no new conception of the
black was required. The old explanations of inherent inferiority continued to
serve and were even reinforced.

The reinforcement came from science through a misapplication of Charles
Darwin's theory of biological evolution. The theory asumed a struggle for
existence between a species and its environmnent as a key factor in the
survival and perpetuation of the species. Darwin never meant and indeed
rejected the notion that the struggle for survival was between members of
the same species. But the theory was extended beyond biology by the "social

Darwinists" to justify a struggle for survival within the human species. Those who wished to, found it easy to believe that blacks were unable to compete successfully against whites in the struggle for existence, a clear sign of black inferiority. White supremacy thus acquired scientific trappings. Black degradation might be unfortunate, but it was the law of life. Social Darwinism sank into the popular consciousness by 1900 and supplied much comfort to white supremacists.

Blacks therefore were tightly boxed in after 1900: economically, politically, socially, ideologically. A great increase in lynching drove home the precariousness of black life. Between 1889 and 1922, more than thirty-four hundred people were lynched in the United States, four-fifths of whom were blacks and the overwhelming majority of these in the South. The worst period was between 1892 and 1899 when more than twelve hundred lynchings took place, most in the rural South in an area of agricultural depression and white frustration. The known statistics take no account of the unrecorded whippings and beatings, rapes and robberies. Defended primarily as a protection of white womanhood, only a minority of lynchings were actually charged to assaults on women. Almost any sign of "uppityness," particularly in black males, whether real, imagined, or contrived, might lead to violence.

In this atmosphere, some white supremacists argued that blacks should be reduced simply to work animals. The Mississippi politician, James K. Vardaman, proposed to abolish education for blacks entirely. Racial relationships reached their lowest ebb in these years, and the issue for blacks appeared at times to be not what kind of existence, but whether they would have any existence at all.

Black Reaction

By the early twentieth century, blacks in the South were shorn of economic independence, disfranchised, segregated, physically threatened, and intellectually bombarded by white assertions of their racial inferiority. In these circumstances, they had little encouragement to act and even less to think. Nonetheless, the reactions of blacks themselves to the threatening world around them in these difficult years are of the greatest importance. Two remarkable black social thinkers and leaders appeared in this period— Booker T. Washington and W. E. B. Du Bois. Their backgrounds and outlooks differed sharply and their disagreements were profound. In thought and action they drew heavily upon their intimate knowledge of black people and a deep understanding of white society as well. Their contrary views both expressed and stimulated a debate among black educators, journalists, and other leaders. The ideas of both men called for programs of action. The result was a rich mine of both thought and experience that is still being worked. The Washington–Du Bois controversy set the broad limits within which most, but by no means all, black social thought and action has proceeded since that time.

The black farmer. Ownership was rare, and poverty, whether a black family owned their own farm or sharecropped, was a reality.

The Washington Approach   Booker T. Washington won acclaim as a national black leader as a result of his famous "Atlanta Compromise" speech, delivered at the Cotton States and International Exposition in 1895. In that speech, Washington laid down the line of argument to which he held for the next two decades. He spoke at the height of the movement to disfranchise, segregate, and repress the black population and he was keenly aware of the power of that movement. He offered a compromise in which blacks would not ask for political or social equality, and in return would be given legal protection, industrial training, and an opportunity to improve their position in the developing economy of the New South. Thus he reassured whites by his denial of black aspirations for equality, yet held out to blacks the promise of ultimate equality on the grounds of their indispensability to the Southern economy:

> The wisest among my race understand that the agitation of questions of social equality is the extremest folly, and that progress in the enjoyment of all the privileges that will come to us must be the result of severe and constant struggle rather than of artificial forcing. No race that has anything to contribute to the markets of the world is long in any degree ostracized. It is important and right that we be prepared for the exercises of these privileges.

Blacks inevitably developed institutions of their own under the reality of segregation, and built their own counterparts of the white society from which they were excluded. Washington actively promoted this self-help movement. He started and stimulated or aided a list of projects, activities, and institutions formidable in number and variety. His own Tuskegee Institute sponsored, along with Hampton Institute, annual conferences for black farmers, demonstrating new agricultural techniques and showing how by thrift and hard work the farmers might improve their lot. This was also the goal of the Farmers' Improvement Society of Texas, which devoted its major efforts to fighting the evils of the sharecropping system by encouraging blacks to raise their own foodstuffs, to buy cooperatively, and to become independent landholders. The National Business League, organized in 1900, proclaimed the doctrine, novel only as applied to blacks, that anyone who tried could succeed; and it publicized plenty of individual examples to illustrate the point. The League also urged blacks to support black business enterprises. Inspired by the black businessmen's example, other professional groups organized: black lawyers into the National Bar Association in 1903; black doctors into the National Medical Association in 1904; black retailers into the National Negro Retail Association in 1913. The National Urban League, founded by the merger of smaller organizations in 1911, and most active in the Northern cities, joined black and conservative white businessmen in aiding urban blacks, many newly arrived from the South.

Black labor unions had a far more difficult task, since laborers found themselves in more widespread and obvious competition with white workers, in contrast to black business and professional men. Black workers in the South organized into a few Jim Crow locals affiliated with the American Federation of Labor, but their recognition was nearly always precarious and their conditions and contracts inferior to those of white laborers. If anything, the movement was mostly the other way: the Georgia railway strike in 1909, for example, was caused by the demand of white railway unions to force black workers out of skilled jobs they had held for years. The flood of unskilled labor in the "new immigration" from southern and eastern Europe created a special hardship for blacks in competition for jobs in the North. Under these circumstances, the American Federation of Labor itself found it easier to control job opportunities by restricting its activities on the whole to craft unionism in the more skilled trades. It was generally a bad time for unions, but the blacks suffered the worst discrimination.

Black social and fraternal organizations began or expanded, frequently tying their activities to economic needs. Black churches sponsored many charitable projects. Local black women's clubs, old folks' homes, orphanages, hospitals, social and literary circles, libraries, day nurseries, and settlement houses multiplied. These organizations were testimonies to the reality of discrimination but offered no challenge to it, and they fitted well with Washington's philosophy of self-help and self-improvement.

Washington exerted enormous influence upon all these activities in the black community down to his death in 1915, aided in no small measure by the favorable publicity he received from the white press. Tuskegee Institute flourished, evidence that the policy of accommodation, of separating economics from politics, would unlock funds both private and public. Many blacks acquired education and accumulated property following Washington's prescription, for these were the natural products of his program. But proportionately their numbers were not great among blacks, and in almost all other respects and in all sections of the country, the status of blacks remained comparatively unchanged or even deteriorated.

W. E. B. DuBois

Washington's acceptance of political and social inequality has been repudiated by blacks in our day. His program prompted critics to charge that he was giving away too much, yielding too readily; but even these critics realized the precariousness of black existence at the time. Any fair judgment of Washington must take into account this fragility in race relations, and also that Washington carried on most of his work in the deep South where conflict was most perilous, a fact that inevitably affected his thinking. It seems clear that with the cultural and physical attacks on blacks, particularly from the 1890s on, black demoralization could have been far greater than it was; and Washington reasoned logically that some finite goal, one that seemed achievable, however distant, was necessary just to hold together the black social fabric.

The Du Bois Challenge   William E. Burghardt Du Bois (1868–1963) represented a stream of black social thought and action in sharp contrast with that of Booker T. Washington. His long and distinguished career carried him far beyond the controversies with Washington, ultimately into the camp of international socialism and African nationalism. Born and raised in

Great Barrington, Massachusetts, he attended the local high school and went to Fisk University in Nashville, Tennessee. Fisk had been founded in 1865 with a liberal-arts curriculum and was designed to train black leaders. While attending Fisk, Du Bois spent summers teaching school in rural Tennessee. Here he became acquainted with the appalling poverty in which Southern blacks lived.

Du Bois attained a youthful ambition by completing his bachelor's degree at Harvard, continued there with graduate studies in history and political science, and received his Ph.D. degree in 1895. In the meantime, with Harvard grants, he studied at Cambridge University and the University of Berlin, and taught briefly at Wilberforce College in Ohio. In 1896, with support from the University of Pennsylvania, he undertook a study of black life in Philadelphia that was published as *The Philadelphia Negro,* the first work in American urban sociology and one that established Dr. Du Bois as a scholar of national reputation.

Atlanta University then invited him to teach in its new department of sociology. Relying upon trained black sociologists, Du Bois began the publication of a series of studies on black problems; and in 1903 he published his great work, *The Souls of Black Folk.* Here he openly challenged Booker T. Washington's educational and social policies, stating that Washington's philosophy "practically accepts the alleged inferiority of the negro." So began the Washington–Du Bois controversy.

A great many blacks could not accept Washington's conciliatory philosophy at all or not in full measure, and it was on the foundation of these sentiments that Du Bois built his opposition. For example, the noted black journalist, John E. Bruce, declared in 1889:

> The man who will not fight for the protection of his wife and children is a *coward* and deserves to be ill-treated. . . . There is no just reason why manly men of any race should allow themselves to be continually outraged and oppressed by their equals before the law. . . . The Negro must not be rash and indiscreet either in action or in words but he must be very determined and terribly in earnest . . . to convince Southern rowdies and cutthroats that more than two can play at the game with which they have amused their fellow conspirators in crime for nearly a quarter of a century.

In 1890, T. Thomas Fortune, editor of the influential black newspaper, the New York *Age,* joined with Bruce and other black leaders to start the National Afro-American League. Blacks from about half of the states were represented, but Northerners predominated at the founding convention in Chicago. Fortune told the convention that "we have been robbed of the honest wages of our toil, we have been robbed of the substance of our citizenship by murder and intimidation. . . . It is time to begin to fight fire with fire." The convention adopted a program of winning over public opinion and appealing to the courts to redress the denial of black rights. The League had little success in the 1890s; it virtually foundered for lack of funds and was quite unable to institute lawsuits. In 1898 it changed its name from League to Council, which sounded less militant and possibly reflected the growing reputation and conciliatory influence of Washington. Washington himself attended meetings of the Council though he was not active in it. The Council languished and finally fell apart in 1909.

A short-run failure, the Afro-American League and Council nonetheless paved the way for a successful effort later. Du Bois and others founded the National Association for the Advancement of Colored People in 1909. Its program and methods were essentially those of the League as Fortune had proposed in 1890.

Du Bois was very reticent about criticizing Washington, whom he acknowledged as one of the great leaders of his race. But their views on education differed so greatly, and Washington was so insistent that industrial and vocational education should be universal for blacks, that conflict here at least was inevitable. Du Bois resented the virtual starvation of his own Atlanta University, with its liberal-arts curriculum, while Tuskegee Institute in comparison received abundant support, and he was insistent that blacks share in American culture in all respects, which included education. As he put it in an address in 1909: "the vocation of a man in a modern civilized land includes not only the technique of his actual work, but . . . as a possible voter, a conserver of the public health, an intelligent follower of moral customs, and one who can at least appreciate if not partake something of the higher spiritual life of the world." And elsewhere Du Bois argued that a "talented tenth" of blacks—those who had a grasp of the whole heritage and workings of white society—was required for black leadership.

By 1904 the rupture with Washington was complete, and Du Bois became the object of bitter attacks from the Washington camp. Washington tried unsuccessfully to get Du Bois dismissed from Atlanta University. Du Bois received strong support from the so-called "Boston Radicals" in particular, led by William Monroe Trotter, publisher and editor of the Boston *Guardian.* In 1905 Du Bois founded the Niagara Movement to counter Washington's influence, and based the organization frankly on protest and agitation.

The NAACP The Niagara Movement shortly merged with the National Negro Committee, another protest group, to form the National Association for the Advancement of Colored People in 1909. The NAACP welcomed concerned whites into its membership, and with the first migration of Southern blacks to the North, with their greater freedom and incomes, the new organization could tap more talent and funds. Du Bois became the editor of its journal, *The Crisis,* and director of publicity and research. Renowned already as a gifted scholar, he now showed his skill as publicist and agitator for integration and full citizenship for blacks.

Du Bois' deep knowledge of history and his firm grasp of the facts relating to the condition of blacks made him virtually invulnerable to attack in debate. He could note, for example, the struggle of the European working classes for the vote and how, once having this, they used political strength to gain recognition for trade unions and to advance social reform. Thus political power augmented economic strength and vice-versa. He insisted that their

The first issue of The Crisis. *The NAACP used the journal effectively to emphasize black achievements and to investigate and publicize instances of discrimination. In addition to activities like campaigns for federal legislation,* The Crisis *also opened its pages to black poets. When asked the purpose of* The Crisis, *DuBois replied that it was to uphold the United States Constitution and its amendments.*

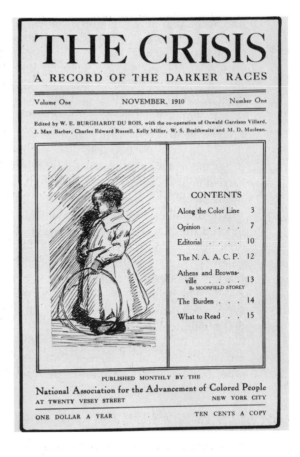

disenfranchisement held back black economic progress, because they could not protect their property rights and income without the vote, to say nothing of their civil rights, about which, however, he did say a great deal. He cited impressive examples of the persecution of propertied blacks to show that Washington's program left blacks essentially defenseless even if they should advance themselves economically. He stated in 1907:

> The voteless Negro is a provocation, an invitation to oppression, a plaything for mobs and a bonanza for demagogues. They serve always to distract attention from real issues and to ride fools and rascals into political power. The political campaign in Georgia before the last was avowedly and openly a campaign not against Negro crime and ignorance, but against Negro intelligence and property-owning and industrial competition as shown by an 83 percent increase in their property in ten years.

Du Bois concluded that the unbridled competition for jobs and income underlay fundamentally the racial question. He strongly urged the admission of blacks into trade unions, the overwhelming majority of which excluded them. He embraced socialist doctrines early and he became more convinced that only common ownership of the means of production would bring an ultimate solution to the racial question.

After Washington died in 1915, Du Bois got a wider hearing. Black newspapers such as the Boston *Guardian,* the Cleveland *Gazette,* and the Chicago *Conservator* supported Du Bois and the NAACP. Many blacks found his challenges too demanding in comparison with Washington's policy of accommodation. Du Bois, however, argued with such authority and reputation, knowledge and consistency, that he simply could not be overlooked. The debate between the two schools of thought was limited largely to the black press and lecture platform. It aroused little interest in white America, which carried on its business as though the black population did not exist. Neither did it involve the majority of the rural black population.

Nor did allies appear on the political front. The Progressive Movement ignored the blacks completely. Woodrow Wilson, however, offered some hope with his proclamation of the New Freedom in the Presidential campaign of 1912. This attracted many black votes since Wilson promised the blacks "fair dealing" and asserted that he would be President of all the people. Du Bois even resigned from the Socialist Party and declared his support for Wilson. In office, however, President Wilson proved to be a great disappointment. He replaced many black office-holders with whites, including the United States Ministers to Haiti and Santo Domingo; and his administration instituted segregation in government lunchrooms, toilets, and other facilities. Blacks protested, but to no avail.

The Beginnings of Change

Max Weber, the German sociologist, once observed metaphorically that the interests of society are the great rails on which humanity moves, but that ideas throw the switches. The statement may be usefully applied to the black experience in the twentieth century; and to a period that began in 1910 to see changes occur and that concluded in 1954 with a Supreme Court decision that declared that segregation in public schools must be ended.

At the beginning of this period, no significant number of whites believed that the interests of society required a change in the status of blacks, and they accordingly remained frozen in the pattern of discrimination. By 1954, however, a significant number of whites, many of them in high places, were urging that the interests of society required breaking the pattern. This shift in attitude was momentous, and ideas about the destiny of blacks in American life won serious national consideration. Underlying these changes were foundations that the blacks themselves began to build early in the century, a task in which they were aided by the great impersonal forces of urban-industrial growth and war.

Migration to the North   In 1910, of ninety-two million Americans, about ten million were blacks; of these, nine million lived in the Southern states,

Children of the city. The mass migration of blacks to Northern cities, provoked by crop failure and economic hardship in the South, was encouraged by black newspapers like the Chicago Defender, *which published favorable accounts of life in the city and poems offering the hope of a new life. Once in the city, blacks were faced with several problems of adjustment, including the harshness of the urban environment in which their children played.*

and the great majority in rural areas. In the decade 1910–1920, some 450,000 blacks left the South, primarily for Northern cities; and within the South itself there was a considerable movement of blacks into the cities. This great internal migration continued in subsequent decades, and more than anything else broke up the static condition of the blacks, released black energies, and gave the racial question a new national dimension.

The primary cause of the migration lay with blacks themselves. People will stay with many miserable situations if they believe these will eventually improve. By this time, however, following the destruction of black political and civil rights and all that went with them, hope had greatly diminished. Economic improvement of individual blacks appeared only to heighten white resentment. White supremacy had exerted itself most tyrannously in

Open air coffee stand in the black ghetto of Philadelphia, from the woodcut
Hungry *by S. G. McCutcheon.*

the rural South, and understandably it was from there that the exodus was greatest.

Natural catastrophes played an important role too. During World War I the Southern cotton crops fell under the ravages of the boll weevil, which caused a great reduction in yields and created a severe depression in the cotton economy. Before the war, yields had averaged 190 pounds an acre. From 1915 to 1924, yields dropped to an average of only 161 pounds, and infestation by weevils became almost complete throughout the Southern cotton states. Serious river floods in 1915, particularly in Mississippi and Alabama, brought further discouragement to Southern agriculture. Southern farm income dropped. For blacks in particular this provided a powerful incentive to leave the region and strike out in a new environment, the city.

Effects of the First World War   The First World War, 1914–1918, upset international migration, greatly stimulated the industrial economy, and drew black soldiers and civilians deeply into American participation in that conflict. All these events worked to the advantage of American blacks.

From 1910 to 1914 approximately a million Europeans had emigrated to the United States each year. The outbreak of war in Europe in 1914 dried up this last mighty wave of the "new immigration," and with it the great reservoir of cheap labor upon which Northern industry had come to rely. Yet the demand for this labor not only remained but accelerated. The Western European powers, particularly Britain and France, shortly began to place orders for American goods of all varieties, and after the United States entered the war in April 1917, the need for labor became insatiable. Blacks thus found jobs in established industries such as iron, steel, coal, meatpacking, railroads, and others; and the war drew them into the new munitions plants, the expanding shipyards, and automobile and truck plants. Blacks as usual received the dirtiest, most backbreaking, and lowest-paid jobs. But income in wages ran from fifty to two hundred percent higher than they had been accustomed to getting in the rural South.

Military service drew 360,000 blacks to active duty. Many of these served overseas, mostly in labor battalions, but several regiments went to the front. The overseas experience at once opened a new horizon for black soldiers, yet made for bitterness as well. In France they found themselves for the first time amidst a white population not greatly concerned about the color question, and here they had a rare opportunity to enjoy freedoms ordinarily enjoyed by whites. Yet they found that military leaves were regulated by the color line, that certain cities and cafés might be off-limits to them by military order, and that white soldiers would spread damaging stories about black soldiers to make the French fear them. The overseas experience generally increased black militancy. A small number of blacks even made some quick comparisons and stayed abroad after the war.

In all branches of the military service segregation prevailed. Blacks demanded the right to become officers, but with rare exceptions military authorities resisted this demand. On the home front blacks were asked to participate in a host of civilian activities such as the Red Cross, YMCA, and bond drives. In keeping with the need for tapping all resources, government agencies began consulting with black leaders. Such invitations in the name of patriotism of course sharpened black aspirations for full citizenship. A war that had been declared to make the world safe for democracy called attention to the absence of democracy for the blacks at home. So a new mixture of impatience and determination came to affect blacks, a mood aggressively expressed by Du Bois in 1919: "We return from fighting. We return fighting. Make way for democracy. We have saved it in France and by the Great Jehovah we will save it in the USA or know the reason why."

The realities did not sustain this mood. For example, William Monroe Trotter, the black journalist from Boston, traveled on his own in the name of American blacks to the Paris Peace Conference in 1919. His intent was to gain an international hearing for the question of democratic rights for blacks at home. The government denied him a passport. Trotter managed to secure a seaman's passport, took a quick course in cooking, and signed on a small steamship as second cook. But all his dogged resourcefulness failed to get him an audience in Paris from either Woodrow Wilson or Georges Clemenceau, the French Premier.

The Chicago riot. In addition to the thirty-eight people killed, six hundred were wounded and a thousand families were burned out of their homes.

The war years, in spite of the general improvement for blacks, prefigured the reaction that was to follow the rising presence of blacks in urban America. In the summer of 1917 a great race riot occurred in East St. Louis, Illinois, prompted by employment of recently arrived black migrants in a factory fulfilling government contracts. Forty blacks were killed in a mob action. Blacks in industry and the service trades tried to influence the American Federation of Labor to relax the color line on trade union membership but made little headway. Unions remained essentially "lily white." In the immediate aftermath of war, some twenty-five race riots flamed throughout the country in the "Red Summer" of 1919, so called because so much blood was shed. The riots consisted of white mob action against blacks who fought back in self-defense. The great Chicago riot lasted thirteen days in July and August, and thirty-eight persons were killed.

A tally of the black ledger for the decade 1910–1920 shows debits in both old and new forms of white resistance to black improvement. The credits, though they appear small, were nonetheless real and solid, unlikely to be undone. The migrations of the decade placed fourteen percent of American blacks in the North, an increase of about four percent. The increase took place almost entirely in Northern cities, particularly New York, Chicago, Philadelphia, Detroit, and Cleveland. In the South as well, more blacks became city dwellers. Nationally, twenty-seven percent of all blacks lived in urban centers in 1910, a figure that increased to thirty-four percent by 1920.

Such changes and fresh trends enabled blacks to build and strengthen new communities and to create centers of political, economic, and cultural influence. From the urban black centers of the North in particular, blacks could venture with greater assurance into the white world. Personal humiliations were common, and violence in racial relations did not disappear. But even while residentially segregated within their urban communities, black life and property were more secure.

Profile: BOOKER T. WASHINGTON

Booker T. Washington (1856–1915) was born on a small Virginia farm, the son of a slave cook and a white man of the neighborhood. Because he was the child of a house servant and because he was freed at the age of nine, his experience as a slave was neither harsh nor long. Rejecting the hard work of the salt furnace and coal mine which his stepfather tried to force him into, he ended up as a servant in the home of General Lewis Ruffner, whose wife befriended him, taught him to read, and began his education. He later worked his way through Hampton Institute in Virginia where he fell under the spell of the principal, General Samuel C. Armstrong, whose philosophy of advice for Southern blacks, given in 1877, Washington adopted as his own:

> Be thrifty and industrious. Command the respect of your neighbors by a good record and a good character. Own your own houses. Educate your children. Make the best of your difficulties. Live down prejudice. Cultivate peaceful relations with all. As a voter act as you think and not as you are told. Remember that you have seen marvelous changes in sixteen years. In view of that be patient—thank God and take courage.

When Washington became head of a new black normal school at Tuskegee, Alabama in 1881, he put into practice there the General's advice and the model of industrial education and the Protestant work ethic that Hampton emphasized. Under Washington's direction the school flourished and became the Tuskegee Normal and Industrial Institute, the best known of the sixty-five black institutes and colleges established in the South by 1900. Washington with his congenial philosophy proved to be an able solicitor of funds and got support from Northern philanthropists such as George Peabody, Andrew Carnegie, and John F. Slater as well as from Northern churches and capitalists. He also impressed the Alabama legislature so much that in 1884 it voted Tuskegee an annual appropriation. As Tuskegee Institute expanded, so did Washington's reputation as a black spokesman, a position confirmed by his famous "Atlanta Compromise" speech in 1895.

Washington was particularly successful in attuning the black cause to traditional American values. For example, he emphasized the land and agriculture as the mainstay of black existence, thus speaking to the traditional idealization of rural life by white Americans. Yet he knew that blacks found it difficult to get jobs in Southern factories because here the competition with whites was most intense. By stressing black self-help and the need for overcoming adversity, he was also emphasizing themes stressed in many a popular novel or tract and going back in time to the days of Benjamin Franklin. Washington was almost incurably optimistic—another American trait—in ignoring examples of prejudice and citing those which revealed harmony and good will between the races.

Even in such matters as segregation and lynching, he was invariably conciliatory and moralistic. He would complain about the inadequacy of separate black public accommodations rather than strike at the inequality exhibited. When he condemned mob violence and lynching, he would point to the harm that lynching inflicted upon whites, their moral fiber, and the reputation of the South.

Few Americans, black or white, have had as keen a sense for the currents of public opinion and custom as Washington had. In contemporary terms he was a first-rate public relations expert and a skilled political infighter, as his enemies in the black population well knew. He was dined by Presidents and received at the Court of St. James's. A superb public speaker, much in demand, he spread his views widely from the public platform and the dinner rostrum. His speeches, well dotted with anecdotes and moral exhortations, were well received by white audiences. Apart from the good will they generated among whites, these speeches conducted a softening-up campaign in the persistent search for philanthropic support for Washington's many educational projects as well as other schemes for the improvement of blacks.

Both Washington and his program seemed relatively simple: do not antagonize; accept. Work for economic and educational advancement, and political and social rights will eventually follow. Yet neither Washington nor his approach was that simple. In some respects he was like a grand master in chess who was able to play a dozen games simultaneously, and win them all. He ran Tuskegee like a benevolent despot, and against those blacks who organized protest movements he employed espionage and sabotage methods that undermined their effectiveness. Yet to the Northern public he appeared the very model of a sane and rational statesman on racial matters, fully in the American tradition. To Southern blacks he was a father figure whose advice many took to good advantage. To the Southern white public, his advice to blacks not to challenge the system made him safe and acceptable. Yet secretly he financed and pushed a series of court suits challenging such restrictions as the grandfather clause in voting, the denial of jury service to blacks, and Jim Crow railroad cars. How he managed to play all these roles as successfully as he did is a source of wonder, and must have cost him much internal strain.

Today Washington's philosophy is inadequate and unrealistic, but this does not suggest that he is undeserving of respect. In the climate of the times, his approach may have been accommodation to white supremacy, but he also kept alive through his work the sense of black identity and pride and of being American in spite of color. And despite the briefness of his life as a slave, neither he nor anyone else who had been a slave ever forgot that fact, and emancipation in itself thus was the great achievement of their lifetimes. Only with a new generation of blacks born free would a new sense of what constituted freedom emerge. And when the generation of ex-slaves, including Washington, passed away, new leaders and new ideas came to the fore.

Chapter 3
AMERICANS FROM ABROAD

The Spirit of the Times:
GOING TO AMERICA

I lived on a farm near the Dalmatian coast with my mother and my sister. . . . We were not too poor, we had a pretty good piece of land and had just bought about forty acres and we had to borrow money to buy that land and I thought if I go to America I can pay it off, earn enough to pay it off in four years, but it would take forever if I stayed, so let's go, I told my cousin Nick, what's the use of sticking around here . . . and besides I wanted to get away from war, did not feel it right to go into the service and serve a king for six cents a day. . . . Some fellows from where we lived came back from America, a cousin brought a trunk with clothes, four or five suits, and shoes, good shoes, two or three hats, he brought a shotgun with him too, automatic shotgun for hunting, and some money, but we found out later he never spent any money in America, maybe fifty cents a day, ten cents was like five dollars in those days. . . . And then we had a neighbor who came home with gold teeth in his mouth, maybe two on the side of his mouth, and I remember when we came out of church and saw him, and then he talked and laughed all the time out of that side of his mouth so we would be sure to see the gold teeth, oh he was a big shot, putting on a show, a fellow like that could buy some land, pay his father's debts, and marry a nice-looking girl. . . . So, let's go, I told my cousin Nick, what's the use of sticking around here. . . . My mother cried, we all cried, she said she would probably never see me again. . . . Oh yes, I said, we'll be back, don't worry, but we never did come back and my mother died. . . . We didn't make a lot of money when we came and we did not want to go back without money, broke, the people around there you come back without American money and they think you are a bum, don't want to work, so we just stayed on. . . . It cost altogether 300–400 crowns for passport, papers, transportation and you had to have 25 dollars in your pockets when you arrived or get it from someone. . . . We took, that's my cousin and I, a little boat down the river to the sea and then we took another boat to Split and from there a bigger boat to Trieste and that's where the big ship was, an English ship, big ship, thirty thousand tons maybe. . . . We stayed there for three days waiting for people from every direction, most wanting to get away from army

Stephen Yakich

service, all under 21, they did not want to serve the kings, mostly single fellows from Poland, Hungary, Yugoslavia, Greece, I don't remember any families, maybe there were some, it was a long time ago, sixty years now, that's a long time, some girls though, not many, coming over to marry someone in America. . . . There were some beautiful girls from Poland, going to marry some fellows in America they had never seen, and they fell in love with some of the fellows on ship, but they couldn't understand each other except they were in love, maybe they changed their minds later about marrying those fellows in America! . . . Naturally we couldn't understand the others, somebody could understand Polish a little bit but not good really, we stuck together because we couldn't understand the other fellows very good. . . . We lived down below, there were a lot of bunks, one on top of you and below, a whole lot of guys stayed there, food was good, meat every day, mostly stew and those English pies with meat, you know how the English make them, for breakfast bacon and eggs or ham and eggs, coffee, three meals a day. . . . It took seventeen days, the ship wasn't moving too fast and it was kind of rough, we stopped at Naples and Gibraltar on the Spanish side. . . . But it wasn't bad at all, we had a lot of fun, we could come out on top and you can have a dance or listen to someone singing, during the day there was mostly dancing, but before we left Trieste pretty soon along comes a small ship from Greece, and lots of them were wrestlers and they would put on a show we could watch. . . . We tried to learn English, how to count the money and to say good morning and ask for something to eat, we tried to learn things like that. . . . And we all wanted to see New York, it was exciting, when we got near New York everybody was up on top, looking out the windows, crowding around trying to find room to see The Liberty, you know, the Statue of Liberty, and pretty soon somebody way on top sees it and shouts See the Liberty! and then everybody shouts The Liberty, The Liberty! yes it was exciting. . . . That was a long time ago. . . . No, I never had any regrets about going to America, no regrets, I probably wouldn't be alive today if I hadn't come to America, lots of guys where I lived got killed in World War I and then more got killed in the Second World War, they fought among themselves then you know. . . . No, I never had any regrets, only regret is that I miss my mother and sister and never saw them again, and I just miss my mother and sister very much, I could afford to go back now, but there's nothing there to see anymore, what would I say, where would I go? . . . They have their own graves, a family place you understand, I guess I could go there. . . .

So remembered Stephen Yakich in 1973, sixty years later.

The Immigrant and America

Immigration has been one of the most significant and continuous experiences in American history. For over three and a half centuries approximately forty-seven million people have pulled up stakes in their homelands and headed for America. But the tide reached its flood in the half-century after the Civil War, when over twenty-five million immigrants made their way to the United States.

These numbers considered by themselves seem astonishing. Yet at no time since the founding of the republic did the foreign-born exceed fifteen percent of the total population. Other countries have had a far greater proportion of foreign-born. In Argentina in 1914, for example, thirty percent of the population was foreign-born. While the millions of immigrants who poured into the United States from 1865 to 1915 seemed in danger of overwhelming in numbers the Americans already on the scene, this appearance was deceptive, because of the heavy concentration of immigrants in certain regions of the country and in the cities. In the Northeast, for example, the foreign-born formed twenty-five percent of the population in 1910, whereas in the South they constituted less than two percent. New York City, the major port of entry, absorbed so many immigrants that it became in effect the largest Jewish, Italian, and Irish city in the world. The statistics on immigration were deceptive also in that large numbers returned to their homelands, especially after 1905, so that the actual net immigration was less than the statistics on entry indicated. Some of those returning were "birds of passage" who came back to the United States. Some even returned home again and then re-entered the United States yet a third time.

Variety of Immigrant Groups   Great though the numbers were, numbers were not the most significant fact about immigration. So many *different* peoples came—this was what has made immigration to the United States unusual. No other country could match this diversity. After a century of independence, Argentina's immigrant population was made up almost entirely of only three groups: Italians, Spaniards, and Portuguese. But the peoples coming to the United States!—Italians, Germans, Poles, Slovaks, Serbs, Croatians, Slovenians, Bulgarians, Russians, Carpatho-Russians, Ukranians, Lithuanians, Letts, Finns, Hungarians, Norwegians, Swedes, Danes, Dutch, French, Flemish, Spaniards, Portuguese, Rumanians, Armenians, Syrians, Albanians, Greeks, Turks, Scotch-Irish, Irish, Scots, Welsh, Japanese, Chinese, Filipinos, Indians, Pakistanis, Mexicans, English, and numerous others—an astonishing variety of peoples seeking a new life.

Such an incredibly varied group—their descendants often intermingling by marriage—has presented a bewilderingly complex picture to other countries in modern times, most of which are composed of a single major ethnic and cultural strain. The writer James Michener has told the story of an American officer in Australia in World War II who was asked to acquaint an audience of Australians, whose origins were relatively simple, with the nature of their American allies. Attempting to convey the idea of a composite mixture of peoples, the American concluded with the unfortunate metaphor that in his veins flowed the blood of Englishmen, Irishmen, Scotsmen, Germans, Italians, and so on—at which point an Australian commented in a loud whisper that the American's mother must have been quite a sporting type. Today it would not be so difficult to get the point across to the Australians, who in the postwar period also opened their doors to different peoples.

The war also showed the capacity of a disparate group to maintain a sense of ethnic pride in its origins in spite of their common American identity. The story is told that on the day after Pearl Harbor an elementary school bus in California pulled up to a corner to pick up a small Japanese-American boy. As he entered the bus there was silence for a moment as he looked down the aisle at the other students, and then he brightly observed, "Well, we sure beat the hell out of you guys yesterday."

The Forces of Assimilation   Indicative as is this story of ethnic pride, the power of the American environment was great, and the presence of immigrant minorities did not result in any fundamental alteration of the main aspects of American life, nor did it significantly change any established institutions. The two-party political system continued; the constitutional division of government powers into legislative, executive, and judicial branches remained unaffected; the separation of church and state was maintained. True, politicians who had immigrant groups within their constituencies found that they had to take into account the interests of such groups when making campaign promises, but there was nothing new in that. The public school movement did not shift its course into another channel, nor did the American reliance on voluntary organizations to get all kinds of things done suddenly disappear. The American private enterprise system was not abandoned. It would, in short, be difficult to find a single significant institution that was significantly changed by the impact of immigration. The presence of such a variety of immigrants unquestionably enriched and augmented American life as a whole. But the immigrants, despite the power of their culture, accommodated themselves to America and its traditions; America did not accommodate itself to them.

Furthermore, the immigrant enrichment of American life was essentially a matter of individual contributions. It is not uncommon for people to cite the scientific discoveries, scholarly books, popular songs or symphonies, political or business achievements attributed to certain immigrants, and then to divide these into ethnic categories and proclaim that this represents the Greek contribution to American life, that the Polish, another the Italian. But this distorts the nature of the immigrant experience. All the achievements that can be listed, and the list is long and remarkable, are the achievements of individuals who came to America and found an environment in which their talents could flourish and be productive. America gave such individuals opportunity, and the immigrants responded to that challenge. Both America and the immigrants benefited by this exchange. But it is a deception to assume that the creative gifts of the immigrant are somehow identifiable as the contributions of some ethnic group. Such contributions became a part of the whole American heritage, and sprang from the nature of American society itself. Few if any of these achievements would have occurred if those who made them had stayed at home and never left for the New World.

It is also important to remember that the immigrant experience was unique in that it was confined to the immigrant generation itself. Those born in America—the children of the immigrants, their grandchildren, their great-grandchildren—were not immigrants. For better or worse, they were Americans. Wrote Vilhelm Moberg of an immigrant mother in *Unto a Good Land:* "The ones she had borne into the world . . . would from the beginning of their lives say what her own tongue was unable to say, *at home* here in America, *back there* in Sweden."

The immigrants themselves, unless they had been small children when they arrived, never became fully assimilated. They were never "melted" down in some vast cultural pot. But neither did they remain entirely Italian, Polish, German, or Russian Jew. To a greater or lesser degree, and on their own terms, they became American. Their children and grandchildren were Americans from the beginning.

What distinguished the immigrants when they came—language, religious customs, social mores and habits, dress, food, the whole paraphenalia of their culture—all began to fade or change in significance under the impact of the American experience. No matter how hard the immigrants might try to preserve these cultural distinctions intact within the framework of their families, they did not succeed. Their children might learn the old tongue in the home, but like their parents they quickly discovered that this was not the language of the business, politics, education, literature, and social life around them. Grandchildren might learn some of the old language, but rarely spoke

*Americanization via the classroom. Public schools provided evening classes
in English and American history to ease new immigrants into society.*

it well. Church services gradually shifted to English, the foreign-language
newspapers faded away until only a handful were left, the foreign-language
theater disappeared, ceremonies were abbreviated or modified.

What people shared in America became the important things in their lives,
not the ethnic differences that set them off from one another. It was science,
technology, industrialism, and the city that shaped and determined the nature of people's lives, not whether they ate pasta or knew Italian. Moreover,
many of the byproducts of immigrant cultures found their way into the
mainstream of American life and were no longer confined to the immigrant
group that brought them. Americans whose parents, grandparents, or great-
grandparents immigrated to the United States still take justifiable pride in
that experience as part of their family history. Ways of cooking certain
foods, the social rituals of family or clan gatherings, taking the time to
observe annually some ceremony maintained out of respect for the past,
participation in celebrations honoring one's origins—all these may persist.
But an American participating in the Columbus Day parade is not a Neapol-
itan, nor is an American marching on St. Patrick's Day a Dubliner. The
Mafia may have been an importation from Italy, but it flourishes in America
not because it is a powerful cultural tradition maintained by the Italians, but
because certain unattractive American conditions encourage it.

The immigrant experience enriched and diversified the American, but did not drastically alter it. The dominant culture prevailed. Stephen Yakich and Phillip Mizel (see the Profile) came to America in 1913 and 1914. There are today no special characteristics that distinguish Michael Mizel, 22, grandson of Phillip Mizel, and David Yakich, 29, son of Stephen Yakich. In any part of the world today, including the lands of their family origins, they would both be recognized for what they are, Americans.

At any rate, who all these peoples were that came to the United States from 1865 to 1915—and indeed on to 1924 when the era of free immigration ended—why they came, and what happened to them in America tells us much about American society and culture during those decades and since.

The Old Immigration and the New

The traditional sources of new Americans in the pre-Civil War period— Western and Northern Europe and Canada—continued to be the main sources for almost thirty years. English, Germans, Irish, Scandinavians, and Canadians arrived in greater numbers than ever before with the single exception of the Irish. Approximately ten million immigrants entered the United States from 1860 to 1890, and 85 percent of them were of the so-called "old immigration"—3 million from Germany, 1.6 million from Britain, 1.5 million from Ireland, 1 million from Scandinavia, and over 900,000 from Canada.

But the greatest wave of immigration was yet to come: the so-called "new immigration" from Southern and Eastern Europe, which began to be significant in the 1880s and by 1896 had passed the old immigration in annual size. These peoples washed onto America's shores by the millions from 1880 until the final restrictive legislation of 1924 ended the long unbroken tradition of open immigration. The numbers in the new immigration were very great: 3.5 million Poles, 4.5 million Italians, 2.75 million from various parts of Russia. In the single year of 1907, 1.3 million immigrants entered the country. Not only the numbers but the variety was far greater than ever before, as subject peoples fled from the Russian and Austro-Hungarian Empires: Poles from Russian Poland and Austrian Galicia; Ukranians and Georgians from Russia; Jews from Russia, Hungary, and Rumania; Czechs, Slovaks, Croatians, Slovenians, Serbs, and Magyars from Austria-Hungary; Greeks, Bulgarians, Italians. They came in what seemed a never-ending stream.

Motives for the New Immigration: Economic   Old or new, the immigrants came for the same basic reason as their predecessors: to find a better life in the New World than they faced in the Old. Economic conditions had caused severe hardships for many. The industrialization of Western and Northern Europe brought with it periods of chronic unemployment and low wages. The great expansion in population in those countries left those on the land with less and less acreage to support a family; a small plot could be

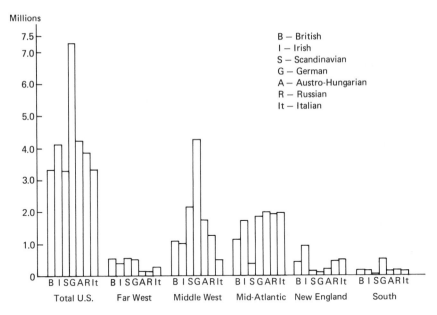

B — British
I — Irish
S — Scandinavian
G — German
A — Austro-Hungarian
R — Russian
It — Italian

DISTRIBUTION OF IMMIGRANT STOCK IN
THE UNITED STATES (1920)

divided only so often and still provide a living. America itself was in part a
cause for the distress of many, since increasing supplies of cheap grain from
America forced farm prices down in Europe, bringing disaster to many in the
Northern and Western countries. The retarded development of industry in
Southern and Eastern Europe left many economies unable to absorb in
factories, mills, and mines the surplus rural population whose capacity to
survive on the land was diminishing. The most primitive economic conditions in rural Russia, village Greece, and on the agricultural estates of
Southern Italy and Sicily chained millions to a vicious system of poverty and
degradation marked by ill health, disease, and inadequate food, clothing,
and shelter.

In a pleading letter to the Emigrants Protective Society in Poland for aid in
getting to America, a Polish father stated bluntly the cry of the dispossessed:

> I want to go to America, but I have no means at all because I am poor and have
> nothing but the ten fingers of my hands, a wife, and 9 children. I have no work
> at all, although I am strong and healthy and only 45 years old. I cannot earn for
> my family . . . and [the children] call for food and clothing and more or less
> education. I wish to work, not easily only but even hard, but what can I do? I
> will not go to steal and I have no work. So I beg the Protective Association to
> accept me for this journey and not only me, but I should like to take with me
> two of my children, a boy 16 and a girl 18 years old. And I beg the Association.
> There are still other people who would readily go to America. They are also
> poor.

America, as it had always done, seemed a paradise to many, especially in
the far reaches of Eastern Europe, who could know little or nothing of what it

was really like. Some, in fact, only now heard of America for the first time, and had no idea where it was. Northern and Western Europeans may have had longer contact with America, but among common people everywhere the basic belief was the same: that the standard of living was higher in the United States than anywhere else in the world—abundant and better food, more attractive houses, more adequate clothing, medical care, education for the young. The land was fertile and rich in minerals, labor was done by machines, wages were high, there was work for all who sought it, taxes were low. It was a tantalizing picture.

"In America you get pie and puddings," wrote a British immigrant, putting it all on the most basic level. An immigrant in Nebraska wrote home that the "soil is unequalled in fertility." A Czech woman returning to her village near Prague reported that America was "rich with opportunities for people not afraid of hard work." And a Polish immigrant wrote home somewhat extravagantly: "I do very well. . . . I have very good and easy work; I can say that I don't work at all, I only stand in an iron-foundry. . . . I have 26 roubles wages weekly, counting in our country's money." A Greek immigrant wrote home to his former employer: "Here people work hard and regularly, and rest only on Sundays, but we fare well. Today, the day I write, is Sunday. I have taken my bath, I have had my milk, and I will pass the day happily. When did I know life with such order in Greece?"

Social Equality   America was not only the land of economic opportunity, it was also the land of social equality. Despite the rising gap between classes and the increase in social distinctions appearing in the United States, the contrasts between American and Old World societies still seemed sharp and clear. George Jacob Holyoke, a British traveler in the United States was struck by what he regarded as the transformation in British working-class immigrants. Whereas in England they had no social contacts with their "masters," in one American town he visited they promptly took him to meet their mayor. In 1891 a German immigrant wrote home to his brother: "And what is nicer yet is the fact that this is a free land. No one can give orders to anybody here, one is as good as another, no one takes off his hat to another as you have to do in Germany." An Italian landowner summed up the transformation America seemed to work on its humble immigrants when he complained about the attitude of those who had been to America and who "walk through the streets as if they were our equals. . . . The worst of it is, signore, that they lose respect for us!"

The irrefutable evidence of the American paradise was the money immigrants sent back home, the letters they wrote, the pictures they posted off, and the dramatic appearance of those who had made it in America and come back home. Stoyan Christowe relates the story of the Macedonian village of Selo when a letter arrived one day from a former resident containing a money order for forty napoleons, more money than anyone in the village had ever possessed. The villagers promptly began borrowing and mortgaging to raise money for the passage to America, and this experience was repeated

Jewish immigrants arriving at Ellis Island.

over and over again. Statistics reveal a close correlation between the amount of emigration and the amount of money sent home in postal money orders; a large number of emigrants were unquestionably financed in their voyages by friends or relatives already in America. Such money was also often used to improve living standards, buy an extra bit of land, pay debts, and get ahead a little. In 1907, some $85 million was sent home to Italy, an immense sum for the impoverished peoples of Sicily and the South where most of it went.

Pictures sent home also created an image of America as the land of wealth, opportunity, and social equality. One immigrant who was a hotel waiter stunned his village friends back home with a photograph of himself seated in an automobile and wearing a large watch chain and a ring. A Pole in Pennsylvania amazed his relatives with photographs of himself attired in a style suitable only to a member of the upper class in Poland. Immigrants who returned home permanently or for visits made a vivid impression. A simple white collar worn by a returned Italian was regarded by friends as a sign of affluence. A Hungarian woman who returned to her homeland to marry and

Advertisement encouraging emigrants to purchase land in Kansas.

settle down told wide-eyed villagers of her days on South Halsted Street in Chicago where she had eaten "thin bread with thick jam on it, and the land was flowing with sausages, lager beer, and chewing gum." A steelworker from Pittsburgh returned to his Yugoslav village and made an incredible impression by telling how he had actually met and shaken hands with President Theodore Roosevelt.

American Persuasiveness These were the most influential channels through which the image of America was cast as a lure before the eyes of the common people of Europe. But many Americans also had a special interest in promoting immigration and worked hard to spread the word through Europe that the chances for a better life were very good in the United States. Manufacturing and other business interests supported various companies, such as The American Emigrant Company, organized to promote emigration among Europeans in order to secure cheap labor for the United States. The great transcontinental railroads, through federal land grants, had large quantities of land along their rights-of-way and sought settlers from abroad by heavy promotional advertising. Shipping interests sought a profit by filling their ships with passengers on the return voyage to America from European ports. Many states, especially in the West but also elsewhere, established immigration commissions to encourage settlement within their boundaries. All these interests had agents abroad flooding Europe with propaganda. They distributed brochures on American prosperity, advertised heavily in European newspapers, planted articles in the press, put up alluring posters, and even stood outside church doors, as in Italy, handing out cards with hymns praising America. Illustrations on brochures frequently showed a "typical" emigrant's progress from a sod house to a fine home. But these efforts were probably important only in providing information to the prospective emigrant on how actually to get to America, and perhaps about the geography of the country. They were rarely effective in persuading people to emigrate. Emigrants in fact, were warned by those who had already been through the experience not to get involved with these American promoters who were more likely to fleece emigrants than to aid them. One Pole warned: "Let nobody listen to anybody but only to his relatives whom he has here, in this golden America."

There were, of course, counter-images of America spread by governments which sought to discourage emigration and publicized hard times in America. There were also returned emigrants who had failed in America and came home broken in health and spirit. But the significant fact was that for most prospective emigrants it was easier to believe in America as the land of hope—the evidence seemed so overwhelming. For those who decided to emigrate, the task of doing so was made easier than ever before by the industrial developments of the last half of the nineteenth century. Technological improvements in the steamship made the Atlantic crossing quicker and safer. Growing trade led to the rise of major steamship lines whose sharp competition drove fares down drastically. The expansion in construction of railroads in Europe made it easier and cheaper for emigrants to reach ports of embarkation. When railroads tied Eastern and Central Germany to the Baltic ports, more emigrants left for America from those regions of Germany than ever before.

And so they came, millions upon millions from all over Europe. Most became part of the American urban scene because the city was rapidly becoming the focal point of opportunity in America, although a surprising number still managed to find their way to rural areas. But it was in the city where the jobs were, and particularly the unskilled jobs, which were the only ones available to immigrants with only peasant or ancient handicraft backgrounds.

Typical Adaptive Patterns   Those from Britain—English, Welsh, Cornishmen, Scots—were widely dispersed and quickly assimilated. Many went into farming and ranching, but large numbers also went into industry. One survey showed that in 1890, forty-eight percent of British immigrants had found jobs in America's factories and mills, many of them as skilled workers. Although most came from the land, the Irish in America were heavily concentrated in the industrial states and the large cities. New York, Massachusetts, Pennsylvania, and Illinois absorbed fifty-eight percent of the Irish, and eighty-one percent settled in cities of more than twenty-five thousand population, especially in New York, Boston, Philadelphia, and Chicago. Most were without skills of any kind and had to rely on the pick and shovel for a

living, often on railroad construction gangs. German immigrants had traditionally sought the land, and now also established themselves on farms, in
the Great Lakes states as well as in the Upper Mississippi Valley. But increasing numbers also ended in urban America, and Midwestern cities such
as Chicago and Milwaukee drew a steadily increasing German element.
Scandinavians, mostly from Sweden and Norway, sought the soil, and most
poured into Minnesota, Iowa, Wisconsin, Michigan, Illinois, and even the
Dakotas. Impoverished French Canadians flowed down into the textile mills
of New England, while others settled in Michigan, Illinois, and Wisconsin.

Many of the southern Italians, although agricultural workers, had lived
crowded together in towns, going out to work each day on large estates. But
few of these Italian immigrants possessed any assets marketable in America
except their muscles, and the majority ended in cities. Some made it to
California's rural counties, but most concentrated in New York, Pennsylvania, and New Jersey. They helped build railroads, did the back-breaking
labor in sewer and subway construction, worked as street-cleaners, became
fruit and vegetable peddlers and bootblacks, poured into the mills of New
England and New Jersey and the mines of Pennsylvania, and sweated it out
in the New York garment industry. In this variety their experience was
typical, although many immigrant groups tended to congregate in certain
industries and kinds of work. Even more than southern Italians, the Jewish
immigrants had an urban background, though many came from villages in
Russia. They too flooded into the cities, especially New York. Many Jews
had been workers in the needle trades, and in America great numbers were
exploited as garment workers. Others became petty tradesmen and shop-
keepers.

The Poles went down into the mines of Pennsylvania, and served as
laborers of all kinds in the major cities, especially New York, Chicago, and
Cleveland. Large numbers also made their way onto the land, taking over the
declining farms of New England and settling on the farmlands of the Middle
West. Other Slavic groups moved into the steelmills and the meat-packing
industry, and served as manual laborers, miners, and unskilled factory
hands.

Some groups engaged in a wide variety of economic activities. The Greeks,
for example, went into barbering, cobbling, and tailoring; or they worked on
railroads, established stores, restaurants, and shoeshine parlors, or put in
time on such menial labor as sweeping in New England mills. Wherever
there was work to do the immigrant was on the job: in housing, office, and
factory construction; grading and paving streets; dredging harbors; building
water-supply and sewer systems; laying gas lines and trolley tracks; constructing railroads; mining; tending machines in factories and mills; supplying the menial services city folk demanded; and working their independent
way in thousands of small stores and shops. Their identification with
urban-industrial America was complete by 1910, at which time more than
two-thirds of the populations of America's eight largest cities were first- or
second generation immigrants. At that time less than eight percent of the
rural population was foreign-born.

*Street peddler with his makeshift display of pastries. Streets lined with
pushcarts offering a variety of necessities were a common sight in
immigrant neighborhoods.*

By the end of the nineteenth century a trickle of immigrants from another
part of the world had joined the stream. These were from China and Japan.
From the 1850s to the 1870s about 238,000 Chinese were brought into the
United States to satisfy labor needs on the West Coast in mining camps and
railroads. Later in the 1890s and in the first few years of the twentieth
century, about 155,000 Japanese also arrived on the West Coast. But racial
antagonisms resulted in restrictive federal legislation beginning in 1882,
which almost entirely eliminated Chinese immigration except under special
circumstances. Similar hostility against the Japanese resulted in 1907 in an
agreement with Japan not to issue passports to laborers in Japan seeking to
emigrate to America, thus effectively curtailing emigration from the Land of
the Rising Sun.

The Immigrant Experience

Life in America was not easy for the new arrivals, not alone because it
demanded sweat and blood in labor, but also because it was so different. The
immigrant literally entered a new world, which challenged ancient values
and beliefs, shattered old loyalties, and bruised the spirit.

New Ways, Strange Customs   In the new environment the immigrants often felt lost and helpless. Pay was low, hours long, and employment precarious. The immigrant worked by the hour or by the piece, not by the season, as most once had done on the land. For many it was impossible to get ahead, and life became a matter of existing from day to day with no assurance of what tomorrow would bring. The work that many did bore no resemblance to the flow of labor on the land, in which every task was related to the single goal of producing food and crops, and there was a sense of wholeness to one's endeavors. Now they turned out only parts of things in factories or a single task in construction, not finished products or whole units of work with which they could identify. The system itself was impersonal, and a man when he was hired was judged not on his qualities as a human being, but on the pure chance of where he was standing in the hiring line when workers were taken on.

Likewise the physical environment was not the world of the living soil with which so many had been familiar, but the cold inanimate world of brick, stone, mortar, steel and iron, of streets and factories. They were confused by constant change: old buildings were torn down, new ones arose; towns and cities expanded; people were everywhere, and more appeared all the time. The immigrants could not raise their own food, or satisfy any of their needs with their own creativity. They had to buy what they needed from strangers in stores, an unfamiliar process. Thus many relied upon peddlers or tiny shops run by their compatriots—both expensive means of purchase.

Religious and Social Comforts

Many of the new Americans were plagued by unfamiliar money problems. Shortage of cash led to wasteful borrowing and credit systems, and to purchasing in small quantities, always costly. Immigrants were often exploited by their own countrymen: by the *padrone* who contracted labor gangs for construction companies at lump sums profitable to himself and the company but giving a minimum to the immigrant signing on; by immigrant "bankers" who recruited laborers in the old country, transported them to America, housed them, found them jobs, and then took a heavy slice of their paychecks; by unscrupulous storeowners whose easy credit brought them profit but bound the borrower to never-ending debt. They were also exploited by Americans who took their money on fraudulent deals in land, insurance, and real estate, and who under the guise of aid to newcomers literally stole their money. One innocent immigrant with several hundred dollars arrived in New York on his way to Kansas. A cab driver took his money, drove him to the Third Avenue Elevated, paid the nickel fare, and told him the train would take him to Kansas City.

Similar problems were faced by laborers who came to the cities from rural America. But American migrants were familiar with change, they knew in

Women on their way to the mills in Fall River, Massachusetts. Immigrant women were a substantial force in the sweatshops and factories of the early twentieth century.

general what was going on, were likely to get a better job, and though the adjustment was hard for them too, it was much harder for the immigrant from the static, backward societies of the Old World from which so many came. The language was different, clothes were different, food was different, customs were different, behavior was different, work was different, the attitude toward women was different. Little wonder that the immigrants so often were swept by feelings of anxiety. They had been cut loose from their moorings and set adrift in strange seas. In our time, even experienced travelers finding themselves in a society far different from their own have feelings of uneasiness, which is one reason why Hilton Hotels have been so successful throughout the world: they provide a familiar base for American travelers to operate from, a reassurance that the world they are familiar with has not disappeared. But the immigrants had no Hilton in which they could drop anchor.

So the bewildered immigrants relied upon other anchors to hold their course steady. One of the strongest was religion and the church. For most of the new immigrants that meant Roman Catholicism, and to a lesser degree Eastern Orthodoxy and Judaism. Faith—Protestant, Catholic, or Jewish—helped to bind many immigrant groups together, to strengthen their identity, to assure them they had not lost everything in moving to the New World.

Religious festivals and celebrations reminded them of days past and helped to provide a sense of community in their lives. The immigrant church provided a center for social activities, especially for women, and often supported the many societies and newspapers that immigrants founded in order to maintain their cultural identity. Many Catholic immigrants attached so much importance to their churches as a binding element in their lives that they demanded the hierarchy give them priests, bishops, and parochial schools of their own ethnic background. But the role of the Roman Catholic church as a stabilizing force in the lives of immigrants was somewhat weakened by the refusal of the Pope (on the advice of the American Cardinal Gibbons) to grant these requests. The tendency of other churches to splinter into various sects after the crossing to the New World also weakened the role of the church as a unifying element. Moreover, among the young particularly, there was a tendency to slide away from the faith of their fathers. Young Stephen Yakich, for example, leaving his Yugoslav village for America, symbolically dropped his crucifix into the sea on the voyage over.

Also important to immigrants in maintaining their identity and cultural composure were the many societies, clubs, associations, and newspapers they established. There were mutual aid societies, singing clubs, folk-dancing clubs, athletic associations, loan associations, theaters, and many others. Yugoslavs, for example, had numerous singing and dramatic clubs, *sokols* for gymnastic and athletic training, and protective and fraternal organizations such as the Slovenian National Benefit Society and the National Croatian Society. Poles had hundreds of societies, some linked into national federations, the largest of which was the Polish National Alliance. Such organizations helped preserve national cultural traditions, and also aided in assimilating new immigrants—seemingly contradictory goals. Since many immigrants came from culturally repressed groups in Europe, organizations were also formed to promote national independence in the Old World. Poles, Czechs, and Slovaks were especially active in such groups by the time of World War I. Immigrants also founded their own newspapers, and by World War I there were hundreds of dailies and weeklies. Many immigrants had paid little attention to newspapers at home, but in America turned eagerly to papers in their own language that not only helped familiarize them with American events, but reported news from home as well. Many such papers became involved in demands for national independence and social and political reforms in the old country.

The one immigrant group not relying upon the Church for unity or seeking to maintain a national cultural identity was the Italian. Coming from the bottom of the social heap the southern Italian immigrant had no commitment to national culture or community. His ties were to family and clan, and his associations rarely extended beyond his home town or village. Moreover, among southern Italians paganism was often stronger than Christianity. Charms and rituals to ward off evil spirits, local saints and madonnas to supplicate and bargain with for aid—these counted for more than Church and God. The usefulness of the Church in providing the Italian with a sense of community was therefore limited.

In the struggle to maintain their cultural identity the immigrants often tended, as time passed, to view the old country with nostalgia, to romanticize the old days. They forgot or thrust into the back of their minds the hardships that had driven them from their lands, and remembered only the good things: the beauty of the forests and streams, the charm of the village tavern or church, the quiet of the fields and the countryside, the dependability of family and human relationships. They often came to resent the letters they received from friends and relatives that in effect denied this romantic image by constant recitals of troubles and problems and by continued requests for money. This perhaps was the final frustration of the immigrants: they could not even enjoy their dreams in peace.

The immigrant experience ended for some with the return to the old country after many years in America. Most of these were from Southern and Eastern Europe. For some who had spent most of their adult lives in America, return provided the last psychological jolt in a lifetime of personal upheavals. For they found, as everyone does, that "you can't go home again." The immigrants had never become fully American like the native-born, including their own children. But imperceptibly their values and attitudes had changed, they had adjusted to the new life, become accustomed to new standards, and the American way had become the familiar way. Now they found it as hard to accommodate to the old society as they had originally to American society. Also they now faced the problem of maintaining their new identity as Americans. They were immigrants all over again, and in their native lands.

Beginning in the 1920s and 1930s, a considerable number who had spent many years in the United States began the long trek home. By the middle 1950s some three million had returned to the lands of their birth. Many of these had retired under pension plans, Social Security, or on successful investments. In 1953, for example, some $15.8 million in Social Security checks were mailed to Greece alone!

Though many were elderly when they returned, their American experience would not let them remain idle or accept things as they were, in village life particularly. Many formed organizations to change things or show how it could be done—to improve a road, build a bridge, repair a church, remodel a school, put up a new mill or an olive press. They might repair the old cottage they had bought and modernize it with the latest in conveniences to show that people didn't have to live as they always had done. They found themselves, in short, dissatisfied with life as they now found it in their homelands. It was unfamiliar, inefficient, and they set out to show how things were done in America. Those who had returned often met in the old country and formed societies to keep alive their American memories and associations!

The Impact of Immigration

Economic Effects   The impact of immigration on American society was clearly very great. Most obvious was the economic effect. The immigrants

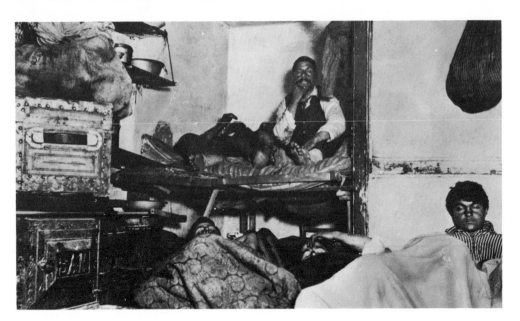

Shelter for immigrants in a Bayard Street tenement in New York. The economic promise of America often disappeared in the oppressive living conditions encountered by immigrants in the cities.

did not bring about American industrialization, but without their labor the process would have been far slower than it was. Investigations in 1907 revealed that in one basic industry after another the immigrants dominated the labor force, and in some they were crucial. Immigrants constituted over sixty percent of the workers in iron, steel, construction, and mining; in the clothing industry almost seventy-five percent. And in industries such as glassmaking, though not dominated by immigrants, native labor was steadily drained away. Had not such industries had new cheap immigrant labor to draw upon, they might not have survived. The age and sex of the immigrants also played a key role since a heavy proportion of the "new immigration" consisted of men between fourteen and forty-five—the prime working years—who were either single or had left their families behind. The Wisconsin economist, John R. Commons, noted this in 1906: "Thus, immigration brings to us a population of working ages unhampered by unproductive mouths to feed."

Immigration also stimulated increased mechanization. Employers saw the advantage of mechanizing so that they could take advantage of the unskilled labor of the immigrant who could easily be trained to feed the machines. The more cheap labor there was, the greater was the temptation for employers to introduce machinery and technological improvements in order to standardize both the task and the product, thus speeding up in yet another way the industrialization of the country.

But immigration also had unfortunate economic consequences. Cheap labor without skills or resources opened the door wide to exploitation. While their labor helped employers get rich, the immigrant workers did not share equitably in the wealth thus created, and their exploited labor therefore widened the gap between rich and poor. Their presence did not create economic classes in America, but it did result in a disproportionate number of people at the very bottom of the economic scale. This was a new thing in America, and it brought with it great human distress.

Social Mobility and Rewards Ironically, at the same time immigration was upsetting the class structure, it was promoting the upward social and economic mobility that had been traditional in this country. The arrival of each new group, to whom only the meanest jobs were available, pushed native Americans and earlier arrivals up the scale a notch. The Congressional Immigration Commission reported in 1907 that in the bituminous coal industry the white-collar jobs were "occupied by native Americans or older immigrants and their children, while the southern and eastern Europeans are confined to mining and to unskilled common labor." On the New York waterfront, Italian laborers pushed Irish workers up the line into the positions of foremen, while French-Canadian and Greek immigrants did the same in the mills of New England. Everywhere in an expanding industrial America this process continually took place: older groups moved up as newer ones took over the lowest level. In spite of the exploitation in this system, it reinforced the tradition of social mobility in American society.

The immigrant experience also strengthened the traditional view that America was a society above all others in recognizing and rewarding merit and talent, that the extent of people's abilities, not the circumstances of their births, determined success and the heights to which they might rise. Dramatic examples of this in business and industry were Carnegie in steel, Cudahy in meat-packing, Pulitzer in publishing, and many others, immigrants all. But there were others whose careers were equally impressive. Michael Pupin, a Serbian immigrant who arrived in 1875 with five cents in his pocket, became a distinguished physicist whose solution for a series of technical problems made possible an effective long-distance telephone system, who constructed the first x-ray tube in America, and whose thirty-four electrical patents made important contributions to that industry.

Political Effects By their sheer numbers the immigrants greatly influenced both the organization and the character of the trade-union movement in the United States. Many labor leaders were immigrant workers: Samuel Gompers of the Cigar Makers and the American Federation of Labor, and Sidney Hillman of the Amalgamated Clothing Workers, for example. Trade unionism in America has always been essentially conservative, opposed to the Marxist concept of class struggle, rejecting the idea of labor parties and radicalism in general. The immigrant group strengthened this conservatism. Most immigrants, of peasant origin, had not been educated to think in terms of politicizing economic problems; they were suspicious of radical change, they had come to America to better themselves as individuals, not as a class; and American trade unionism reflected these sentiments. There is no evidence that the American trade-union movement would have been different in any case, but immigrant influence reinforced and strengthened those widely accepted American beliefs which shaped unionism in America.

The immigrants also reinforced the tradition of American political parties in appealing to various interest groups for support. Leaders of large ethnic groups recognized the value of bloc voting and used that power to advantage. Politicians in cities dominated by immigrant voters played upon their sense of nationality. Even today politicians talk about the "Polish vote," or the "Italian vote."

Influence on Religion In religion also the immigrants had a major impact on American life, reinforcing the diversity of religion in America. In 1973 over two hundred separate religious bodies existed in the United States, some sixty of which had been brought in by new immigrant groups. There are eighteen categories for the Eastern Orthodox Churches alone. More important than the variety of sects was the introduction of Catholicism and Judaism on a major scale into America. The net result was that what had been essentially a Protestant country now became a nation principally colored by three major religious faiths rather than one: Protestantism, Catholicism, and Judaism. It is also likely that the influx of immigrants, whose faith was by and large very strong, revitalized religion in America as a force for conservatism just at the time when American Protestantism was coming under liberal influences. Most of the newly imported faiths were traditional in view, rigid in structure and ritual, unyielding in their beliefs, and powerful in their hold upon their members. In the strength of their faiths and the power of their conservative influence, these churches challenged American Protestantism to a similar commitment. In the twentieth century this challenge was taken up particularly by the fundamentalist Protestant churches.

Finally immigration left its mark upon American culture in the broadest sense. American culture was obviously enriched by immigrant customs, habits, institutions, traditions, and interests. The Yiddish theater and the German singing club enriched American society and made it more cosmopolitan. Individual immigrants of humble origin became artists, writers, scientists, statesmen, and educators. American life was enlivened by a diversity of ethnic restaurants, by a variety of literary and musical traditions, by festivals and ceremonies from ancient homelands, by the variety of languages passed on from one generation to the next. Since colonial times ours had been a society marked by cultural diversity, and so it remained in the time of the new immigration.

Anti-Immigrant Sentiment and Restriction

But there were doubts and misgivings. Even in colonial days there were protests against the unchecked immigration of peoples who seemed about to overwhelm by their numbers the local inhabitants. Benjamin Franklin had complained about the Germans in Pennsylvania. And the influx of Irish Catholics early in the nineteenth century had raised the fear of an alien Papist influence on American institutions, a fear that turned mobs loose on the streets and had the pernicious effect of introducing nativism into American politics. There had been attempts to restrict immigration or at least to impose strict naturalization requirements.

But immigration continued to flow freely, and in the second half of the nineteenth century reached flood proportions. Few protested, for obvious reasons: the United States needed the immigrants, and not merely as laborers. Immigrants were living proof that American ways and institutions were superior. Immigration was a psychological boost to the American spirit, to American pride. Americans delighted in boasting to the world about those whose talents would have been smothered in the repressive atmospheres of their homelands but which flourished in America's open and democratic environment. Americans also took pride in their own compassion in welcoming the humble and the ordinary. To most Americans, Emma Lazarus's words inscribed on the Statue of Liberty really meant what they said:

> Give me your tired, your poor,
> Your huddled masses yearning to breathe free,
> Send these, the homeless, tempest-tossed, to me;
> I lift my lamp beside the golden door.

Americans had long been taught that their country was "an asylum for all mankind," and the new immigration proved the truth of that teaching. Eminently practical, Americans also recognized that they also needed the immigrants to promote their own well-being. A writer in the *North American Review* in 1892 declared that because of immigration "our almost limitless resources have been partially developed, forests leveled, railroads built, and canals dug . . . and the wilderness has been made to blossom."

Rise of Anti-Immigration Feeling

Yet by 1900 a countersentiment emerged against the new immigrants from Southern and Eastern Europe which was to culminate in the restrictive legislation of 1917–1924. In part this feeling sprang from humanitarian impulses. As early as the 1870s relief agencies were disturbed by the arrival of impoverished and confused immigrants whose distressing condition not only placed a heavy burden on public health and aid facilities, but handicapped the immigrants themselves in their search for a place in American life. Legislation establishing physical examinations and vaccination requirements, and trying to set minimum standards for shipboard accommodations was put into effect on both sides of the Atlantic. These laws did not restrict the number of immigrants, but did help to implant in the American public mind the idea that there were disadvantages in the influx of millions of the poverty-stricken and the helpless.

Strengthening the sentiment for restriction were religious fears, often tied to nationalistic and economic factors. Essentially this was a reactionary Protestant response to Catholic and Jewish immigration. The chief organ of this view was the American Protective Association, founded in 1887, whose 500,000 members lived mainly in the Middle West. The APA's vicious propaganda against Catholicism included proposals for restricting immigration and requiring stricter naturalization laws. Outside the APA many people became alarmed at the rising influence of the Irish Catholics in politics, especially in certain cities. An outburst of anti-Semitism among poorer Western farmers and urban workers sprang largely from economic resentment, and this also fed restrictionist sentiment.

Racist arguments also began to influence public opinion, mainly directed against the Southern and Eastern Europeans. Under the influence of Social Darwinism the idea of the superiority of the Anglo-Saxon race as the prime carrier of civilization began to take hold in the United States, where those who regarded blacks as inferior were already accustomed to racist thinking. Prominent intellectuals and political leaders declared that Eastern and Southern Europeans were "beaten men from beaten races," biologically inferior to the Anglo-Saxon stock of Northern and Western Europe. The conservative lawyer, Madison Grant, in his book *The Passing of the Great Race* wrote of

> a large and increasing number of the weak, the broken and the mentally crippled of all races drawn from the lowest stratum of the Mediterranean basin and the Balkans, together with hordes of the wretched, submerged populations of the Polish ghettos. Our jails, insane asylums and almshouses are filled with this human flotsam and the whole tone of American life, social, moral and political has been lowered and vulgarized by them.

The purity of the Anglo-Saxon race was seen to be in grave danger of being diluted and corrupted. The distinguished progressive sociologist, E. A. Ross, declared that these groups had a "pigsty mode of life," that they threatened American social standards with "their brawls and animal pleasures," and their "coarse peasant philosophy of sex." Such attitudes were rejected by the more realistic and scientific-minded, such as the lawyer Clarence Darrow, who commented: "Purity of the Anglo-Saxon race! The greatest race of sons of bitches that ever infested the earth. Mind you, if there is such a race, I am one of them. . . . But I do not brag about it; I apologize for it."

Economic factors also favored restriction of immigration. Organized labor was increasingly perturbed by the use of immigrants as strike-breakers and by the willingness of new immigrants to work for low wages. A labor paper declared in 1909 that "The Poles, Slavs, Huns and Italians come over without any ambition to live as Americans live and . . . accept work at any wages at

The fears of those who favored restrictions on immigration are expressed in this cartoon, which attributes the problems of radicalism to hordes arriving from foreign shores.

all, thereby lowering the tone of American labor as a whole." Although American industrialists profited from cheap immigrant labor and were therefore cautious about taking a restrictionist stand, many American businessmen did become alarmed after the Haymarket riot of 1886 at what they saw as the influence of communism, syndicalism, and anarchy introduced into the labor movement by radical immigrant agitators. Public outcries against the radicalism of immigrants had no basis in fact and produced no restrictive legislation, although a national organization, the Immigration Restriction League, founded in 1894, pushed for a strong literacy test which would have discriminated against immigrants from Southern and Eastern Europe. A literacy-test bill did get through Congress in 1897, but it was vetoed by President Cleveland, who pointed out with some irony that such a bill would hardly keep out radical agitators who were practically guaranteed to be literate.

Progressivism also made its contribution to anti-immigrant sentiment. Many of the problems Progressives dealt with centered in the cities where immigrant concentration was heaviest. Political exploitation of immigrants seemed to lie at the heart of corrupt political machines. The economic and social problems of the city inevitably involved the problems of immigrants. Most Progressives believed that the immigrant could be drawn into American life, and hence promoted programs of Americanization, especially in education. Progressivism clearly sought to aid the immigrant, and in many ways did so. But it also pointed to the immigrants as the center if not the cause of many social, political, and economic problems, and made them appear to require constant aid, protection, and guidance if such problems were to be kept under control.

Running through all these elements of concern was the visible difference that marked so many of the new immigrants as a people apart, who bore little resemblance to the immigrants of old. For those Americans who rubbed elbows with the new immigrants in the cities, this was a matter of no small significance. They thought the immigrants babbled in strange tongues, often wore "funny" clothes, had odd social habits, ate strange-smelling foods, treated their women differently, clustered in their own sections of the city, and stuck together at work. They were different, and the old tribal instinct to view the outsider with caution was reinforced with each successive wave of immigrants.

All these factors contributed to anti-immigrant sentiment and restrictionist policies. Individually they probably meant very little, and even together they tended to slip to the background in the full flush of prosperity, growth, and reform in the first decade and a half of the twentieth century. Nevertheless, they represented an attitude of mind arising out of the new America: the suspicion that America no longer had the capacity to absorb unlimited numbers of newcomers, that assimilation of immigrants of whatever origins into one grand American cultural scheme was not the simple matter it had once seemed to be, that there were problems enough in making industrialism work and cities livable without yearly taking in hundreds of thousands of people to whom this way of life was unfamiliar. Moreover, the intense feelings of nationalism generated by World War I and the disillusionment with the peace and with the Europe that came out of it, combined to make Americans suspicious of foreigners and foreign influences. A powerful feeling for national homogeneity developed. A journal as liberal as the *New Republic* could state in 1916 that "Freedom of migration from one country to another appears to be one of the elements in nineteenth-century liberalism that is fated to disappear. The responsibility of the state for the welfare of its individual members is progressively increasing. The democracy of today . . . cannot permit . . . social ills to be aggravated by excessive immigration." And so the uneasy feeling grew that American nationality and character could not be maintained through the continued influx of peoples different (and hence presumably inferior) in race, ideas, and culture. The net result was a literacy-test law passed over President Wilson's veto in 1917, and then in 1921 and 1924 came a restrictive quota system based on national origins limiting immigration to 150,000 a year and sharply discriminating against Eastern and Southern Europeans. And so an era in America history ended. The day of free immigration was over.

Profile: PHILIP MIZEL

Philip Mizel: born Pesach Elia ben Yitschak Isaac Mizel, December 15, 1897, in the small town of Kopul near Minsk in Russia; parents Jewish; died October 20, 1971, in the very large city of Chicago in the American Midwest. Only one of over a million and a half Jews who left the empire of the czars and sought in the New World a better life than he thought faced him in the Old. Nine children in the family. Three never made it past infancy, two died as a consequence of World War I, another was killed in World War II. Three were to make it to America. In baseball terms, a respectable .333 batting average; in human terms, an agonizing record.

No one starved, but it was not an easy life. A cow provided milk for the family and for sale. There was plenty of bread, cheese, and vegetables, not much meat, eggs from chickens kept in the house, and fruit only for the ill. The family made their limited living by early contracting with local landowners for their fruit crop, which they then sold to merchants. It was a chancy business, but an older daughter developed a knack for estimating a crop to within a few bushels. Once the contract had been settled, the family moved into the orchard to protect it from birds, animals, and thieves until harvest time.

The father died of exposure a few days after his team and wagon had broken through the ice on a lake. With his older brother in the army, young Pesach at the age of thirteen became the head of the family. For three years he struggled to make a go of things, and then the family decided he should leave for America. Letters from relatives had been picturing a life of opportunity for the enterprising and hardworking while letters from his older brother in the Russian army indicated that particular future was a dead end. Unable to raise the money, sixteen-year-old Pesach accepted the offer of cousins in America to pay for his passage. He made his way to a Baltic port and, lost in the anonymity of steerage, sailed for America in the summer of 1914 just before the war broke out in Europe.

After landing in New York, he went directly to a cousin's home in Sioux City, Iowa, where he transformed himself into Philip Mizel, enrolled in a night school to study English, and got a menial and back-breaking job in a butcher shop for $2.50 a week. After a few weeks he was fired for suggesting that his labor was worth more than $2.50 a week, and so he decided to strike off on his own. With his cousin's backing, he purchased a horse and wagon and became a peddler of brooms, notions, yardgoods, and other items, traveling through Iowa and South Dakota from farm to farm. Gentle, kindly, and honest, he established a remarkable rapport with farmers and their wives, and he never forgot their hospitality.

But peddling is a way to get started, not to get ahead, and in 1917 young Phil settled in Mitchell, South Dakota, a prairie farm town of about nine thousand population where he began a business dealing in metals, hides, furs, and used automobile and truck parts. He was a hard worker, the war boomed his business, he borrowed heavily for expansion from a local banker who had taken a paternal interest in him, and as he remarked years later, thought himself "a real big shot"—wearing $25 silk shirts, buying expensive shoes, trying to smoke fancy cigars.

Since his first paycheck in Sioux City, he had been sending money home to his family in Russia and paying off his obligations to his cousins. Now in 1920 he made arrangements to bring his mother and two younger sisters to America. It took a long time to work out, and by the time they arrived in November 1921, he was also arranging for his marriage to Esther Martinsky, a young Jewish girl he had met on his travels as a peddler. His future mother-in-law was a widow whose family came from Lithuania and who had embarked years before on the unusual venture of homesteading in South Dakota on her own with her five children. Attractive young Jewish fellows were not exactly growing on trees in South Dakota and she and her daughter had kept the young peddler in mind. At any rate, Phil purchased a small house in Mitchell and in January 1922, he, his bride, his mother, and his two sisters moved in.

It was an awkward time to suffer his first and only financial disaster. He had sold a very large shipment of hides to a firm in Wisconsin, and while the shipment was on the way, the hide market collapsed, the Wisconsin firm went bankrupt, and Phil was left holding hides for which he was heavily committed financially. His banker advised him to file for bankruptcy himself, but he had not come to America, he said, to abandon his obligations. It was years before his debts were paid.

He became a car dealer and expanded the original business of hides, furs, and automotive parts. He later branched out into coal and wool, and ultimately founded an automobile finance and loan company. He formalized his commitment to America by becoming a citizen in 1926, and regarded voting and paying attention to public issues as a duty and a responsibility. He became a recognized and respected part of the community. He worked incessantly, six days a week and many times on the Sabbath, from seven or eight in the morning to ten or eleven at night. He never took a real vacation in his life. Behind him lay the grim days in Russia and his early days of false success in America, and he labored as though these experiences were always breathing down his neck.

He remained devoted to his Jewish traditions, and during high holy days took his wife and sons to Sioux Falls, Sioux City, Des Moines, or Minneapolis so that they could observe the holy days in a synagogue. A traveling rabbi came by once a year for a month to teach the boys Hebrew. He kept a kosher home, and when the rabbi came by once a year, Phil visited his farmer friends and bought chickens, turkeys, and ducks which were strung up in the cellar to be properly killed. Occasionally kosher meat was ordered from Des Moines. But in between times, as one of his sons later remarked, "we ate an awful lot of tuna fish sandwiches." It wasn't easy to be Jewish in South Dakota. Not in the sense of facing discrimination, for Phil never felt its presence, but because he did feel isolated from any Jewish community. And it was this deep urge which prompted him finally, after World War II, to move to Chicago where he founded a finance company with his three sons. But as he painfully discovered, the severing of his roots in South Dakota, where he had spent almost thirty-five years, proved harder than emigrating from his home in Russia. As a result, whether in Chicago or in South Dakota, the sense of being a stranger in the land never left him.

A kind and gentle man, generous to a fault, shrewd in business, outwardly calm and never known to lose his temper, within he was consumed by a passion to succeed, not just in the American business world, but in a deeper, more fundamental way. He had the feeling that he was starting the family all over again in the New World, far from home, and that he, not his grandfather or great-grandfather was the founder, the patriarch, that it was all up to him, and if he failed the end of the line had been reached, that there was no one to fall back upon except himself if this name, this family were to mean something. And who is to say that this was unworthy, or that he did not succeed?

Chapter 4
THE LAST
FRONTIERS

The Spirit of the Times
THE END OF SOMETHING

In Chicago in 1893 at a meeting of the American Historical Association, a young professor named Frederick Jackson Turner from the University of Wisconsin read a paper on "The Significance of the Frontier in American History." In the eighty years thereafter, historians and others spent so much time defending, attacking, augmenting, and subtracting from what Turner said that there are times when the paper seems more important than the frontier. Perhaps its impact can be compared to that of another frightening discovery that Americans have quite recently made: that there are limits to their natural resources just as there were limits to free land.

Turner's language was rhetorical, almost poetic, and critics sometimes appeared to resent his eloquence as much as his ideas. The following is an example of his dramatic style:

> Stand at Cumberland Gap and watch the procession of civilization, marching single file—the buffalo following the trail to the salt springs, the Indian, the fur-trader and hunter, the cattle-raiser, the pioneer farmer—and the frontier has passed by.

The heart of his thesis was simple enough: "The existence of an area of free land, its continuous recession, and the advance of American settlement westward, explain American development." Simple, but in its time bold.

As proposed by Turner and later elaborated by many others, the frontier thesis evolved into a complex theory explaining why the Americans turned out to be the kind of people they were. It was the frontier experience that Americanized the immigrant, that provided the environment in which democracy, both cooperative and individualistic, could flourish, that promoted the American sense of nationalism, that gave rise to those traits of materialism, social mobility, disregard for tradition, and optimism that presumably distinguished Americans from their European cousins. In taking this strong nationalistic view of American uniqueness, Turner and others were reacting against those who wished to trace the origins of all American institutions and ideas back to their beginnings in Europe. In proposing that American society developed from the simple to the complex, from the primitive to the civilized, and that this was a process repeated over and over in a succession of westward-moving frontiers, they were also reflecting the influence of evolution on historical thinking.

Turner had a sophisticated and creative mind, and he hardly intended to suggest that the influence of the Western world stopped short at the three-mile limit off the Atlantic shore, that there were no European influences on American life. Nor did he wish to imply that other environmental influences, such as the city, had no impact on American development. He was well aware that the influence of the frontier was not entirely benevolent and constructive. But he wanted to extend the perspective from which people viewed America and thus broaden their understanding of American society, and he was certainly correct in the assumption that the frontier had a great deal to do with shaping American society and thought. It would be unusual, to say the least, if the lives of those who lived through the frontier experience had not been shaped to a greater or lesser degree, for good or for ill, by that experience.

Turner was also correct in noting that a new situation had arisen in American development when a line of frontier settlement could no longer be drawn on the Census Bureau maps. The Superintendent of the Census had declared in 1890:

> Up to and including 1880 the country had a frontier of settlement, but at present the unsettled area has been so broken into by isolated bodies of settlement that there can hardly be said to be a frontier line. In the discussion of its extent, its westward movement, etc., it can not, therefore, any longer have a place in the census reports.

Although a great deal of land yet remained to go under the plow, a westward movement and a social process that had persisted for generations had now ended. The show was over. Turner ended his paper with this dramatic announcement:

> What the Mediterranean Sea was to the Greeks, breaking the bond of custom, offering new experiences, calling out new institutions and activities, that, and more, an ever retreating frontier has been to the United States directly, and to the nations of Europe more remotely. And now, four centuries from the discovery of America, at the end of a hundred years of life under the Constitution, the frontier has gone, and with its going has closed the first period of American history.

If this were the case, then the question was not only how significant the frontier had been in the American past, but how significant for the future would be its passing. For here was a society whose values, ideas, attitudes, habits, and institutions had been greatly shaped by the experience of the frontier. Could these values, ideas, attitudes, habits, and institutions survive under the impact of a new and very different set of experiences, in the world of factory and city? Not only could they survive, but would they be useful if they did survive? Could a democracy forged in the crucible of the frontier work in the new America? Or would democracy have to be redefined within the context of science and technology, city and factory? Turner had declared that "the unchecked development of the individual was the significant product of this frontier democracy." By the end of the nineteenth century that kind of individualism had helped create a world marked by the concentration of wealth and by inequality of opportunity. And what would also be the consequences of an attitude of mind, arising out of the frontier experience, which saw nature's resources as inexhaustible and infinitely exploitable for personal gain, in a world of expanding science and technology, of voracious machines whose demands upon nature's stores were vastly greater than the limited and almost casual demands of a frontier age? Turner himself in 1921 noted that the question now was "how large a part of the historic American ideals are to be

The Oklahoma land rush. After the Civil War an excitement over the opening of new territories seized Americans and settlers rushed in a fever pitch to claim land as soon as the threat of Indian attack was lessened and homesteads had been surveyed.

carried over into that new age which is replacing the era of free lands and of measurable isolation by consolidated and complex industrial development and by increasing resemblances and connections between the New World and the Old."

For three-quarters of a century America has been struggling to answer such questions as these. And in the settlement of the last frontiers left in America in the latter decades of the nineteenth century, it is possible to see how the forces of a new America of factory and city entered into the frontier experience itself, altering and changing its character so much that by the time Turner spoke in 1893 the frontier had not just ended but its last days bore little resemblance to what it had been in past generations. Thus, in the last frontiers, it is not just the past that is revealed but the future as well.

The End of the Frontier

The days when the major energy of Americans was devoted to moving westward and settling the land were pretty well over by 1900. Yet so vast was the country, and so great its growth, that in the years from 1860 to 1912 far more settlement had actually taken place in the West than ever before in the nation's history. Except for its early penetration by a handful of the intrepid, an immense area between the Missouri and the Sierras was untouched, undeveloped, unexploited. Bypassed by earlier generations who dismissed its treeless expanse as "the great American desert," this vast region west of the Mississippi was carved into fourteen new states by 1912. Rather than a barren desert, it turned out to be one of nature's great treasurehouses.

This region was the last great frontier, the last West, and its conquest had all the vitality, color, and roughness associated with the dramatic encounter between the individual and nature that for so long had characterized the American experience. Yet the development of the last frontier not only helped speed the process of industrialization that was taking place at the same time, but that industrial development in turn governed the settlement of the West. This last frontier experience therefore bore little resemblance to the frontier experience of previous generations. Yet ironically this was the frontier that overshadowed every other. For ordinary Americans of modern times it has been the only frontier they have known much about, and it has come to stand for all that the frontier was supposed to represent in American history. It was not the Mohawk Valley or the Kentucky of Daniel Boone that gave contemporary Americans their picture of the frontier past. It was Tombstone and Deadwood, Abilene and Dodge City, the frontier of cowboys, grizzled prospectors, gunmen, and homesteaders. Not the frontier of the Five Nations of the Iroquois or the rebellion of Pontiac, but the frontier of Sitting Bull and Crazy Horse, the Little Big Horn and Wounded Knee. This was the frontier turned into legend by countless short stories, novels, plays, movies, and television programs: a legend created so artfully and absorbed so fully that the streets of Dodge City are as familiar to most of us as our own neighborhoods. And why not? We've ridden down them on a thousand noons.

What was it really like?

The Mining Frontier

From the time of the first settlements in the seventeenth century, people had dreamed of discovering the secret riches of the earth, its precious gold and silver. But the first great success in the United States did not come until the discovery of gold in California in 1849. By the late 1850s these discoveries led many prospectors to believe that if precious metals were to be found on the western side of the Sierras and Rockies, why not the eastern slopes as well? And so the search began. The territory they entered belonged either to the United States government or to various Indian tribes—a legal distinction that did not bother those who dreamed of sudden wealth. So they moved into what is now Nevada, Colorado, Idaho, Montana, New Mexico, Wyoming, Arizona, and South Dakota. For a decade and a half prospectors, miners, and the assorted crew that followed them were drawn through mountain

The solitary prospector panning for gold. The image was a romantic one that belied the arduous, backbreaking work that usually resulted in wealth for only a few. Through the painstaking process of sifting through sand for gold dust and an occasional nugget, most miners managed only to break even.

and desert by strikes and rumors of strikes. Though many boom towns rose to only momentary glory and then sank into dusty death, thousands of square miles were brought to heel and partly settled as a consequence.

The Great Boom

The process began in Colorado in July 1858 when a small strike near what is now Denver brought an initial rush of would-be prospectors to the hills of the Pike's Peak country. Though little gold was found, fantastic stories

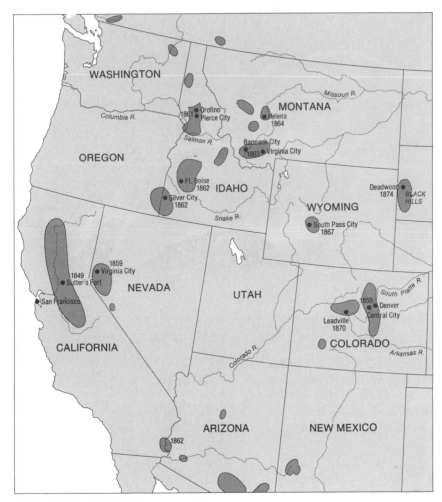

THE MINING FRONTIER (1860–1875)

spread eastward and by the following June more than a hundred thousand people were scattered through the eastern Rockies on a frantic search for gold that proved so futile that over half had departed by midsummer. But then the first big strike was made on the north fork of Clear Creek. With the presence of gold now a certainty, the search widened; each new strike, big or small, extended it. Throughout the West news of strikes sent miners dashing off to the new area. In Nevada, gold discoveries on Davidson Mountain in the Washoe district marked the opening of the famous Comstock Lode, although it was not known until 1873 that the lode grew wider as it went deep within the earth, making it one of the richest finds in history, some $200 million worth. Other strikes in Nevada in the 1860s included those in the

Frontier justice dispensed from a saloon. Roy Bean was one of the most publicized of the unorthodox judges of the West. A merchant who followed the construction of the Southern Pacific Railroad, Bean's prestigious appearance encouraged people to come to him to settle disputes despite his lack of training in the law. That informal practice and the fact that a real judge was over two hundred miles away soon led even the Texas Rangers to bring prisoners to him for justice. Eventually he was officially made a justice of the peace and he carried on his tradition of serving up his rather flamboyant opinions with pre- and post-trial drinks.

Esmeralda and the Humboldt Mountains. In the 1860s and 1870s came strikes in Arizona, Idaho, Montana, Wyoming, and in the Black Hills of South Dakota.

In all these strikes, thousands of wealth-seekers from everywhere poured in, mining towns sprang into being with instant populations, and the pressure for orderly development led to rough-hewn local government by mass meeting and vigilante justice as well as to demands for the establishment of territorial government and federal law.

Mining towns were much alike everywhere on the frontier. They all drew an assorted crew of prospectors, miners, gamblers, ladies of easy virtue, saloon keepers, merchants, desperadoes, lawyers, editors, farmers, all attracted by the prospects of excitement and easy wealth. Prospectors and miners were drawn by the lure of the quick strike, merchants by the high prices of goods, saloon keepers by the endless thirst of miners, prostitutes by the profits to be made by their availability in communities overwhelmingly male, gamblers by the easy pickings at the card tables, farmers by the high price of produce, professionals by the high cost of their services. They came from all over the country and from all walks of life, and they were frequently on the move from one mining town to the next. Many such instant communities were extraordinarily cosmopolitan. Virginia City, Nevada, had five newspapers and a stock exchange. Idaho City's population of 6,000 enjoyed a hospital, a theater, a fire department, and three newspapers. At the Gem Theater in Deadwood, the Mikado once ran for 130 nights. Such towns were expensive places, especially in the early days. Flour sold for $28 a hundred pounds, chickens for $5 each, butter for $1.20 a pound, all far above the price of food elsewhere. No wonder farmers moved into the fertile valleys nearby!

There was always an early clamor for government, and a foreign traveler in the Denver area in the winter of 1858 observed with amusement the demand by the handful then present for territorial status:

> Making governments and building towns are the natural employments of the migratory Yankee. He takes to them as instinctively as a young duck to water. Congregate a hundred Americans anywhere beyond the settlements and they immediately lay out a city, frame a state constitution and apply for admission into the Union, while twenty-five of them become candidates for the United States Senate.

Local government was at first based on the mass meeting which elected a chairman, picked three or four "judges," and passed laws regulating procedures for claim-staking and the size of claims as well as for settling disputes. Criminals attracted by the chance of loot were frequently dealt with by vigilante committees which hunted down outlaws and administered swift justice by hanging. But what mining towns wanted was regular law and order, and this was attainable only by territorial status and then statehood. It was the demands of the mining frontier that first brought territorial governments into the last frontier.

Modern Influences   But the nature of mining, for all its flamboyant and wide-open character, by the 1870s began to reflect the industrial-business society developing elsewhere in the country. Science, technology, corporate business, and industrial demand took over, and the transient, individualistic, picturesque aspects of the mining frontier receded into the background.

The experiences of Nevada and Colorado illustrate the impact of science and technology. In Nevada the full exploitation of the famed Comstock Lode was made possible only by remarkable engineering feats providing a massive water system draining lower levels of the mines and the construction of some 180 to 190 miles of underground galleries and shafts. In Colorado, the introduction of large-scale smelting resulted in the saving of almost all the valuable metals present in ores, most of which had been lost in older and cruder processes. Much of this was due to the work of Nathaniel Hill and Richard Pearce, both of whom had scientific training in Europe as well as in America. The discovery of lead in Colorado ores resulted from the work of

August Meyer, a trained metallurgist. This discovery made Leadville, Colorado, a major producer of that metal. The establishment in Colorado in 1879 of a Rocky Mountain division of the United States Geological Survey brought a scientific survey of the Leadville region that became known as "the miner's bible," so great was its value. Similar surveys were then prompted elsewhere. Colorado also provided an example in the 1890s of advanced technology in the first use of electricity as a source of power in the mines.

Everywhere in the West from the 1870s on, business corporations moved in to dominate mining. The Homestake Mining Company, which exploited the major gold mines of the Black Hills, and the Anaconda Copper Company, which became the major power in copper mining in Montana in the 1880s, illustrate this trend. The search for valuable minerals was also influenced by industrial demand. The extended search beyond gold and silver for lead- and copper-bearing ores indicate the expanded needs of industry. Copper was essential for the construction of telegraph and electric lines. Railroad construction throughout the West also became a vital link in the process, making possible the large-scale exploitation of discoveries by providing transportation and by lowering costs.

What happened on the mining frontier by the 1870s, therefore, was that mining and the search for exploitation of mineral resources became an integral part of the whole fabric of the new America. Corporations replaced small outfits, trained geologists replaced grizzled prospectors, sophisticated machinery and technology replaced crude mechanical processes operated by one man or a small group. And the traditional search for gold and silver—in themselves valuable to the expanding financial empires of the new America—broadened to include other essential minerals. The trend was unmistakable. A frontier in the old sense of the word was rapidly being transformed into a large-scale industrial operation.

The Cattle Frontier

Perhaps the most colorful aspect of the last great frontier, and certainly the most enduring in legend, was cattle raising: the open range, the long drive, the cow town, the roundup, the cowboy, and gun fights on dusty main streets. From 1865 to 1887, the cattle frontier flourished on the treeless expanse of the Great Plains from the Canadian border to Texas. There had always been a cattle frontier of sorts—from colonial days to the first half of the nineteenth century—out on the edge of settlement where land was plentiful and people few. But the last cattle frontier had a peculiar distinction.

The Open Range   It began after the Civil War when the financial prospects seemed exceptionally encouraging if only the millions of cattle running free in Texas could be gotten to Eastern urban markets. Cattle that were worth two to four dollars a head could bring ten times that or more in Eastern cities. The solution was the long drive. Railroads were pushing West

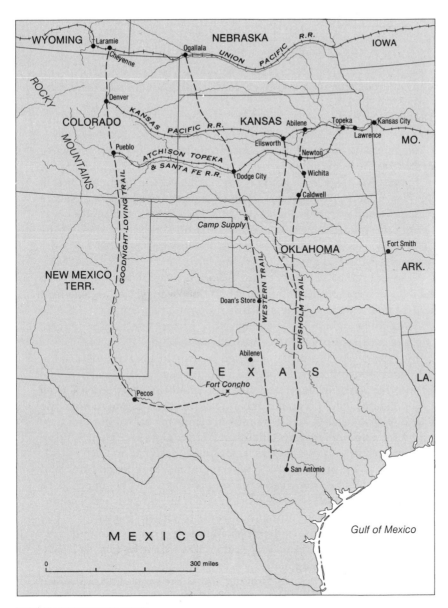

THE CATTLE FRONTIER

across the plains, and if the cattle could be driven to rail terminals, their value would be enormous. An unsuccessful attempt was made in 1866 to drive a herd North through the wooded and settled terrain of Missouri. But a Chicago stockman named Joseph McCoy concocted the successful scheme of driving cattle through the open range of the public domain to the new rail terminal at Abilene, Kansas, which provided connections to Chicago and the meat-packing companies of the Middle West. In 1867 the first herds of Texas steers, aproximately thirty-five thousand, made it to Abilene, and the following year over twice that number. Ellsworth, Newton, and Dodge City subsequently became key Kansas cow towns on the western rail system, and over four million cattle were driven to Kansas rail terminals before the long drive passed into history.

Within a short period, as the railroads pushed across the northern Plains and into the Colorado Territory, cattle-raising developed in these areas also. Texas longhorns were bred with eastern cattle to produce a more attractive breed. By 1880 the cattle industry was in the saddle everywhere on the Great Plains. Ranges were stocked from Texas through New Mexico, in the Indian Territory, in eastern Colorado and Wyoming, up through western Kansas and Nebraska, and north to Montana and the Dakotas. Meat from the cattle frontier fed the mining towns, railroad construction crews, the cities of the East, and a good deal of Europe. Millions of acres of free grass seemed a guarantee of wealth, and ranches based on control of water rights to streams and creeks were staked out everywhere, though no legal rights of ownership existed in most instances. Roundups and branding every spring and fall kept herds identified and their owners satisfied. Common agreement as to who owned what range rights plus a willingness to protect one's claim by force held the system together and made it work—for a time.

But by 1880 the profits to be made led to overstocking and devastating competition among thousands of ranchers. Foreign and Eastern capital flowed into the West in huge amounts, and small-time operators flocked West by the thousands. To protect themselves, ranchers began to fence the range land (often illegally), to file fraudulent claims for title to the land they needed—some two million acres under the Desert Land Act alone—and to form cattlemen's and stock-breeders' associations designed to keep outsiders off the ranges, to supervise and control roundups, to settle disputes, and to restrict the number of cattle allowable on the range. The boom collapsed in the winter of 1886–1887 when deadly blizzards and sub-zero temperatures killed at least eighty percent of the cattle on the northern Plains.

The days of the cattle drive and the open range were over. Grass and cattle had to be properly managed, and that could only be done by fencing legally acquired lands, by restricting herds, and by growing hay to provide winter feed. The dominance of the cattle frontier was at the same time threatened by the advance of sheepmen who invaded the Plains in the 1880s, which led to deadly warfare between sheepherders and cowboys, and the advance onto the Plains by homesteading farmers. When it was all over, the settled, established, fenced ranch survived. Better cattle were produced and shipped direct from home ranches, but the day of the wide-open cattle frontier was gone.

Even in its days of glory, the cattle frontier reflected and was shaped by the forces of industrial-urban America. It was the growing cities which needed to be fed that provided the lure of great profits; it was the railroad that brought the cattle and the market together; it was the technological achievements of the refrigerated railroad car, cold storage, and the tin can that made possible the full exploitation of that market in the United States and abroad; it was the appearance of the great meat-packing corporations that provided the essential middleman services for turning steers into beef; and in the end it was the entrance of corporate control—in the form of the Prairie Land and Cattle Company and the Capitol Freehold Company, among many others—that not only took over much of the cattle industry but helped transform the cattle frontier of the open range into the permanent ranches of an organized and typical business.

The Great American Legend   The cattle frontier passed into history, but its legend has survived. Far more than any other frontier in time or place, it became deeply embedded in the American mind as the embodiment of all that was meant by "the West." And it survived not so much as it actually was but as the Americans (and practically everybody else) wished it to be.

The cattle frontier had all the ingredients of high drama. The long drive: thousands of longhorns on the move, stretching over the horizon, "gaunt, dust-caked, nervous" . . . the threat of stampede from any sudden noise . . . open to harassment by Indians or by outlaws . . . swimming the herd across the Colorado or the Cimarron or the North Platte . . . dust-filled days of drought or the clouded rain-soaked days of the spring or summer storm . . . the terror of fire in the prairie grass . . . ninety days to Abilene, six months to the northern Plains on a trail fifty yards to two miles wide . . . death for animal and man.

The roundup: thousands upon thousands of cattle driven in from the range, milling, bellowing . . . the air hazy with dust for miles around . . . cowboys in perpetual motion and chuckwagons dotting the landscape . . . fires and sizzling branding irons . . . cutting out cattle . . . eighteen to twenty hours a day in the saddle for weeks on end.

The cowtown: stock pens, railyards, boarding houses, saloons, dance halls, gambling dens, red-light houses . . . dull, drab, and dusty most of the time . . . tumultuous, jammed, corrupt . . . brawls, shootings, gambling, debauchery . . . release from tension and strain.

The cowboy: a strange figure, set apart . . . most of the time on horseback . . . wide-brimmed sombrero, high-heeled boots, chaps over woolen trousers, bright handkerchief around the neck, six-gun . . . lonely . . . hard-working . . . exploding in town and sometimes dying there, prematurely.

The sheer physical pain of cowpunching, the endless hours and days in the saddle, dust in your teeth and rain down the back of your neck, uninterrupted sleep a longed-for luxury, the unrelenting and uninspiring sameness of chuckwagon chow, the occasional binge in some sleazy town and the rotgut hangover, the monotony of male companionship, the loneliness of night watch on a herd or riding the range or even on the trail when the nearest other rider might be half a mile away, the low wages, a future the same as the present, enlivened only by the next order from the Montgomery Ward catalogue. No Americans in their right minds are thinking of that

The long, long line.

day-to-day reality when the cowboy gallops across the screen of their imaginations. They are thinking of how the historian Walter Prescott Webb once described the cowboy as he passed into legend. There was

> something romantic about him. He lives on horseback as do the Bedouins; he fights on horseback, as did the knights of chivalry; he goes armed with a strange new weapon which he uses ambidextrously and precisely; he swears like a trooper, drinks like a fish, wears clothes like an actor, and fights like the devil. He is gracious to ladies, reserved toward strangers, generous to his friends, and brutal to his enemies.

No pain or dullness here. And not exactly the summing up that Jim McCauley made of his life as a cowboy:

> All in all I got out of cowpunching is the experience. I paid a good price for that. I wouldn't take anything for what I have saw but I wouldn't care to travel the same road again, and my advice to any young man or boy is to stay at home and not be a rambler, as it won't buy you anything. And above everything stay away from a cow ranch, as not many cowpunchers ever save any money and 'tis a dangerous life to live.

Since the days of the cattle frontier, Americans have been raised on the myth, not the reality. The American has always been drawn to the lone figure enduring great odds, holding firm to the simple virtues, and the rest of the world be damned. A Swedish film critic maintained in the 1950s that the best way to understand American foreign policy was to see the western *High Noon,* and he may have had a point.

What is clear is that the Americans romanticized what was already a kind of romantic reality. The cattle frontier dramatized our eternal obsession with

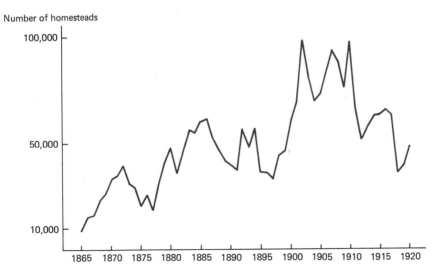

Number of homesteads

HOMESTEADS GRANTED FROM PUBLIC LANDS (1865–1920)

the conflict between individual and nature, individual and individual, and all the virtues the Americans saw in these conflicts: courage, determination, perseverance against great odds, the integrity of the individual. In a society already rapidly moving indoors into factory and office, a society defined by city streets and far from open spaces, a society in which the individual disappeared into an anonymous mass, a society where risk and danger lay in misjudging the stock market or the distance of your hand from the maw of the machine—in such a society the West of the cattle frontier seemed to represent what life ought to be. The superficialities stripped away, the elementals revealed: the earth beneath, the sky above, and the horizon distant; on your own; everyone with the final arbiter and equalizer on the hip; and the good and the best will somehow triumph.

The Farming Frontier

The cowboy might conquer many enemies in reality or in myth, but one he could not conquer: the farmer. After 1870 a wave of people surged over the Great Plains, settling a larger area of land than in all previous American history. From 1607 to 1870 some 407 million acres had been settled; between 1870 and 1900 more than 430 million acres were occupied, 225 million of this in farm land, 37 million more acres than had been farmed from 1607 to 1870. Even more land went under the plow after 1900 than in the thirty years before. The people came from abroad and from the neighboring states to the East. In the 1880s Iowa, Missouri and the states of the Old Northwest saw over a million people go West to the Great Plains.

Land Speculation   Although presumably the opening of the Plains would enable the humble farmer to obtain land under the Homestead Act of 1862, the tragedy was that by and large these immensely fertile lands passed first through the hands of speculators of one kind or another. Probably only one acre in nine actually went directly to small farmers. They were for the most part compelled to purchase land from two private sources: the great transcontinental railroads which had been given grants from the public domain totalling 181 million acres, or from speculative land companies which had purchased control of the lands granted to the states under the Morrill Act of 1862, had fraudulently acquired millions of acres directly from the Land Office, or had acquired reservation lands sold by Indians or disposed of by the government. Speculators and corporations altogether acquired over 500 million acres as opposed to the 80 million acres dispensed through the Homestead Act, and some of this land had been obtained by fraud. Free land for the farmer was a myth. Federal land granted the states under the Morrill Act was purchased by speculators for as little as fifty cents an acre and resold to farmers for anywhere from five to ten dollars an acre. Or farmers could purchase land from the federal land grant reserves held by the Union Pacific for one to fifteen dollars an acre. They could get good land all right, but they had to pay for it.

The Hardships of Farming   But getting the land was the least of their problems. The Great Plains were rolling lands, covered with coarse grass and an incredibly tough sod, lacking the flowers, shrubs, and trees characteristic of the East, limited in game with the rapid extinction of the buffalo, swept by constant winds, cursed with a rainfall lighter than they were used to. More acres were needed for successful farming than elsewhere, and the technical problems involved in turning this vast area into one of the world's great granaries were considerable.

Farming on the last frontier bore little resemblance to that on earlier frontiers in the forested areas of the East, and success came only with the resources and skills of industry, technology, and science. The tough prairie sod was broken by improved chilled-iron and steel plows with a specially designed mold-board. Natural materials for fencing to protect crops from animals and other trespassers were lacking, but the need was met by the invention and mass production of barbed wire. The first few thousand pounds were sold in 1874, and by 1880 over eighty million pounds of it were being sold annually. The necessary transportation was provided by that workhorse of industrial America, the railroad. Trains hauled the farmers' grain to market, and brought them machinery for their fields, clothes for their families, wood to construct permanent homes and barns, coal to heat with, canned and processed foods.

The problem of water was never totally solved. Deep subsurface water could be reached only when drills were invented in the 1870s that could penetrate to the necessary depths. Ingenious technical adaptations of the windmill took advantage of the constantly blowing winds to raise water to the surface, although it was not until the 1890s that windmills were cheap enough for most farmers to afford. Scientists proposed new methods of cultivation known as dry farming: deep plowing, sparse planting, and frequent cultivation to remove weeds, all of which made the most efficient use of rainfall. They also introduced new types of wheat which required less water and were more suited to the harsh environment of cold winters and hot summers. Varieties of "hard" wheat imported from northern Europe and Russia proved highly successful. But they required new milling processes to make flour, a technological achievement first developed in Minneapolis mills in 1871 and put into full operation elsewhere by 1880. Improved mechanical methods for storing and handling grain also developed in the 1870s with the appearance of the elevator alongside railroad tracks where conveyor belts stored the grain and later transferred it to freight cars.

Mechanization   The most important advance, however, was mechanization on the farm itself. Farming on the Great Plains was necessarily large-scale farming—at least 360 acres were required in contrast to the 40 to 80 acres that could be farmed for profit in the East. After the Civil War a number of new machines and improved versions of older ones came into existence, using steam power by the 1890s. Spring-tooth harrows; checkrowers; grain drills; listers which dug a deep furrow, planted the corn, and covered the seed in one operation; harpoon forks, spring-tooth rakes, hay loaders and baling presses for the handling of hay; cord binders and headers for handling grain; advanced threshing machines with self-feeders, bandcutters, and automatic weighers; corn cultivators; disk gang plows; and many others. By 1900 as much as $101.2 million had been invested in farm machinery. The results were dramatic. By the 1890's the United States Commissioner of Labor was able to report that mechanization had reduced the time spent in cultivating an acre from 61 hours to 3 for wheat, from 39 to 15 for corn, and from 66 to 7 for oats. Labor costs per acre went down from $3.55 to .$66 for wheat, $3.62 to $1.51 for corn, and $3.73 to $1.07 for oats. Similar savings in time and cost occurred for other crops.

In various other ways the farming frontier was affected by the forces of the new America. Corporate farming, which has come to dominate American agriculture, was started on the Great Plains. By the 1880s a number of corporations farming tens of thousands of acres had appeared, using hundreds of machines which at planting and harvest time rolled across the landscape like mechanized armies. The cost of farming on the Plains—especially the purchase of land and equipment—depended on modern financing as surplus capital from industrial growth was channeled into mortgage investments in the West. And the effects flowed the other way too. Mechanization of agriculture stimulated the manufacture of farm machinery. And the produce of the Great Plains went to feed not only America but Europe as well.

The consequences in productivity were impressive. Wheat production soared from 152 million bushels in 1866 to 675 million bushels in 1898. Corn

*The combine harvester. When Cyrus McCormick invented the reaper in
1830 he initiated the eventually complete mechanization of the harvesting
process. The combine followed quickly in 1836, cutting and threshing grain
with one machine. However, it was not until late in the nineteenth century
that big-team hitches were developed that could use up to thirty horses,
greatly expanding the capacity of the machine.*

production skyrocketed from 730 million bushels in 1866 to 2.3 billion
bushels in 1898. So great was agricultural production that it contributed to a
disastrous decline in the price of agricultural produce, land rents, and land
values in Europe. By 1900 over 225 million bushels of wheat were being
exported, American farm produce made up three-quarters of the country's
total exports, and accounted for the nation's favorable balance of trade in the
last quarter of the nineteenth century.

Economically the farming frontier quickly became a gigantic enterprise.
Gone was the independent farm where the family raised its own food, made
its own clothes, tools and equipment, and raised a small surplus for market
to buy the essentials they could not make or produce. In its place was a
business operation with all the advantages and woes of commercialization.
Farmers became victims of price declines stemming from their own productivity, of high costs for machinery and for the transportation and storage of
their produce, and of excessive interest charges on money borrowed to buy

PRODUCTION OF PRINCIPAL
CROPS (1860–1920)

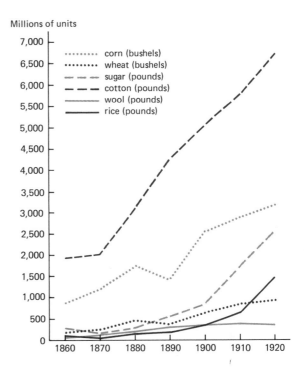

Millions of units

....	corn (bushels)
....	wheat (bushels)
– – –	sugar (pounds)
— — —	cotton (pounds)
————	wool (pounds)
————	rice (pounds)

ever more land and machinery. Cursing the corporations, the banks, the railroads, and the grain elevators, the farmers of the Plains joined with their brethren elsewhere and sought in 1892 to relieve the pressure by taking political action. The Populist party, dominated by the farmers of the Great Plains, offered some interesting and useful proposals but failed to get off the ground. Farmers were unable to see that their failure in profits like their success in productivity sprang from the degree to which farming had become enmeshed in the larger economy, and that their problem could not be solved for the farmers alone. When general prosperity brought higher prices and a more stable income to farmers by 1900, farm protest faded away.

Life on the Farming Frontier The harshness of the Western environment made life often seem grimmer than for the pioneer farm family of old. It had not been easy in the Eastern forest lands. But there had always been plenty of water, game abounded, there were wild berries and fruits, the trees cleared provided wood for houses, tools, furniture, utensils, fences, and fuel.

On the Plains the environment was not so generous. Early settlers had to live in a nine-by-twelve-foot dugout carved out of the side of a hill or ravine, or in an eighteen-by-twenty-four-foot sod house built out of sod bricks cut from the tough prairie turf and made, as one early settler remarked, "without mortar, square, plumb, or greenbacks." Though cool in summer and warm in winter, such homes were hard to keep clean. Dirt got into everything, and when it rained, dirty water dripped on family, beds, and food. It was a great relief when there was enough money to bring in material for a regular wooden house, but families often stayed for several years in a sod house before they could grow and sell enough wheat to pay for such a luxury. Families originally had to make do on clothes as well. One settler noted that "After we had been there a short time we carried our wardrobe on our backs and our feet stuck out." Clothes were sometimes made of grain bags patched with flour sacking. In the early years food was limited and monotonous. Sugar and coffee were luxuries, and farm wives were hard put to come up with a varied and healthful diet. Corn was an early staple, and the *Nebraska Farmer* once printed thirty-three different ways of making it palatable.

Life was especially difficult for women. Working from before dawn until after dusk, beaten by the sun and parched by the wind, limited in resources, lacking the consolation of trees, flowers, and green grass, often isolated from neighbors and miles from town, they endured more than they lived. That chronicler of life on the plains, Hamlin Garland, wrote that faced with the miseries of farm wives "my pen refused to shed its ink," so sad was the story.

But as settlement spread, farm families found relief in going to church in the small towns dotting the Plains, in visiting neighbors, in hunting, sports, and work parties or bees. Baseball reached the Plains in the 1870s, and in 1874 Milford, Nebraska played Seward, Nebraska in a four-hour game on the open prairie—no backstop, no masks, no gloves, just a ball and a bat. Milford won, 97–25. Bees were held on all occasions, usually to help a neighbor in need, occasionally to build a church or a one-room school. Visits were enormously popular, lasted one or more days, and involved the whole family. Dancing was popular, as it had always been on the frontier, and dances were held on every possible occasion. A prairie paper reported one dance as follows:

> About 60 persons were present; crammed into a room some 14 by 20 feet in size, in the center of which two sets of cotillion were compelled to "all saschey." The honest sons and daughters of the soil were there in their plain garbs; widows and widowers in whom the blaze of passion had burned the carbon of life to a cinder were there; chins were there that showed the eider down of tender teens and the heavy hand of time's reproach; the tender maid just swelling with the truth of nature's possibilities, and the mother holding the unweaned offspring to her bosom were there. The polished gentleman of travel who speaks 5 languages fluently and correctly, and the tobacco chewing bummer who does not speak one correctly were there; the mild and the harmless, the swaggering and armed, and the gay young man from town were all there. To set the meaner elements of that heterogeneous mass in motion, whiskey was introduced. In a little while it could be smelled in the air, upon their breaths and clothes, seen in their eyes and noticed in their balance, and down the throats of half the party. Even the cat-gut caught it and slewed among the minor and major keys in reckless disregard of tone. Halters to teams were cut, whips stolen, the road strewn with fence posts, three or four fights ensured, pistols drawn, and bedlam mirrored. We have told enough; numerous other things happened that won't do to tell.

The Last Frontier of the Indian

The success of the mining, cattle, and farming frontiers came at the expense of the Indian tribes that occupied this vast area—the last chapter in one of the saddest stories in American history. A contemporary Indian remarking on the uneven exchange between the red people and the white observed with bitter irony that of course the white people had provided the Indian with valuable gifts, such as antibiotics to combat the diseases introduced by whites into the New World.

Indian Culture   The record of the New World Indians is remarkable for their achievements. They produced over fifty crops now valued in the world, including corn, tobacco, the potato, avocado, pineapple, squash, kidney and lima bean, peanut, chocolate, and pumpkin. They domesticated the stingless bee, the llama, the muscovy duck, and the turkey. In medicine they produced quinine, cocaine, ipecac, witch hazel, oil of wintergreen, petroleum jelly, and other pharmaceutical products. They invented tepees, moccasins, canoes, rubber balls, hammocks, pack baskets, toboggans, and snowshoes. There is little doubt that the development in European thought of the concepts of a better life on earth, and in the natural rights of the individual—which shaped the thought of Locke, Montaigne, Montesquieu, Voltaire, and Rousseau—was influenced by accounts of Indian life in the New World where a remarkable equality prevailed among the common people. Nothing in Europe in the fifteenth and sixteenth centuries equalled the democratic constitution of the Iroquois, which provided universal suffrage for women as well as men. The Iroquois confederacy of the Five Nations was a stimulating precedent for the union of the American colonies. Cherokee chiefs, as well as those of many other tribes, were regarded as servants of the people and took no decision until the issue at stake had been discussed in the councils of the people and agreed upon there, a contribution of considerable significance to the whole concept of the public will.

New World Indian culture was incredibly diverse. In 1492 there were probably about 700,000 Indians living in the present continental United States, divided into at least 200 distinct cultures and languages and marked by hundreds of dialects. The warlike Natchez had a class society and an elaborate social system topped by a king known as the Sun, whose power was absolute and whose person was so sacred that ordinary mortals could speak to him only at a distance, and who was carried in a litter to avoid profaning his feet by touching the ground. The Pueblos were peaceful, classless, cooperative, and so tightly organized that the individual was compelled to conform to the general will of the people or be totally isolated socially. The Cheyenne had warrior societies to maintain military discipline and internal order. Among the Apaches it was every man on his own. The typical housing for Indians of the Northeast was the conical structure covered with bark, the wigwam. Later on the Plains it was the tepee, a hide-covered tent.

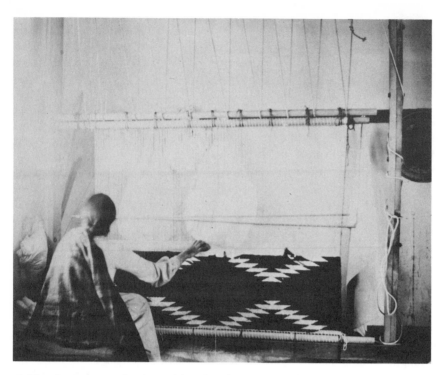

A Navaho woman at her loom. Though Indian art varied from region to region in materials and design, there was a common tradition of art shared by all tribes that was essentially functional. Art was used to decorate utilitarian articles or to distinguish ritual objects, in which the art itself was a part of the object's sacredness. All tribes shared as well the effects on their art of contact with white civilization. As they began to produce objects solely for trade to whites their art lost its functional relationship.

Some tribes emphasized premarital chastity, others did not. Some practiced polygyny, some polyandry, some were monogamous. Some gave women a major voice in council, others did not. Long before 1492, many tribes kept slaves acquired in war or by trade. As late as 1825, 15,563 Cherokees held 1,277 black slaves. A majority of tribes tortured captives beyond belief, the captive accepting the torture as a test of his will and courage, and the captors as a test of their ingenuity. Some tribes resisted every contact with whites. The Cherokees, on the contrary, sought to adapt to the new civilization, and by the 1830s before their forcible removal west of the Mississippi by President Jackson, had their own government with a written constitution, a two-house legislature, their own written language, printing presses, schools, churches, a newspaper, and a successful economic order. Some tribes engaged in warfare for glory, others for profit. In some areas, as in the Pacific Northwest, the supply of food from fishing, hunting, and wild plants was so abundant that there was no need for agriculture. Elsewhere agriculture developed extensively and provided the main food supply.

Indian Adaptability While diversity was the dominant characteristic of Indian culture, all Indians had two things in common. First, they were all human; the New World held no secret fountain of youth and health for them any more than it did for the whites who sought it. Indians died in battle, in childbirth, in the first years of life. They suffered from respiratory and pulmonary ailments, tumors, dental problems, and infections that struck them down in the prime of life. Being human, they also sought to turn to advantage what came their way, and when they did their lives were changed: in the long run disastrously, but in the short run often to their benefit. The Navahos took the white people's sheep and developed a remarkable weaving industry. Out of that came new and elaborate rituals and an astounding poetic mythology. The metal tools of the white people gave the Indians of the Northwest the means for a great creative outburst of carving and sculpture that ranks high in any catalogue of artistic achievement. The unintended freeing of the horse by the Spanish allowed wild horses to multiply and spread on the Plains, and it was the horse that made possible the Plains culture which began about 1700 when the Sioux were pushed westward by the eastern tribes who were themselves being thrust west by white settlement. By 1800 other tribes had also mounted and moved onto the Plains along with the Sioux: the Blackfeet, the Cheyennes, the Kiowas, the Commanches, the Arapahos, the Crows, and the Piegans. A brand new culture evolved based on the horse and the buffalo.

The second thing all Indians held in common, despite great variation in rituals and ceremonies, was a special affinity with nature. Lacking scientific knowledge and hence any capacity to control and direct the world in which they lived, they sought to establish a relationship with it that would spell out satisfactorily their own role and thus give meaning to their lives. The Indians viewed life as a vast and intricate web of natural and supernatural forces. Survival depended upon maintaining the proper relationship between the two. Their goal was to bring themselves as part of nature into harmony with the supernatural forces governing all life, and thereby to acquire guidance for all their activities from day to day. To accomplish this, the Indian sought visions, practiced rituals, engaged in elaborate and complex ceremonies, and fervently worshiped tribal and personal deities. Whether the Zuñi were seeking rain or the Sioux the buffalo, religious ceremonies had to be carefully followed and medicine signs sought. Unable to control nature, the Indian developed a profound respect for, indeed awe of it which was utterly absent in the attitude of the white invaders.

It could properly be said that all Indians also had one more thing in common—the menace of white civilization. In the beginning it did not appear that way. The Indians were many, the settlers few. The Indian was dominant, generous in offering help in the ways of the forest and New World agriculture, and curious about European technology. But once settlements appeared and growth was certain, the outcome was clear. Basically, the problem was that Indian culture was too fragile to survive contact with encroaching Western civilization. Even with the best of intentions and the most decent attitudes of first the European and then the American settlers, Indian culture would eventually have gone under. But the best of intentions were rarely present, so the story became a shameful as well as a tragic one. But unless the Europeans were to ignore the Western Hemisphere completely after its discovery, or the Americans later to confine themselves voluntarily to a limited area, the result would have been much the same.

Throughout the colonial period, relationships between whites and Indians had depended on local conditions and leadership, upon which was superimposed the complicated maneuverings of the European powers who were competing for domination in the New World and willing to use Indian allies in pursuit of their goal. The result was about what would be expected. Brutality and slaughter, decency and respect on both sides, and the steady extension of white settlement. After independence, from 1778 to 1871, the relationship was formally defined by treaties, a process that at least implied recognition of the sovereign rights of the Indian tribes, even though the reality did little to bear out the implication. Some 370 treaties were written in this period, almost all of them forced on the tribes for the purpose of getting land, rights of way, or direct control over the Indians. In most cases, the Indian nations were promised land elsewhere, hunting ranges, and guarantees into perpetuity. None of these promises was kept. The process was inexorable. By the eve of the Civil War, the Indians east of the Mississippi had been reduced to fragments of their former size, become extinct, or been moved west of the Mississippi.

The End of the Trail   By 1860 the last free Indians were flourishing in the West, roaming over almost half the United States in a region stretching from the edge of white settlement in eastern Kansas and Nebraska to the Sierras, from Canada to northern Texas. The dominant tribes were those on the Plains. The horse enabled the Plains Indians to rove over a vast area, to fight efficiently, and to conquer the buffalo with ease. Pulling an A-shaped frame, the horse could transport relatively heavy loads, so that possessions increased and tepees grew in size. Possession of the white civilization's rifle and cavalry sword, along with the powerful Asian bow, made the Plains Indian a deadly fighter and hunter.

This Plains culture had been developing for well over a hundred years, and by 1860 was at its peak. It centered on the buffalo, which occupied the Plains by the millions. The buffalo was the principal supplier of all needs. It provided a rich, seemingly endless supply of food. Women turned the hide into blankets, clothing, and shelter: moccasins, headdresses, shirts, mittens, leggings, dresses, and covering for the tepee. The hide was also used as a canvas for painting. Thread and bowstrings were made from sinew; tools

An Indian camp in South Dakota.

from bones; cups and ladles from horns; water bottles from the stomach; and fuel from the dung.

Porcupine quills, beads, feathers, and paint were used ornamentally with skilled artistic effect on clothing, pouches, weapons, and ceremonial trappings. Men artists decorated tepees with paintings displaying a striking virtuosity.

The Plains tribes were warlike, and from war came honor and prestige. But killing an enemy was not in itself a major goal. Rather, the aim was "counting coup" by stealing an enemy's horse or simply by touching the enemy with the hand or a "coup stick." The Plains Indians loved sports, war being the greatest sport of all. They also played lacrosse, engaged in foot and horse races, and played games of chance. Stories in the form of myths and legends provided a cohesive element in a tribe's culture and history.

As someone once observed, the Plains Indians enjoyed life immensely. They wanted to be left alone, and by and large were, before 1860. The trappers and traders who entered the area were almost always welcomed hospitably, and whites passing through were rarely molested.

But after 1860 their days were numbered. Miners, cattlemen, and farmers moved in. The Indian's own efficiency as a hunter was already reducing the supply of buffalo and white hunters in an orgy of killing completed the job. With the buffalo gone and the area rapidly being occupied by whites, the Indian had come to the end of the line by the 1880s. The policy of segregating the Indians on reservations, occasionally followed earlier, now became the government's principal instrument for dealing with them. By 1887 most of the tribes had been assigned to lands considered unfit for white settlement. There were uprisings and protest, but no hope. No incident involved more than a few hundred Indians at most. One of the most dramatic was that of the Nez Percés who left the reservation in 1877, waged a campaign lasting seventy-five days and ranging over a thousand miles of wild country with federal troops in pursuit, and finally surrendered a few miles from the Canadian border and freedom. In the surrender ceremony, one of their chiefs, Chief Joseph, spoke these words, which seemed to symbolize the tragic story of the Indian:

> I am tired of fighting. Our chiefs are killed. Looking Glass is dead. Toohulhulsote is dead. The old men are all dead. It is the young men who say yes or no. He who led the young men is dead. It is cold and we have no blankets. The little children are freezing to death. My people, some of them, have run away to the hills and have no blankets, no food. I want to have time to look for my children and see how many of them I can find. Maybe I shall find them among the dead. Hear me, my chiefs. I am tired. My heart is sick and sad. From where the sun now stands I will fight no more forever.

The Reservation System The reservation system itself was a terrible failure although it is true that without it genocide might have been the result. If it had been fully and honestly supported it might have avoided major human suffering, although it could never have preserved Indian culture intact. But it was not supported fully and honestly, nor did its administrators have any conception of the cultural problems involved. Honest and sympathetic Indian agents made the best of an unfortunate situation, but the dishonest defrauded the Indians by diverting supplies for their own profit, using shoddy materials, making unethical contracts for supplies, and letting Indian land be illegally used for the benefit of cattle and timber men. Allowing missionary activity on reservations was destructive of Indian religious beliefs and demoralizing to many. Competition among missionaries for the privilege of saving heathen souls confused many Indians and provoked Chief Joseph to angry opposition: "They will teach us to quarrel about God as the Catholics and Protestants do on the reservation. . . . We may quarrel with men sometimes about things on this earth, but we never quarrel about God. We do not want to learn that." Government educational facilities were inadequate and their personnel often poorly trained, even if one assumes that white education was appropriate for Indians, which it probably was not. Many youngsters were sent away to the 148 Indian boarding schools which had been established by the end of the century, an often frightening and certainly a disagreeable experience for the children and parents alike.

Missionary and educational activity suggested clearly that the intent of the government was to "Americanize" the Indian. The passage of the Dawes Severalty Act of 1887 confirmed this intent to end the old tribal life and to channel the Indian into white civilization. Under the law, the president had the power to allot reservation land to individual Indians. Each head of a family could receive a quarter section of 160 acres, and smaller amounts could go to others. Title was to be held in trust by the government for twenty-five years. Indians accepting allotments were compelled to live apart from their tribes. Citizenship was to accompany acceptance of an allotment. The assumption that a law could suddenly transform the tribal Indian into a small independent farmer proved unworkable. Most Indians did not know the essentials of modern farming methods, they had no credit for the purchase of tools, equipment, and supplies, and local assessors often taxed their land excessively. Corrupt leasing practices, illegal seizures, and unethical guardianship and inheritance techniques by whites defrauded many Indians of their lands and the income from them. The net result was that between 1887 and 1934, when the law was finally changed, some 86 million acres of Indian land out of a total 134 million had passed from the hands of the Indians.

Decline of Indian Population   By the end of the nineteenth century and the opening decade of the twentieth, the American Indian was in a bad way. The census figures of 1890 and 1900 recorded that there were between 237,000 and 248,000 Indians. There is no accurate way to assess the decline to this number from the estimated 700,000 on the continent in 1500. Recent studies have indicated, however, that slaughter in war was not a principal cause. From 1798 to 1898 between three thousand and six thousand Indians were killed by U.S. soldiers, and it seems improbable that white civilians could have accounted for anything like an equal number. In the same period Indians killed approximately seven thousand soldiers and civilians. There were no great battles between Indians and United States army units. Of the 1,240 recorded military encounters between Indians and soldiers from 1798 to 1898, most were between bands of eight to twenty young warriors and a troop of thirty to sixty soldiers. Nor could intertribal warfare be regarded as a major cause of decline. Though warfare was a way of life for many tribes, killing was not in itself a major objective. The Iroquois war to exterminate the Huron in the middle of the seventeenth century was the exception, not the rule.

What does seem clear is that Indian societies were radically reduced or wiped out by disease. Europeans introduced to the New World diseases against which the Indian had no natural resistance. Measles, venereal disease, Asiatic cholera, and especially smallpox wrought havoc among whole tribes. The annihilation of the Mandans by smallpox in 1837 is one example among many. Some were driven to the verge of extinction, others reduced to impotence by killing diseases. Moreover the old way of life was destroyed by contact with whites and the steady encroachment of settlement. Confinement to limited areas, and then segregation on reservations, impoverished many tribes, weakened health through inadequate diet and poor living conditions, and left many open to the scourges of pneumonia, tuberculosis, and other diseases. Liquor, to which Indians were an easy prey, ravaged the health of many and contributed to early death.

Indian culture, whatever its variations, had been based on a deep and profound relationship with the open world of nature. When that world was replaced by the closed world of the reservation, or the 160 acres of the small farmer, Indian culture disintegrated. Authority passed from the hands of tribal councils to the U.S. government; ceremonies and rituals were forbidden; the practice of artistic skills had little meaning when the world they represented disappeared, and so they fell into disuse; myths and legends were forgotten, since the occasions for their telling no longer existed. With all these gone, tribal loyalties blurred. When Indian culture lost the living stage upon which it had so long performed, the Indian sense of identity dimmed and weakened.

Most Indians now lived in poverty. They had the lowest incomes of any group in the nation, they were cursed with the highest death rate, plagued by disease, and demoralized by the prospect that the future would be much the same. By 1920 it became apparent that Indian culture was disintegrating and that a majority of Indians were living in intolerable conditions. The attempt to turn the Indian into a white man had been disastrous. Near the end of the colonial period, a French traveler had written:

> For, take a young Indian lad, give him the best education you possibly can, load him with your bounty, with presents, nay with riches; yet he will secretly long for his native woods . . . and on the first opportunity he can possibly find, you will see him voluntarily leave behind him all you have given him, and return with inexpressible joy to lie on the mats of his fathers.

But by 1920 there was no bounty and there were no mats to return to. The painful search for a substitute was to occupy increasingly the attention of many Indians as well as whites for the next half-century.

Conclusion

When Turner in 1893 read his paper on the significance of the frontier, the frontier had not only ended but its character for a quarter of a century had been greatly altered from what it had been earlier. Individuals may have staked their mining claims, run their cattle, and tilled their acres as they had always done on the frontier, but overall things had sharply changed. Science and technology had become major accomplices in the conquest of the wilderness. The demands of factory and city had become more important in dictating the settlement and development of the West than the needs of individuals. And corporations rather than individuals had taken over the exploitation of the resources of the West.

In the process, the Indians who had roamed this vast expanse and in their own way owned it, suffered the final humiliation, as the land which was the lifeblood of their culture was taken from them.

The conquest of the last frontiers was inevitable, but that is not to say it was all good.

The pioneer woman and her family at home on the frontier.

Profile: NANNIE TIFFANY ALDERSON

Born in Virginia in 1860, married at twenty-two to a wandering cowpoke she had met on a visit to Kansas who now wanted to settle down, going in 1883 to make do on a small ranch in Montana, widowed in 1895 when her husband was kicked in the head by a horse, ranching on her own in 1906, flat broke in 1919, Nannie Tiffany Alderson finally said the hell with it, settled down with one of her married daughters, and got around to telling her story in 1942 when she was in her eighties. No big name in the settlement of the last frontiers, just one of the ordinary people who did the job, she accepted with remarkable good spirit what came her way and she made the best of it, which is what a great many women of the West did.

The only things she said she had going for her were determination, a knowledge of how to make hot rolls, and a "vague" idea that her petticoats ought to be plain. She got an inkling of the new country as it really was when they left Miles City, Montana, on the last leg of the journey, a hundred miles across the prairie in a spring wagon:

> Already the grass had started, and the country was prettily tinged with green. But it was a big and bare country, with only scattering pine trees and the cottonwoods in the river bottoms to break its vast monotony. In all the years of my marriage, I never had trees over my head; they could have been planted, but we never lived long enough in one place for them to grow.

Her first home was "a maverick shack," a shelter thrown together for men who had been cutting timber in the Wolf Mountains and who had abandoned it when their scheme fell through: a dirt-roofed, dirt-floored cabin, with one door, one window, two rooms, and a pair of antlers over the door from which dangled a human skull she later learned had been picked up on the battleground of Lame Deer. Though they had plenty of meat, milk, and butter when she found time to make it, and a meager garden that provided some vegetables, supplies of every other kind were brought in once a year from Miles City: hundred-pound sacks of flour and sugar, great tins of coffee, sides of bacon, and canned goods galore. But none of this mattered—it was simply a way-station on the road to something far better. "We didn't expect to live on a ranch all our lives—oh, my no! We used to talk and plan about where we would live when we were rich—we though of St. Paul. It all looked so easy . . . in no time at all we'd be cattle kings."

But it didn't work out that way. And what Nannie Alderson learned how to do that first year, she was still doing years later: washing, ironing, making bread, churning butter, preparing butchered beef, hauling water, putting up preserves, repairing clothes, sewing, and cooking dishes she had learned from bachelor cowboys. When she got her "new" house, a four-room cabin this time, it was burned down by Indians, and they had to start all over again.

The isolation bothered her as much as anything else. She rarely saw other women. A neighboring rancher's wife was a good friend whose company she enjoyed, but they lived thirty-five miles apart and "those thirty-five miles of winding river bottom and high grassy divide were like a Chinese wall dividing us, and we saw each other only twice a year." No wonder parties were so popular, and "people would drive to them from miles and miles away, all bundled up in a wagon with their babies in their arms." The Aldersons once got invited to a party being given over a hundred miles away. But by that time Nannie Alderson had the first of her four children, and although the invitation was a temptation she refused to go that far with a baby.

Medical care was a long way off, and for the most part they were on their own. Nannie Alderson had a little kit of medicines she had gotten in Kansas on a visit. It contained a number of bottles of pills and a set of directions on which pills to take for colds or fever, stomach trouble, and what not. The pills, she confessed, all looked alike and tasted the same, but they either had some magical properties or her family had fantastic constitutions, because they got well every time.

The Montgomery Ward catalogue, which the Aldersons had after 1885, helped to bring the outside world a little closer. "The wish book," she called it, and her children learned to read from it. From the time they got the catalogue in the fall until Mr. Alderson took his cattle to Chicago to sell, they would all pore over its pages, carefully choosing the things they wanted, revising the list endlessly. When he returned he brought back a special trunk filled with each child's order.

But the Aldersons never really made it, and they finally sold out and moved to Miles City where he became a deputy assessor. Shortly afterwards he was killed, and Nannie Alderson was on her own. She ran a boarding house, then a store, was postmistress in a small town, finally borrowed money in 1906 and bought a small ranch and started over—"a cattle queen, with thirty-five cows, and an outfit consisting of a thirteen-year-old boy and a girl." Together with her young son and daughter, she had built their herd up to 950 cattle when the market collapsed in 1919 and they lost everything. Nannie was sorry for her son, but figured he was young and could make it again. "While as for me, I was sixty years old, and I'd been broke so many times before that I could face it. When you have lived without money as much as I had, it loses a great deal of its power to hurt you."

Her friends told Nannie Alderson that she had led a difficult life. "Perhaps," she said at eighty, "but I don't think an easy one is ever half so full."

Chapter 5
AN URBAN-INDUSTRIAL GIANT

The Spirit of the Times
THE RELIGION OF SUCCESS

In the half-century after the Civil War vast industrial enterprises developed, enormous personal fortunes were made, abject poverty grew, more farmers turned into factory workers, towns were transformed into great cities, corporate wealth and power appeared on a scale never before known.

The dominant figures of the age were its great businessmen who defended with vigor the new society and their own role and position in it. It was not easy in a society founded on the principle that all people are created equal and have an equal right to pursue happiness, to defend inequality in the control and distribution of wealth. But businessmen, supported by a number of educators, ministers, writers, and social scientists, took up the task with assurance.

Lack of self-confidence was never a weakness of business leaders. George Baer of the Pennsylvania and Reading Railway declared that "the rights and interests of the working man will be protected and cared for not by the labor agitators, but by the Christian men to whom God in his infinite wisdom has given control of the property interests of the country." The lines of communication between defenders of the business system and the Almighty were open and active twenty-four hours a day. The popular preacher, Henry Ward Beecher, whose own income was a gratifying $20,000 a year, was pleased to pass on in the depression year of 1877 the word that "God has intended the great to be great and the little to be little. . . . I do not say that a dollar a day is enough to support a working man. But it is enough to support a man! Not enough to support a man and five children if a man insists on smoking and drinking beer. . . . But the man who cannot live on bread and water is not fit to live."

Others went beyond the argument implicit in Beecher's views that only individuals of high morality acquired wealth to contend that God "has placed the power of acquisitiveness in man for good and noble purposes." In short, you make money in order to do good to others. Not to seek wealth, therefore, was to avoid one's Christian duty, a view with obviously limited appeal.

*The Labor Day crowd on Main Street in Buffalo. By 1900 the energy and
promise of the city reflected the success of the businessman.*

The argument that enjoyed the greatest popular support in defending the
dominance of the business class was that which emphasized that the system was
wide open, that anyone could achieve fame and fortune if he were hard-working,
frugal, virtuous, and intelligent. The Americans had always had faith that people
could get ahead by their own efforts. Indeed, there were enough self-made men to
make the argument seem almost self-evident. The idea was popularized in biographies, in school books, in stories and poems, in magazines and newspapers, in
commencement addresses across the country. Most who wrote in this vein did so
not to manipulate the facts in defense of great wealth and private enterprise, but
simply because they believed what they saw. After all, Thomas Edison went from
newsboy to inventor, Rockefeller from poverty to power, Andrew Carnegie from
immigrant lad to the mightiest steel king in the world.

The popular writer Horatio Alger, Jr., played upon this theme in some 119
stories for boys, with typical titles like Ragged Dick and Strive and Succeed. And
William Makepeace Thayer in biographies and books for schoolboys such as The
Ethics of Success and Men Who Win, flooded the market on another level. Russell
Conwell, a self-made lawyer and editor, played the same theme in a famous
address, "Acres of Diamonds," which he delivered across the country an incredible
six thousand times to over thirteen million people. Conwell emphasized that
material success could be won right in your own back yard, not by chasing
rainbows. Orison Swett Marden, an orphan who worked his way through college
so successfully that he emerged with a small fortune of $20,000, saw his first book,

Pushing to the Front (1894), through 250 editions. He too emphasized that individuals, if they made the effort, could triumph over all odds and achieve success. Surrounded by all this fact and fiction it is little wonder that few objected to the observation made by the founder of the Coca-Cola Company, Asa G. Chandler, that "The most beautiful sight that we see is the child at labor; as early as he may get at labor the more beautiful, the more useful does his life get to be."

Millions of Americans accepted the doctrine of success, even those near the bottom of the heap, though their own circumstances may have seemed an obvious denial of it. But it gave them hope, and it bolstered the existing order—an undeserved bonus for America's business leaders.

The Expansion of Industry

Of all the changes that have affected humanity in its development, those which have marked the emergence from agriculture to industry and the extensive use of the machine have been among the most significant. Such changes have altered the total way of life: social habits, ideas, political behavior, artistic ventures, ways of looking at the world and assigning meaning to it.

Thus when any people completes the transformation from an agrarian to an industrial base, the way they accomplish this and what it means for them is a matter of major interest. For the Americans this transformation took place in the half-century after the Civil War. Industrialization had, of course, begun much earlier. The foundations of an industrial America had been laid by 1860. But it was not until after the Civil War that the use of machines became a dominant force. The process then took place so rapidly that most Americans had little time to contemplate its meaning, judge its consequences, or assess where it was taking them.

Let us get some measure of this growth. In the last four decades of the nineteenth century, the production of anthracite coal rose from four million to sixty million tons a year, and bituminous coal production skyrocketed from three to two hundred million tons a year. Since coal was the chief source of power, these figures suggest the immense growth of industry. New sources of power in the form of natural gas and electricity had appeared by the end of the century, and were to expand rapidly. By 1912 the total electrical horsepower used in industry had risen to 13 million, and in addition nearly 40,000 miles of railway and trolley track were electrified.

In the key industry of iron and steel, production totaled over nine hundred thousand tons in 1860, almost all in iron, since steel was still difficult and expensive. By 1900 iron and steel production had boomed to some 26.8 million tons a year, almost half of that in steel, which had now become cheap and easy to produce by the new Bessemer process. By 1900 the United States was producing one-third of the world's iron and steel, and had replaced Great Britain as the major producer.

The same growth took place in manufacturing. From 1860 to 1900 the number of factories and machine shops rose from 140,000 to 512,000, the

*Laying the final rail joining the Union Pacific and the Central Pacific at
Promontory Point, Utah. Everyone, from construction workers and
prostitutes to a minister and Leland Stanford, the president of the Central
Pacific, was on hand for the historic moment on May 10, 1869, when the
East and West were united with a spike of California gold.*

amount of capital invested in manufacturing had risen from $1 billion to $12
billion, the value of manufactured products from less than $2 billion to
approximately $13 billion, and the number of workers in manufacturing
from one and a half million to over six million. Less than twenty years later,
the number of manufacturing enterprises had increased some 32 percent
over 1900, capital invested had grown more than 250 percent, and the value
of products had risen 222 percent.

Industrial expansion could also be measured in the development of the
nation's railroad system, a key factor in industrial growth. In 1861, there
were some 30,000 miles of track, much of it poorly linked. By 1900, there
were over 193,000 miles of track, most of it efficiently organized. This constituted some 40 percent of the world's total railroad mileage and was greater
than that of all European nations combined. By 1910 track had increased to
some 257,000 miles, although much of that increase was in double tracks,
spurs, and expanded terminal facilities. By the end of the nineteenth century
more capital was invested in railroads than in all manufacturing combined.

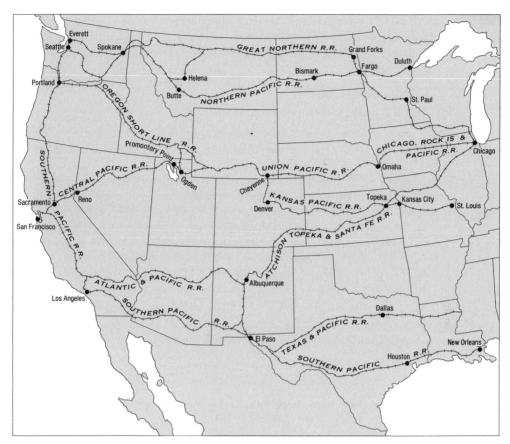

THE DEVELOPMENT OF THE RAILROADS,
1850–1900

An additional measure of industrial growth lay in consumer goods: food, tobacco, leather, silks, rubber, furniture, hardware, clothing, and textiles. The per capita value of such products almost tripled from $60 to $172 from 1860 to 1900, and since prices declined as population expanded, this suggested an even greater increase in production than the figures reveal.

Finally, industries small or nonexistent in 1860 had become giants by 1900. The oil industry, which produced two to three million barrels a year during the Civil War, hit the hundred-million mark in 1903, and that was only the beginning. The automobile industry did not exist in 1860, and in 1900 produced only 4,000 cars. But by 1915 over 970,000 automobiles were rolling off the assembly lines every year. By 1919 the industry ranked second only to steel and was turning out a product valued at nearly $4 billion.

By 1894 the United States had become the major industrial nation in the world. By 1914 it was producing as much as Great Britain, France, and Germany combined, her three nearest rivals.

What factors accounted for this astonishing achievement? The ingredients in the American success story were many, and suggest the complexity of the task facing any modern nation that seeks to travel the road that will lead it to industrialization.

Natural Resources   Natural resources are essential for industrial success, and a nation that has to seek them elsewhere faces special problems. Great Britain, lacking many natural resources, took the road to imperialism in its search for raw materials to feed its machines. The United States was singularly blessed in natural riches and under no such compulsion to search elsewhere until well into the twentieth century. Basic American resources were probably greater than those of any other people in history. More than half the known coal reserves of the world lay within American borders. Iron ore was extensive, not only in the East and South but in the Midwest, particularly in the vast Mesabi range in Minnesota. In oil the Americans were similarly blessed, and the same was true of other minerals—copper on the Michigan peninsula, in Montana and Nevada; gold and silver in South Dakota, California, Colorado; lead in Missouri, Illinois, Colorado; manganese in Virginia. A third of the continent was covered with timber of unparalleled value, and there were great rivers which could be used for hydroelectric power.

Capital   The Americans were equally fortunate in capital for industrial growth, with one significant difference: that a crucial segment of the capital which underwrote American industrial expansion came from abroad. European investors had poured in some $3.4 billion by 1900, and by 1914 over $7 billion. This meant that less saving was demanded of the American people out of the national income, far less for example than was demanded of the British in the last half of the eighteenth century and the first half of the nineteenth. In short the Americans paid a much smaller price for industrialization. There was also domestic capital from a variety of sources: from the surplus created by past industrial development, from the profits of commercial ventures, and from agricultural wealth. The Americans of course welcomed the influx of capital from Britain and the Continent, which let them do more than they could have done on their own. And though there were to be some rumblings about the power of the London money market in American affairs, there were few real fears of undue foreign influence. In the twentieth century this situation was reversed and American capital has flowed abroad—a flow so heavy as to raise fears in a number of countries of undue American influence and a new and subtle kind of imperialism.

Labor   Industrialization in this basic stage of expansion demanded a large and fluid supply of cheap labor. Though part of the labor force was domestic, largely from the increasing flow of rural folk to the cities, the United States found most of its cheap labor in the millions of immigrants who poured into the country from 1880 to 1920. Whereas many who came from Northern and Western Europe in the forty years after the Civil War settled in the West on farms and in small towns, most other immigrants ended in America's cities where they furnished the labor force for the new industrial society.

Markets Industrial development and expansion depend on demand for the products of the machine, and if a nation does not have a market at home it must, as with natural resources, search elsewhere. With a limited population, Great Britain was compelled to seek vast markets abroad for its industrial products, thus helping to propel Britain into imperialism. There was no such problem for the United States, even though she exported more and more manufactured products in tobacco, textiles, oil, and other goods. Basically, America found her market at home in her expanding population. Through natural increase and the heavy tide of immigration, the American population tripled from thirty-two million in 1860 to seventy-six million in 1900, and then to ninety-seven million in 1914.

Technological Innovation and Invention Industrial growth depends heavily on a continuing wave of new techniques, devices, products, ways of doing things, and on willingness to put new knowledge to work. The half-century after the Civil War saw hundreds of innovations, in a kind of chain-reaction, all eagerly accepted in order to increase production and expand efficiency. The Bessemer process made cheap steel available for the first time, and the Siemens-Martin process made possible the conversion of even poor-grade iron ore into steel. The discoveries leading to artificial refrigeration, the telephone, the electric lamp, the internal combustion engine, and dozens of other products created whole new industries. Ford's development of the moving assembly line altered production methods drastically as it was adopted by one industry after another.

Americans embraced such changes almost obsessively. Foreigners visiting American factories were constantly astonished at the eagerness to put new knowledge to work. At the end of the nineteenth century, an English observer, W. C. Steadman, commented that "The American workers do not work any harder than their English brethren, the tendency being to use improved machinery of the latest type, and should a new machine be put in today and a better one come out tomorrow that will turn out more work it will be put to one side for the latest and the best, no matter what the cost." Perhaps he was thinking of Andrew Carnegie, who two months after the completion of a new steel plant learned of a new method that would lower costs, and promptly rebuilt the plant.

Although Americans were ingenious and inventive—witness Ford's assembly line and Edison's electric lamp—much discovery and new knowledge came from Europe, including artificial refrigeration and the new processes for making steel. But the Americans were quicker to use invention and

Carnegie's Homestead, Pennsylvania steelworks in 1886. An absolute fascination with the Bessemer process turned Carnegie's energies to steel production on the threshold of an era when steel was beginning to be understood as a replacement for iron. In 1867 the United States was producing only twenty thousand tons of steel. By 1900, largely through Carnegie's efforts, production had risen to ten million tons.

discovery than others. Moreover, American industrialists pioneered in establishing industrial research laboratories and subsidizing research in the nation's colleges and universities.

Government Government was important in the expansion of industry, an extension of its role as established before the Civil War. During the war government contracts stimulated some industries, favorable banking legislation was passed, the tariff was raised to some 47 percent to protect native industries, and policies permitting contract labor among immigrants provided a cheap work force for many factories and railroads. By an unparalleled generosity in making the public domain available to railroad, mining, and timber interests, these took a great leap forward. The Mineral Act of 1872 and the Timber and Stone Act of 1878 permitted vast amounts of the public domain that were rich in mineral and timber resources to pass into the hands of mining and lumber companies for as little as $2.50 an acre, a price less than the value of a single log from one tree. The government was equally

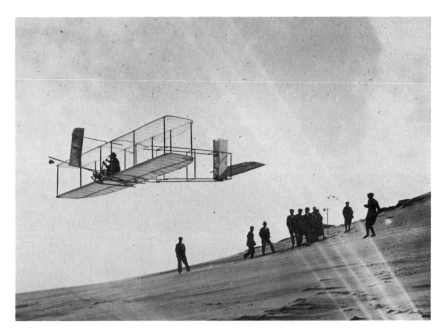

A Wright plane in flight. After several attempts with gliders and elaborate experiments that resulted in the information necessary to design a vehicle that could lift itself and fly, Orville made the first flight of 120 feet. Within five years the Wrights had a contract with the U.S. War Department for the first army plane. By 1909 they had formed a company, and flying was an industry.

generous to the railroads, particularly the builders of the transcontinental lines. These companies received cash loans of millions, and as direct subsidies over 130 million acres of the public domain.

Government aid went beyond even this. The executive branch again and again aided business in times of trouble with workers, sending federal troops in major strikes, such as the railroad strikes of the 1870s and the Pullman strike of the 1890s. The courts were as friendly as the President. A famous but typical instance was the Supreme Court decision of 1889 in a case between the State of Minnesota and the Chicago, St. Paul, and Milwaukee Railroad. The Minnesota legislature, faced with the arbitrary and unreasonable fixing of high passenger and freight rates by the company, had authorized a state commission to fix fair rates. The Court declared this action unconstitutional, thus freeing the railroad to do as it pleased in the matter.

Business Leadership   Any nation seeking to industrialize must, regardless of its economic system, be able to draw men of talent into the economic arena. Most able men tend to go where the rewards are, a fact which tells us much about a society's values. In the last half of the eighteenth century the most talented men in America were in public life, because Americans then placed a high value on public service. In the last half of the nineteenth century America placed a high value on material success, and hence to business leaders went the rewards of prestige and power. There were dozens of remarkable business leaders: Jay Gould, William Vanderbilt, Collis P. Huntington, James J. Hill, Edward Harriman, all of railroad fame; there were John D. Rockefeller in oil, Andrew Carnegie in steel; Jay Cooke and J. Pierpont Morgan in finance; William A. Clark in mining; Armour and Swift in meat-packing; and many others. The desire for wealth obviously motivated these men. Americans have always tended to feel that even though you can't take it with you, you can't go far without it. But the rewards lay not in money alone. Most of these men early acquired far more wealth than they needed. They were lured by the challenge of a new arena of human activity where the stakes were high, and the excitement considerable. The opportunity to build something new and bigger than ever before must have provided great personal satisfaction. And there was the lure of power. In this new society wealth meant power, social and political as well as financial. For many people of talent the urge to attain and exercise power is irresistible.

And these were people of talent. They had great organizing ability, the skill to bring together the resources of minerals, labor, and capital. Andrew Carnegie described the process in his own field perhaps too simply but correctly:

> Two pounds of ironstone mined upon Lake Superior and transported nine hundred miles to Pittsburgh; one pound and one-half of coal, mined and manufactured into coke, and transported to Pittsburgh; a small amount of manganese ore mined in Virginia and brought to Pittsburgh—and these four pounds of materials manufactured into one pound of steel, for which the customer pays one cent.

Carnegie declared this achievement of his to be one of the wonders of the world. Humility was not one of his major attributes.

Such men were able not only to see opportunity but to seize it. Rockefeller's early move from the produce business into oil refining is a case in point. Though many of them were not highly educated, they saw the advantages of trained staffs and technical experts. They adopted new techniques in management and organization and supported the rise of technical schools to insure a future supply of trained people to serve their interests.

The great business leaders also had an enormous capacity for work. Although they all had the means to enjoy a life of leisure and contemplation, and even to dabble in the fleshpots, few were tempted. They stayed on the job and rarely retired, at least voluntarily.

Most of them were willing to use almost any means to further their ends. They turned to monopoly to gain domination although it was against the law; they were not averse to political corruption; they gouged the public in prices if they could; and if force was necessary they used it. Rockefeller

The age was one of widespread exploitation and corruption due to the power wielded by politicians as well as industrialists, as depicted in this cartoon by Thomas Nast attacking the infamous Tweed Ring. Boss Tweed's power extended over the New York City police, the district attorney, the courts, and most newspapers.

relied upon rebates despite their illegality, he sabotaged his rivals' companies, he bribed public officials, and when taken to court or ordered to appear before a legislative investigative committee did not hesitate to lie or take the Fifth Amendment if it served his purposes. Considering all this, it would seem that Rockefeller's response, when asked how he acquired his wealth, that "The good Lord gave me my money," was perhaps giving the Almighty credit He did not deserve.

Yet few felt guilty about such activities. Since they were engaged in mighty tasks, anything was justified. Collis P. Huntington once wrote to one of his agents that "If you have to pay money to have the right thing done, it is only just and fair to do it. . . . If a man has the power to do great evil and won't do right unless he is bribed to do it, I think the time spent will be gained when it is a man's duty to go up and bribe the judge." In remarking upon George Pullman's monopoly in sleeping cars, Carnegie commented that "It was well that it should be so. The man had arisen who could manage and the tools belonged to him."

The American Tradition   A final factor contributing to America's industrial success lay in qualities that had been encouraged and developed in the American people by the American experience itself. The conquest of the wilderness had demanded ingenuity, determination, self-reliance, cunning, courage, and ruthlessness. Moreover, the Puritan tradition had left us committed to hard work, thrift, and efficiency. And out of the democratic heritage of the country had come the conviction that people should have no restraints placed upon their capacity to assert their talent, to rise to the top, to go where their abilities led them. All these qualities, which had been strengthened by the very nature of the American experience in the past, were useful to an emergent industrial nation. Furthermore, the total American experience had always been shaped by the desire for material gain. Immigrants had been so motivated, settlers had been pressured by it as they sought to rise above mere survival, and the seemingly unlimited resources of the land had been an open invitation to all to take what they could and improve themselves in the process. And it was industrialism which offered the hope that perhaps at last enough could be created by the machine to provide well-being for all.

The Growth of Cities

Paralleling industrial expansion was the equally rapid and extensive growth of cities, extending the trend established before the Civil War. In 1860, 1 American out of 6 lived in towns of over 8,000 population. In 1900, 33 percent lived in such towns and cities, and by 1910, 38 percent. In 1860 there were 141 towns of more than 8,000 population; by 1910, there were 778. In the half-century after the Civil War new towns appeared from nothing, established towns grew into cities, and cities turned into metropolises. By 1910, 24 percent of the American people lived in 25 metropolitan areas composed of cities surrounded by smaller cities and towns in vast urban environments. In the Middle Atlantic states, almost 45 percent of the population was concentrated in such areas.

This growth, of course, took place at the expense of rural America. While the rural population doubled from 1860 to 1910, the urban population increased seven times over. Between 1880 and 1890, over two-fifths of the townships of Pennsylvania, three-fifths of those of New England, and two-thirds of those of New York saw a sharp decline in population. Rural losses occurred even in the Midwest. Half of Indiana's townships showed a decline of population, although the state's total population expanded. There were abandoned and vacant farms everywhere as rural Americans deserted the traditional life in the country for a new life elsewhere.

The phenomenon of urban growth was national in scope, and in many cities spectacular. New York went from 1,175,000 in 1860 to 4,766,000 in 1910. Philadelphia, over 1,500,000 in 1910, had grown threefold. Chicago exploded from 110,000 in 1860 to 2,185,000 in 1910, to become America's second largest city. In the single decade from 1880 to 1890, Omaha went from 30,000 to 140,000. Everywhere there were similar stories of growth: in the South, the Midwest, and the far West, as well as the East.

Urban Blight   Like industrial expansion, urban growth was rapid, unplanned, and unregulated. In consequence the cities were far from attractive places to live in, even for the wealthy who increasingly sought to maintain homes in the country. Cities were dirty, smelly, noisy, unhealthy, for the most part ugly, and plagued by crime.

The great cities were marred by the ugliness of the tenements—depressing, airless firetraps of 4 to 6 stories into which were packed scores of people. A New York City sanitary police report in 1890 noted 101 adults and 91 children in a Crosby Street tenement, and this was not unusual. As late as 1900, New York City still had 2.4 million people jammed in tenements. The density of population was incredible. Jacob Riis reported in 1890 that New York City's 330,000 persons per square mile far surpassed the worst crowding in Old London, which never exceeded 175,000 per square mile. This density extended to the streets. Any picture of an American city at high noon in 1900 shows an incredible congestion of people, streetcars, wagons, and carriages—as bad as in any American city today at the rush hour. Few streets were paved. It was not until the late nineteenth century that asphalt paving made its appearance, gradually replacing brick, cobblestones, and wooden blocks. Most streets were simply dirt roads. In Chicago in 1890 only 628 miles of streets were paved, out of a total of over 2,000 miles, and less than half of those were asphalt. Most streets were quagmires when it rained and dust piles when it was dry.

The unattractiveness of the rising cities was made worse by the general lack of parks, playgrounds, and recreation areas. Only an occasional city had the luck or foresight to provide these, such as New York City's famous Central Park—and even Central Park was smaller than originally planned. Many cities had more land set aside for the comfort of the dead than of the living. Newark, New Jersey set aside less than one percent of its land for parks, and almost twice that for cemeteries. The average American city at the end of the nineteenth century had little distinction or charm; most were monotonous in their ugliness.

Pollution   Cities, moreover, were the unhealthiest of places. The incidence of disease was higher than anywhere else, and no wonder. Sanitary conditions were appalling. In many cities sink and slop water was dumped into the gutters. Only a small percentage of homes had water closets, and human waste ended in the nearest river or lake, or was deposited on land where it frequently contaminated wells of drinking water. Manufacturing wastes from Camden, New Jersey, were poured into the Delaware River, while on the opposite side Philadelphia dumped its raw sewage into the same river from which, incidentally, the city also drew much of its drinking water. The Chicago River flowed through the city into Lake Michigan, carrying a freight of garbage, human waste, dead animals, and refuse. In most cities garbage disposal was inadequate, and piles of refuse accumulated in streets and vacant lots. The smoke from factories and the ashes and soot from the new elevated railroads added to the general pollution.

The horse posed a major pollution problem. Everyone today is well aware of the automobile exhaust, but in the fifty years after the Civil War the exhaust of the horse was monumental. In 1900 there were three to three and a half million horses in American cities, the prime movers of freight and passenger traffic. Electric trolley lines after 1880 cut down the number of city horses, but even in 1890 some twenty-two thousand horses and mules were still pulling streetcars in New York City. The price in sanitation was high. The average horse deposited about twenty-two pounds of manure a day, and when he gave up the ghost he deposited himself as well. Maltreatment was common; the average working life of a streetcar nag was only about two years. Injured or dying horses were simply killed where they lay, creating an additional health problem. As late as 1912 the city of Chicago was removing over 10,000 carcasses a year when disposal units could get to the task. (In 1968, Chicago had to remove from the streets the carcasses of some 24,500 abandoned automobiles.) In rain pedestrians waded through liquefied manure; in dry weather it blew about as dust. If health officials deplored the situation, flies delighted in it. Billions of them spread disease throughout the cities.

Heavy concentrations of people always make it easier for infectious diseases to spread. The death rate in America in 1900 was less than 20 per thousand, but in city slums it rose as high as 38 per thousand, and among slum children soared to 136 per thousand. One Chicago precinct reported that three out of every five newborn infants did not live to their first birthday. The killers were varied: pneumonia, diphtheria, scarlet fever, typhoid, tuberculosis, measles, and a multitude of other ailments. Little wonder that the anticipated life-span of a newborn male city dweller was ten years less than for a child born on a farm.

Cities were also noisy. *Scientific America* reported in the 1890s that it was nearly impossible to hold a conversation on a New York City street-corner. The iron shoes of horses and the iron-tires of wagons and carriages clopping and clanging on brick and stone created a maddening din. A traffic study in 1885 counted some 7,811 horse-drawn vehicles passing a single busy corner in New York City in one day.

Crime   Cities were plagued by crime and terrorized by fire. Though crime was not unknown in rural America, it was a grim feature of city living.

Tenement children in their only playground.

The poverty-stricken slums were training-grounds for criminals. Boys learned early to steal from sidewalk displays and roll drunks. Thus prepared they could move into the gangs that operated in all cities, holding up pedestrians and banks, robbing stores and warehouses, engaging in shootouts with rival gangs as well as the police. Corruption among law-enforcement officials increased the problem.

Although the statistics on crime showed an increase by the 1880s and 1890s so great as to be proper cause for alarm, at least part of the rise came from laws that were essentially class legislation: laws on vagrancy which struck at the homeless, the unemployed, the bewildered drunk who had the misfortune also to be poor. Public prosecutors who were often paid by the case welcomed such laws and enforced them for their own profit but for no gain to society except to remove the helpless briefly from the streets.

Fire and Fire Prevention The horror of fire in congested areas was great, particularly since so much construction was of wood. It was not until late in the nineteenth century that fireproof materials such as brick and steel began to be used significantly in urban areas. Moreover, only late in the century did cities begin to switch from volunteers to full-time paid municipal firemen and use improved firefighting equipment. The possibilities for disaster were demonstrated in 1871 in Chicago where the great fire of that year wiped out the center of the city. The damage exceeded $200 million. While this was a catastrophe not equaled until the fire accompanying the San Francisco earthquake of 1906, fire damage in American cities rose steadily year by year.

The rising cities with their congestion, crime, unhealthy atmosphere, and noise were very different from what most of their inhabitants were used to. Most immigrants came from rural backgrounds, as did many Americans. For most of these the city was a startling physical contrast to what they had known, and to which it was hard to adjust. But profound psychological differences between rural and urban living also complicated people's lives.

City Life   Country families were physically isolated and longed for company. They sought out their neighbors, though they may have been miles away. They got to know each other well, and found a common bond in the similarity of their lives. Small towns and villages gave shared intimacy which made them like a large family in which everyone knew everyone else, including the more private as well as the more public aspects of each other's lives. Despite its disadvantages and dissatisfactions, country living gave a deep sense of community and social intimacy.

In the city, the problem was not physical isolation. People were very close, on the streets, in factories and shops, in apartment houses and tenements. But social contact was limited and transitory. In the city it was impossible to know even a fraction of the people you came in contact with. Jammed into crowded streetcars, people had no opportunity to establish any kind of relationship, except perhaps that required to keep someone's elbow out of one's ribs. With factories located away from residential areas, workers by the hundreds swarmed to work from different districts, most of them unknown to one another. In shops and stores, customers were often waited on by people they had never seen before. Human relationships tended to be segmented, anonymous, and impersonal. The people you worked with were not necessarily your neighbors, and your neighbors not necessarily your friends, nor were the people you found beside you on the streetcar or sidewalk, or encountered in stores. Josiah Strong observed in the 1890s that "You may be separated from your next neighbor by only a few inches, and yet for years never see his face or learn his name. Mere proximity does not imply social touch." In the great ocean of the city, many found themselves always swimming in unknown waters.

Where more personal relationships exist, social controls and attitudes tend to be relaxed, easygoing, and informal. Where social relationships are distant, social controls and attitudes tend to be more formal, rigid, and institutionalized. The relationship between farmer and hired hand was close and easygoing. The hired hand, if he had no home of his own, ate with the family and worked beside the farmer in the fields. But in the city, factory workers never saw the factory owner, much less sat at the table with him.

They stood outside the factory in the hiring line and a hard-eyed boss admitted them or not, for reasons beyond the workers' ken. In a small town, a native who had drunk too much in the local saloon would in all likelihood be steered home and deposited on his front porch by a friend or the constable who called him by his first name. In the city the drunk and disorderly— the very terms had changed—were all too likely to be hauled away in the police wagon and dumped in jail overnight.

As if this were not enough, there was in the city a certain loss of independence. Country people relied mostly upon their own efforts and resources. They dug their wells or carried their own weapons for defense; their own horses and wagons provided transportation; they took from the environment to build their homes. The city dweller had to rely on others for goods and services. For you cannot raise your own food in a tenement or even an expensive townhouse. In the city there were no open prairies or forestlands from which to cut sod or trees. If half of New York's residents rose at dawn and headed with a bucket for the East River to draw water for the day, many would be trampled to death.

Food came into the city from the country by train and was dispersed to stores from great markets. Public water systems had to be constructed. Streetcar and elevated railway systems had to be built. Fire and police departments had to be organized. City folk were dependent upon these for their survival, and whether laborer or banker they could not have made their contribution to the diverse and complex economy of the city without these goods and services provided by others. Some of them were provided by collective public action, others by private enterprise, but the city could not have existed without them. There can be little doubt that this interdependency challenged the rural heritage of individualism, forcing city people into different modes of thinking. Understandably, this was hard to get used to.

Unless you were born and raised in this new environment, which most were not, the life of the city made many people perpetually uneasy and uncomfortable. A verse published in 1898 recounted the joys and charms of rural life, and continued:

> Contrast with this the city life
> With all its bustle and its roar;
> Its howling greed, its angry strife
> That tramples down each feeble life
> Which vainly struggles to the fore;
>
> Its brawling crime and snarling death;
> Its cries of want and wild despairs;
> Its dust and smoke which stifle breath;
> Its foul effluvia of death;
> Its catacombs of human lairs;
>
> Its seed of whirlwind, crops of tares;
> Its hells of woe, its devils' cares;
> Its folly-shops of sham-faced wares;
> Its tolls, its panders and its snares.

The Lure of the City   Yet despite its drawbacks the city had immense attractions and advantages. With the expansion of industrialism it became the center of economic opportunity. Here were the jobs in factories, mills, stores, banks, warehouses, railroads, telegraph offices. Here centered the need for labor in construction. Here could be found the multitude of other tasks that made up the expanding and increasingly complex economy. It was in the city that the wealth of the nation was concentrated, and the opportunities for acquiring one's share of that wealth. For many, of course, the city was bitterly disappointing. For others, its advantages were an open-sesame to prosperity and wealth. What ultimately drew people to the city was the same dream that had earlier drawn them to the New World—the dream that here their fortunes would take a turn for the better. If the dream failed, it was hard to retreat to the land. So if people failed they stayed where they were or sought another chance in still another city.

The city also possessed the magnetic pull of its cultural and intellectual institutions. It possessed the wealth and the audience to support theaters, operas, concerts, museums, clubs, universities, and the publishing of books, magazines, and newspapers.

Cultural Interests   It was no coincidence that the half-century after the Civil War experienced a cultural expansion equal to the industrial. Banker Henry Lee Higginson helped found the Boston Symphony Orchestra in 1881. In 1883 the Metropolitan Opera of New York came into being, backed by Vanderbilt and others. Continuous vaudeville was introduced in 1885. The University of Chicago, which rapidly became one of the great institutions of higher learning, was founded in 1892 with Rockefeller support, and earlier, in 1876, Johns Hopkins University, a unique institution devoted almost entirely to graduate study, opened its doors. There were over 2,800 daily newspapers by 1909—five times the number published in 1870—and the circulation of the greatest urban papers, such as Pulitzer's New York *World*, had passed the million mark before the end of the century. New magazines came on the scene: *Scribner's, Ladies' Home Journal, McClure's*, the *Forum*, among many others. Between 1881 and 1919, Carnegie provided for the establishment of over 2,500 public libraries.

The city therefore represented for many another kind of dream than that of sudden wealth. It promised to stimulate the mind and the senses, to reveal new horizons, to open a new and exciting world filled with people and activities that would make life far richer than was possible on the farm or in the village. For young people to whom rural America semed drab, limited, and monotonous, the city dazzled the imagination. Hamlin Garland, in his autobiographical *A Son of the Middle Border*, described the first time he went to a theater in a town near Chicago and saw Edwin Booth in *Hamlet*. He "trembled with anticipatory delight," and "had a distinct realization that a shining milestone was about to be established" in his life. The experience, he recorded, "filled me with vague ambitions and a glorious melancholy."

The first issue of Scribner's *magazine.*

Closely related was the lure of the city as a beehive of human activity. The greatest pleasure of rural families, as the history of the frontier amply shows, was to break their isolation and be with other people—visiting neighbors for a day, or perhaps attending church services miles away not just for spiritual but for social comfort.

There was no problem in the city about this kind of isolation. On Broadway you could see theatrical stars, chorus girls, artists, writers, producers, composers. On Longacre Square was Rector's, a celebrated restaurant where twenty dollars bought an elegant supper for five, including champagne and cigars. Less than three miles away you could eat with working men in a place where fifteen cents bought soup, meat stew, pickles, bread, pie, two schooners of beer, and a cigar or cigarette.

You could see "the Dresden doll," Adele Ritchie, starring in *A Runaway Girl* at the Fifth Avenue Theater, or the *Floradora* sextette at the Casino Theater. You could marvel at the fabulous Waldorf-Astoria on Fifth Avenue, the largest and costliest hotel in the world: 1,000 bedrooms and 765 private baths, numerous public rooms, state apartments, and restaurants. In the notorious Tenderloin, from Madison Square to 48th Street between Fifth and Ninth Avenues, were the gambling resorts, brothels, restaurants, and dancehalls where customers were openly solicited by prostitutes, and all the other tawdry aspects of New York lowlife.

Fifth Avenue north of 50th Street was dominated by the homes of the very rich, modeled after Renaissance palaces and French chateaus. At Fifth Avenue and 65th Street, for example, was the white French Renaissance palace created for Mrs. Astor by Richard Morris Hunt and paid for by William Astor to the sum of over two million dollars. Below 14th Street was another aspect of the great city: slums packed with immigrants where dress, custom, food, language, even appearance were strikingly different. Between the Bowery and the East River was the ghetto inhabited by East European Jews, where among others you could see the beard, skullcap, and long-skirted kaftan of elderly survivors of a Polish pogrom. Shop signs were in Hebrew and you heard more Yiddish than English on the streets. West of the Bowery was Little Italy which reflected the life of southern Italy. Below this was Chinatown, where men of the older generation still wore braids and Chinese dress and women were hidden from public view. On Greenwich and Washington Streets near the Battery, you could wander past the coffee houses and bazaars of Turks, Syrians, and Arabs. Near St. Mark's Place along Second Avenue were the brightly lighted cafes, sidewalk terraces, and gypsy musicians of Little Hungary. And so it went. The Bohemian quarter, the German colony, the Greek district. A visit to New York City was like a trip around the world. With its varied peoples and cultures, its incredible variety of human activity, its mixture of the exotic, the commonplace, and everything between, little wonder the city seemed the most fascinating place in the world.

New York was the apex of the American urban world, but all cities had some glamor. No matter what your taste, in the city you could find if not always afford satisfaction for it. No matter what your interests, in the city you could find people who shared them. Someone once remarked that it required a city of one million to provide him with the twenty to thirty congenial friends he needed to live a satisfying life. No farm community could match these attractions. This is why rural America seemed monotonous and the city exciting.

Poverty and Wealth

The new America of factories and cities was a land of extremes—enormous wealth on the one hand, great poverty on the other. The wealth created by the machine and concentrated in the cities was controlled by a handful of people. By 1910, the top one percent of the population owned at least forty-seven percent of the national wealth and received about fifteen percent of the national income. An earlier estimate in 1893 by a statistician of the Census Bureau suggested that the top nine percent of America's families owned seventy-one percent of the wealth. In 1900, Andrew Carnegie's income from his steel interests alone was $23 million a year, and this at a time when there was no income tax and the wealthy paid very limited property taxes. John D. Rockefeller's income at the turn of the century was about $100 million and he was worth probably $1 billion. This is personal wealth staggering to the imagination.

The wealthy entertain themselves.

The Wealthy American Such wealth meant living on a grand scale with pleasures, luxuries, and entertainments denied to other Americans. It meant that any taste, any desire, any whim could be satisfied. Only the lives of Indian maharajas, Italian Renaissance princes, and Turkish potentates approached it.

Almost all the wealthy built themselves magnificent palaces. The Vanderbilts had seven palatial residences along Fifth Avenue in New York whose total cost exceeded $12 million. They also had other residences. William K. Vanderbilt had an $11-million resort home at Newport and another on Long Island which contained 110 rooms. George W. Vanderbilt's famous home in North Carolina was built in imitation of the castles of the Loire Valley in France. It possessed a tapestry gallery, a print room, a huge banquet hall, forty master bedrooms, and a library of over 250,000 volumes. The estate itself covered 203 square miles and on it Vanderbilt's extensive experiments in forestry and agriculture required more men than were employed by the United States Department of Agriculture and had a larger budget.

The houses of the wealthy were often as much museums as residences. Agents of the rich searched Europe for the finest Flemish tapestries, ancient Greek statues, sixteenth-century French furniture, Italian Renaissance paintings, rare books and manuscripts, the work of the great goldsmiths, precious porcelain, and scores of other treasures. To the distress of many

Europeans, these works of art flowed in a steady stream into the homes of America's élite. Many Americans developed a taste for the art they acquired—J. P. Morgan, for instance. Others simply viewed such treasures as evidence that in art as in everything else the best goes to those who can afford it.

Some homes were in themselves composite works of art. William C. Whitney's mansion had gates from the Palazzo Doria in Rome, a ballroom from a French castle, painted ceilings in the banquet hall and drawing room from the palaces of Genoese and Roman princes, a corridor from an old French monastery, and many stained glass windows from medieval churches. Europe seemed to have been looted by rich Americans more successfully than it had ever been by barbarian hordes, in proof that the checkbook is mightier than the sword.

Nor did the wealthy want for entertainment. The James Hazen Hydes, whose fortune came from insurance, once gave a costume ball costing over $200,000. Competition was keen in such matters. For the occasion, Hyde hired the famous architect Stanford White to turn the main ballroom at Sherry's restaurant into a replica of the Hall of Mirrors at Versailles. The floor was covered with rose petals, the walls adorned with thousands of orchids, the guests were in court costume, the waiters in livery, and entertainment was provided by the famous French actress, Gabrielle Rejane, who had been brought over for the occasion.

The rich also dined well. Randolph Guggenheimer gave a dinner for forty at the Waldorf-Astoria on February 11, 1899. The Myrtle Room had been turned into a garden with flowers in bloom and birds (some of which had been borrowed from the zoo) in full throat. The menus were painted in gold on scraped and polished coconuts, and the dinner consisted of Buffet Russe, Cocktails, Small Blue Point Oysters, Lemardelais à la Princesse, Amontillado Pasado, Green Turtle Soup Bolivár, Basket of Lobster, Columbine of Chicken, Roast Mountain Sheep, Jelly, Brussels Sprouts Sauté, New Asparagus, Mumm's Extra and Moët & Chandon Brut, Diamond Back Terrapin, Ruddy Duck, Orange and Grapefruit Salad, Fresh Strawberries, Blue Raspberries, Vanilla Mousse, Bonbons, Coffee, and Fruit.

The slightest whim did not go unsatisfied. At their summer place or "cottage" in Newport, Mrs. Belmont had Chinese artisans construct a genuine red and gold lacquered tea house. They neglected to provide the means for making tea, so she had a miniature railroad built from the pantry of the cottage to the tea house over which servants rode serenely, carrying tea for guests.

There were those who scorned display and lived relatively simply and unostentatiously—Rockefeller, Carnegie, and Morgan, among others. Yet even Morgan found it convenient to have homes in New York City, Highland Falls, and England, as well as a retreat in the Adirondacks, special suites in Paris and Rome, a private Nile steamer available for his use in Egypt, and his famous 320-foot steam yacht *Corsair III*, which he used in preference to the common public transportation of ocean liners for crossing the Atlantic and cruising the Mediterranean.

By the end of the nineteenth century the rich seemed out to create a new breed of American, the machine-age aristocrat. Most of them sought to establish the validity of their claim by their manner and style of living. To provide the final confirmation they had begun to marry their daughters to European nobility. In this as with their palaces, their art, and their entertainment, they relied upon the power of the purse. Husbands were purchased, with price no object. The marriage contract between Consuelo Vanderbilt, who must have been one of the most beautiful women in the world, and the Duke of Marlborough gave the Duke $2.5 million in railroad stock with guaranteed annual interest of four percent for the rest of his life. Although the nature and amount of the wealth may have differed—horses instead of railroads—certain Indian tribes had been accustomed to making similar arrangements.

The Urban Middle Class   Contrary to the impression of many foreigners, not all Americans were rich. There was also a substantial urban middle class, the technicians, salaried professionals, clerical workers, salespeople, public and corporate service personnel—the fastest-growing segments of the population. While the American population as a whole was increasing two and one-third times from 1870 to 1910, this group was expanding eight times from 756,000 to 5,610,000. Meanwhile the older urban middle class, the independent professionals, the small manufacturers, the merchants and small businessmen merely doubled in size by 1910 to some 3,260,000. The savings of both groups poured into the economy—into railroads, insurance, banks, and manufacturing. By 1900 there were an estimated 4.4 million stockholders in American corporations, and by 1917, 8.6 million.

In the great cities these Americans lived in brownstone or brick row houses; their counterparts in the smaller cities and towns had spacious and attractive homes on tree-lined avenues. By 1910 these homes had electricity, indoor plumbing, and telephones. The automobile, which only a decade before had been the plaything of the rich, was increasingly found parked outside middle-class homes. These houses were filled not with the looted treasures of Europe, but with the products of the American economy. Many by 1900 were losing their gloomy Victorian character with its potted plants, heavy mahogany furniture, and marble-topped tables. Gilded reproductions of Louis XVI furniture came in along with a host of figurines, vases, miniatures in gilt frames, and paintings by unknown artists. A more liberal use of white paint brightened interiors considerably.

Not given to the extravagances of the rich, the middle class yet lived a pleasing life. Those at the top patronized good restaurants, attended the theater, and sent their sons to college. Most middle-class families lacked the mobility of the rich—the ability to vacation elsewhere in the country or abroad was to come decades later. Most had a servant or two, drawn from the pool of female immigrants. It did not take an enormous amount of money to live the minimum pleasant life within the middle class. An income of $1500–2000 a year, provided one exercised economy, bought a great deal

West Seventy-Third Street, New York City, 1889. The brownstones of the middle class begin to shape the city.

as the twentieth century began, especially in the smaller cities and towns. A family with an income of ten or even five thousand dollars a year could live very well indeed, with few worries beyond the unnecessary but common one of how to acquire even more than they already had.

The Urban Worker and the Poor   But the price of triumph as the most advanced industrial nation in the world was high. The wealth was badly distributed. Millions lived in poverty, despite the many opportunities for working people to improve their condition. In 1890 the average yearly income of nonfarm wage earners was $486. This was barely enough to provide adequate food, clothing, and shelter for a family of four, and offered no opportunity for saving or protection against serious illness or unemployment. Obviously many people earned far less than this average. The same situation prevailed in 1909, when $500 a year was regarded as necessary for a decent standard of living. As late as 1915 a federal commission discovered that between one-third and one-half of all American workers in mining and manufacturing did not earn enough to buy adequate food, clothing, and

*At work in a sweatshop. Low piece-rates and dangerous working conditions
characterized the small shops set up in tenements to produce cheap
handmade articles like clothing, artificial flowers, and cigars and cigarettes.
The high unemployment rate kept the sweatshops filled despite the
conditions, and attempts to regulate them failed in the late nineteenth
century.*

shelter. Not surprisingly, a survey of six large cities revealed that twelve to
twenty percent of all children were not getting enough to eat.

Skilled workers, such as those in the building trades, were not in want.
Many could save money, buy homes, and even acquire additional property.
The rise of building and loan associations among immigrant working-class
groups, such as the Bohemians in Chicago, suggests that large numbers of
workers got along successfully. The millions of dollars that immigrants sent
home yearly suggests that savings were large even among low-paid workers,
but only at a sacrifice. Yet an individual workingman or woman with no
family could manage satisfactorily on $1.50 a day. An unskilled hand truck-
man in a factory on Chicago's West Side in the 1890s earned $9 a week, but
his board and room cost him only $4.25, and he later recorded what he got
for that sum:

> In the tenement house in Chicago we breakfasted at half past six in the
> morning, had a porridge, meat, a vegetable, we had all the coffee we wanted
> for breakfast, and excellent bread—all . . . was well prepared. For our mid-day
> meal at each man's place was a steaming bowl of soup. It was replaced with a
> plate containing a slice of roast beef of some sort, and two or three vegetables,

and an abundance of bread, and after that would come dessert, usually pie—or sometimes a pudding. In the evening, after our day's work was done, we had a simpler meal, some cold meat and a hot vegetable, with an abundance of bread, and we finished up with a fruit.

Not exactly comparable to dinner at the Waldorf-Astoria, but certainly a far cry from starvation. But what an individual could get by on for $1.50 a day was nearly impossible for a family.

Jacob Riis reported in 1900 that while $1.50 a day was standard for unskilled labor, he had found women working for as little as 30 cents a day, and this was not uncommon. Even reasonable wages made no provision for unemployment, a constant hazard of the working class, and many workers were unemployed as much as four months a year.

There is no way to describe adequately the misery of the extremely poor. But reports from the time give some idea of the grimness of life, especially for those at the very bottom. Riis, in *How the Other Half Lives*, quoted a report from the Association for the Improvement of the Condition of the Poor in New York, which described a family living in a garret in a tenement:

> The family's condition was most deplorable. The man, his wife, and three small children shivering in one room through the roof of which the pitiless winds of winter whistled. The room was almost barren of furniture; the parents slept on the floor, the elder children in boxes, and the baby was swung in an old shawl attached to the rafters by cords by way of a hammock.

Riis described another family as follows:

> There were nine in the family: husband, wife, an aged grandmother, and six children; honest, hard-working Germans, scrupulously neat, but poor. All nine lived in two rooms, one about ten feet square that served as parlor, bedroom, and eating-room, the other a small hall-room made into a kitchen. The rent was seven dollars and a half a month, more than a weeks wages for the husband and father who was the only bread-winner in the family.

The French observer, Paul Borget, found in the Italian part of the Bowery two rooms on the street level, "small as a boat's cabin," in which eight men and women were "crouched over their work, in a fetid air, which an iron stove made still more stifling, and in what dirt!" In the Jewish quarter in New York he found "hunger-hollowed faces," and "shoulders narrowed with consumption, girls of fifteen as old as grandmothers, who had never eaten a bit of meat in their lives." Robert Hunter, who did a major study of poverty in America at the turn of the century, described workers on their way in early morning to a factory in Chicago: "Heavy, brooding men; tired, anxious women; thinly dressed, unkempt little girls, and frail joyless lads passed along, half-awake, not uttering a word." Investigations in Chicago among working-class families in the poorer wards revealed small children unattended at home, often tied up while other members of the family were out working, and left only a chunk of bread to eat during the long day.

In such conditions prospects seemed bleak indeed. A Chicago laborer said bluntly: "Land of opportunity, you say. You know damn well my children will be where I am—that is, if I can keep them out of the gutter."

It is hard to generalize about living conditions, since human beings differ in their response to circumstances. Many among the rich threw their money about with no restraint. Others looked with contempt upon spending that served only vain display. Among the lower classes there were those who ordered their lives with thrift and efficiency within their income, provided for their families, saved, and gradually improved their condition. Others spent inefficiently, cared little for the welfare of their families, and viciously exploited the labor of their own children.

It is clear, however, that wealth in the new America was badly distributed, and its maldistribution warped the lives of many, rich as well as poor. It weakened the presence of decency in human relationships, reduced compassion, lessened respect for others, and in some perverted fashion seemed to transform greed into a virtue. The economic system worked for many, but for vast numbers it did not.

Profile: ANDREW CARNEGIE

From the cottage of a Scottish handloom weaver in Dunfermline to Skibo Castle on Dornoch Firth via Pittsburgh, from a $1.20-a-week bobbin boy to the second richest man in America, from a shrewd saver of pennies to a philanthropic dispenser of over $350 million—few make journeys of such distances. But Andrew Carnegie did.

Carnegie was one of the great examples of the American gospel of hard work, thrift, common sense, native ability, and the ability to seize opportunity by the throat. Arriving in America in 1848 with his father, mother, and brother, Andrew at thirteen began work in a cotton factory as a bobbin boy and engine tender. He was a messenger in a Pittsburgh telegraph office at fourteen, then telegrapher, and at eighteen he was noticed by Thomas Scott of the Pennsylvania Railroad in true storybook fashion and made Scott's private secretary and personal telegrapher at the incredible sum of $35 a week. "I couldn't imagine what I could ever do with so much money," he later recalled.

But Carnegie did know what to do with his $35 a week and with subsequent raises as he moved up the ladder with the Pennsylvania Railroad. He invested it. By the time he left the Pennsylvania at the age of thirty in 1865 he had interests in the company that held the Pullman sleeping-car patents and in various iron enterprises. He went into bridge-building, bond-selling, oil wells, and other ventures, and in 1873 started the J. Edgar Thomson Steel Mills and was on his way. He was then 38 years old. Five years earlier he had written himself a memo: "Thirty-three and an income of $50,000 per annum! . . . Beyond this never earn—make no effort to increase fortune, but spend surplus each year for benevolent purposes. Cast aside business forever . . ." He had gone on to record that to devote himself wholly to making money "must degrade me beyond hope of permanent recovery."

But alas for good resolves made in the flush of youth. He went on to make a very great deal of money, and apparently did not feel that it degraded him in the least, although some workers at the Carnegie plant at Homestead in 1892 during the bloody strike of that year might have agreed with his prediction if they had known about it. And his competitors in steel production who had a hard time competing with his methods during his rise to power might on this matter have found themselves for once in agreement with him.

But economic shrewdness and foresight, which Carnegie possessed in abundance, are hardly synonymous with degradation. His skillful use of integration in industry illustrated these qualities well. His Edgar Thomson Steel Works was a primary supplier of steel rails, which required a steady supply of pig iron. So he acquired blast furnaces to make pig iron. Blast furnaces require good coke, so he joined forces with Henry Frick, who controlled the greatest source of coke in the world. He also acquired control of the best of the Mesabi Range iron-ore property through long-term leases. For transportation, he then built an independent railroad line to Pittsburgh from Conneaut Harbor on Lake Erie. He also built a fleet of lake steamers to carry his ore. By 1900 he had tied together all the elements in the making of steel, the Carnegie Steel Company was earning profits of $40 million a year, producing four-tenths of the steel made in the United States, and Carnegie's wealth and power were enormous. Faced in 1900 with a threat by the manufacturers of finished steel products that they would make their own steel, Carnegie set out to beat them by building his own mills to manufacture finished tubes, wire, nails, hoops, and rods. But, significantly, the problem was solved by a combination of the competitors into a new super-corporation, the United States Steel Company, the first billion-dollar corporation in America. Carnegie sold out his interests for $250 million.

He then turned his attention to matters other than business—at 65. A number of years before he had published an article entitled "The Gospel of Wealth." The gist of it was that the people who accumulated wealth were merely trustees of what was, after all, the result of the labors of many people, not just of the people who possessed it. Since the rich obviously had extraordinary talents—witness the ability to create their fortunes in the first place—they should clearly be the ones responsible for putting this wealth to the best public use. It could be argued that capitalists might share their wealth as they went along by higher pay to workers, lower prices to consumers, and even a few taxes to governments which do occasionally spend money for useful public purposes. But given Carnegie's faith in the capitalistic system of his time one can understand and scarcely criticize his belief that wealth, which was essentially created by the community, should ultimately be returned to the community.

Nor were the things he planned unworthy. Being a writer, a friend of writers and scholars, and believing that his own mind had been nourished by the reading of his youth, Carnegie turned his thoughts and his fortune to making books available to others. His faith in books and education was not common among businessmen of that time. He gave some $60 million for public library buildings, and at least $60 million more for colleges, universities, and educational research. He established a number of philanthropic foundations, including the largest, the Carnegie Corporation of New York. He took a special interest in international peace, and he gave millions to a foundation created for that purpose. His total benefactions were over $350 million, over $60 million of which went for libraries, education, research, art, music, and other causes in the countries of the British Empire, and the rest in the United States.

Carnegie sincerely believed that these great gifts would benefit the common people and help improve the general condition of humanity. Today we know that it takes more than even this kind of personal generosity to make much progress at such a monumental task. But it would be hard to say he did not try, which is what he had done all his life anyway in accumulating his wealth, and few Americans would be inclined to hold that against him.

Chapter 6
SOCIETY AND CULTURE

The Spirit of the Times
POPULAR CULTURE

Life was serious in the new America, and factory and city created tensions and pressures that demanded release if sanity was to be preserved. Yet the urban environment by and large was not suitable for the kinds of recreation and entertainment Americans had traditionally sought as relief from the labor of the day. But the city did offer a variety of activities for all classes of people that made life more tolerable and indeed enjoyable than it might otherwise have been.

The legitimate stage appealed more to the educated classes, though only a few American playwrights, such as Bronson Howard, Augustus Thomas, and Clyde Fitch, dealt in the kind of drama and social comedy that analyzed the new world being created in America. So European imports, especially masters like Shakespeare, dominated the legitimate theater. Quite apart was the popular theater of melodrama and farce. Cheap prices, from ten to thirty cents, made this entertainment available to the urban masses. In New York the Bowery Theater, the People's, the Windsor, the National, and many like them in other cities, were places of friendly informality, clamorous and disorderly. Beer was served continuously, house policemen tried to maintain some decorum, and actresses often joined members of the audience for a drink.

Melodramas on the pitfalls of city life were extremely popular and their titles suggest their tone: typical were Under the Gaslight, Only a Working Girl, and Nellie the Beautiful Cloak Model. Virtue always triumphed even though it may have been a rare commodity in the real world outside. Poverty may have been the condition most people wished to avoid in reality, but in the melodrama it stood for decency. "An honest shop girl is as far above a fashionable idler as heaven is above earth," proclaimed one heroine who coincidentally happened to be a shop girl. Melodramas on western themes were the most popular in the years before 1900, bringing to urban audiences a taste of wild excitement absent in their own lives, and often made more thrilling by the appearance of real-life Western heroes such as Wild Bill Hickock, Buffalo Bill Cody, and others who re-enacted on the stage their own adventures, and a few more besides. The excitement of melodrama was

Early movies bring a new form of entertainment to New York City.

enhanced for its cheering audiences by elaborate stage settings featuring train wrecks, horse races, stage holdups, Indian attacks, and ships sinking at sea.

Burlesque was almost as popular as melodrama, especially for the lone male in the city, and the reason could be found in the advertising: "50—Pairs of Rounded Limbs, Ruby Lips, Tantalizing Torsos—50." In 1895 Sam T. Jack was the "King of Burlesque," and burlesque dominated many theaters and road companies.

Vaudeville—variety entertainment for the whole family—was also popular. All major cities had at least one vaudeville theater, and most had several. The acts included acrobats, trained dogs, trick bicycle riders, jugglers, magicians, dancers, comedy acts, and often a one-act play or farce. Top vaudeville stars of the 1890s included Weber and Fields, Lillian Russell, Sandow the Strong Man, Pat Rooney, and the Cohan family. Dominant in organizing and extending vaudeville across the country were Tony Pastor, B. F. Keith, and F. F. Proctor.

Besides all this there was the night-life of urban America—the dime museums, dancehalls, shooting-galleries, bowling alleys, concert saloons, music halls, and other places of entertainment which ranged from the respectable to the sinister. In the major cities there were scores of music halls and concert saloons where you could be served drinks by scantily clad waitresses and listen to musical and other entertainers. There was also the common saloon where the working man could feel completely at home with his fellows in an inexpensive place where he was accepted just as he was, no questions asked. Moralists may have proclaimed the saloon a place of sin because of the five-cent beer, but it was a temporary retreat from both home and work that seemed essential to the peace of mind of many of America's working class.

In the first decade of the twentieth century a new form of entertainment appeared: the motion picture which had its origins in the peepshows of the 1890s based on Thomas Edison's invention, the Kinetoscope. A nickel was inserted in the machine, and an eye to the peephole gave the novel pleasure of seeing tiny figures actually moving. Other inventors quickly found ways to transfer these images to a large screen. The potentialities of the new medium were revealed in 1903 in The Great Train Robbery, and soon theaters called nickelodeons were operating by the thousands, where for a nickel you could see a twenty-minute show. In a single year, 1907, three hundred opened in New York City alone, and Harper's Weekly reported that 200,000 people a day were visiting them.

Between 1908 and 1914, many movie makers moved to Los Angeles and Hollywood where the sunshine, which was then still available, was of particular advantage to early photography. By 1914 both producers and exhibitors had learned the basics of the craft and the industry was set for its great leap forward.

The early movies in the nickelodeons inevitably brought forth cries of condemnation. Darkened theaters alone implied a tone of dubious morality, to say nothing of the threat to the nation's morals from what took place on the screen. When the first kiss was shown in a movie based on a play, a Chicago critic wrote in disgust:

> In a recent play called The Widow Jones you may remember a famous kiss which Miss May Irwin bestowed on a certain John C. Rice.... when only life size it was pronounced beastly. But that was nothing compared to the present sight. Magnified to Gargantuan proportions and repeated three times over it is absolutely disgusting.... Such things call for police interference.

From the beginning the motion picture was mass entertainment, and it was to be the major form of mass entertainment until the advent of television.

All over urban America the need for entertainment and recreation was increasingly satisfied not by direct participation, but vicariously through watching others perform, as the theater and movies attest. This also held true for a number of sports, especially horse racing, boxing, football, and baseball. Direct participation seemed possible only for members of the middle and upper classes, who began to take up such activities as golf, tennis, bicycling, croquet, and sunning and swimming at exclusive beach resorts such as Newport.

But the need for leisure activities was great for all classes, and providing satisfaction for it became a major business in the new America.

Women and the New American Family

The Changing Family   The family was deeply influenced, indeed altered, by the impact of the urban-industrial society. It became more and more fragmented as it gave up one after another of its traditional functions. In rural and village America, the family had functioned as a single economic, social, even political and military unit. Now in the world of great cities and factories these responsibilities were being eroded. On the farm and the frontier the family had been involved in one economic endeavor—working to make the farm succeed. All had their tasks and all worked closely together. But now the family dispersed as its members took on different tasks outside the home: father as factory worker, mother and older daughter as domestic servants, store clerks, or office help, young son as newsboy or machine-tender in a mill. Even in middle- and upper-class families, shops and small businesses had once been largely family enterprises. Now well-to-do families no longer regarded even maintaining the home as a family enterprise, but increasingly relied on servants. Sons were often sent to college to succeed their fathers in business, but even this meant passing on to other hands the responsibility of training.

Recreational activities were earlier defined and shaped by the family, often tied to its economic life, and geared naturally to the seasons. In the city there was little opportunity for this kind of cooperative pleasure, and recreation became commercialized entertainment, a business in itself. Significantly, the members of the family often went their separate ways seeking the various entertainments offered by the city.

Primary educational and religious responsibilities likewise drifted away from the family in the new America. To the degree that earlier Americans had faith in the value of education and religious belief, the family had always been regarded as the institution where these values were first preached, practiced, and maintained: teaching their letters to the young, reading aloud from books, the evening Bible session. In the city the public and private schools increasingly assumed total responsibility for education, including the task of training the young for a useful economic life. Religion increasingly became associated with Sunday and the church, and less and less an integral and natural part of family life itself. In the new America, too, the family as the basic unit of protection disappeared. The rifle over the fireplace to be taken down when danger threatened had no place in urban America, where organized police departments assumed the function of protection. A family unit integrated socially, culturally, and economically had in the past so many interests in common that its political views were one, despite the fact that only the husband had the right to vote. But now the man of the house no longer spoke for all when he cast his ballot.

The Role and Status of Women   This fragmentation of the family had a marked effect on women. The new America offered opportunities for women to move outside the home and participate in the larger active world of society. Especially was this true about jobs. In 1870, 14.8 percent of women over sixteen years of age were employed; by 1910 the percentage was 24.3. Between 1890 and 1905 20 percent of all workers employed in manufacturing were women, and by 1910 there were over 7.5 million in the labor force. They worked in factories and mills, as domestic servants, as clerks and office help, as telephone and telegraph operators, in nursing, and teaching. They did not get the best jobs, nor were they paid as well as men. There were few women in the professions, though the first breakthroughs had been made. By 1900 there were only a few women doctors and lawyers, and their practices were severely limited in scope. But the admission of women to colleges after the Civil War, and the establishment of women's colleges such as

Women's suffrage demonstration in 1917. The increased involvement of women in projects of social reform as well as the added numbers obtaining college degrees swelled the ranks of the suffragists. In the late nineteenth and early twentieth centuries the movement gained a respectability it had not known in its earlier years and established sufficient support in Congress to obtain passage of the Nineteenth Amendment.

Vassar, Wellesley, Smith, and Bryn Mawr by male philanthropists, did create and encourage the slow trend toward the entrance of women into the professions.

Participation in the labor force despite the lowly status of the jobs open to them gave women a degree of financial and social independence from fathers and husbands that few had before. As one mill girl commented: "I like to be independent and spend my money as I please." Not only young single girls escaping parental domination took to the labor market, but also married women. This trend was stimulated by the appearance near the end of the nineteenth century of the day nursery, which enabled many women with preschool children to move outside the home and be exploited by men other than their husbands. In 1890 some 13.9 percent of working women were married, and the figure rose slowly but steadily from then on.

Many middle- and upper-class women now became involved in a variety of activities outside the home. Taking advantage of an old American habit—

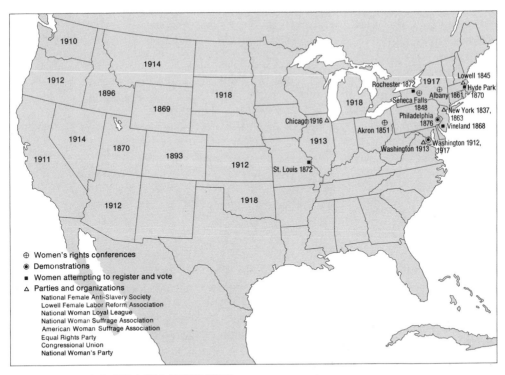

THE WOMEN'S SUFFRAGE MOVEMENT

the urge to organize—they plunged into activities traditionally not part of the role of wife or mother. The number and variety of such organizations reflected the explosive energy of the female sex. Women formed patriotic societies such as the Daughters of the American Revolution, the Colonial Dames, and the United Daughters of the Confederacy. They formed professional and educational organizations such as the American Association of University Women. They challenged male fraternal orders with their own, such as the Order of the Eastern Star. They founded the National Consumer's League, the Junior League, and the National Women's Trade Union League. They established literary, artistic, and scientific clubs, and these banded together in 1889 as the General Federation of Women's Clubs, which in 1904 broadened its interests to include such social concerns as public education, child labor reform, sex education, and other matters. By 1914 the General Federation had over one million members. Under the leadership of Frances Willard, the Women's Christian Temperance Union took after the evil of drink, but it also supported such diverse reforms as labor legislation protecting female workers, the kindergarten movement, and international peace through arbitration. Women also organized to secure legal and political rights. By the time of World War I a majority of the states had granted women the right to own and control their own property, allowed wives to retain their own earnings, permitted wives to sue and make contracts, and removed restrictions on remarriage after divorce. Moreover, between 1869 and 1900 four Western states granted women the right to vote, and by 1914 seven more states had done so. And throughout the country many localities had also granted political rights to women including the franchise. Success on the national level came in 1920 after World War I, although Jeanette Rankin of Montana took her seat in the House of Representatives in 1917 before the passage of the Nineteenth Amendment, which finally granted women the vote.

Some held that all this energy directed outside the home further weakened the family. But given the social, economic, and physical circumstances of the urban family in the new America, the broadening role of women unquestionably introduced a new element of strength into the American family since it gave to wife and mother powerful ties and associations with the larger aspects of society beyond the family which heretofore had been available only to husband and father. Partners in marriage now had more in common in these ties and associations than they had possessed before.

The growing independence of women was accompanied by a rise in the divorce rate, from 27 to 86 per 100,000 population in the years from 1867 to 1906, from fewer than 10,000 actual divorces per year to more than 72,000. This was both a percentage and a number far greater than in any other country, in fact larger than in the rest of the Western world combined. Most divorces took place in cities, and most were sought by and granted to women. Divorce laws were liberalized in a number of states, and by 1916 one out of every nine marriages ended in divorce.

Also related to the movement for women's independence, and a product of urban-industrial growth, was the decline in the size of the family. Before the Civil War the number of births per thousand people had been in the forties. After the war it dropped to the thirties, and after 1900 down into the twenties. Statistical studies have shown that this drop took place in every kind of urban family: white, black, immigrant, and native. Yet the open challenge to the large family was raised largely by educated women of the middle and upper classes. The situation may not have been as extreme as that implied by a woman physician who noted in 1904 that "Among my patients I find that the majority do not want any children; certainly not more than one." That sounds like the Zero Population Growth movement of the 1970s. Nevertheless, the existence of such an attitude at the beginning of the century signified a departure from the past. And it disturbed many Americans, including President Theodore Roosevelt, who was moved to denounce publicly those who did not marry or want children.

New attitudes also appeared toward birth control, a subject long taboo. Earlier efforts to publicize birth-control methods had been smothered by religious opposition and antibirth-control legislation, but the movement was revived by Margaret Sanger, who organized the National Birth Control League in 1914. The League quickly acquired branches in various states, and despite opposition and even jail sentences for those distributing birth-control literature, its influence steadily grew.

Changing Attitudes Toward Sex Opposition to birth-control propaganda was, of course, part of the larger hostile attitude toward any public discussion of sex. But late in the nineteenth century a determined effort began to bring sex into the arena of public discussion. Three forces nourished this effort: the determination to improve the moral environment by eliminating or reducing prostitution, the rising alarm in the medical profession about the incidence of venereal disease, and the growing recognition that women had sexual desires and powers just as men did—that a women could "electrify" both herself and her male partner. Although the motives behind these forces may have differed, they fed into a broad movement that revised traditional attitudes toward sex and sexual behavior. Prostitution had rested upon the assumption that men needed sex or their health would suffer, but that good women had no such feelings. The doctors who founded the social hygiene movement pointed to the horrors of syphilis and gonorrhea which could be, and often were, visited upon innocent wives infected by their husbands. This approach blended with the gradual recognition that women too possessed strong sexual passions, and that sexual fulfillment could be found in marriage.

These forces combined to decrease prostitution, to extend the role of physicians in treating venereal diseases, to promote a powerful movement for sex education, to weaken the double standard of morality, and to give greater recognition to the role of women in the sex act. Many conservative people saw all this as the last stage on the road to hell. And it is true that sensationalists and those who saw themselves as the advance guard of a new freedom often took advantage of these developments to justify open discussion of any aspect of sex. But it is also clear that by 1900 or so a healthy change had set in. The human body, as Walter Lippmann noted in 1914, was no longer regarded "as a filthy thing"; it was now possible to tackle by modern educational and scientific methods diseases that before had gone unchecked and untreated simply because it had been looked upon as socially repulsive even to mention their existence. And a new and more appreciative attitude toward women as equals had made its appearance.

The American Home As is true for people who live in cities everywhere, the vast numbers of Americans who moved into the cities experienced a radical change in living. Where space is at a premium, few can afford it. In 1904, for example, only forty private homes were constructed in New York City. Multifamily dwellings thus became the standard—apartment or tenement. The change was drastic. No yards, no grounds, no trees, lawns, or gardens. No integration between home and nature, land and people. No views of fields and woods from the window, no sunsets or sunrises seen on the horizon of your own land. No trees to climb for the young or barns to venture into, no attics to explore. No flowers or food from your own garden.

Smaller living quarters not only affect the birth rate. The loss of contact with nature and the difficulty of private relaxation create new tensions and contribute to the tendency to seek escape in the commercial diversions of the city and to form new ties outside the home. Thus institutions as diverse as the theater, the saloon, the labor union, the youthful street gang, and the women's club become safety-valves for the urban family.

Family life also reflected the new urban-industrial America in other ways. More and more family chores became simplified or commercialized. Most clothing was ready-made. If not, the task was made easier by the home sewing machine. Bread, cereals, canned fruits, and vegetables were prepared commercially. Clothing could be sent out to commercial laundries. Iceboxes serviced by commercial companies eased the problem of storing and preserving foods. The city offered a greater choice in foods, herbs, and spices, thus broadening taste and enjoyment.

Children and the Young   Just as the new America of factory and city drew women outside the home, so it also drew children, with some unfortunate results. By 1900 almost two million children between the ages of ten and fifteen were employed. They worked in factories, mills, and mines, they labored at home on piece-work with the rest of the family; they were out on the streets as newsboys, bootblacks, peddlers, delivery and messenger boys. Such labor was a far and painful cry from doing chores on the farm or being an apprentice in a craftsman's shop. Young workers were often harmed in health and well-being, and long years at labor deprived many of any opportunity for social, cultural, and mental development. Life as a child laborer frequently became a tattered passport to a similarly deprived life as an adult.

Before 1900 little serious attention was paid to the problem of child labor. There were laws, but most were unenforceable or were ignored. Between 1902 and 1909, however, forty-three states passed tough child labor laws or amendments to existing ones which abolished night work, established an eight-hour day for those below a minimum age, and removed many children from the labor market by compulsory school-attendance laws. Beginning with Delaware in 1909, states also began to pass general laws forbidding the employment of children under fourteen.

Living in fragmented families in slum conditions, many of the young were forced outside the home for satisfactions no longer available within it. Juvenile delinquency became a serious problem. Gangs formed in which boys found the discipline, authority, group identity, and purpose lacking in their families. Crime led to a more intensive and earlier interest in the young than did the exploitation of their labor. Crime, after all, takes from the pocket of the ordinary citizen, while labor, even that of children, tends to fill it. At any rate, new views toward the reformation of the young offender came into being, based upon the assumption that the young should not be treated as criminals, but as wards of the state which should try to provide the care, custody, and discipline parents failed to provide. The work then being done in mental hygiene and psychology resulted in the juvenile court (where not the crime but the conditions producing it were the issue), the appearance of the child guidance clinic and the foster home, and the movement in many states to grant pensions to mothers and widows with dependent children.

Child laborers on the midnight shift at the Indiana Glassworks. The National Child Labor Committee attempted to enlighten the nation with photos like this one as to the horrors of conditions for children at work, whose accident rate was three times that of adults.

Interest in bringing the juvenile offender back into society was only part of a larger interest in children in the fifty years after the Civil War. Child-raising became a matter of much study by experts, including those in the new field of psychology, and their advice and opinions were disseminated by popular writers. Although working-class families lacked the time and means to explore the question of how children should be raised, this was not true of middle- and upper-class parents, especially mothers. Child-study clubs sprang up in many cities before the end of the nineteenth century, such as the Child Study Association and the National Congress of Mothers founded in 1897, and many new journals appeared which focused on child study, among them *The Child Study Monthly.*

By 1900 the idea of infant depravity had virtually disappeared from theological debates and the minds of parents. It was now assumed that children could be brought up as decent human beings by proper training. "Children," declared one writer, "can be trained in almost any direction." It was also assumed that character could be built into children, and society thus greatly improved over the long run. All this placed a major responsibility on parents. Parenthood was no longer a natural matter of instinct and Biblical guidance, and a new emphasis was placed on seeking the advice of experts and even training in the art of being a parent. This task was made more difficult by the rising view that children should not be deprived of the pleasures of being children and should be considered as individuals in their own right. This made the exercise of parental authority delicate indeed.

Many Americans still believed that children should be trained in the fear of God's punishment, and the new ideas were criticized by those who feared that the shrinking influence of religion in the home would diminish the authority of the parent as God's special agent in the family.

Yet the very circumstances of the urban family forced the development of new ways of enriching and filling the lives of the young. For example, recreation became more organized. Before 1885 there were no city playgrounds. In Boston in that year, social workers and others introduced the notion of supervised play for city children by sponsoring sand gardens as free playgrounds. The movement for organized activities and parks for the young evolved rapidly, led after 1905 by the Playground and Recreational Association of America. After 1900 the Boy Scouts, Girl Scouts, and Campfire Girls were established to acquaint the young with a nature to which they had no access in the city, and to build their character through programs of citizenship and self-reliance.

Children's books, too, reflected the new attitudes. Preaching books and tracts virtually disappeared, and children could now read fantasies and adventure stories. *Treasure Island* by Robert Louis Stevenson, Howard Pyle's editions of the stories of Robin Hood and King Arthur, L. Frank Baum's tales of the wonderful land of Oz, Beatrix Potter's stories of Peter Rabbit and other little animals, Palmer Cox's stories of *The Brownies*—these and many other books had one thing in common. In them individuals were placed in varied circumstances in which they had, so to speak, to make their own way to find their true selves, test their characters, explore what the world had to offer.

Education and Learning

Public Education Education also changed radically in the decades after the Civil War, notably through expansion and broadening of the curriculum. The old conviction that a democratic republic required an educated citizenry continued. The rising tide of immigration also generated the feeling that those from abroad were an easy prey to political manipulation, and part of the drive for more education sprang from the desire to "Americanize" the immigrants and especially their children.

At the same time industry and technology demanded educated workers and specialists. Blueprints had to be read, accounts kept, letters written, instructions followed, reports rendered. Business recognized the need for

Percent of population 17 years old

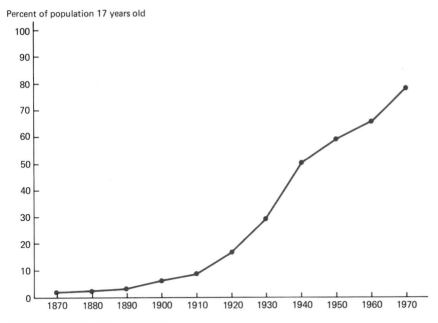

HIGH SCHOOL GRADUATES

trained executives and a host of specialists such as lawyers, engineers, geologists, chemists, and the like. Commercialized agriculture required farmers educated to take advantage of developments in scientific farming and farm management.

The net result was a broad expansion in public education. Total expenditures rose from $63 million in 1870 to $426 million in 1910. The number of public high schools rose from around three hundred in 1860 to over six thousand by 1900, and eight thousand by 1914. The total number of high-school pupils per thousand of the population increased from less than five in 1898 to more than seventeen by 1914. The illiteracy rate steadily dropped during these decades, from about twenty percent in 1870 to half that by 1900, though both black and immigrant illiteracy, especially the former, remained high.

The system also changed in curriculum and approach. On both elementary and secondary levels the curriculum was broadened. Between 1860 and 1890, literature, geography, history, civics, and nature study entered the elementary school, and domestic science, drawing, and manual training followed after 1890. The high school curriculum also reflected the belief that secondary education should prepare students not just for college, but for the jobs needed in an industrial society. Consequently courses in bookkeeping, typing, shorthand, woodworking, metalworking, printing, mechanical drawing, agriculture, and domestic science opened a whole new area of educational opportunity.

There were also changes in approach and point of view. By 1914 the ideas of John Dewey had become highly influential. Dewey was critical of traditional education as authoritarian, boring, and useless in its emphasis on rote learning, and unrealistic in its separation of intellectual life from the more practical and vocational. Dewey saw the public school as the chief agency for reforming society. The school should form a total experience within which the child learns how to solve problems not only as an individual but also a member of a group. Dewey argued for the adoption of teaching and learning methods that would promote the flowering of both the individual and the group. If the young grew through such learning, both society and the individual would profit.

Yet in spite of the advances made, elementary and secondary public education still faced serious problems. Although teacher-training institutions expanded in number and state requirements certifying teachers were raised, many teachers were still often poorly prepared. There were not always adequate funds for facilities, equipment, and books. The achievements were greater and the gaps between intent and reality narrower in the cities, but even so the average schooling in 1914 was only a little above six years. For more than ninety percent of America's young, elementary school was their only formal contact with education. Only eleven percent of young people between fourteen and seventeen were in high school in 1900, and there were fewer than ninety-five thousand high school graduates in the entire country. Sixty years later there were almost two million high school graduates, and ninety percent of this age group was in school. If the goal in 1900 was education for all, its attainment was still some way ahead.

Colleges and Universities

Similar expansion and change occurred in higher education. In 1869 the situation in America's colleges and universities was probably worse than it had been before the Civil War. Most were small and were dominated by the churches that had founded them. Teaching was almost entirely by recitation, a stifling method at any level and especially in college. The curriculum was rigid and limited; discipline problems were widespread, indeed probably the major concern of professors. And most institutions had little contact with the larger intellectual and social life of the nation. Little wonder that fewer students in proportion to the population went to college in 1869 than had in 1826. But in the next half-century a major revolution occurred in higher education.

Both public and private colleges expanded. The state-supported university came into its own by the end of the nineteenth century. New private institutions were founded by American millionaires. Rockefeller gave $30 million for the University of Chicago, and in California the railroad tycoon Leland Stanford founded Stanford University with a gift of some $20 million. Between 1878 and 1898, the urge to see their names associated with the learning few of them possessed prompted millionaire philanthropists to donate

Number of degrees

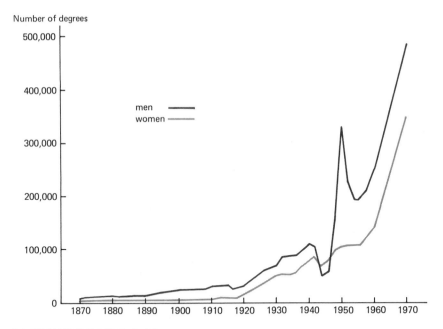

BACHELOR'S DEGREES CONFERRED

more than $140 million to higher education. More and more students went to college. Between 1870 and 1910, while the population of the country doubled, the number of students in college increased five times. This increase extended to graduate study as well. There were a mere 191 graduate students in 1871, but 9,370 in 1910. Increasing sums were spent on libraries, laboratories, and research equipment; professional societies were organized in all fields of learning, such as the American Historical Association, which was only one of some 120 such societies by 1900. And there was a steady increase in the number of professional journals.

One significant change was the disappearance of sectarian control of private institutions. Businessmen replaced ministers on boards of trustees, scholars replaced clergymen as presidents, and the faculty was judged by its academic qualifications, not its religious faith. In both public and private institutions there was a growing commitment to the expansion of knowledge. This commitment was greatly influenced by the experience of the German universities in which thousands of Americans had been trained by 1900, and it led not only to an emphasis on a faculty continually engaged in research, but to the steady development of graduate and professional schools.

Paralleling these changes were important reforms in method and curriculum. The recitation method was replaced by the lecture, the discussion section, the demonstration, the seminar, and work in the laboratory and the field. Subjects long neglected now began to dominate the curriculum: the natural and physical sciences, the social sciences, modern languages, and literature. The newly introduced elective system gave students greater choice on their own and provided a challenge to professors no longer guaranteed a captive audience. Requirements were raised for professional studies, particularly law and medicine where training had been unbelievably lax. President Eliot of Harvard had noted that "the ignorance and general incompetence of the average graduate of American Medical Schools . . . is something horrible to contemplate." And Harvard led the way in requiring a B.A. for admission to the schools of law and medicine, a three-year course of study that included written examinations, the case-study method in law, and laboratory work in medicine.

The net result was the full involvement of the colleges and universities in the life of the nation. Out of them came scholarly work and ideas that profoundly influenced American society and thought.

In philosophy, for example, the work of Josiah Royce, Charles Pierce, William James, and John Dewey, especially the latter two, gave rise to America's unique contribution, the school of pragmatism. Both James and Dewey emphasized that ideas must be related to experience to be of value. James conceived this largely in terms of the individual, Dewey in terms of society. Both provided a new point of view: that the mind, human intelligence, was an instrument to control and direct humanity's environment, that the only test of the "truth" or validity of an idea was its effectiveness in promoting individual or social well-being, its capacity to help individuals solve their problems.

Such an approach gave encouragement to those unwilling to accept as "natural" and "right" the social and economic conditions they saw about them, and who therefore turned to studying those conditions with the intent of changing and improving them. Such scholars rejected the arguments defending the existing social and economic system as the natural order of things, and prominent scholars such as John R. Commons, Richard T. Ely, Walter Weyl, Edward A. Ross, Charles A. Beard, and others engaged in investigation of working-class conditions, the nature of politics and government, the operations of the business world, the role of government regulation, the conservation of natural resources, the causes of social discontent, the effects of immigration, and other aspects of American life.

This close alliance between universities and the world of affairs can be illustrated by the experience of the University of Wisconsin in developing what became known as the Wisconsin Idea. The Wisconsin Idea rested on the assumption that higher learning was a crucial function of society, that all citizens should benefit from it, that research should be used in the interests of the people, that the higher learning should be related to the professional and practical needs of the state and its people, and that the University should be used to enrich the lives of the citizens of the state. The faculty at Wisconsin became famous for its researches into the problems of the new America, its willingness to carry its learning directly to the people of the state, and its close ties with the state under the leadership of Progressive Governor Robert LaFollette, who put faculty experts on various state commissions and consulted with them on economic, social, and political matters.

In other ways as well, higher education became an intimate part of the life of the nation, especially in response to scientific and vocational demands. Scientific and technical schools increasingly became an integral part of higher education. The University of Wisconsin created its agricultural college in 1868, and established civil and mechanical engineering schools in 1870 and 1877. Harvard established a Graduate School of Business Administration in 1908, and Columbia a School of Journalism in 1912.

Such development in turn produced a change in attitude toward the value of a college degree in the world of business. The new industrial society needed trained people, and company after company began to lay down regulations requiring a college degree for executive promotions. The noted corporation lawyer, James B. Dill, declared that "the demand today is for trained minds, devoted to specific lines of work."

Yet the course of higher education was not smooth. Faculty salaries were not impressive. The average in a hundred institutions in 1893 was $1470, comparable to the wages of a skilled worker. The teaching schedule often overburdened the faculty and left them little time and energy for research. President A. Lawrence Lowell of Harvard in 1903 criticized the trend toward specialization, arguing that if carried too far it could end in the isolation of learning from society and thought. Furthermore, much scholarship in America merely imitated Europe scholarship. Original thought, such as Frederick Jackson Turner's thesis on the significance of the frontier in America, or Thorstein Veblen's *Theory of the Leisure Class,* was the exception, not the rule. Too many professors, like William Graham Sumner, accepted the dominant ideas of European economists and sociologists and echoed them, however eloquently, in support of the status quo. The rising influence of businessmen also often restricted the work of liberal professors—the sociologist E. A. Ross, for instance, was removed from Stanford by trustees who found his views incompatible with theirs.

For students too all change was not necessarily healthy progress. Specialization and the elective system often meant a proliferation of courses, some of which had no real value, no solid base of recognized courses upon which specialization could rest, and often a degree which did not add up to either a liberal or a specialized education. Moreover, the growth of colleges brought commercialized athletics, which weakened the argument that colleges and universities were the center of the nation's intellectual life. Football became a business. By 1899 when Yale had won 46 straight games, scoring 2,018 points to her opponents' total of 29, it had become clear that something was rotten in the stadium. Eligibility rules meant nothing: a University of Wisconsin player who graduated in 1892 was still playing on the team in 1900, when he was a member of the faculty. The game had become so rough, in response to the apparent blood-lust of great crowds, that in 1903 forty-four players were killed and uncounted others were seriously injured. In 1905 the President of the United States was forced to intervene in an attempt to clean up the game. Students, on the assumption that all brain work and no riots make for a dull life, frequently poured out on the streets to the distress of the local populace. Wisconsin students would hit the pavement at the cry

William Jennings Bryan speaking at Chautauqua, New York. Founded in 1884 as a summer school for Sunday school teachers, the Chautauqua movement developed rapidly into a broad program of adult education. Eventually the name was applied to lecture and concert series that moved from town to town and that enjoyed immense popularity until replaced by the radio.

of "Varsity Out," and once kept the Madison police station under siege until the President of the University showed up late at night in his pajamas and persuaded the students to call it a day.

But in spite of all the difficulties, handicaps, and problems, by the eve of World War I education and learning had progressed far beyond what anyone in 1865 would have thought possible, and the groundwork had been laid for the future achievement of the United States as the great exponent of mass education and one of the world's great centers of learning and scholarship.

Formal achievements in education and learning suggest that all this took place in schools, and that the masses of the people were quite divorced from learning. But America had always had a commitment to narrowing the gap between the life of the intellectual and the life of the people. The move to extend education through public elementary and secondary schools, and the opening of college opportunities to those with talent, were both a part of this commitment. But much took place beyond those doors.

The development of the university extension system—which saw the faculty at Wisconsin in the single period 1912–1914 give 1250 lectures in 525 Wisconsin communities to an audience of over 370,000 people—opened up new areas for enriching the minds of ordinary people. The development of the public lecture circuit known as the Chautauqua promoted this same goal. Although many Chautauqua performers were more entertainers than educators, many distinguished scholars and writers made contributions to popular enlightenment.

The growth of private correspondence schools, offering courses on the arts, business, technical, and vocational subjects, fed the appetite of Americans for knowledge. At least three hundred were in existence by 1918 and though some were frauds, most were genuine. The appearance of books for as little as ten cents a copy, such as the Standard Library, the Munro Library, the Leisure Hour Series, and many others, made available books that ordinary people would not otherwise have known of. The same held true for the book business of the mail-order houses, such as Sears Roebuck, which sent to villages and farmhouses books by the millions, even though their offerings tended to be limited. The expansion of the public library movement, aided enormously by the generosity of Andrew Carnegie, and the rise of the mass-circulation newspapers and magazines, also helped to extend the knowledge of the common citizen. Little wonder that James Bryce, an English scholar familiar with the United States, wrote that in America "The average of knowledge is higher, the habit of reading and thinking more generally diffused, than in any other country."

Science

Practical Applications In applied science—in putting knowledge to practical use—the Americans were preeminent. Science had value that could easily be seen in the inventions and technological developments that underwrote the success story of American industrial growth and national wealth. So Americans understood and supported research geared to produce practical, measurable results. The greatly expanded work of the United States Coastal Survey, the Smithsonian Institution, and the Naval Observatory, for example, built upon accepted tradition. The development of research and agricultural experiment stations under the United States Department of Agriculture, created in 1862, also seemed sensible and reasonable. The work in 1893 of Theobald Smith of the Department's Bureau of Animal Industry on the cause and prevention of Texas fever, which was killing thousands of cattle, proved the worth of practical research in an area that directly affected the lives and fortunes of many Americans.

Moreover, the rise of scientific and technical schools and institutes after the Civil War could be easily justified to the ordinary citizen as well as to the business world which reaped the benefits of their studies and the talents of their graduates. Before the end of the nineteenth century the Massachusetts Institute of Technology, Worcester Polytechnic Institute, Stevens Institute of

Technology, the Case School of Applied Science, and others had appeared, while major institutions such as Princeton, Dartmouth, and Rutgers had founded scientific schools, and other universities had greatly expanded their existing scientific schools and departments. The recognized value of practical research was also reflected in the rise of industrial laboratories in the great corporations.

One reason why medical research was well supported was its obviously practical benefits. The work of Dr. Walter Reed in discovering how yellow fever was transmitted by a certain species of mosquito, as well as the work of Major William Crawford Gorgas of the Army Medical Corps in controlling yellow fever and malaria among workers in the building of the Panama Canal, illustrate the point. So does the national campaign against tuberculosis, launched in 1904, which cut the death rate almost in half from 1900 to 1920.

But in all these cases, and others, the basic research from which these practical developments came, such as the development of the germ theory of disease, had taken place in Europe, and the Americans were simply applying original work done elsewhere. In fact, Americans had played no role at all in the most important scientific discoveries of the nineteenth century. The theory of evolution, the atomic structure of matter, the principles of electromagnetic induction and electrolytic action, the discovery of microorganisms, the concept of conservation of energy—none of these was the work of Americans.

Pure Science   Pure science, original research, was far down on the priority list in America, not only in appreciation of its value but in willingness to support it. There simply did not exist in America a genuine scientific tradition. It would be difficult to maintain that there was when the membership of the American Association for the Advancement of Science in 1900 was less than two thousand and included not only professionals but teachers, clergymen, doctors, and others simply interested in science. The American astronomer, Simon Newcomb, stated the problem clearly:

> The various deficiences in the incentives to scientific research which we have described may be summed up in the single proposition that the American public has no adequate appreciation of the superiority of original research to simple knowledge. It is too prone to look upon great intellectual efforts as mere tours de force, worthy of more admiration than the feats of the gymnast, but not half so amusing and no more in need of public support.

This is not to suggest that no original work took place in America during these decades—quite the contrary—but such work was the labor of a handful of dedicated individuals whose endeavors went unappreciated by the public, often misunderstood by their colleagues, and in sum could not be compared to the achievements of European scientists.

But those Americans who did engage in original scientific study made major contributions. One example was Josiah Willard Gibbs, professor of mathematical physics at Yale for over thirty years until his death in 1903. Few men had Gibbs's command of the abstract language of mathematics; his editors confessed they did not know what he was talking about, and he was therefore virtually unknown in the United States though recognized in Europe as a genius. It was Gibbs who laid the foundations for physical chemistry. Although at the time his work seemed to have no practical value, it later proved to have extensive applications in metallurgy, mineralogy, petrology, and theoretical chemistry, and provided the basis for the manufacture of hundreds of plastics, drugs, dyes, and organic solvents.

Original work was also done by the physicist Henry Rowland, who revolutionized spectrum analysis, the study of the elements, by comparing their different wavelengths of emitted light. This led in 1888 to his famous "Photographic Map of the Normal Solar Spectrum." Equally if not more impressive were the achievements of Albert Michelson in measuring the speed of light. Seemingly as distant from the practical as an invisible star, Michelson's work was used by Einstein and contributed to the development of the nuclear physics of modern times.

Literally more down to earth were the experiments of the biologist Jacques Loeb, who studied the reactions of living matter to physical and chemical stimuli. And the biologist Thomas Hunt Morgan made fundamental discoveries about heredity in his study of the common fruit fly, demonstrating that physical characteristics are transmitted from one generation to the next by genes. He thus laid the foundations of the new field of genetics. No ordinary American in his right mind would have contributed ten cents to a study of the fruit fly, but the uncovering of the laws of inheritance ultimately led to the improved breeding of livestock and plants.

The Influence of Evolution   The impact of these and other isolated accomplishments was little felt by the general public at the time. But certain scientific developments occurring abroad in the nineteenth century had a profound felt impact on American society and thought in a variety of ways. Chief of these was the work of Charles Darwin on the evolution of species, set forth in his books *Origin of Species* (1859) and *The Descent of Man* (1871). In science, of course, the impact of evolutionary thought was immense. The work of many American scientists in botany, zoology, geology, biology, and paleontology was geared to testing the theory of natural selection, and Morgan's work on fruit flies contributed to a major modification of the theory by proving the role of mutations in the modification of species. Othniel Marsh's expeditions uncovering ancient fossils in the American West provided clear evidence of evolutionary change.

But Darwin's theory of evolution had a deep and lasting effect outside science. It lay behind the new ideas on the function of the mind that formed the basis of pragmatism in philosophy. It helped change traditional views about children and shaped the science of psychology. It enormously influenced the new view in legal thinking that the law is not based on immutable principles but arises out of experience and in response to changing conditions in society. It shaped the thinking of historian Frederick Jackson Turner who saw society in America evolving from the simple to the complex under the impact of the frontier experience. Through the popularization of Darwin's ideas by his fellow countryman, Herbert Spencer—which was carried on by Americans such as William Graham Sumner—the idea of natural selection was used to justify the existing economic and social order of capitalist America. It was argued that the great captains of industry got where they were by a process of natural selection, "the survival of the fittest," in Spencer's classic phrase. Ironically, Darwinian thought also influenced those reformers and social critics of the existing order who turned the theory of evolution to their advantage by arguing that the reforms they proposed were a more advanced stage in the social evolutionary progress of humanity.

The power of science is no more clearly seen than in its impact on life beyond the arena of science. Just as the Newtonian science of the eighteenth century enormously influenced the social, economic, cultural, and political ideas of that time, so Darwin's thought had the same extended influence in the nineteenth- and twentieth-century world. It challenged many existing ideas and assumptions, and it disturbed the dull and the unimaginative who are always fearful of change. Its impact was invigorating. It opened new doors of understanding, new approaches to life itself, new avenues of exploration. In fact, successful criticism of many aspects of the Darwinian view and its application promoted further creative thought which helped to enlarge the horizons of knowledge.

Religion

Religion and Evolution   But in one area of life evolutionary thought appeared to be devastating, since it seemed to deny the ultimate meaning of life itself. This area was religion. Evolutionary thinking, whether defined by Darwin in terms of the natural world of living things or by the geologist Sir Charles Lyell in his theories on the evolution of the earth itself over immense periods of time, raised a direct challenge to the Christian concept of a universe brought into being in one act of creation by a God who had determined the final nature and character of all living things at the moment He created them.

Scientists of religious conviction as well as theologians at first found it impossible to reconcile evolution and religion. President Barnard of Columbia College, himself a distinguished scientist, declared in 1873 that the existence of God and the immortality of the soul were incompatible with organic evolution. The theologian Charles Hodge maintained in 1874 in answer to the question *What Is Darwinism?* that "a more absolutely incredible theory was never propounded for acceptance among men." Yet gradually many liberal theologians as well as scientists loyal to religion came to see Darwinism and Christianity as completely compatible. The distinguished Harvard botanist, Asa Gray, defended Darwin vigorously, finding this position not at all challenging to his deep religious convictions. Popular minister Henry

Dwight Moody at the pulpit. An extremely successful shoe salesman with a deep interest in religion and social welfare, Moody began his evangelical career by inviting itinerant men he met on streetcorners and in boardinghouses to share his pews at church. He eventually abandoned his business to become a city missionary. He was never ordained and had little formal education, but his preaching of God's fatherly love captured the minds of businessmen and college students as well as the poor and uneducated.

Ward Beecher, a convert to evolution, argued that evolution was "the deciphering of God's thought as revealed in the structure of the world." The Harvard philosophy professor, John Fiske, in a series of popular books did more than anyone to reconcile religion and evolution, arguing that evolution was simply "God's way of doing things."

Science also shook religious convictions when modern scholarship was applied to studies of the Bible by philologists, anthropologists, and students of comparative religion. Most of this work was done abroad, but it was translated and publicized by American scholars. These studies showed that the Bible had been put together over a long period from a variety of writings. It contained confusions and errors that raised questions about its divine origin. Other studies showed that features thought to be unique to Christianity were found in other religions as well. A number of clergymen faced heresy charges at the turn of the century for accepting these new views of the Bible, but the concept that the Bible was less revealed truth and more a literature of ethical guidance and wisdom gradually spread through the seminaries and among the educated public.

The Church   None of these developments seriously affected the church as an institution, and in fact it grew in numbers and wealth after the Civil War. The major Protestant denominations by 1916 more than held their own: the Methodists and Baptists and their affiliates had a membership of some seven million each, the Presbyterians holding at over two million, the Lutherans about a million and a half, and the Disciples of Christ, Episcopalians, and Congregationalists following after.

Immigration, as in the past, influenced the church greatly, helping the continued expansion of the Roman Cathlic Church in America. From some three million members in 1860, the Catholic Church expanded to over sixteen million in 1910 through the heavy migration from southern Europe. Although anti-Catholic sentiment persisted, its effects were tempered by the great skill of the American Cardinal Gibbons in making the Church an accepted American institution. He supported the American doctrine of the separation of church and state, defended democracy, proclaimed the church to be the friend of the worker, and successfully opposed the desire of immigrants to have priests of their own national origin and their own schools.

Jewish congregations also multiplied as hundreds of thousands of Jews came from the Russian and Austro-Hungarian Empires from the 1880s on. The various reform, moderate, and orthodox Jewish groups that came to America also faced problems of unity and identity.

The American taste for new religious experiences continued to be satisfied with the appearance of new sects. One of the most successful of the scores that rose and then shrank or disappeared was Christian Science, founded by Mary Baker Eddy who was divinely inspired, according to her followers, to proclaim that matter has no real existence, only mind, and that therefore sin, disease, even death, were only illusions of the mind. Such illusions could be dispelled by putting the mortal mind in harmony with God, the Eternal Mind. Although bitterly denounced in established churches and the conservative press, Christian Science flourished, gaining adherents especially among the middle class where urban life produced its own special tensions seeking release.

The strength of religious yearning was also demonstrated by the still powerful force of evangelism. The most prominent of the revivalists was Dwight L. Moody, who reached great audiences by praising the fundamentals of Christian dogma, declaring that the Bible was not made to be understood but only to be accepted, and persuading thousands to return to God by his sincerity and avoidance of hysterical emotionalism if not by his learning.

Millions of Americans, of course, refused to abandon their literal faith in the Bible. They remained unaffected by the new ideas, and some even tried to legislate Christianity into the Constitution by an amendment declaring Christ to be the ruler and the Bible the law in America.

But by World War I many Americans were adjusting their views on the supernatural to accord with the world they saw unfolding about them. The extent of religious expression today testifies to the capacity of Americans to accommodate their spiritual and their secular views without denying either.

Literature and the Arts

Writers and artists were as much influenced as anyone else by the impact of industrial growth and its problems, the tense environment of the city, the conflicts of the economic order, the challenge of science to traditional values. In one way or another the new America greatly affected cultural life.

Literature   On the popular level, romantic and sentimental writing had an immense success. F. Marion Crawford took his numerous readers abroad in novels set in Italy or distant India. General Lew Wallace's tale of Christianity, *Ben Hur,* sold over two and a half million copies. Charles Major delighted the chivalrous with *When Knighthood Was in Flower.* Owen Wister idealized the West in *The Virginian,* building upon the popularity of adventure stories in the dime novels and introducing a new phrase for use by the insouciant: "When you call me that, smile!" Country and small-town life was romanticized in Edward Noyes Westcott's *David Harum,* while James Whitcomb Riley did similar honors in verse. Jack London opened up a new frontier of adventure in the frozen North. Sentimental tales of pure heroines and gallant heroes, long-suffering wives whose husbands reached for the bottle as frequently as the authors of such stories did for the inkwell, poor but honest boys who rescued the daughters of millionaires and became partners in the grateful fathers' firms—the market for such stories was bullish.

It is often said that this outpouring had little to do with the realities of American life, or indeed any life anywhere, past or present. And serious writers and critics deplored what they regarded as sentimental blather. Their observations went unheeded. And in a way these critics were wrong. For popular literature was intimately related to the new America. Life was a serious business; and when picking up a novel to read, the urge for many was overwhelming not to read about the life they had to face every day but about life in other worlds and times where virtue triumphed and things turned out well. None of it may have been "true" or "real," but it was a relief from the pressures of a reality most urban people knew only too well.

The more serious and talented took up the pen to different purpose, determined to explore the social crises of the world they lived in, to probe into the problems of human motivation in a new society, to pursue the elusive goal of the meaning of existence—to provide, in short, a "realistic" view not just of the American but of that curious animal, the human being. They had no wish to comfort readers with a false world, but to show the real one as it is.

The greatest of the realists was Mark Twain, who detested hypocrisy, sham, and injustice, and was merciless in deflating the pompous and pretentious. He could poke fun at anything with a delicious and penetrating wit. Introduced once on the lecture platform by a lawyer who rocked back and forth and talked with his hands in his pockets, Twain drawled that it was the first time he had ever been introduced by a lawyer who kept his hands in his own pockets. Twain had no use for the pious who felt superior to everyone else, and once told a story about a woman who complained at being ill in spite of her godly life. Twain told her the trouble was she had never smoked, drunk, or chased men, so she had nothing to give up in return for improved health—she was, he said, a sinking ship with no moral ballast to throw overboard. This was the Twain of the lecture platform, an immensely popular entertainer.

As a writer he was equally popular, delighting readers with novels, reminiscences, and travel sketches. Out of a tour of Europe and the Holy Land

Henry James.

came *Innocents Abroad* (1869), a classic portrayal of the American's contemptuous view of the Old World in all its decay and corruption. He provided vivid, realistic pictures of the mining West in *Roughing It* (1872), of the new capitalist-industrial America in *The Gilded Age* (1873) which he wrote with Charles Dudley Warner, of his own village boyhood in *Tom Sawyer* (1876), and of the steamboat age in *Life on the Mississippi* (1883). His masterpiece was *Huckleberry Finn* (1885), one of the great American novels.

No one could equal Twain at drawing characters to expose the weaknesses of society. Huck Finn may be an illiterate rustic boy, a pain to the genteel with his deviltry and activities frowned upon by established society. But in aiding the slave Jim from motives of natural decency, Huck revealed the hypocrisy of his "betters." And in Jim, who had the nobility of character lacking in those who would enslave him, was brilliantly exposed the shallowness of conventional values. In vividly recreating down to the last mist curling off the Mississippi a time when the American seemed truly free in the world of nature, Twain brought home, as few have ever done, the contrast between the natural world and the corruption of individuals in society, a theme that has influenced American literature before and since. At the end Huck says: "But I reckon I got to light out for the Territory ahead of the rest, because Aunt Sally she's going to adopt me and sivilize me and I can't stand it. I been there before."

Important in the development of realism was William Dean Howells, editor of the *Atlantic Monthly* and *Harper's Magazine*, the most influential literary critic of his time, and author of several widely read novels. Howells promoted the works of the great foreign writers, including Tolstoy, Ibsen, and Zola, and encouraged young writers such as Stephen Crane, Hamlin Garland, and Frank Norris. He urged that writers maintain "fidelity to experience," and although the middle-class world he realistically dealt with so often in his own fiction obviously did not encompass the whole scope of experience, yet within his range he practiced in his own novels what he preached in his criticism. In his great novel, *A Hazard of New Fortunes* (1890), he created a realistic panorama of New York life from rich to poor, indicting the course industrial development had taken.

Some of the younger writers heightened realism to what was called "naturalism," which was much influenced by Darwinian thought. Standing almost dispassionately aloof, they saw individuals so influenced by the powerful forces of heredity and environment that their destinies were beyond their control. Stephen Crane, before his premature death at twenty-nine, had written *Maggie: A Girl of the Streets,* the tale of a slum girl driven to prostitution and eventual suicide; *The Red Badge of Courage,* a study of men in battle; and a number of shorter stories, including "The Open Boat," a powerful statement of the indifference of the universe to humanity.

Frank Norris, who also died young, exposed the animal passions of man in *McTeague,* and in *The Octopus* and *The Pit* explored political and economic corruption. A more powerful writer was Theodore Dreiser, the first in this age to deal realistically with sex and to question conventional morality, as in *Sister Carrie,* who instead of ending in the streets rose to Broadway stardom over the bodies of the men who desired her. Dreiser also looked realistically at economic corruption in *The Financier* and *The Titan.* Less fatalistic but equally realistic was Hamlin Garland whose *Main-Travelled Roads* explored the grim aspects of rural life.

The greatest literary artist of the era was Henry James, who was not popular in his own day but gained a towering reputation later. A profound observer with a complex style, he wished "to leave a multitude of pictures of my time." He had a great talent for creating situations to illuminate his characters. Like Twain he was deeply interested in the fate of the individual—often a sophisticated and intelligent woman caught up in the complexities of society. Living almost entirely in Europe, James nevertheless remained in this interest essentially American. He often examined in his international novels the problem of the innocent American confronting the subtleties of European society. His early major achievements were *The American, The Bostonians,* and *The Portrait of a Lady,* while his later triumphs included *The Wings of the Dove, The Ambassadors,* and *The Golden Bowl.*

The most original poet of the later nineteenth century was Emily Dickinson, whose verse began to appear in print only in 1890, four years after her death. An almost total recluse, she flitted about her New England home "quicker than a snake's delay" (to use her own delicate phrase for a bird in her garden), and even her neighbors rarely saw her. Little aware of the outside world, her poetry revealed an inner world of her own.

At the end of this period, on the eve of the First World War, there began a poetic renaissance, and a number of new voices were heard: Carl Sandburg,

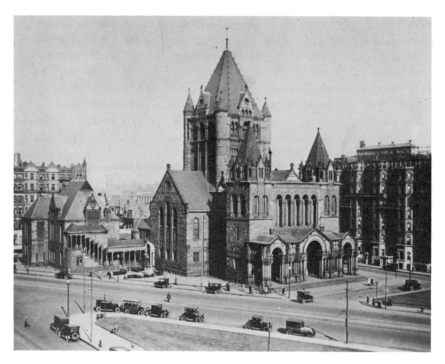

*Trinity Church in Boston. When Richardson's design for the church won
the competition in 1872 it established his reputation as the architectural
leader of the age and established America as architecturally independent in
the international community.*

Edgar Lee Masters, Robert Frost, Ezra Pound, T. S. Eliot, and others, but their
greatest impact would be felt as part of the cultural revolution after the war.

Architecture, Painting, and Sculpture In a booming America architects enjoyed a varied business in the design of office buildings, railway
stations, warehouses, churches, public buildings, and homes for the wealthy.
But their imaginative talents were considerably less than their opportunities.
The result was a hodgepodge of borrowed styles—classic, gothic, and renaissance, all with a heavy Victorian stamp. By the 1880s the Roman style had
come to dominate through the influence of Henry H. Richardson, who had
built Trinity Church in Boston in 1872. The Columbian Exposition—the great
world's fair held in Chicago in 1893—provided a golden opportunity for
original design, but except for Louis Sullivan's Transportation Building the
chance was muffed. A warmed-over classicism prevailed, imposing but
hardly related to either Chicago or America at large, and through the Exposition reached throughout the country.

But change was underway. The skyscraper, a notable American innovation, was developed in Chicago, where first William Jenney and then others
took advantage of steel-frame construction and the invention of the elevator

Long Branch, New Jersey, *a painting by Winslow Homer.*

to shoot commercial buildings up into the sky. But the great original was Louis Sullivan, who developed the concept that "form follows function" and sought to create buildings to suit their uses, succeeding notably in the Wainwright Building in St. Louis in 1890 and later in such buildings as the National Farmer's Bank in Owatonna, Minnesota. Sullivan's apprentice, Frank Lloyd Wright, was to surpass the master. Wright practiced "organic" architecture: designing buildings from the inside out, blending them into the natural landscape, and using materials that would carry out these aims. In the early 1900s Wright designed homes in suburban Chicago and a few buildings elsewhere that began an influence that was to become significant in later decades when his best work was done.

In painting the influence of Europe was strong. American painters trooped abroad and the training and experience they got there greatly improved their work. Some found the Old World the more invigorating artistic climate, among them James McNeill Whistler, John Singer Sargent, and Mary Cassatt. Others took the opposite course: Winslow Homer, Thomas Eakins, and Albert Ryder remained in America and generally stayed close to their homes in Maine, Philadelphia, and New Bedford, Massachusetts. Homer and Eakins were essentially realists. Homer, who had a mania for detail and accuracy, chose many of his subjects from the New England scene and after 1880 turned to the sea for his subject matter. Eakins had a real grasp of human anatomy, and some of his most extraordinary pictures were of surgical operations. Ryder, however, was a thorough romantic, whose brooding, mysterious paintings, such as *Death on a Pale Horse*, were admired by only a few. In the years just before the First World War a new group of young painters, known as the Ashcan School, shocked the art world with their realistic portrayals of the meaner aspects of city life—saloons, tenements, rundown markets, and pushcart peddlers.

Sculpture, too, tended to be heavily derivative, following European trends, and as a consequence was marked by much mediocrity. Most sculptors, like painters, were trained abroad. The outstanding sculptor of the period was Augustus Saint-Gaudens, who was trained in Paris and did many memorials to heroes of the Civil War. Probably his most famous work is the memorial for Mrs. Henry Adams in Rock Creek Cemetery in Washington.

There was clearly a growing appreciation of painting and sculpture in America. This could be seen in the growing number of museums, the presence of commercial art galleries in the major cities, the growth and expansion of art schools and academies, the commissions to painters and sculptors, and the number of private collections such as that of J. P. Morgan. By the 1880s and 1890s, nearly every wealthy man in Boston was able to adorn his home with paintings, statues, and other works of art brought home as mementos of at least one trip abroad. But most Americans downgraded the work of their artist countrymen. When the famous Armory Show was held in New York in 1913, it was the European importations, not the American works, that attracted attention, and outsold the American by five to one. The Cézannes and Van Goghs, the Redons and Gauguins, the Matisses and Picassos—these made the works of American artists seem tame indeed.

Music As in the other arts, interest in serious music increased until by 1900 there were symphony orchestras in the major cities, and by World War I the Metropolitan Opera in New York with Toscanini as conductor and Caruso as leading singer had become one of the chief opera companies of the world. But again the major talent was European. Musicians felt that they had to be trained abroad. America's only serious composers were Edward Mac-Dowell and Charles Ives, and nobody heard much about Ives until the 1930s.

The vigor of American music lay in other fields. John Philip Sousa made the brass band and the marching song into an expression of American pride easily appreciated by ordinary Americans, and Victor Herbert in his light-hearted operettas created a body of melodies everyone could hum with ease. The power of folk music continued—railway gang songs, cowboy songs, and songs from rural America. Rarely written down, frequently altered and changed, these gave expression to many aspects of American life.

The most original music in America came from the blacks, first ragtime and then jazz. Originating in New Orleans at the turn of the century, jazz broke away from the customary musical conventions, created new rhythm, and made improvisation into a fine art. Picked up by white musicians, jazz moved out of the South during World War I. Though it did not become a national phenomenon until decades later, it profoundly influenced music both here and abroad.

Change and America

A new America came into being between the Civil War and World War I, an America of machines and cities, science and technology. Nothing remained untouched by this transformation, which affected economic, social, and cultural institutions and altered familiar habits and values.

Although this transformation made America rich and powerful beyond any state in history, it created problems seriously threatening the democratic heritage of the nation and thrust the United States on the world stage unprepared for leadership just when Europe was about to explode after a hundred years of relative peace. In responding to these two challenges, the United States was caught up by two antagonistic forces: reform and war. When both had run their course an era had ended and a new one begun for both America and the world.

Profile: MARK TWAIN

Born as Samuel Langhorne Clemens and dying as Mark Twain, America's most celebrated humorist was fond of saying that he came into the world in 1835 with Halley's Comet and expected to go out with it when it came again in 1910. And he did—one of the few occasions when his expectations were fully realized. Clemens took his famous pen name in 1863 when he was writing for the Virginia City, Nevada, *Territorial Enterprise.* "Mark Twain" was a river term meaning two fathoms, or about twelve feet—a depth just safe enough for navigation. It was an appropriate choice, for his life was a voyage in such waters. He scraped many a sandbar, but survived for seventy-five years.

Twain's life was a long protest against the transformation of America from an easygoing, rural, frontier society to a fast-paced, urban, industrial, technological society. It probably is not fair to say that Twain never grew up while the country did—that would be uncomplimentary to him and too complimentary to the country. But it is fair to say that his heart lay in his vision of an earlier America of simple virtues, and he idealized that earlier America of his boyhood in Hannibal, Missouri and his young manhood in such books as Tom Sawyer, Life on the Mississippi, and the first part of Huckleberry Finn. But he poked fun at his own repainting of the past when he had Huck Finn say, "Mr. Mark Twain he told the truth, mainly."

What he did not like was the society that replaced the America of his boyhood. He detested the hypocrisy, greed, and cold inhumanity of capitalism and technology that he believed corroded social, cultural, economic, and political life. He was disgusted by political corruption, and delighted in references to "Congressmen and other bandits" and in writing that "whiskey was carried into committee rooms in demijohns and carried out in demagogues." And he abhorred the way Americans worshiped and pursued money, declaring that the idea was "to get it dishonestly if you can, honestly if you must." In A Connecticut Yankee in King Arthur's Court (1889), he seemed to be praising American technical ingenuity, but in the end technology and science destroyed all, Twain's prediction of the fate of mankind.

Yet paradoxically, Twain was as attracted by the shimmering lures of the new society as any other American. He was drawn to dreams of quick wealth, of becoming a millionaire. When he went West to the Nevada Territory with his brother in 1861, he was swept up in the gold and silver fever, staking and selling claims and investing in mining stock. Later, when he had plenty of money from his lectures and books, he poured tens of thousands of dollars into schemes to make more: a steam generator, a steam pulley, an engraving process, and most heavily in an unsuccessful typesetting machine that wiped him out financially. In 1884 he also established his own publishing company, convinced he could make more money than by having his books published by others.

Despite his contempt for a technological civilization, he was fascinated by machines, as his fruitless investments demonstrated. And he was far from unwilling to put technology to his own use. He bought an early Remington typewriter and became the first American author to submit a typewritten manuscript. And what he later referred to as the best years of his life—when he was a pilot on the Mississippi—were spent sailing that mechanical marvel of the time, the steamboat, up and down the great river.

Though he denounced the new capitalism, he counted millionaires among his friends, including Andrew Carnegie, William Rockefeller, and Henry Huttleston Rogers of Standard Oil who, at the time of Twain's financial troubles, took over the management of his affairs and saved him from ruin. Moreover, Twain loved to live well and spend money. He idealized the simple life of his boyhood, but he early dreamed of affluence. After his marriage in 1870, he and his wife, who had considerable money of her own, built an elaborate house in Hartford, Connecticut, where for twenty years they lived in style with their three daughters. In 1881 alone Twain spent over $100,000, which in those times was truly living in the grand manner.

Mark Twain was one of the most popular Americans of his time and the most successful author the country had ever had. He traveled widely on lecture tours, lived abroad for a number of years, and was acclaimed everywhere. His fellow citizens delighted in his ability to poke fun at others as well as at themselves. He wrote and spoke in the language of ordinary people, giving stature to the American language. His humor was contagious and his satire softened by comic exaggerations. He was an extraordinary performer on the public platform—as actor Hal Holbrook's recreation of an evening with Mark Twain has brilliantly demonstrated—and his books revitalized American literature.

But despite his popularity and success, Twain was racked by increasing inner despair. Modern society depressed him more and more with the years. And the illnesses and deaths of family members made life seem pointless. Bitterness and despair came over him, and his humor turned black as he described his contempt for "the damn'd human race." "If you pick up a starving dog and make him prosperous, he will not bite you. This is the principal difference between a dog and a man." Yet he didn't set himself above others, confessing that what one sees in the human race "is merely himself in the deep and private honesty of his own heart."

Like many Americans, Mark Twain was both the beneficiary and the victim of his society. The new America gave him fame, fortune, and opportunity, but it had destroyed the happy time of his boyhood in that "white town drowsing in the sunshine of a summer's morning" where the majestic Mississippi rolled its mile-wide tide.

Chapter 7
THE END OF AN ERA: PROTEST, REFORM, AND WAR

The Spirit of the Times
POWER AND CORRUPTION GROW

By the opening of the twentieth century industrial growth and development had created as many problems as benefits, as much misery as pleasure, as much despair as hope. True, America's total wealth made her the richest state in history. There now existed a variety and range of goods far beyond anything deemed possible before, increased productivity and mass production steadily reduced prices and thus made goods available to more and more people, and the expanding economy offered opportunity for many people to improve their lives materially and socially.

But a high price was being paid for this growth and development. Millions lived in poverty without the benefits of a full dinner pail. The health, energy, and spirit of many children were weakened by the exploitation of their labor. The rapid extension of the use of women in the labor force afforded opportunity for many to achieve a certain independence they had little possessed before, but their labor was callously exploited in menial and unimaginative tasks at wages far below those granted to men. And for all workers in the new America, the hazards of industrial labor were great. Working conditions were often unhealthy, unsanitary, and unsafe. Robert Hunter, in his study of working conditions in the early twentieth century, estimated that a million workers were killed or injured on the job every year. In 1901, 1 out of every 399 railroad employees was killed and 1 out of every 26 was injured—an appalling figure. Although a number of states had passed laws regulating such matters, few had adequate provisions for enforcement.

A political cartoon attacking John D. Rockefeller's Standard Oil Company. The company was incorporated in 1870, combining the largest oil refineries in Cleveland. Within nine years it had engulfed not only its rival refineries in Cleveland but oil production facilities in other cities as well. By 1879, through subsidiaries and associated companies, it controlled approximately 90 percent of the refining capacity of the country.

THE MONSTER MONOPOLY.

Disregard or contempt for human dignity and life—hardly a dominant American attitude in earlier times—now seemed too often to prevail among all classes. The factory owner who refused to install safety equipment, even though workers were maimed and killed, on grounds that it was "cheaper" to do without, was contemptible by any standard. Equally contemptible was the worker who sent his children into the labor market and complained on their death that he was deprived of his rightful income. Things rather than human beings sometimes seemed to have top priority in the American scheme of values.

There were other disturbing developments. By 1900 many people were concerned about the exercise of power in this country, both economic and political. Earlier, power was rather broadly dispersed in society. Now it appeared to be concentrating in the hands of a few.

By 1900 America was dominated by the corporation, especially the supercorporation. The age of the individual proprietorship was over. In 1899 corporations produced 66 percent of all manufactured goods, and ten years later 79 percent. But corporations, no matter how large, suffered disadvantages in efficiency, profits, and power in any wide-open system of competition. And they often found themselves at the mercy of other companies upon whom they depended for supplies or markets. The answer was combination, which not only brought together former competitors in the same field, such as several oil-refining companies, but the vertical integration of a whole industrial process from raw materials to finished products. Rockefeller discovered the advantages of combination when he created the Standard Oil Trust. Later the holding company achieved the same purpose. By 1904 there were 318 such giants, either trusts or holding-company operations. Of these

82 had been organized before 1898, and 234 with a capitalization of over $6 billion between 1898 and 1904. The economic power of these combinations was enormous, and they were controlled by a handful of men.

Paralleling this concentration of industrial power was a concentration of financial power. The expanding economy had generated a steady stream of savings pouring into banks and insurance companies. By 1899 America's financial institutions possessed assets of $9 billion; by 1911, over $28 billion. An expanding industrial economy needed capital, and those who controlled these assets possessed great economic power. By 1904 there were two main financial empires in existence, one dominated by the House of Morgan, and the other by the Rockefeller interests. After 1907 these two merged through interlocking directorates and exchange of stock into one informal association. A Congressional investigating committee, the Pujo Committee, revealed in 1913 that the Morgan-Rockefeller interests together held 341 directorships in 112 banks, insurance companies, railroads, industries, and public utility corporations whose resources or capitalization totaled more than $20 billion. Although this did not imply any day-to-day direction of the affairs of such concerns, it did suggest a powerful central influence and direction of policy. And it clearly implied that a handful of men possessed extraordinary power over America's economy and the lives of Americans.

The same trend toward a concentration of power had appeared in the political arena. Political machines were not unknown before, but since the Civil War the cities had seen the creation of political empires almost as powerful as those in industry and finance. Growing cities needed goods and services: transportation (elevated railways, trolley lines, streetcar systems), sewer lines, streets, lighting, water supplies, public buildings, maintenance, equipment, and a host of other facilities and services. The cities with their expanding populations, varied tastes, and anonymity, offered opportunity for vice on the grand scale: gambling, prostitution, liquor, crime. Newcomers from abroad knew little of American ways and needed help in finding relatives, getting a job, finding a place to live, and aid in time of trouble.

Shrewd political leaders used these circumstances to create powerful and wealthy organizations which came to dominate much of the political life of the nation. Politicians literally sold contracts and franchises to private businessmen to provide the goods and services the cities needed. And through control of the police and even the courts, they were able, at a price, to provide the protection vice needed to survive and flourish. By aiding the new immigrants, even to making them instant citizens, they acquired the votes to stay in power. It was all highly profitable. In city after city, political bosses such as Richard Croker of New York became millionaires, associated with reputable business leaders (William C. Whitney was a friend of Croker), and survived the sporadic attempts of reformers to break their political power. The result was that by the end of the nineteenth century much of the political power in the country was concentrated in the hands of a few powerful bosses.

Overall, the new America seemed increasingly a flawed society. What had happened, as more than one foreign visitor observed, was that the Americans apparently had been so busy trying to get ahead that they had no time left to make their society a decent and fair place for its citizens to live in. Yet this was the very goal to which Americans had traditionally been committed.

The changes wrought in life and society had produced conditions and problems that, if left unattended, would seriously threaten the democratic character of American society. Techniques, institutions, and ways of doing things that had worked in an earlier America to insure that democratic character were no longer adequate. New approaches, new attitudes, and new techniques were called for. The Americans responded to this challenge in a variety of ways.

Protest and Reform

The drive to reform urban and industrial America climaxed in the first decade and a half of the twentieth century in the Progressive movement. But Progressivism was both preceded and nourished by other efforts. Workers, who suffered materially from the unchecked growth of an industrial-capitalist system that denied them a fair share of the benefits of that growth, rose in protest and developed weapons to defend their interests. Spiritual leaders concerned about the conscience of the church, indifferent in the midst of suffering, began to take an active role in seeking answers to the problems created in the new society and sought to redirect the energies and resources of their institutions in that direction. By the opening of the twentieth century the time was right for a major effort at reform that would make sure that America's economic, social, and political institutions reflected the democratic ideas to which the nation had presumably committed itself over a century before.

The Response of the Workers: Labor Organizes For workers the answer to the problems of low wages, long hours, and poor working conditions lay in the same technique used by the great captains of industry and capital: combination. Helpless when acting as individuals—just as many a company discovered itself to be—workers increasingly perceived that their strength lay in organization.

In the half-century after the Civil War, therefore, workers increasingly turned to union organization and to their only real weapon, mass withholding of their labor by means of the strike. Thousands of strikes took place in these years, against great odds. The courts frequently refused to uphold the right to strike, to boycott, and to bargain collectively. Employers fired strikers and hired "scabs" (nonunion workers) to replace them; they blacklisted union organizers; they employed spies and private armies against unions; they organized employers' and citizens' committees to combat unionism. Governments, from cities to states to nation, were willing to use police and troops to break strikes. Newspapers were willing to denounce unionism as un-American, an alien doctrine preached by anarchists, communists, and socialists.

The Knights of Labor Unions were organized anyway, primarily among craft and skilled workers rather than among the vast numbers of the unskilled or the semiskilled. It was the cigar makers, the printers, the iron workers, the carpenters, the machinists, the railroad men who organized.

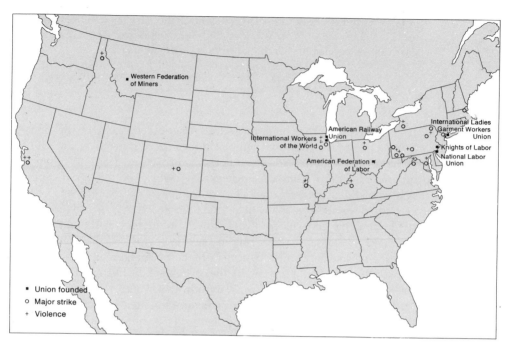

THE DEVELOPMENT OF MAJOR UNIONS

By the 1870s, some 300,000 workers belonged to national craft unions, while others had been organized into new unions embracing such trades as railroading. The only serious challenge to this type of organization came from the Knights of Labor, an organization that boomed spectacularly in the 1880s, reaching a membership of over 700,000. The Knights sought to organize by industry rather than by crafts, and welcomed blacks, women, and unskilled workers as well as skilled craftsmen. Indeed they were open, they said, to anyone who did honest labor, denying admission only to lawyers, bankers, and saloonkeepers. But ineffective leadership, confused social goals, and a series of circumstances that saw the Knights incorrectly associated with the Haymarket Riot in Chicago in 1886 destroyed them.

The AFL   The American Federation of Labor, an organization of national craft unions, appeared in 1886, and it was the AFL that set the goals and pattern of union organization in America. Starting off with a total of 150,000 members, the AFL reached 1,676,000 in 1904 and over 2,000,000 by 1914. Earlier attempts to unionize workers had been heavily influenced by social and political issues. The AFL, under Samuel Gompers, rejected this approach and concentrated on the bread-and-butter issues of the job itself: better wages, shorter hours, and improved working conditions. AFL leaders viewed union organization as a practical device for the protection of the worker's basic interests. Said Gompers: "The trade unions are the business

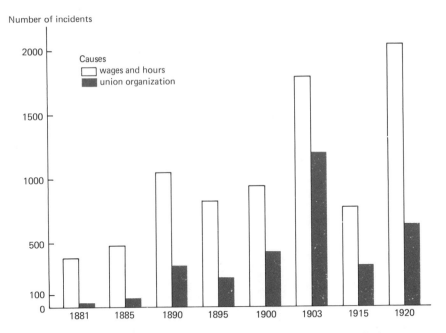

Number of incidents

Causes
☐ wages and hours
■ union organization

THE POWER OF THE UNIONS: INCIDENTS OF WORK STOPPAGES

organizations of the wage-earners." Their goal was defined with equal plainness. In testimony before the United States Commission on Industrial Relations in 1914, Gompers declared that the AFL sought "to accomplish the best results in improving the conditions of the working people, men, women, and children, today and tomorrow and tomorrow—and tomorrow's tomorrow; and each day making it a better day than the one that had gone before."

Although Gompers favored political power, urging workers to make "an intelligent use of the ballot" and to support legislation in their interest, he steered the AFL away from direct involvement in politics and toward the relationship between employer and worker. Through this approach the AFL also sought to counteract the dehumanizing effects of the new industrial system in which employers tended to treat workers as commodities. Henry Stone, a railroad official, expressed this employer attitude with painful bluntness: "If I wanted boiler iron, I would go out on the market and buy it where I could get it cheapest, and if I wanted to employ men, I would do the same." The AFL, by seeking recognition of the worker's role as a human partner in the industrial system, and by pushing for a fair share within the system, sought to restore a lost dignity to working people.

Strikes and Violence The intense opposition of employers to union organization, and to the strike as a device to force improvement in working conditions, combined with worker frustration and bitterness to produce some of the most unpleasant violence in the nation's history. Few strikes occurred without some disruption, but several were ferocious.

*John L. Lewis and Samuel Gompers.
Gompers, the cigar union organizer
who became president of the
American Federation of Labor, was a
powerful personal force in sustaining
the organization. Lewis, equally
dynamic, headed the United Mine
Workers and established the Congress
of Industrial Organizations when a
dispute arose within the AFL over
organization by craft versus by
industry.*

In 1877, a strike began on the Baltimore and Ohio Railroad in response to a wage cut. It spread until about two-thirds of the railroad mileage of the country had been affected. Violence broke out in several cities as troops were called in. Several dozen people were killed, many more were wounded, and a great deal of property was destroyed. Similar large-scale violence occurred in 1892 at the Carnegie Steel Company plant at Homestead, Pennsylvania, where at one point a deadly all-day gun battle, including the use of a cannon by strikers, raged between three hundred Pinkerton guards and members of the Amalgamated Association of Iron and Steel Workers. Ten lives were lost, scores of people were injured, and much property was destroyed. In these and other devastating strikes, such as the Pullman strike of 1894, and the violent strike by silver miners in Idaho, the combined forces of employers, law enforcement officials, troops, and public opinion brought crushing defeat for the workers and grave setbacks for the cause of unionization.

The tragic irony of all this was that on many occasions public sympathy initially lay with workers, but shifted the moment they took to protest and violence. Increasingly fearful as the public might have been about the amassing of capital in the bank vaults of the nation, they were far more fearful of the mass organization of men on the streets. People tend to react most strongly to the obvious, the visible, the near. And workers on strike were nearer, more obvious, and more visible than vast aggregations of stocks and bonds.

Workers were not averse to relying upon armed force. Mine workers won a strike in 1898 by virtue of their superior marksmanship, as one commentator described the victory. But by and large violence erupted only when employers brought in armed guards and troops. And much violence, especially destruction of property, came only at the hands of hoodlums and others eager for loot and excitement, as in the railroad strike in Pittsburgh in 1877. But strikers got the blame and were portrayed as men out to destroy the country. A clergyman at the time of the Pullman strike described its leaders as "a junto of men, who stand ready to strike in the dark ... at everything we hold dear, our very altars and our firesides." And the New York *Times* referred to the strikers as undisciplined mobs composed of scoundrels, thieves, blacklegs, and murderers. Given the conduct of many business leaders, such denunciations could as well have been applied to them, but seldom were.

In consequence, the workers had a hard time protecting and defending their interests. Yet by 1900 the union movement was entrenched as a significant technique for getting economic opportunity and security for American workers.

The Response of the Church

The rise of an urban-industrial America also had its effect on the thought and actions of many religious leaders, particularly Protestants. Although the church had always been concerned with poverty, crime, greed, vice, and general wickedness, it had assumed these to be matters of personal sin related to weakness of character. Poverty was a punishment for sin, prostitution a sign of immoral character.

Yet increasingly it became clear that many people were poor not because they were wicked but because of the way the economic system worked; that women turned to prostitution and men to crime not for love of evil but as the only alternative to misery. Salvation of the soul is fine, but offer a starving man a choice between bread and salvation and he is likely to prefer the bread. In fact, workers increasingly became estranged from the church in the decades after the Civil War simply because its traditional emphases seemed totally irrelevant to their basic needs.

At any rate, these pressures brought about a movement within the Protestant churches in America, and to a certain extent among Catholic and Jewish congregations, which sought to develop as great a concern for the social body as for the individual soul. The result was an involvement by the church in social and economic affairs. The basic motive behind this involvement was the conviction that the ethic of love ought to be put into practice. This practical effort took three forms: the rise of the institutional church, the appearance of private agencies inspired by religious belief to engage in social work, and the Social Gospel.

The Institutional Church The institutional church was a movement designed to turn the church into a fulltime institution responding to the needs of parishioners. The Catholic church had traditionally been a center of social activity, but the American Protestant church had been a one- or at best a two-day institution confining its contact with parishioners to preaching about the fate of their immortal souls.

A number of urban churches, led by the Episcopalians and Methodists, began to move in a new direction. Under the guidance of D. W. S. Rainsford, St. George's Episcopal Church in New York, which stood in a tenement district, established vocational training classes, recreational activities for all age groups, a cooperative grocery, and vacations at the seashore for children. Working-class families returned to St. George's in droves, and its membership rose from 87 in 1882 to over 4,000 in 1897. The new Congregational Church at Elmira, New York, contained a library, lecture rooms, and a gymnasium. In many other cities, similar activity turned churches into full-time institutions open seven days a week, providing aid projects for parishioners and serving as centers for social activities of all kinds.

While the institutional church proved to be a useful response to certain immediate needs, its scope was clearly limited. Private agencies with religious motivation broadened the coverage. Originating in England the Salvation Army began its work in America in 1880, providing temporary food and shelter for the destitute while beating the drum for their salvation. Settlement houses, modeled on Toynbee Hall in London, appeared in many American cities, Jane Addams' Hull House in Chicago being one of the most celebrated. Settlement houses, as Hull House proved, were especially useful for immigrants, and their concern centered on such matters as the health of children, vocational training, legal aid, political action on the local level, and a dozen other matters that involved the lives of their neighborhood clientele.

The Social Gospel Of even greater importance was the Social Gospel, the movement that brought the church into the broader arena of social reform. Its most prominent spokesman was Walter Rauschenbusch, whose service as pastor of a slum church changed his views and prompted him to argue in a series of important and influential books that America's industrial system was run on principles "antagonistic to the fundamental principles of Christianity." Rauschenbusch supported the trade-union movement, cooperatives, proposals for income-tax laws, old-age pensions, minimum-wage laws, and other measures designed to improve the lot of working-class Americans. Although some clergymen became socialists, the majority affected by these ideas were moderate. But they helped to involve the church in the drive to regulate big business and to protect the interests of workers. Many churches established commissions to study and report on social and economic problems; seminaries began to reflect the new emphasis in their training of young ministers. By 1908 the General Conference of the Methodist Episcopal Church was calling for a shorter work day, abolition of child labor, regulation of working conditions for women, and the highest wage industry could afford. The newly established Federal Council of Churches adopted the same program, and many ministers and their more liberal and concerned followers found themselves involved in active work for legislation to accomplish these goals. This new interest of many urban churches contributed greatly to the favorable public opinion toward the political movement known as Progressivism.

The Progressive Movement

Although the settlement house, the Social Gospel, and even the extended activities of trade unionism after 1900 could properly be regarded as part of the larger environment of Progressivism, the Progressive movement was essentially a reform impulse operating through the traditional channel of democracy in America—political action.

The Progressive spirit for reform in the first decade and a half of the twentieth century invaded both political parties and indeed brought about the creation of a third, the Progressive party led by Theodore Roosevelt in 1912. The reform influence operated on all levels of politics and government—municipal, state, and national, and it encompassed a wide range of social, economic, and political proposals. Its strength as well as its weakness came from its breadth of interest and approach. Few Progressives were fully committed to or identified with all the causes associated with the movement. Some indeed assumed that the adoption of one particular reform might well solve all the ills of mankind. Even Woodrow Wilson was guilty of this kind of exaggeration when he declared of the short ballot that it was "the key to the whole problem of the restoration of popular government in this country"—rather a heavy responsibility to assign to so simple a document.

If there was not always agreement on the priority of the multitude of reform proposals, there was general agreement that reform was essential if democracy was to survive. A major spokesman for Progressivism, Walter Weyl, wrote in 1912 that "Reform is piecemeal and yet rapid. It is carried along divergent lines of people holding separate interests, and yet it moves toward a common end. It combines into a general movement toward a new democracy."

Support for Progressivism was broad throughout American society. Its success in passing innumerable proposals for change could not have occurred had this not been true. It is customary to think of Progressivism as a middle-class movement dominated by middle-class values. While it is true that the leadership tended to come from middle-class America—businessmen, lawyers, engineers, editors, journalists, clergymen, college professors, and the like—when the votes were counted it was clear that workers, native and immigrant alike, had much in common with the middle class in seeking reform. And if a desire to correct injustices in America's social, economic, and political life represented middle-class values, then obviously more Americans regarded themselves as middle class than the statistics measuring such status would normally suggest.

"What's the use? The more I talk, the better she likes him!".

Robert La Follette was a candidate for the Republican nomination for president in 1911. But his inability to gain more than regional support drove the liberals to Teddy Roosevelt.

It would, however, be correct to say that if Progressivism was an affair of the conscience—which is what Kansas editor William Allen White called it—and if conscience implies guilt, then Progressivism was indeed middle class. Surely the working class had no cause to feel guilty that America's economic system had turned out the way it had. Workers were victims, not perpetrators of the system. Nor were there very many in the upper class who felt guilty about the wealth and the power they were enjoying so grandly. The rich tend to feel guilty only when age begins to diminish their capacity to enjoy wealth and power.

But the middle class had, and still has, a remarkable talent for self-criticism. Brought to an awareness of injustice and wrongdoing through the exposures of social, political, and economic evils by the so-called "muckraking" newspapers and magazines, the middle class set out to correct abuses. At the same time it lashed itself, and took a perverse pleasure in being lashed for allowing such things to happen in the first place. William Allen White observed that "in the soul of the people there is a conviction of their past unrighteousness." Perhaps what was involved was a secular version of the Biblical visitation of the sins of the fathers upon the children. In short, what the middle-class Progressive generation, or rather their fathers and grandfathers, had done was to concentrate so much on getting ahead that they had abdicated their sense of civic and social responsibility. Now that had been recovered, and it was felt to be everyone's duty to correct things. What occurred was a widespread revival of concern about social responsibility, the duty of the citizen to see to it that government and society were decently formed and operated. Theodore Roosevelt expressed this feeling when he said: "No hard and fast rule can be laid down as to the way reform must be done; but most certainly every man, whatever his position, should strive to do it in some way and to some degree."

Many of America's corporate leaders supported those aspects of Progressivism which would lead to a more efficient and tightly organized economy better serving their own interests. Certainly Progressivism did not lessen the commanding role played by America's capitalist elite in the decisions that governed American society. Rather this role was strengthened as government at all levels became more directly involved in economic life, and the ties between government and business became deeper and more intimate.

Labor Reforms   In short, what occurred from 1900 to 1915 was a coming together of many forces, a coalescing of motivations: worker demands for an improved life; trade union programs for improved conditions of work, hours, and pay; a new awareness on the part of many churches and religiously oriented people that the Christian ethic should be practiced in the social, political, and economic arena, not just preached in the pulpit; a rising concern among the middle class that democracy had gotten lost in the urban-industrial shuffle and should be regained; a sense of shame on the part of many that their pursuit of selfish goals at the expense of civic duties and social responsibilities had led to much political, social, and economic abuse; an intellectual conviction that all problems could be solved sensibly by the application of expanding knowledge if people were willing to make the effort; and the corporate drive for efficiency. All these came together to produce a decade and a half of active reform. What were the results?

Conditions did improve for working people, more among those unionized than others. The average work week moved down to 55.2 hours a week by 1914. Greater attention was paid to the health and safety of workers, a move prompted by state and national legislation as well as by corporate initiative. Workmen's compensation laws were passed. Progressive state legislatures sought to limit the hours of labor for women and children. Real wages increased, stimulated in large part by an expanding productivity.

Importantly, attitudes toward labor began to change. Although the courts retained their unfriendly view of unions, strikes, and boycotts, their attitude toward the fate of workers began to shift as the courts moved in the direction of upholding legislation dealing with improvements in working conditions. In the Clayton Act of 1914, Congress specifically denied labor to be a mere commodity, and Progressive Presidents Roosevelt and Wilson consulted with labor leaders. A federal Department of Labor was created.

Reform in Business   At the other end of the economic spectrum conditions also changed. The trend toward bigness and concentration in American business was not halted, despite a number of successful antitrust suits by the federal government; but such suits did instill a certain caution in the business community. And on both state and federal levels regulation of business enterprise to curb excessive power, to correct abuses, and to introduce the public interest into business decisions became accepted practice. Regulatory agencies such as the Federal Trade Commission and numerous state industrial, railroad, and public utilities commissions made it clear that the arrogant freewheeling days were over. Corporate, income, and inheritance taxes were enacted as brakes on the accumulation of unlimited wealth. Many elements in the world of big business began to acquire a sense of respect for a new power in the economic field—the power of government—and to develop a sense of social responsibility about their own role in the affairs of the American community.

Social and Political Reform   The social arena also changed for the better, though far too much responsibility for such change was left to the states and consequently too much remained undone. But concern for the fate of the disadvantaged joined with a new sense of broad social responsibility to produce some significant legislation. Mothers' assistance programs, old-age pension provisions, school-attendance laws, more aid to public education, pure food and drug laws, and other measures helped to improve the social environment. Conservation measures initiated a new concern for the natural environment upon which people depended for their survival.

Great stock was also placed in political reform as the key to accomplishing other changes, the assumption being that democratization of political and governmental processes, practices, and institutions would inevitably lead to a clear realization and expression of the needs of people in a new kind of world. This was an assumption not always warranted. On the grounds that more efficient ways of doing things would also be democratic, innovations such as the commission and manager form of city government were introduced in various communities large and small. City planning commissions, executive budgets, and the merit system in civil service were also experimented with for the same purpose. Experts were brought into government on all levels to serve on various commissions, and legislative reference services were established in many states, all with the intent of bringing expanding knowledge to bear on modern problems. To eliminate or reduce the possibility of political corruption and government by special interests, a number of reforms were adopted: direct election of United States Senators, corrupt practices acts, antilobbying laws, the initiative, the referendum, the recall, and the direct primary. The women's suffrage movement culminated in the Nineteenth Amendment in 1920.

Reforms Still Needed   These are simply examples of the many and varied measures which marked the period of reform from 1900 to 1915. Progressives felt that they were embarking upon a great crusade to remake

American society, restore rule to the people, and turn a modern urban-in-dustrial society into a model of democracy in which the old principles were applied in new ways. To a surprising extent, they succeeded. But their optimism turned out to be not entirely justified. Much work needed to make America truly democratic went undone, even ignored. Little or nothing was done to protect the rights of blacks, Indians, and other minorities. The right of labor to organize and act collectively remained unassured. A hopeful movement to provide medical care for all was killed almost at birth. Efficiency in government did not necessarily mean democracy in government, and devices such as the initiative could be used as skillfully by special-interest groups as by the people at large. Political bosses managed to survive the onslaught of reform. No provision was made for continuing social and economic change and reform. The reform movement was not radical in the sense of drastic change, and it is clear that a number of people supported reform not because they believed in it for its own sake but because they preferred reform to the violence, chaos, and protest they feared would take place without it.

Nevertheless the reforms of this period were significant for American society. They laid the basis for future achievement. The movement for reform brought many people to an awareness of the fundamental fact of a modern urban-industrial society: that the parts of such a society are interdependent, and damage to one affects all the rest. Reform showed that a sense of responsibility toward others was crucial in a modern society. And reform in this period showed that the people had at hand in the instrumentality of their government a means of exercising that responsibility. The reforms of the first years of the twentieth century demonstrated that many Americans had not lost a sense of their own democracy, their faith in the adaptability of democratic principles to new conditions and changing times.

America and World War I

Whatever the success of Progressivism in improving the lives of Americans, this effort was cut off by the outbreak of what used to be called the Great War, into which the world was drawn in 1914. This first world war of the twentieth century forced the Americans to reassess their view of the role the United States should play in world affairs, and brought home to all the painful fact that industry and technology had not only changed the United States in the past half-century but the rest of the world as well.

The American Role in the World: The Isolationist Myth   Behind American involvement in World War I lay a long period of uncertainty about the American role in the world that stretched back to colonial days and the beginnings of the Republic. From the beginning the Americans had seen themselves as a new society embarked on a course separate and distinct from that of other peoples; but they also knew they were a product of European civilization, and that their fate was intertwined with that of Europe. The American colonies had been caught up in the wars of the European powers struggling for control of the New World. Although the lives of most colonials were not directly touched by these great conflicts for empire, colonial troops had fought in such wars, outlying settlements had sometimes been swept up in the shifting tides of battle, and the long-range development of the North American colonies had been finally determined by the British victory in the wars for empire on the North American continent.

Moreover, the War for Independence had taken America onto the continent of Europe in search of allies against Britain. Independence and nationhood seemingly left the Americans free of involvement in European affairs, free to go their own way with a minimum of contact with a decadent Europe. Both Washington and Jefferson emphasized the importance of avoiding entanglement in the affairs of Europe, and their warnings became an important element in American thinking about the rest of the world and particularly the European world. Most Americans in the new democratic nation, therefore, preferred to see their country as primarily a "model for all mankind"— an example from which others could learn. They agreed with Henry Clay who argued that America's role in the world was to keep freedom's "lamp burning brightly on this western shore as a light to all nations."

But this conviction did not keep the nation from being affected by events taking place elsewhere. The attempt to remain aloof from the Napoleonic wars seriously affected the American economy and involved the new nation in clashes with Britain. Throughout the nineteenth century an expanding America gradually moved outward into the world arena where contacts with and involvements in the affairs of other peoples became inevitable. In the first half of the nineteenth century most of these contacts took place on the North American continent in the course of American expansion and did not seem to violate the American commitment to remain aloof from contact with others. But by the eve of the Civil War a rapidly increasing export trade, numerous contacts with the Far East including the American role in the opening of Japan, other Pacific interventions such as in Hawaii, and the imperial visions proclaimed by such public figures as William Henry Seward (Secretary of State from 1861 to 1869), all indicated that total isolation from the larger affairs of the world was more myth than reality. Nevertheless, at the end of the nineteenth century Henry Cabot Lodge was probably expressing a sentiment held by a majority of Americans when he remarked that "Our relations with foreign nations today fill but a slight place in American politics, and excite . . . a languid interest. We have separated ourselves so completely from the affairs of other people."

New Pressures Outward

While it was possible to express this extreme isolationist position, certain events in the second half of the nineteenth century confirmed a different reality. The United States took part in many international exhibitions and

*The landing of the marines at Guantanamo. A sensational press that
emphasized Spanish atrocities while ignoring equally cruel Cuban practices
in warfare, a humanitarian sympathy for insurgents struggling for their
independence, and an aggressive nationalistic interest in expansion
precipitated American intervention in the Cuban civil war and consequently
war with Spain.*

fairs, joined in international conferences on the standardization of navigation
charts and the delineation of international time zones, engaged in scientific
expeditions ranging from polar exploration to botanical studies in South
America, and probed outward to open up Japan and establish interest in
numerous Pacific and Caribbean islands. More and more Americans began
to operate overseas as missionaries, students, tourists, scholars, and especially businessmen who engaged in commercial, trading, and industrial
operations over all the continents of the world and many of its islands. The
merchant marine, the navy, and the consular and diplomatic services expanded to meet the needs of these ventures overseas.

As the United States changed from an agrarian to an industrial economy, it
was forced to become more world-oriented. Science, technology, and business practices increased American agricultural productivity, even as more
and more land went under the plow, and stimulated a search for new mar-

kets overseas for the heavy surplus from American farms. As industry and technology became more sophisticated, the need for overseas markets as well as the need for new sources of raw materials became apparent.

All these developments led to a rising American interest in the rest of the world and a growing realization of our unavoidable involvement in world affairs. The nineteenth century climaxed with the melodramatic war with Spain in 1898 and the American acquisition of overseas territories as a consequence of the war. The Spanish-American War gave Cuba a nominal independence under American guidance, brought Puerto Rico, Guam, and the Philippines under direct American dominion, and provided the occasion for the annexation of Hawaii.

This outward expansion of the United States by war began a new era in American history. For there was more to it than the mere acquisition of additional lands—a process, after all, the United States had engaged in during the first half of the nineteenth century. More importantly, the war marked a significant change in attitude on the part of most Americans, stemming from the recognition that the United States was now one of the great powers. The Americans reacted in various ways to this new sense of their power in the world. For some it involved simply a sense of exhilaration that the United States now possessed the power to give the back of its hand to the bullying authority of an Old World power—Spain. For others, notably many American businessmen, the acquisition of Hawaii, the Philippines, and other territories opened the door to expanded trade opportunities in the Far East. For still others, our power provided the means to spread the benefits of Western and especially American civilization to backward peoples. And for some, particularly a group of influential governmental, business, and military leaders, the war was the logical beginning of a new American empire based not so much on colonies as on a dynamic American economic and political influence in the world and backed by naval power.

These views found expression in disturbing actions: the brutal suppression of a Filipino independence movement after the Americans took over the islands; persistent American interference in the internal affairs of Central and South American countries, including military intervention; the failure to extend American constitutional rights to those peoples who came under American rule as a consequence of the war; the aggressive expansion of American economic interests everywhere in the world; and an increasing tendency on the part of the United States to shoulder its way into world politics, as in Secretary of State John Hay's pronouncement of an Open Door policy for China and President Theodore Roosevelt's mediation of the Russo-Japanese War.

These actions and others caused problems for the United States and indeed divided the American people. Their consequent influence on the American role in the world was considerable, particularly in the development of the idea that the United States as the major power had a responsibility to involve itself actively in world affairs for the sake of peace and order, although peace and order on whose terms and for whose purposes became a matter of dispute.

An increasing involvement in world affairs was inevitable, though the particular course it took after 1898 was not necessarily decreed by fate. For by 1900 a new kind of world had come into being. Even though most peoples still wrested their existence from the soil, the world itself was now dominated by the forces of industrialism and technology. The desire to open up areas to meet the needs of the industrial countries for markets and raw materials steadily drew even primitive societies into the orbit of world affairs. The telegraph, the oceanic cable, the steamship, the railroad, the whole paraphernalia of modern communications as it then existed linked the world together in a way before undreamed of. The products of industrial mass production began to find their way into humble villages, and native peoples in different parts of the globe found themselves laboring in tin mines or on rubber plantations owned by corporations based in industrial nations on the other side of the world. By the eve of World War I, the world had become a great economic and political unit—not through formal organization, but because what happened in the Congo had import in Brussels, and what happened in London had an impact on the Malay peninsula.

In such a world, it would be difficult indeed for a major nation such as the United States not to be concerned or affected. When war broke out in Europe in 1914, most Americans retained the old sense of aloofness from foreign entanglements, but the day had long passed when there was no need to make decisions about our relation to such a conflict. In World War I, all the accouterments of a world dominated by industry and technology put pressure on America. Modern communications placed the war before us day after day. The Americans may have believed that the war was not their business, but they could not avoid making a decision about it, and in this sense it was indeed their business. Industrialism and technology did not guarantee United States participation in the war, nor did our status as the major industrial-technological power in the world of 1914. But these facts did mean that the United States would be affected by the struggle, and it became clear to Americans that involvement would help us to determine an outcome favorable to what were then perceived to be the interests of the United States.

The Decision for War

The decision for war, which took almost two and a half years to reach, involved two stages: first the rise of sympathy and support for the Allied Powers, and second the development of a rationale for entrance into the war on the Allied side.

The matter of sympathy and support for the Allies was quickly settled. There were elements in the country hostile to Britain and others unwilling to condemn Germany. The Irish had carried to America their longtime antagonism against English rule, the large German population in America had a natural reluctance to take a stand against the homeland of their fathers, a number of other Americans entertained suspicions of British manipulations

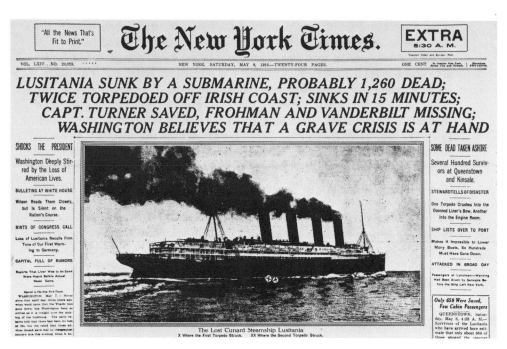

"All the News That's Fit to Print."

The New York Times.

EXTRA
5:30 A. M.

VOL. LXIV...NO. 20,923.   NEW YORK, SATURDAY, MAY 8, 1915.—TWENTY-FOUR PAGES.   ONE CENT

LUSITANIA SUNK BY A SUBMARINE, PROBABLY 1,260 DEAD; TWICE TORPEDOED OFF IRISH COAST; SINKS IN 15 MINUTES; CAPT. TURNER SAVED, FROHMAN AND VANDERBILT MISSING; WASHINGTON BELIEVES THAT A GRAVE CRISIS IS AT HAND

SHOCKS THE PRESIDENT

Washington Deeply Stirred by the Loss of American Lives.

BULLETINS AT WHITE HOUSE

Wilson Reads Them Closely, but Is Silent on the Nation's Course.

HINTS OF CONGRESS CALL

Loss of Lusitania Recalls Firm Tone of Our First Warning to Germany.

CAPITAL FULL OF RUMORS

Reports That Liner Was to Be Sunk Were Heard Before Actual News Came.

SOME DEAD TAKEN ASHORE

Several Hundred Survivors at Queenstown and Kinsale.

STEWARD TELLS OF DISASTER

One Torpedo Crashes Into the Doomed Liner's Bow, Another Into the Engine Room.

SHIP LISTS OVER TO PORT

Makes It Impossible to Lower Many Boats, So Hundreds Must Have Gone Down.

ATTACKED IN BROAD DAY

Passengers at Luncheon—Warning Had Been Given to Germans Before the Ship Left New York.

Only 650 Were Saved, Few Cabin Passengers

QUEENSTOWN, Saturday, May 8, 4:28 A. M.—Survivors of the Lusitania who have arrived here estimate that only about 650 of those aboard the steamer

The Lost Cunard Steamship Lusitania
X Where the First Torpedo Struck.   XX Where the Second Torpedo Struck.

The sinking of the Lusitania. *One of the reasons that ultimately forced the United States into the war was Germany's decision to destroy any merchant ship attempting to trade with the Allies. While America was still neutral German U-boats were responsible for the deaths of at least two hundred Americans, most of whom perished when the* Lusitania, *carrying munitions to Great Britain, was torpedoed.*

in the international money market, and many intellectuals had a long-standing respect for German culture and scholarship. But these views were overwhelmed by others. America's roots lay in England: much of our culture, institutions, and ideas rose out of English experience. The nation also had strong sentimental ties with France stretching back to French aid in the Revolution. Moreover, a series of German actions—the violation of Belgian neutrality, submarine warfare, attempted sabotage of American industry, and the attempt to get Mexico to declare war on the United States should America enter the war on the side of the Allies—greatly angered Americans. These circumstances, combined with British control of the communications lines to the New World and her skillful use of atrocity propaganda stories about German soldiers, produced a preponderance of sentiment favorable to the Allies and hostile to Germany and her partners.

This sentiment was paralleled by active support, particularly since the circumstances of America's declared neutrality favored Britain, whose navy controlled the seas. The neutrality policy proclaimed by Wilson meant in theory that we would sell supplies to both sides, but in practice it meant that the Central Powers were denied access to America's industrial production. A huge trade quickly grew with the Allies—from $825 million in 1914 to $3.2 billion in 1916—while that with Germany dwindled to a few millions. The same held true with loans. To purchase war supplies in the United States after their cash ran out, the Allies needed loans, and by 1916 American bankers had provided over $2.2 billion.

Sympathy and support were one thing. Going to war, however, was quite another matter. Many factors worked against such an action. Though not a dominant element in American thought, Christian pacifism had been persistent since the 1840s. The peace movement had been founded in the United States, it had never died out despite setbacks, and it revived in 1914. In the popular mind, moreover, there had always been an aversion to involvement in the affairs of Europe, a decadent and corrupt society in contrast to America. That element in Progressive thought which perceived so many modern problems to stem from the selfishness of economic interests was now applied to war. Progressive Senator Robert LaFollette of Wisconsin argued, for example, that war talk was promoted by "munitions manufacturers, stock brokers, and bond dealers" who would make "enormous profits" if America entered the war. The humanitarian element in Progressivism that was concerned about harsh working conditions for workers could just as easily be aroused by the inhumane slaughter of war. Fear, clearly justified, that reform itself would be set aside by war also fed antiwar feeling. Wilson's own desires, despite his sympathy for Britain and France, also carried weight. His influence was enormous, and he was determined to avoid war.

But important as these factors were, there were others that worked in the opposite direction. Of great importance was the growing feeling, which Wilson himself came to share, that if Germany were to win the war, her victory would pose a threat to the future security and well-being of the United States. The assumption was that a victorious Germany would pose many uncertain problems for America's future role in the world. What would happen if Germany were to dominate Europe, to encroach on the British Empire overseas, to disrupt the whole Atlantic community of which the United States was a part? Unforeseen problems of adjustment and association would arise, presumably damaging to American markets, sources of raw material, trade routes, and commercial dealings. In February 1917 the *New Republic* noted that "on the two shores of the Atlantic Ocean there has grown up a profound web of interest which joins together the western world. . . . If that community were destroyed, we should know what we had lost. . . . The passing of the power of England would be calamitous to the American national interest. . . . What we must fight for is a common interest of the western world, for the integrity of the Atlantic Powers. We must recognize that we are in fact one great community and act as a member of it." Fear of what the world would be like if the Allies lost was of course sheer speculation, but the fear was real and it exerted a profound influence.

Of equal importance was the growing belief, which Wilson firmly held, that America as a great power had a responsibility for leadership in world affairs. In his second inaugural address he said: "The greatest things that remain to be done must be done with the whole world for stage and in cooperation with the wide and universal forces of mankind. . . . The tragic events of the thirty months of vital turmoil through which we have just passed have made us citizens of the world. There can be no turning back." This leadership was not to be sought for any selfish national interest, but to promote the interests of humanity and the cause of democracy and justice in the world. In his call for a declaration of war, Wilson declared that the United States had "no selfish ends to serve." Rather, "We are at the beginning of an age in which it will be insisted that the same standards of conduct and responsibility for wrong done shall be observed among nations and their governments that are observed among the individual citizens of civilized states."

What Wilson was doing here was to revive the old image of America's role as an influence for good in the world. In the past this role had been essentially passive—America was an example from which others could learn. Now it was to be an active role, shaping the circumstances of world events to create conditions favorable to the promotion and preservation of democracy in the world. On April 2, 1917, in his call to Congress for war, Wilson made this point clear:

> It is a fearful thing to lead this great peaceful people into war, into the most terrible and disastrous of all wars, civilization itself seeming to be in the balance. But the right is more precious than peace, and we shall fight for the things which we have always carried nearest to our hearts—for democracy, for the right of those who submit to authority to have a voice in their own governments, for the rights and liberties of small nations, for a universal dominion of right, by such a concert of free people as shall bring peace and safety to all nations and make the world itself at last free.

And so the United States entered World War I, thus insuring an Allied victory. Even more significantly, involvement marked the American entrance onto the world stage as a dominant and active molder of world affairs. From here on, whether the Americans liked it or not, or recognized it or not, more and more of the nation's time, energy, thought, and resources would be devoted to this role, and what the Americans did or did not do would play an increasing part in deciding the course of human affairs.

Mobilization for Victory

To function successfully, a modern society requires a high degree of organization and centralized control. Nowhere is this more evident than in the mobilization of society's resources in wartime. "It is not an army that we must shape and train for war," said President Wilson, "it is a nation." In modern war all areas of life become involved in the conflict: office, shop, factory, mine, farm, home, school. All talents and skills are drawn upon: workers, businesspeople, farmers, housewives, artists, writers, historians, psychologists, scientists, doctors. So it was in World War I. Nothing like this had occurred before in the nation's history.

The Administrative Accomplishment   The President was given such extensive powers to organize the country for war that one Senator complained, "We might as well abdicate and make the President a king." Special agencies were created and established ones were given new assignments. There were mistakes, inefficiencies, waste, and even opposition, but organization of the nation's economic, social, and cultural resources for war purposes by and large succeeded, indicating the degree to which an industrial-urban-technological-scientific society is already geared to organization and centralization.

Manpower was mobilized by the Selective Service Act of May 1917. Almost ten million men were registered and classified—"the first great standardization of human material in mass production" in American history, as one observer later called it. Some 2.8 million men were drafted, and 2 million more volunteered. Over 2 million served overseas. Many objected to being rounded up for slaughter. There were an estimated 300,000 draft dodgers, a number of whom managed to disappear in the mass anonymity of modern society, the ranks of the peasantry in Mexico, or the attics of their parents' homes. While the Selective Service Act provided for religious conscientious objectors, it did not for those objecting on other grounds. About 4,000 men openly refused military duty. The majority were assigned to agricultural or industrial work camps under conditions resembling prison life, some accepted noncombat duty in the army, and several hundred determined holdouts were sent to prison.

Economic mobilization took place in four major areas: industry, transportation, fuel, and food, each with its own administrative board. The War Industries Board, under Bernard Baruch, controlled both civilian and military production, setting prices and priorities, establishing rules of standardization in manufacturing products, and recommending consolidation of businesses. The Railroad Administration, under Secretary of the Treasury William McAdoo, made schedules and rates uniform, organized the railroads into an integrated system based on regional units rather than companies, directed all freight and passenger traffic, and promoted consolidation and pooling of operations. The Fuel Administration, headed by Harry Garfield, consolidated production and promoted mechanization, achieving a twenty percent increase in coal production and a fifty percent increase in oil. The Food Administration, run by Herbert Hoover, fixed prices and profits, put marginal land back in production, promoted volunteer "land armies" to provide agricultural labor and to increase home and community gardens. Crop production, already up by 1917, increased even more. Wheat production, for example, went from 619 million bushels in 1917 to 904 million in 1918. Food exports rose from 12.3 million tons to 18.6 million.

In addition to these aspects of economic mobilization, the government also paid serious attention to the effective use of labor, establishing a National War Labor Board and a War Labor Policies Board to settle labor disputes, to establish wage and hour standards for the major war industries, and to promote cooperation between management and labor. Many strikes were prevented, and union organization was encouraged, so that membership rose

Women joined the labor force in the mobilization effort.

by over two million. The government also mobilized the financial resources of the nation to support the war, relying upon five major bond drives to raise about two-thirds of the cost of the war. The rest came from over $10 billion in taxes, including a steep income tax, an excess-profits tax, and an increased inheritance tax. The price paid for the war is reflected in the rise in the public debt of the United States from slightly less than $3 billion in June of 1917 to $25.5 billion in June of 1919. The direct cost of the war was over $33 billion.

Social Mobilization   Social mobilization was on an equally impressive scale. The goal was conformity in public opinion backing the war. The Espionage Act of June 1917 and the Sedition Act of May 1918 provided fines and imprisonment for anyone who by word or deed interfered with or criticized the war effort. Along with prosecutions under these acts went the work of the Committee on Public Information, headed by George Creel, which deluged the country with propaganda and encouraged citizen suppression of any opposition to the war.

The Espionage and Sedition Acts and the Creel Committee created an atmosphere of hysteria that has had no parallel in the nation's history. More than a thousand persons went to prison, and thousands more were harassed and subjected to humiliating indignities in violation of their civil rights.

*Loyalty parades, like this one in New York in 1917, were used to promote
patriotism and support for the war effort.*

Banning the teaching of German and the playing of Wagner and Beethoven,
and renaming sauerkraut "liberty cabbage" were mild absurdities.

Other matters were more serious. Investigators from the Department of
Justice raided organizations presumed to be dangerous, seized papers and
destroyed property without warrant, arrested people on no evidence, and
built up a volunteer army of citizens reporting on their neighbors. Socialists,
radicals, union organizers, and pacifists were special prey. The socialist candidate for governor of New Jersey denounced the sending of troops to France
and was quoted as saying Tom Paine was greater than George Washington,
for which he was indicted, tried, convicted, and sentenced to five years in
federal prison. Ninety-five members of the Industrial Workers of the World,
a labor organization held in great suspicion, got long jail sentences. And over
twelve hundred striking copper workers in Arizona were rounded up by
vigilantes, herded into cattle and freight cars, and shipped out of the state,
some ending in California jails, others abandoned in the New Mexico desert.

The foreign language press and radical newspapers were attacked. One
German-language paper was charged under the Espionage Act and three of
its officials were sent to prison because its translations of innocuous reprinted material differed from the originals in such a way as "to depress
patriotic ardor." The socialist paper *The Masses* was suppressed because its
editor, Max Eastman, wrote that the war "was not a war for democracy. It did

not originate in a dispute about democracy, and it is unlikely to terminate in a democratic settlement."

The demand for conformity reached out to affect other citizens as well. Teachers were particularly susceptible to attack. In schools and colleges across the country, teachers were removed on the slightest grounds. At Columbia, Wisconsin, Michigan, Washington, Illinois, Minnesota, Cornell, Virginia, and other universities, professors were fired for disloyalty, including a University of Wisconsin professor who humorously noted of a superpatriotic colleague that he wore two liberty buttons—one on his lapel, and one on the seat of his trousers so his patriotism would be visible even when he wrote on the blackboard. One public school teacher was discharged because he maintained "a neutral attitude" when the subject of anarchism was discussed in his class. Another was dismissed for taking driving lessons from an unnaturalized German. Casual but intemperate statements by ordinary citizens landed them in jail. A Texan was sent to jail for saying "Wilson is a wooden-headed son of a bitch." Critical comments about the Red Cross or the YMCA got people into trouble. Citizens failing to subscribe for a stipulated amount in local bond drives were called on in the middle of the night, threatened with having their names published on "rolls of dishonor," horsewhipped, or tarred and feathered. The producer of a movie on the American Revolution received a ten-year jail sentence because the movie contained a scene showing British brutality, thus insulting our ally. Ironically, such hysteria did not exist in either Britain or France, whose peril was certainly far greater than that of the United States.

Mobilization of American society during the nineteen months the United States was actually in the conflict produced no significant military contribution in ships, airplanes, tanks, and artillery. The time was too short for that. But the American contribution was major in the essentials of food, fuel, and munitions. And the million and a half men who fought in France were crucial in the defeat of Germany's forces on the western front.

The long-range impact of the war was considerable. The trend established in the Progressive era of concentrating power in the hands of the federal government, expecially the executive branch, was accelerated. The role of government in organizing the economy clearly demonstrated that it could be a partner with business in the drive toward consolidation and efficiency, which not only reflected corporate interests but also the dictates of an industrial-technological system itself. Finally, the work of the Creel Committee demonstrated the ability of a modern government to propagandize its own people and guide their behavior for its own purposes, creating a problem that has been with us ever since.

The Insane Conflict

There was an aura of insanity about World War I. Europe had not experienced a major war for a hundred years, and people had no idea of the horrors and devastation modern war would bring. For the young it seemed at first a great adventure, as they marched off to the strains of "Tipperary," "Die Wacht am Rhein," and "Over There." The young English poet Rupert Brooke, finding himself in 1915 a member of the expeditionary force destined for Gallipoli, exulted, "It's too wonderful for belief. I had not imagined Fate could be so kind. . . . I suddenly realize that the ambition of my life has been—since I was two—to go on a military expedition against Constantinople." Romantically he looked ahead and gave purpose to his death:

> If I should die think only this of me:
> That there's some corner of a foreign field
> That is for ever England.

A generation later there was little chance that such lines could be written. A young American coming out of the devastating battle of Tarawa in the British-owned Gilbert Islands in the southwest Pacific wrote these lines in 1943 in parody of Brooke's:

> If I should die think only this of me
> That there is some corner of a foreign atoll
> That is forever safe to British commerce.

Cynicism also overtook the generation of 1914–1918, but not at the beginning of the conflict.

Not only the young lacked a realistic conception of modern war. At the beginning French generals were sending men in brightly colored uniforms and singing the *Marseillaise* against barbed wire and machinegun fire. When steel helmets were issued to the British army, one general refused his men permission to wear them because it would be a sign of cowardice. Young English officers new on the front were reminded that before going over the top they must check to make sure the senior regiment was on the right. American generals arriving in France brought white horses so they might ride in triumph through liberated cities. The American painter John Singer Sargent, in France to paint battle scenes, was dumbfounded to discover that fighting took place on Sundays. As late as 1917 there were British and French generals who, despite the desperate situation of their armies, were distressed by the arrival of American troops because they did not wish to share the glory of battle. To the end of the war there were officers in rear areas who pored over maps and sent men into battle with no real idea of what the front lines were like. One officer, seeing the front for the first time, burst into tears and cried out, "My God, were we really sending men into this?"

Trench Warfare The conflict that developed was one of trench warfare, something no one had anticipated. Hundreds of miles of complicated trenches, dugouts, and underground fortifications were constructed by both sides, denying any freedom of maneuver. Ghastly battles raged in cramped and tiny areas as each side periodically sought to smash and overwhelm the other's defenses. Hundreds of thousands of lives were lost for a gain of a few hundred yards, or at best a few miles. Ten months of struggle at Verdun in

War in the trenches of the Argonne Forest.

1916 altered the front lines less than four miles and cost 976,000 casualties. Trench warfare meant living for weeks in a ditch, under perpetual bombardment by enemy artillery. It went on constantly, the daily casualties being called "normal wastage" by the British. And when artillery opened up before an assault the effect was literally unimaginable. On the morning of March 21, 1918, the beginning of the last great German offensive of the war, six thousand heavy German guns opened fire simultaneously on a narrow front upon which the assault was to be focused. In Barrie Pitt's study of the last year of the war, *1918,* he described the effect of that intense bombardment as follows:

> At times the fire grew so intense that the very laws of nature seemed in abeyance. The air vibrated with shock, black layers danced in the fog, fixed objects flickered to and fro, and in the light of mounting flame and fire the mist became a crimson, yellow-shot effervescence. The thunder and crash of explosion became a norm which was no longer heard, as senses numbed and violence and horror increased. . . . In the forward posts and the front line, the slaughter during the opening hours of the offensive had been horrific. Entire platoons had been wiped out in seconds, men had been killed by the flying fragments of their friends' bodies, buried in collapsing trenches, trodden to death by those seeking room to dodge their own.

To attack or go "over the top" against the enemy was equally horrifying. One American soldier recorded the experience in this fashion:

> All the while shells are screaming over our heads, throwing up great geysers of mud all around us. . . . There is a cry for help. The section which includes Dave Barney has been buried by a shell. . . . We dig them out again. . . . Ten minutes later they are all blown up and buried again. . . . Dave is the only one of them left alive. . . . We moved forward. . . . We fell into mud and writhed out again like wasps crawling out of plums. . . . Shrapnel was bursting not much more than face high and the liquid mud from ground shells was going up in clouds and coming down in rain. . . . The dead and wounded were piled on each other's backs.

Death was so much a daily reality that many became callous, detached, or even casual about its presence. The sensitive were driven out of their minds, to suicide, or to deadly cynicism. The English poet Siegfried Sassoon wrote with searing bitterness

> . . . pray you'll never know
> The hell where youth and laughter go.

The war ended November 11, 1918, with the final exhaustion of the German armies, taking with it the best of an entire generation of young men and wiping out all the romanticism and innocence which had marked the beginning of the great conflict.

Aftermath   World War I was an unmitigated disaster, utterly pointless, a senseless affair from beginning to end. For the ultimatums, threats, counterthreats, and mobilizations that swept country after country in Europe after the assassination of the Austrian Archduke Franz Ferdinand at Sarajevo on June 28, 1914, reflected the worst aspects of nationalism. It was a classic case of how national fears, national pride, national honor could lead nations down paths catastrophic to the desires of ordinary people. It was a classic case of nations arming to the teeth to defend their "interests," and then finding themselves compelled to put their armies to the test when suspicions about the motives of their neighbors became aroused.

In retrospect, it might well have made little difference who "won" the war, with or without the participation of the United States. It is difficult, at any rate, to imagine consequences more devastating to Europe and the world than those which actually took place. The loss in human life alone was staggering: more than 8.5 million were killed out of a total of over 30 million casualties, and millions more civilians died. Nor did the war produce the results the European nations had in mind when they blundered into it. Once the war began all thought they were fighting to preserve a familiar order of things in which their own places would be secure. But quite the contrary happened. Looking back, Winston Churchill observed that "Authority was dispersed, the world unshackled, the weak became the strong, the sheltered the aggressive, and a vast fatigue dominated collective action."

The Signing of the Treaty of Versailles in the Hall of Mirrors, 1919. *From the painting by Sir William Orpen.*

Traditional balances of power were upset, and the war produced social disorder, economic chaos, political instability and unrest, revolution, and psychological wounds of the deepest nature in the countries most severely shaken by the conflict. The German, Austro-Hungarian, and Russian empires were destroyed, and that of the British shattered beyond repair. Revolution turned Russia to communism; fascism came to Italy,and strong men rose to power in other states; economic chaos and psychological despair in Germany brought Hitler into office and turned vengeance from a primitive urge into public policy; a political malaise settled over France; and everywhere disillusionment and cynicism marked the attitudes of people toward the institutions and social arrangements, concepts and values that had brought their countries to the sorry and dreadful pass in which they found themselves at war's end. Far from being the war that ended war, the conflict laid the groundwork for an even more terrible war to come.

Profile: WOODROW WILSON

Woodrow Wilson (1856–1924) as both a reform President and a wartime leader is traditionally and properly thought of as one of America's great presidents. His accomplishments were significant, he had qualities of the highest order, and his impact on American political thought and action was great. He had his faults and failures. He lacked Lincoln's humility and capacity for tolerance of those who disagreed with him, two limitations that contributed to the failure of Wilson's postwar policy and hence weakened the ability of the United States to play the role in world affairs that he thought it should.

Nevertheless, his career was extraordinary. He studied law, acquired a Ph.D. in government and history at Johns Hopkins University, joined the faculty at Princeton in 1890, became its president in 1902, became Democratic governor of New Jersey in 1910, and won the presidency of the United States in 1912 in a three-way race.

His choice of an academic career does not suggest political ambitions—college teaching is seldom a springboard to the presidency—and he was fifty-four when he first ran for office as governor of New Jersey. But he had grand ambitions and he yearned to be great. While still in graduate school he expressed these in a letter to his future wife, writing that "a sort of calm confidence of great things to be accomplished has come over me." And at Princeton, when it appeared that an academic career was his only destiny, he wrote a friend: "I do feel a very real regret that I have been shut out from my heart's first—primary—ambition, which was to take an active, if possible a leading part in public life and strike out for myself . . . a statesman's career."

His ambitions were not unwarranted, given his abilities. In his years at Princeton he acquired a national reputation for his public addresses and essays published in such leading magazines as the <u>Atlantic Monthly</u>, many of which were collected and published in book form. Though not a profound thinker he was perceptive, had a remarkable clarity of expression, and a talent for catching the essence of a thought in a striking phrase. On the public platform these qualities made him impressive and effective and few possessed his ability to bring people around to his point of view.

Though his views up to the time he accepted the Democratic nomination for governor of New Jersey were hardly noted for their liberal character, in his campaign and then as governor he made it clear that he was his own man, not the Democratic machine's, and he put through a series of important reform measures that won over progressive elements throughout the state and propelled him onto the national political scene within two years. In offices where he could act strongly—the governorship and the presidency—his liberal democratic instincts came to the fore. He believed that people were essentially decent, and once told his daughter Eleanor that "most people are fundamentally good—of that I am sure. Don't let a few cheap and dishonest ones hurt you." He believed that democracy offered opportunity to all, eloquently declaring that

> Nature pays no tribute to aristocracy, subscribes to no creed or caste, renders fealty to no monarchy or master of any name or kind. Genius is no snob. . . . It affects humble company as well as great. It . . . chooses its own comrades, its own haunts, its own cradle even. . . . This is the sacred mystery of democracy, that its richest fruits spring up out of soils which no man has prepared and in circumstances amidst which they are the least expected. . . . The test of every American must always be, not where he is but what he is. That, also, is of the essence of democracy.

Too much can probably be made of Wilson's tendency to view issues in a moral light, thus preventing compromise. In a much-quoted remark to a colleague at Princeton who noted that there were two sides to every question, Wilson replied, "Yes, a right side and a wrong side." And once when asked by reporters about his position on a bill he was promoting in the Congress, he said, "When you get a chance just say that I am not the kind that considers compromise when I once take my position." Yet in his career Wilson on numerous occasions changed his stand and demonstrated an ability to get along with those who disagreed with him.

Nevertheless, deeply ingrained in his beliefs was the conviction that service to humanity was the highest duty one could perform. He also believed that some people, among whom he unquestionably included himself, were better qualified for this task than others. This is a view which, if you consider that the stakes are high enough, can lead to the assumption that you know what is best for others better than they do themselves and that it is therefore your moral duty to act for them.

In essence this is what happened to Wilson in World War I. He regarded war with moral repugnance, had no wish to see the United States involved, and successfully kept the nation out for two and a half years. When forced to change his stance and lead America into the war, he had to place the action on the highest grounds possible. The cause would be war to save the world for democracy, war to end war. Victory alone was not enough, as he recognized better than most. Out of victory must come a plan to prevent this catastrophe from happening again, and so he became committed to the League of Nations as a way to save the world from itself.

It was a useful proposal, but Wilson viewed it in terms of a mission so grand and all-encompassing, so noble in purpose, that no alteration was possible. Minor compromises would have secured ratification in the United States Senate of both the Peace Treaty and the League, and would not have weakened the League's chance to prove itself in the arena of world affairs. But Wilson was unable to compromise. In his mind the method had become totally identified with the goal; the League was world peace. In September 1919, on his speaking tour across the country to rally public support for his position, he prophetically noted that "I can predict with absolute certainty that within another generation there will be another world war if the nations of the world do not concert the method by which to prevent it." It is debatable whether a League of Nations of which the United States was a member would have prevented another world war, but certainly its chances of success would have been considerably better than they turned out to be.

Wilson's tragedy was that faced with one of the great decisions of his life, he failed to recognize that there is more than one road to Rome. He became a prophet, not a leader. It is a dangerous matter to take on one's shoulders the burden of saving mankind, and to assume that you alone have the key to salvation.

The strain of his speaking tour was too great. He collapsed and suffered a stroke. Most people when suffering a massive physical illness reassess themselves, and in their appreciation of survival are likely to adopt a more relaxed view of life's problems. Not so with Wilson. His stroke seemed to make him more intractable than ever. Though he had recovered his mental powers by the time the Treaty came up for consideration in the Senate, he refused to give way, and without concessions from him the Treaty died. So did he, unrelenting, in 1924.

Part Two

MODERN TIMES

1919–1975

1919	Red Scare
1920	Eighteenth and Nineteenth Amendments
1921	Washington Disarmament Conference; Treaty of Versailles rejected
1923	President Harding's death; Teapot Dome Scandal
1927	Lindbergh's flight to Paris; pact to outlaw war
1929	Panic and depression
1932	Franklin Roosevelt elected
1933	The Hundred Days of New Deal legislation
1935	Wagner (National Labor Relations) Act
1940	Roosevelt elected to third term; first peacetime draft
1941	Pearl Harbor attacked; U.S. in World War II
1945	Germany and Japan surrendered; Roosevelt died; United Nations founded; A-Bomb dropped at Hiroshima
1946	Cold War began
1947	Truman Doctrine announced; Marshall Plan for European recovery; Taft-Hartley Act to regulate labor unions
1948	Truman elected over Dewey in upset
1950	U.S. assisted UN in Korea; Joseph McCarthy led Red Scare
1954	*Brown* v. *Board of Education of Topeka* (racial segregation illegal); U.S. involved in Southeast Asia
1960	John F. Kennedy elected; New Frontier program
1963	Kennedy assassinated; civil rights demonstrations
1964	Gulf of Tonkin Resolution; Civil Rights Act
1965	Voting Rights Act
1968	Richard Nixon elected
1972	Detente with Russia and China; withdrawal from Viet Nam began; Watergate incident during election campaign
1974	President Nixon, in danger of impeachment, resigned
1975	War in Vietnam ended

Chapter 8
THE
TWENTIES

The Spirit of the Times
A GOLDEN, TROUBLED AGE

The 1920s has often been portrayed as a decade when the Americans momentarily lost their heads, much like some respectable gentleman who suddenly realizes that his fortieth birthday is at hand and his youth is behind him, and he finds himself in a strange town and takes off on a last fling. A decade of speakeasies and bathtub gin, flappers doing the Charleston, jazz, gangsters in flashy suits, college boys careening about the countryside in Stutz Bearcats, everybody shooting for a fast fortune on the stock market, expatriates sipping wine in the bistros of Paris, youth burning the candle at both ends with Edna St. Vincent Millay.

And in a way, that was the sort of decade it was. It did have a zany quality about it, including the inevitable day of reckoning, of sobering up in the cold gray dawn of depression. The critic Malcolm Cowley, looking back on the twenties, wrote that it was great to be alive in that decade, "yet on coming out of it one felt a sense of relief, as on coming out of a room too full of talk and people into the sunlight of the winter streets."

But the twenties were much more than an interlude of casual irresponsibility. They were the decade when the forces and experiences long influencing the shape of American society and thought came to abrupt maturity—when disappointed idealism turned to disillusioned skepticism which emerged with explosive suddenness to become the dominant tone of the emotional climate. In this sense the 1920s mark the emergence of America as we know it today. A new world came into being that was quite different from the world of only a decade before. It was hard to get used to at first: you did not know whether to be exhilarated or frightened, and almost no one understood the full implications of this new world and the direction in which it was moving. Little wonder that the impact of its arrival created problems of adjustment and concern with which we are still struggling half a century later.

Given all this, it is not surprising that the 1920s are familiar to us today in a way no earlier decade is. It is not mere nostalgia that makes us able to see ourselves as living in the 1920s, whereas we cannot really visualize ourselves as living in the

The transformed landscape of the 1920s. Products—automobiles,
refrigerators, packaged foods—shaped lifestyles more than any other force in
the past.

America of 1900 or of 1860. For the twenties is contemporary America on a reduced
scale, the America of automobiles, highways, radio, motion pictures, vitamins,
airplanes, big business, organized crime, ethnic consciousness, minority protest,
mass advertising, mixed faith and doubt, and a host of other phenomena we
associate with our own time. Not quite the same of course, for ideas change and
expand, attitudes shift, circumstances alter. But the last six decades form a recog-
nizable whole, they are parts of one pattern, and they have things in common that
they do not share with the decades before 1920.

Industrial Expansion and the Boom

In the 1920s America's urban population for the first time surpassed its rural
population. By 1930 69 million out of 123 million Americans were classified
as city dwellers. It was especially significant that the population increased by
one-third in cities over 100,000 in size, for the size of the city was one
measure of the industrial concentration it represented. The change was underscored by the fact that 13 million left the farm in the 1920s. Industrial
growth paralleled the astonishing expansion of the cities. Manufacturing

increased by 64 percent, and at the opening of the decade was contributing three times as much as agriculture to the national income. Industrial productivity as a whole almost doubled in the 1920s. The financial resources behind this industrial expansion also increased dramatically. Total banking resources doubled, while the resources of life insurance and building and loan associations expanded threefold.

This surge of industrial expansion rested in part on the development of mass advertising and new and refined sales techniques, which made people product-conscious. It was also aided by the extensive application of Frederick Taylor's principles of "scientific management," improved techniques for handling employee relationships. But the fundamental causes were technological. The moving assembly line first used by Henry Ford enormously increased production. It was in the 1920s that industry adopted electricity as its major source of power. And thousands of innovations in machinery and mechanical processes continually increased production and cut cost, so that the same number of workers were employed in manufacturing in 1929 as in 1920.

Productivity in major industries such as petroleum, steel, and telephones expanded several times over. Previously insignificant industries such as chemicals and synthetics exploded in productivity. The production of rayon alone increased over 6,000 percent, and together with celanese, an artificial silk, created the synthetic textile industry. Established industries such as construction also boomed as factories, office buildings, houses, apartments, and stores multiplied. As the automobile freed people from the city, suburbs expanded: the borough of Queens (New York City) doubled while Grosse Point (Detroit) grew 700 percent. Everywhere was heard the sound of the hammer and the rivet. Roads and highways were built on a vast scale to accommodate the automobile. The auto industry became the single most important in America. In economic terms alone, to say nothing of its social and cultural impact, it transformed American life. By 1929 over 4.8 million cars were rolling off the assembly lines each year, and there were some 26 million cars and trucks using the new highways. The ratio of cars to people was about one per family. The rise of the automobile industry lay at the heart of the new American industrial system: it was the major consumer of rubber, glass, nickel, and lead; it purchased 15 percent of the steel produced in America; it was the major stimulus for the extraordinary growth of the petroleum industry; it created the demand for good roads and highways; it stimulated scores of other businesses from gas stations and garages to roadside motels and billboard advertising. Directly or indirectly it gave employment to over 4 million workers.

All this constitutes only a partial catalogue of the industrial expansion of the 1920s, one of the wonders of the modern world. No other nation even came close to this achievement. The major economic problem of this incredible growth was that the number of affluent consumers did not increase at the same rate as the goods produced. Failure to recognize and deal with this problem contributed to the breakdown after 1929.

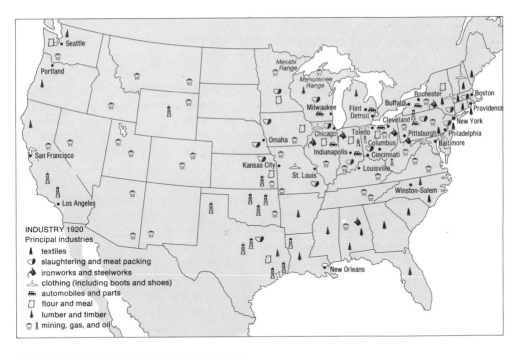

INDUSTRY 1920
Principal industries
- textiles
- slaughtering and meat packing
- ironworks and steelworks
- clothing (including boots and shoes)
- automobiles and parts
- flour and meal
- lumber and timber
- mining, gas, and oil

THE EXPANSION OF INDUSTRY BY 1920

Prosperity—and Want But for the time being, all this expansion brought remarkable prosperity. Total national wealth almost doubled from what it had been on the eve of World War I; per-capita income was higher than it had ever been in the world; wages were at an all-time high and hours had been cut, the average work week being slightly more than forty hours. But there were areas in the economy that did not share in this broad prosperity. Agriculture received only twelve percent of the national income although it still had forty-five percent of the population. Soft-coal mining and the textile industry were experiencing hard times, and their labor force suffered accordingly. The average rate of unemployment in the decade was just under five percent. Only twenty-five percent of the national income went to the lower forty percent of the population, while half the income ended in the pockets of the top twenty percent. Even though prosperity for the society as a whole was greater than ever, millions yet lived in want and squalor. Productivity by itself was clearly not the final measure of economic achievement, although those who did the producing seemed to be under the impression that it was.

Even so, the growth of the twenties did increase the extent and scope of material comfort and pleasure as never before. Even people with low incomes now had a greater choice in the way they could spend their money. It became clear, for example, that many would prefer to save on food and clothing in order to buy an automobile. And for those with adequate incomes, the list of things to buy became very long indeed. In this sense industrial growth changed the lives of millions of Americans. The automobile made people far more mobile than ever before. The great American habit of visiting acquired new flexibility and ease, and the modern movement to the out-of-doors, to "seeing America," began. The electrification of homes, except on farms, brought not just cheap illumination, but a host of electric servants: refrigerators, washing machines, sewing machines, toasters, vacuum cleaners, and many more. And beyond comfort and convenience lay pleasure. Radio sales rose from $60 million in 1922 to $852 million by 1929, opening up new vistas of information and entertainment. Though much that came over the airwaves was not worth hearing, there were operas and symphony concerts, and the beginnings of what was to become in the next decade a great informational network. Already a significant form of entertainment when the decade opened, the motion picture became a major source of inexpensive pleasure for the masses by the end of the decade. By 1929 weekly attendance was over 100 million—almost once a week for every person in the country. Technological improvements, including the introduction of sound before the end of the decade, made the movies a major industry. By 1930 there were over 23,000 motion picture theatres, more than $2 billion were invested in the industry, and it employed over 325,000 people.

Thus the 1920s brought great change in living habits, desires, and values, in what people regarded as important and what they wanted out of life. And this held as true for those of meager income as for the affluent. Ford's Model-T was selling for $290 in 1926; what was once a toy of the rich had become a mechanical servant of the humble. Once only the well-to-do could command the pleasure of the opera house or concert hall; now a flick of the radio dial could bring fine music to the home. The concept of the good life was being radically changed for ordinary people everywhere.

The Glorification of Business   Another impact of industrial expansion was the glorification of the business system and its leaders for making all this possible. Despite the obvious fact that a variety of people had a hand in creating the new prosperity—scientists, engineers, inventors, technicians, workers skilled and unskilled, and even government—many people attributed this achievement largely to the private enterprise system and its managers, the business leaders of the country. President Coolidge, who had a knack for the trite but pithy phrase, observed that "the business of America is business," and blandly pronounced that "the man who builds a factory builds a temple, and the man who works there worships there." If the coal miner or the farmer had doubts about the profundity of these remarks, or the cultural values they reflected, many others did not. And they were encouraged in their conviction by business itself, which was seldom guilty of modesty. Expanded public-relations departments in many businesses proclaimed that the crude excesses of business leaders belonged to an earlier age, called attention to the rising philanthropic activities of the business community, and noted the benevolent concern of corporations for the communities in which they operated.

One day's production of Model T's. Ford's decision to concentrate on a single inexpensive model made possible the application of mass production techniques to the automobile industry, and created a vehicle accessible to millions.

The businessman, far from appearing as the arrogant proponent of his own self-interest who could be denounced as the cause of anybody's troubles, as had been true in the 1890s, was now a figure of almost pious regard. A major example of this new respect was the veneration accorded Henry Ford. A group of college students in the 1920s voted Ford the third greatest figure in world history, placing him after Jesus Christ and Napoleon. It is hard to say how far the public at large saw American business as the highest achievement of civilization, as one business writer proclaimed, or felt that businessmen knew better than anyone else what was good for the country. But in much of the public press, business was accorded the highest praise and everything seemed to be analyzed in business terms and judged by business standards. In his book, *The Man Nobody Knows*, a best-seller in the middle of the decade when the boom was at its peak, the popular writer Bruce Barton described Christ as one of the great businessmen in all history: "He picked up twelve men from the bottom ranks of business and forged them into an organization that conquered the world." Christ's preaching became salesmanship and the parables "the most powerful advertisements of all time." Businessmen sat high in government, dominated the boards of colleges, and served as lay directors of churches. If a large number of Americans were not under the impression that business was one of the great achievements of the ages, they were remarkably quiet about it.

The Growth of Materialism   The drive for material gain and comfort was nothing new in American life. It had been a powerful motive in immigration, it drove many to seek greener pastures in the West, and it had always been an element in democratic aspiration. But now so many material things seemed within grasp that it seemed to overshadow all other values, and was not a means to an end but the purpose of life itself.

Many foreign observers of our "unheard of triumphs in all spheres of material aggrandizement" felt uneasy with this preoccupation. The Latin American critic of the United States José Enrique Rodó found the North Americans lacking in public and private morality, in sensitivity, and in culture, as a consequence of this obsession. Even American science was less a search for truth than for something useful. The German professor of aesthetics and philosophy Richard Müller-Frienfels felt that America had made quantity, not quality, the measure of life, and he saw our mechanization and materialism as stifling the human personality. André Siegfried, a perceptive French observer, noted that America "is a materialistic society, organized to produce things rather than people." Sigfried saw originality and individual talent smothered under a baleful materialism, with human beings as standardized as the products they consumed.

Of course there were other things going on in America, in religion, in the arts, in the pursuit of knowledge. But many Americans judged even these activities in material terms. A book was good if it sold a million copies, a play was judged on how long it ran, a church was assessed on the size of its membership, a scientific discovery for its contribution to the national wealth. America's incredible industrial success in the twenties exalted materialism in the hierarchy of values, and created problems our society has been struggling with ever since.

The Environment   The industrial-technological explosion of the 1920s also had a massive impact on the natural environment. From the time of the first settlements the environment had undergone extensive change. We cut down trees, destroyed wildlife, and plowed the prairies. With the rise of industry forests were mutilated, natural resources gouged out of the earth, rivers loaded with industrial wastes. Inevitably, the explosive growth of the 1920s speeded this process enormously. New industries spewed their wastes into air and stream. The earth was ravaged for the raw wealth needed to satisfy the appetite of the machine. The automobile began its career of befouling the air. The sudden unplanned expansion of towns and cities steadily ate into farm lands and created widening stains of macadam and steel, tied together with ribbons of concrete. Few things indicate the extent of the American commitment to an expanding industrial society like their lack of concern for the natural world. People were cheered for their exploitation of nature, not for what they did to protect it. In the general euphoria about the artificial wealth created, few gave any thought at all to the natural wealth destroyed.

Science the Liberator

Behind the machine beat the creative impulse of scientific knowledge, and business clearly recognized this fact. By 1927 over a thousand of the largest firms were supporting their own research and development laboratories out of which flowed new products and improved industrial processes. It was obvious to most that the application of scientific knowledge was rapidly changing the nature of American society. Nor was there any doubt in the minds of most that all this was beneficial. Science was extending human horizons and making life fuller and more attractive. More and more sophisticated machinery appeared to be removing the age-old curse of backbreaking labor, reducing the need for long hours, and opening the possibility of increased leisure. Through such achievements as the automobile, the airplane, the radio, and the motion picture, science appeared to be providing people with control over time and space and thus giving them greater power than ever before to shape their own destinies. Scientific advances had also improved health and extended the life span. By 1930 the life expectancy of a newborn baby in America was sixty years, unprecedented in human history. The toll from diseases such as tuberculosis, pneumonia, and diphtheria dropped sharply. An antitoxin for scarlet fever was developed.

Most basic research was still done abroad, though the American skill in applying it was unmatched. But by the 1920s American scientists in university laboratories and private research institutes began to pay more attention to basic research. World War I had proved the value of projects without immediate practical application and showed that basic research was best done in universities. This led to a new attitude in governmental, industrial, philanthrophic, and academic circles. The International Education Board and the General Education Board backed by Rockefeller funds, the National Research Council, the Guggenheim Foundation and others poured funds into the upgrading of scientific training in key American universities as well as European scientific institutes; the best of America's young scientists were sent abroad on post-doctoral studies; the topnotch Europeans were brought to American institutions. Doctoral students and degrees tripled in the 1920s, and by the 1930s the groundwork had been established for American leadership in theoretical and basic scientific research. The 1920s also saw the first steps by corporate laboratories in basic research, beginning with DuPont's commitment in 1927. And through the public press the Americans gained a popular knowledge of basic research in genetics, astronomy, and physics that promised a greatly improved understanding of humanity, nature, and the universe. In a multitude of ways, therefore, science seemed to the average American of the 1920s a force for good.

Science and Doubt   At the same time science and its influence were producing among intellectuals disillusionment and doubt. The machine was seen as dehumanizing, not as humanity's servant but as the master of more and more people tied to its operation and its products. The values of the machine took precedence over human values. Lewis Mumford argued in 1923 that mass production kept workers from any sense of participating in the creation of a whole product, and hence alienated them from the fruit of their labor.

New glimpses into the world of the atom, where particles were so small as to be almost beyond comprehension, and the world of stars so vast as to frighten thought away, showed people a universe in which they were an accident of unimaginable insignificance. As science advanced, the supernatural, which had once given meaning and comfort to human existence, retreated. The English philosopher Bertrand Russell stated his pessimistic view of what all this meant, and a number of American intellectuals agreed.

> That Man is the product of causes which had no prevision of the end they were achieving; that his origin, his growth, his hopes and fears, his loves and his beliefs, are but the outcome of accidental collocations of atoms; that no fire, no heroism, no intensity of thought and feelings, can preserve an individual life beyond the grave; that all labors of the ages, all the devotion, all the inspiration, all the noonday brightness of human genius, are destined to extinction in the vast death of the solar system, and that the whole temple of man's achievement must inevitably be buried beneath the debris of a universe in ruins—all these things, if not quite beyond dispute, are yet so nearly certain, that no philosophy which rejects them can hope to stand.

This could scarcely be called a philosophy of comfortable optimism.

The growing skepticism of some American intellectuals was well expressed by Joseph Wood Krutch in his book *The Modern Temper* in 1929. The problem, he wrote, is that science has increased our power but not our happiness or our wisdom: "We are disillusioned with the laboratory not because we have lost faith in the truth of its findings, but because we have lost faith in the power of those findings to help us as generally as we had once hoped they might help." Intellectuals are always asking why society is not as attractive as they think it should be. In an earlier age, they had found an explanation in people's misusing the word of God. Now they found it in people's abusing the word of science. Few ordinary Amerians in the 1920s were aware of these uncertainties and doubts, but they were to color the national mood increasingly in the years to come.

Social and Cultural Change

More Freedom for Women The demands for labor in World War I had drawn women into the labor force in large numbers in a variety of jobs. With the economic expansion of the 1920s, even more women entered the labor market. By the end of the decade more than ten million women held jobs. But for the most part positions in the economic world were not open to women on an equal basis with men. While some women served in managerial positions or heaved cargo on the waterfront along with male stevedores, they were the exception, not the rule. Women continued to be regarded as

THE DECLINING BIRTH RATE

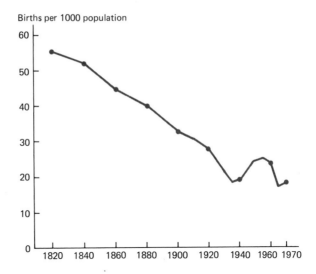

Births per 1000 population

particularly suited to clerical and secretarial positions, to teaching in elementary schools, to serving customers in stores and shops. Even in such jobs their pay was rarely equal to men's. Yet jobs did help to provide a degree of freedom for more and more women, the idea of women working, especially in the cities, became respectable, and wives helped to support their families, a role traditionally confined to men. Yet only ten percent of married women were employed outside the home. Unmarried women with jobs often lived on their own in apartments, resident hotels, or boarding houses. In any case, working gave women a degree of freedom and choice that they increasingly felt entitled to.

Women entered the 1920s with the right to vote granted by the Nineteenth Amendment passed in 1919. Yet the right to vote did not produce the significant changes in political life that many women had anticipated. The critic and social commentator H. L. Mencken had gleefully predicted that the chief result of women's suffrage would be that adultery would replace boozing as the chief pastime of politicians. As it happened, the expectations of neither Mencken nor the feminists were realized. Many women failed to exercise the vote, many were indifferent to the issues, and many simply voted as their husbands suggested. Since many men behaved in exactly the same fashion, perhaps this was one area at least in which women achieved equality. Occasional women went into politics, lobbying for a cause or even running for office. But politics in general remained a man's world.

Weakening Family Ties Trends long observed in the American family accelerated in the 1920s, especially in cities. The birth rate steadily declined, dropping from twenty-four per thousand to less than nineteen by 1930. Farm families continued to be large, but this was more than offset by the decline in the cities, where smaller families reflected many aspects of modern urban

Percent of population 14 years old and over

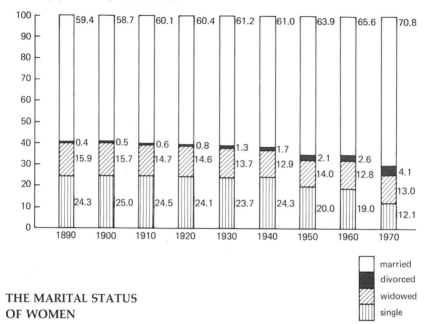

THE MARITAL STATUS
OF WOMEN

married
divorced
widowed
single

society: the availability and social acceptance of contraception, the more confined space of urban apartments, the greater influence of a materialism, which found many parents preferring to provide well for one or two children than inadequately for more, and the desire of more and more women not to be confined as closely to home and hearth as a large family required.

For a long time the school, the factory, government, and mass entertainment had been steadily taking over varied social and economic functions the family had performed in the past and which bound it together. That trend too was greatly advanced in the 1920s, and it is easy to see why. With mass education a reality by then—eighty-two percent of the five- to seventeen-year-olds were in public schools—the young spent more time in the classroom and with their peers than with their families, and the school and peer group exerted greater influences in values, attitudes, and standards.

A great variety of social activities drew all family members out of the home as individuals, but rarely any longer as families. Men went to club or lodge meetings, such as the Masons or the Elks, women went to jobs or to social or service groups, young people went to the myriad of organizations and sports now available to them, and all went to the movies of their choice, often as individuals, not as a family. Almost the only influences in modern urban life that drew families together were the radio and the automobile. Family members often grouped together around the radio in the evening to listen to a favorite program, and although the young soon learned to commandeer the car for an evening, family outings by automobile were common. One father commented that "I never feel as close to my family as when we are all together in the car"—although the contact may well have been more physical than social.

So the success of a modern family tended to rest on two functions that previously had been minor: the personal relationships between husband and wife, and between parents and children. Given the delicate structure of such relationships and their relative unimportance in the past, the modern family faced difficulties of monumental proportions. An understanding and knowledge of human relationships was required of which few Americans were capable. It is not surprising that by 1929 the number of divorces had risen to 205,000 and the United States had the highest divorce rate in the world with the possible exception of the Soviet Union.

Psychology and Sex   Many urban middle-class women wanted marriage to provide personal satisfaction, to be a partnership, not a relation between superior and subordinate. Consequently the help afforded by psychology became more and more important, either directly through psychoanalysis and counseling, or indirectly through books and articles. For many women manners, behavior, and even dress became symbols of the demand for sexual equality—witness the short skirt, the skimpy dress, bobbed hair, smoking in public, drinking, even entering the speakeasy as casually as the beauty salon.

The turn to psychology for better understanding of marital relations was extended to a search for guidance in child-rearing. Dr. John B. Watson's ideas on behaviorism became widely popular. Watson argued that environment was the key factor in child-rearing, and that if parents manipulated the environment properly they could turn their children into anything they wanted them to be. The validity of this assertion was completely open to question, but even if it had not been, parents discovered that the environment of the city was more than they could counteract, especially since the young spent more and more time outside the home. The young soon found in the automobile a mode of escape from parental observation and control.

It has often been said that the 1920s saw great liberalization in sexual relations. The point is open to some question. Some moralists believed that women's fashions, drinking, "erotic" dancing, youthful partying without chaperones, and similar freedom of behavior was immoral. But it is doubtful that drinking illegal as opposed to legal liquor had much to do with sex, or that short skirts and peculiar hats led to licentious behavior. What is clear is that sex was much talked and written about, in conversation, magazine articles, books, plays, movies, and advertising. Indeed it was in the 1920s that America began its great love affair with sex.

Much of this discussion, which in its openness and extent did constitute a significant change, was stimulated by the popularization of the ideas of Freud. Increasing attention had been paid to psychology before World War I

Sigmund Freud

and Freud's ideas had become familiar to intellectuals and to the medical profession. By 1916 some five hundred people calling themselves psychoanalysts were operating in New York City alone, and the use of psychological testing during the war had made many Americans aware of the spreading influence of this discipline. In the 1920s psychology attracted attention for the aid it could presumably offer marriage partners and parents, and in other ways became a major fad. Books appeared on such topics as the psychology of your golf game, and you could get *Ten Thousand Dreams Interpreted* through the Sears and Roebuck catalogue. Over all this hovered the presence of Freud. In the discussion of sex there was the popular if erroneous impression that Freud was in essence providing people with a license for indulging their appetites, and that sex was the principal motivation in human behavior.

The overall effect was a startling contrast to the mores of the past. Men and women in mixed groups discussed sexual inhibitions, and words once scrawled on fences dropped lightly off the tongues of "enlightened" ladies in living rooms. The young talked about, and perhaps engaged in, petting or necking, which caused Lloyd Morris to observe later that the word "neck" ceased to be a noun, suddenly became a verb, and could no longer be located anatomically with any precision. Tin Pan Alley took up the subject, and crooners were soon singing songs like "Hot Lips" and "Burning Kisses." Magazines such as *Paris Nights* and *Flapper Experiences* played upon the theme to commercial profit if not intellectual enlightenment. Advertising began to work sex into its copy, resulting, as one observer noted, in the transformation of soap from a cleansing agent into an aphrodisiac. Before censorship arrived at the end of the decade, the movies created the American love goddess, of whom one of the earliest was the "vamp" Theda Bara, a type who has been with us in one form or another ever since. Movie ads promised "brilliant men, beautiful jazz babies, champagne baths, midnight revels, petting parties in the purple dawn, all ending in one terrific smashing climax that makes you gasp." Near nudity in the films was not uncommon. A number of writers such as the dramatist Eugene O'Neill and the novelist Conrad Aiken used Freudian themes as major tools for understanding human motivation, and less able writers used sex to expand their bank accounts.

Much of the evidence that there was a sexual revolution—whatever that is—probably reflected more than anything else the rising demand for equality by women and the growing independence of youth. Open discussion of sex, however much it distressed the older generation and the rural population, helped to eliminate hypocrisy and stimulate healthier attitudes toward one of the basic drives of human nature. The cheap commercial exploitation of this more open attitude by advertising, the movies, and writers making money out of sensationalism was one of the less attractive aspects of this broadened attitude.

Literature and the Arts

The rising sense of alienation in serious writers and intellectuals of the 1920s opened a large gap between them and the rest of American society. The literature of the 1920s was by no means optimistic in tone, nor did it accept the widespread values of the business cult. A volume published in 1922 edited by literary critic Harold Stearns, *Civilization in the United States,* took the view that American society had become culturally barren and intellectually sterile through the impact of materialism, technology, and business. Yet the decade produced one of the great outpourings of literary talent in American history: Fitzgerald, Hemingway, Faulkner, John Dos Passos, Sinclair Lewis, Thomas Wolfe, Sherwood Anderson, Eugene O'Neill, T. S. Eliot, Carl Sandburg, Robert Frost, and others. Lewis, Hemingway, Faulkner, and O'Neill were later to win Nobel prizes, and all began their significant work in the twenties.

A Generation of Protest   Some writers, such as Sinclair Lewis, set out specifically to chronicle the shallow materialism, moral corruption, and vulgarity of middle-class American society. In *Main Street* and *Babbitt* Lewis criticized the materialism and narrowness of the business and social world of the middle-American small city. In *Arrowsmith* he portrayed the medical profession as equally materialistic. In *Elmer Gantry* he showed how church and clergy also had become tainted by business values, focusing on a caricature of the evangelist Aimee Semple McPherson and her money-making temple in Los Angeles. And he closed the decade with *Dodsworth,* not so

F. Scott Fitzgerald, his wife Zelda,
and daughter Scottie celebrate
Christmas in Paris.

much this time a contemptuous as a sympathetic portrait of a successful but decent American businessman who lost his soul and self in pursuit of the dollar.

By and large, however, the serious writers of the time were not concerned with exposing specific aspects of American society in Lewis's journalistic and sociological vein. Their disappointment with America was shown in their indifference to it, their flight to Paris, and their increasing concern with the individual rather than with society, with the inner experience of the individual or of a region rather than with the country as a whole. They rejected the idea of society and perceived meaning only in the individual perception of experience. Hemingway's Lieutenant Frederick Henry in *A Farewell to Arms* turned aside in disgust from society's values as expressed in the experience of World War I:

> I was always embarrassed by the words sacred, glorious, and sacrifice and the expression in vain. We had heard them . . . and read them, on proclamations that were slapped up by billposters over other proclamations, now for a long time, and I had seen nothing sacred, and the things that were glorious had no glory, and the sacrifices were like the stockyards at Chicago if nothing was done with the meat except to bury it.

Hemingway's preoccupation with the individual under pressure was expressed in a brilliantly concrete and evocative style in his stories of war, bullfighting, hunting, and other forms of violence, in his *The Sun Also Rises* and *A Farewell to Arms*, and in a number of short stories. Equally intense and

George Gershwin at the piano.

modern but more profound were the brooding explorations of O'Neill in his dramas on the inner psychological agony of individual personalities, as in *Beyond the Horizon, The Great God Brown,* and *Strange Interlude.* And Scott Fitzgerald, in his portrayals of the "jazz age" in *This Side of Paradise,* and the idle rich in *The Great Gatsby,* caught the fatal weakness of the age in its frantic pursuit of false values as no other writer managed to do, even though he himself was infected by that weakness. "Here was . . . a new generation," he concluded in *This Side of Paradise,* "dedicated more than the last to the fear of poverty and the worship of success, grown up to find all gods dead, all wars fought, all faiths in men shaken."

Although the critic George Jean Nathan may have been exaggerating, he clearly expressed the essence of this social rejection when he wrote:

> The great problems of the world—social, political, economic, and theological—do not concern me in the slightest. If all the Armenians were to be killed tomorrow and if half of Russia were to starve to death the day after, it would not matter to me in the least. What concerns me alone is myself, and the interests of a few close friends. For all I care the rest of the world may go to hell at today's sunset.

For serious writers in the twenties, then, society aroused no sense of responsibility as it had done in the past; only the self seemed valid. Yet in this they were like many other Americans of the decade, whose freewheeling pursuit of the material good life also meant an abandonment of any sense of social responsibility.

American Music Grows Up Except for literature, only music among the arts was strikingly original, although music, painting, sculpture, and architecture all reflected to some extent the effects of technology in a prosperous urban society. By 1925 technology, in the development of electrically transcribed recordings, had improved fidelity, although old-style phonographs prevented their widespread enjoyment until much later. Radio of course also broadened the audience for music and greatly extended the variety available. Major schools of music—Eastman in Rochester, New York; Juilliard in New York City; and Curtis Institute in Philadelphia—were founded in the 1920s, greatly extending the number of superbly trained American performers and making them the equal of those in Europe. Interest in music prompted the spread of musical training in high schools, colleges, and universities. By 1920 there were 73 permanent symphony orchestras, 55 chamber-music groups, and 576 choral societies. America still had to import conductors for her top-flight orchestras, among them Serge Koussevitsky and Arturo Toscanini, as well as most of her operatic stars, although a few Americans emerged of a quality high enough to star at the Metropolitan.

Aaron Copland, George Gershwin, and Howard Hanson became in the 1920s the first American composers to acquire international reputations. And it is worth noting that two of them experimented with the most original element in American musical development: the emergence of jazz, or rather jazz-influenced music. Real jazz, as it came out of New Orleans in the spiritual march, the hot music of Storyville dives, and the blues vocal, gradually acquired a hearing in America, but was long limited to black audiences. But the white adaptation, "Dixieland jazz," became popular and was successfully taken up and promoted by such greats as Louis Armstrong, Jelly Roll Morton, and blues singer Bessie Smith. Jazz enormously influenced American music, even in altered form, and George Gershwin showed its versatility in *Rhapsody in Blue, An American in Paris,* and his opera *Porgy and Bess.* Jazz and its influence spread throughout the world with such impact that someone once noted that, except for modern plumbing, jazz seemed to be America's only contribution to world culture.

Some Major Painters The painting of the twenties, though America produced major artists such as John Marin, Georgia O'Keeffe, and Max Weber, had no audience in America comparable to that for literature and music, and was heavily influenced by European innovators, particularly Cézanne. Other modernist trends included abstractionism, cubism, and various experimental forms that seemed particularly apt expressions of a mechanistic-urban culture. Neither sculpture nor architecture were innovative in the 1920s. The growth of the country obviously offered work and creative opportunity in commissions for public and private buildings. But most architects took the work and ignored the opportunity. The inevitable demand for World War I memorials gave sculptors equal opportunity, but with them also there was no creative break from the traditional. The chief exceptions in architecture came from a handful of men such as Frank Lloyd

Brooklyn Bridge *by John Marin.*

Wright, whose work had started earlier. Significantly, however, the rise and expansion of schools of architecture made universities centers for the study of modern design. Thus the University of Michigan invited the Finnish architect of advanced ideas, Eliel Saarinen, to join its faculty.

Education for All

The chief development in education in the decade of the twenties was the final commitment to mass education, in college as at lower levels. A prosperous America not only could afford this, the very nature of a modern industrial technological society required it. By 1928 we were spending more on education than the rest of the world combined: almost three billion dollars a year. The United States had achieved mass elementary education by 1920. High-school enrollments doubled from 1920 to 4.4 million in 1930, which meant that half those of high school age were in school, a proportion unequaled anywhere in the world. In 1920 the colleges were jammed with 600,000 students, but by 1930 that figure had doubled. On the graduate level the rate of increase was even greater: over 2,000 Ph.D.s were awarded in 1930 as against some 500 in 1920.

The Broadened Curriculum   There were other significant changes. It came to be assumed that the schools should teach basic health and hygiene, give training for citizenship and safety, aid in the Americanization of immigrants, give instruction on the dangers of alcohol and tobacco, provide recreational and socializing opportunities, and take on other functions. Few educators resisted these intrusions, and the public by and large approved, since family and church no longer performed these functions.

Moreover, a modern society increasingly required men and women trained in the vocational tasks of an urban-induatrial world. By the end of the 1920s many school systems had extensive vocational programs that were more a replacement than a supplement for the academic. Thus many high-school students learned to handle jobs in commercial offices, in the building trades, printing, automotive and appliance repair work. But to do this successfully required a heavy investment by school districts, many of whose taxpayers objected to the cost if not the purpose. Consequently many schools had only "shops," which became dumping grounds for students not academically inclined, and where the best that could be hoped for was learning how to use a hammer and saw.

These additional responsibilities obviously cut into the capacity of the schools to fulfill their original academic function. Nevertheless, children did as well or better than a generation earlier, primarily because teaching was more effective. Teachers were better trained, methods were improved, and library resources were greatly expanded.

The Colleges Specialize   In colleges and universities also there were significant changes. Although the cost of a college education increased, this did not prevent a rapid rise in enrollments. Some old-fashioned people complained that higher education was a waste of time, but the specialization of a complex society made it a necessity, not a luxury. Engineers, scientists of all kinds, social scientists, and other professional specialists were essential. Business itself had become so complex that the person who rose from the ranks was now more the exception than the rule.

Schools of engineering and business expanded greatly, and were responsible for much of the increase in male enrollment. Businesses became committed to the college-educated in their recruitment programs. Private philanthropic funds in the millions of dollars, channeled through the National Research Council, the General Education Fund, the American Council of Learned Societies, the Social Science Research Council and similar agencies, contributed to an astonishing leap forward in the quality of research and training. Public funds for state universities and colleges increased. Critics at home and abroad complained that mass higher education in the United States was lowering standards and flooding the colleges with young people not much interested in or capable of university work. Certainly the colleges admitted many young people seeking only a good time and the status of a degree. But by 1930 higher education in America had reached its highest level in the nation's history, had shaken off its dependence on Europe, and had advanced to a position of world leadership in the sciences and in the social sciences.

Social Unrest

Religious Tensions   Religion and the church were also much affected by the pressures of the 1920s. The churches prospered with the general prosperity of the decade. Their wealth grew steadily and their membership increased. By 1930 half the population claimed some church affiliation, a significant increase over past decades. Yet these figures reflect no deep religious experience. Many clearly felt, as one church-goer put it, that "Even if going to church doesn't give us anything else, it at least gives us the habit of going to church," not exactly a reflection of deep piety. For many people church-going came to be simply ritualistic, a social rather than a religious experience. Many churches were in part at fault. Liberal churches were often involved in social work, and in trying to compete with secular activities for the attention of their parishioners they tended to become secular themselves. Some clergymen, too, were swept up in the cult of business—indeed many churches had heavy business investments—and promoted religion in their sermons as though they were advertising cigarettes. They sometimes urged prayer on their parishioners as a way to improve their economic fortunes and achieve business success.

The rising tempo of modernism inclined many urban churches, though certainly not all, to an accommodation between religion and science, an accommodation which played down traditional views on doctrine. This influence became widespread as the five leading theological seminaries adopted liberal views. This development in itself tended to lessen the traditional distinctions between denominations. At any rate, a survey in the twenties revealed that few Protestant divinity students believed in hell and damnation, the Bible as divine inspiration, or the Virgin Birth.

The tensions these developments produced between modernists and fundamentalists were more acute than at any earlier time because more than religious differences were involved. For the fundamentalist position rejecting the theory of evolution was deeply rooted in rural America though it was also preached from many city pulpits, and the modernist position was centered in the city though it had adherents in the countryside. In a decade that saw the dominance of the city and all the forces of technology, industrialism, and big business that had made the modern city, rural America often felt that its back was to the wall. It was the city that lured the young and manipulated the national wealth, and where the key economic decisions were made affecting their lives. It was the city that sheltered foreign influences, housed the universities where the young were shorn of the ideas of their parents, where entertainment and pleasure diverted people from honest toil. Even in the poorer rural areas urban influence touched the lives of the people in one way or another. The result was the last sharp tension between city and country.

Rural America might well have made a rational defense of its way of life as well as a rational critique of the city—as indeed it did in part—but the tension exploded in a controversy between religion and science that brought credit to neither. This was one of those curious battles in which the opposing forces, by the very nature of things, were not really on the same battlefield but

Clarence Darrow and William Jennings Bryan at the Scopes trial. Bryan was the dedicated reformer who had refused to adapt to modern developments in science and who had become increasingly rigid and intolerant of views that differed from his own. Darrow was the unorthodox criminal lawyer who had begun his career by seeking amnesty for the defendants in the Haymarket riot and then committed himself to political and labor cases. His brilliant cross-examination of Bryan exposed the reformer's bigoted views but failed to establish a review of the constitutional issues. Bryan died five days after the trial ended, and the original law was repealed in 1967.

fought madly as though they were. Fundamentalism was conservative socially, economically, politically, and culturally as well as in matters of religious faith, but it opposed the forces of modern America on religious grounds by attacking the scientific knowledge of humanity and the universe that had come to symbolize the forces of modern America. The scene of the struggle was primarily in the Southern and border states where the contrast between town and country was sharpest. By 1925 five states had some kind of anti-evolution laws put in their statute books by rural-dominated legislatures. In that year the Tennessee legislature, with great reluctance and under immense political pressure, passed a law forbidding any teaching that denied the story of divine creation as related in the Bible. The contrast between rural

and urban America is indicated by the fact that when one of the Northeast-
ern states had a similar bill introduced forbidding any teaching that human
beings had evolved from lower animals, the bill was referred to the Committee on Fish and Game.

At any rate, the law was deliberately challenged in Tennessee, and the
Scopes trial took place, high-school teacher John Scopes being charged with
violating the law by teaching evolution. The most famous trial lawyer in
America, Clarence Darrow, took over for the defense, while William Jennings Bryan, who had long crusaded against the materialism he saw smoth-
ering America's spiritual life, aided the prosecution. The roles both science
and religion could play in the enrichment of people's lives were completely
lost sight of, to say nothing of the point of legislating belief of any kind.
Bryan asserted that the world was created on October 23, 4004 B.C., and yet
admitted that he himself "interpreted" the Bible to conform to his own
views, thus undercutting completely his contention that the Bible was to be
taken literally. Scientists abandoned their presumed objectivity by declaring
that Bryan was demanding to see a monkey or a jackass turned into a man
although he was a good example of the reverse. So it went. Scopes was found
guilty and fined, the State Supreme Court threw out the conviction on a
technicality, and refused to rule on the constitutionality of the law itself. The
whole affair was probably the worst possible example of the changes
wrought in America by the 1920s and the problems and tensions those
changes had produced.

The Red Scare   The years just after World War I were marked by a
continuation of the repressive attitude taken during the war. This was ex-
emplified by the so-called Red Menace threatening America after the Bol-
shevik Revolution in Russia, by the unprecedented wave of strikes after the
war, and by a wave of attacks on federal officials and other prominent
persons by unknown parties sending bombs through the mails. Using federal and state wartime legislation, authorities moved against what they regarded as radicalism. The Lusk Committee of the New York State Legislature investigated not only the Communist party, the Socialist party, and the
Social Labor party, but the Amalgamated Clothing Workers Union, the
International Ladies Garment Workers Union, and other unions, and found
them all a menace to the nation. It claimed that schools, colleges, and
churches were under subversive influence, and it denounced such well-
known and respected Americans as Jane Addams of Hull House, Clarence
Darrow, John Dewey, Helen Keller, Judge Ben Lindsay, Father John Ryan of
Catholic University, and many others. The committee also forced the expul-
sion of five New York state legislators who had been elected on the Socialist
ticket.

The federal government was equally energetic. The offices of the Seattle
Union-Record were raided and closed, the Socialist New York *Call* and the
Milwaukee *Leader* were denied the use of the United States mails, and Victor
Berger, editor of the *Leader*, was denied his seat in the United States House of

Representatives to which he had been duly elected by the voters of Milwaukee. This panic carried over into the deportation insanity of 1920 when the United States government rounded up some 4,000 persons it claimed were radical subversives and managed to deport about 700 of them before the process was brought to a halt by public pressure instituted by well-known and respected lawyers and public figures.

Ethnic and Religious Intolerance Although this brand of hysteria faded under public pressure and exposure, it was succeeded by other developments equally dubious. The closing of immigration by the National Origins Act of 1924 may have been due anyway, and it certainly paralleled the actions of European nations that had begun to restrict emigration. Even so, the act showed both ethnic and religious discrimination, reflecting Anglo-Saxon intolerance of Southern and Eastern Europeans, Jews, Catholics both Orthodox and Roman, and Asians. The irony of this discrimination was that although it limited immigration to 150,000 to be drawn largely from Britain and Western Europe, it said nothing about immigration from the countries of the Northern Hemisphere. And in the twenties some 900,000 Canadians, many of whom were French Roman Catholics, and 500,000 registered immigrants from Mexico plus several hundred thousand more who entered without formal declaration, poured over the borders north and south—the very kind of people whom the ethnically and religiously intolerant were trying to exclude on the grounds that America must be kept racially and culturally "pure."

The Ku Klux Klan The lurking suspicions against alien and dangerous influences coalesced around the Ku Klux Klan, which flourished as the major hate organization of the decade. The growth of the Klan was little short of phenomenal, especially in rural areas, though its influence was strongly felt in the cities as well. Revived about 1915 from the Reconstruction period, it grew from some five thousand members in 1920 to between three and five million by 1925 and was antiblack in the South, anti-Catholic in the Midwest and Far West, and anti-Semitic in the East. Today we may wonder how an organization that operated under the guise of white-robed conspiracy, employed terrorist tactics, and was opposed to so much, could find members at all. But its opposition to anything it regarded as "un-American"—Catholics, Jews, blacks, divorce, short skirts, flirtatous women, gin-drinkers, and immigrants—struck a responsive chord in the hearts of many rural and urban Americans upset by the rapidity of change in America and not knowing what to do about it. Though it denounced blacks, Catholics, Jews, and immigrants, the Klan actually exerted its main pressure on Anglo-Saxon, Protestant Americans from whom it sought to exact a rigid moral behavior its own leadership was unable to demonstrate. The conviction of the Midwest leader of the Klan for rape, assault, and manslaughter brought about popular exposure of its killings, floggings, and threats, and the Klan collapsed. While it

The move North saw the rise of the urban ghetto—physically isolated, dilapidated, and crowded housing shaping the lives of its inhabitants.

was a frightening example of how people could be misled, it was as short-lived as a meteor that flared and burned away in the atmosphere of public exposure.

The Improving Status of Blacks

More disquieting in the long run was the continued ill-treatment of blacks and Indians. Yet the circumstances of black Americans were changing significantly in the twenties. The closing-off of unrestricted immigration left an economic gap that drew more and more blacks to the cities. By 1930, approximately 1.4 million—some twenty percent of the total black population—had moved to Northern cities where prosperity gave opportunity for employment. Yet this opportunity remained limited for the most part to the poorest jobs. The cities provided the world of the ghetto where blacks were free to be themselves without having to shift to another role in the presence of whites, and where concentration gave them a sense of political power for the first time since Reconstruction. But the black ghettos were also centers of degradation in many ways. Disease, crime, and infant mortality rose sharply; exploitation by white landlords forced rents up sharply and properties were allowed to deteriorate; overcrowding intensified. And despite the slow rise of a black middle class, by the end of the twenties there were only about fifteen thousand black college graduates and only forty who held Ph.D.s. Though greatly reduced, there was lynching in the South and rioting in the North. Although attempts were made to secure a federal antilynching law, these foundered under Southern filibusters. Yet migration to Northern and Southern cities improved black education, sharpened black aspirations, and drew them along with millions of other rural Americans into the orbit of a modern urban society.

Marcus Garvey and the UNIA The continued and undenied frustration of black Americans was dramatically underscored by the astounding momentary success of the Universal Negro Improvement Association founded by Marcus Garvey, a black from Jamaica. Garvey saw himself as a kind of black Zionist, but without the unifying heritage behind him which had kept Jews for centuries proclaiming "Next year in Jerusalem." He played down the struggle for equality in America while telling blacks of the promise of an eventual united and independent African motherland. He proclaimed an Empire of Africa and made himself its first president. Since the struggle for equality appeared to be making little progress at home, the black working class hailed the African future Garvey so glowingly painted. He toured the country organizing UNIA branches everywhere; he encouraged cooperative ownership of stores, laundries, hotels, and restaurants. His paper, *The Negro World,* had a circulation of 200,000 and recalled for blacks a glorious African history. The First International Convention of the UNIA was held in New York at the opening of the decade. Auxiliary groups that were to serve the new African Republic paraded through the streets, smartly uniformed: the Universal Black Cross Nurses, the Universal African Motor Corps, the Black Eagle Flying Corps, and others. Before an audience of 25,000 at Madison Square Garden, Garvey proclaimed:

> We are the descendants of a suffering people; we are the descendants of a people determined to suffer no longer. . . . We shall now organize the 400 million Negroes of the world into a vast organization to plant the banner of freedom on the great continent of Africa. . . . If Europe is for the Europeans, then Africa shall be for the black peoples of the world.

Garvey then undertook his ill-fated Black Star Line, a steamship enterprise to transport blacks to Africa with the first beachhead in Liberia. By 1924 the whole project was in financial trouble. The Liberian government began to protest and got support from the British and French, who had no desire to see black nationalism let loose on their own African territories. Garvey was accused of mail fraud, imprisoned for two years, and deported in 1927.

Established organizations such as the NAACP and the National Urban League felt that the flamboyant parades and emotionalism of the UNIA were damaging to the public image of blacks, and they certainly resented the inroads Garvey made on their own leadership in the black community. Most

Marcus Garvey in the uniform of the "Provisional President of Africa" on his way to a UNIA rally at Madison Square Garden.

middle-class blacks were convinced that Garvey's African Republic was an illusion, and that efforts wasted on it would detract from the crucial struggle for equality at home. But Garvey made a deep impression. He created the first mass movement among blacks, and demonstrated the power and unity of black identity and pride.

The Harlem Renaissance While Garvey tried to involve American blacks in a continent most knew nothing about and in a cultural past no one had any recollections of, two movements far more realistic if less dramatic were based on the assumption that blacks were Americans, not potential Africans. The first of these was the so-called Harlem Renaissance, a creative movement among black writers and artists which, though sometimes patronized by whites on the grounds that it represented the superior primitive virtues of blacks amidst the sophisticated vice of a business civilization, nevertheless clearly revealed the extraordinary talent latent in the black population. Though a number of such writers had begun their careers before and many continued long after the twenties, their sudden recognition publicized the cause of black equality. The work of James Weldon Johnson, Langston Hughes, Countee Cullen, Alain Locke, Claude McKay and many others in prose and poetry constituted a remarkable achievement and a revelation to many whites who saw, as it were, the black world for the first time. While not a national movement, it showed clearly the creative powers of black Americans freed from the confines of the rural South. Of equal importance it promoted another movement, that of awareness of their role in

American history and development. This had begun in 1915 with the establishment by Dr. Carter Woodson of the Association for the Study of Negro Life and History. As editor of *The Journal of Negro History,* Woodson greatly stimulated research and writing in black history, promoted an annual Negro History Week, and supplied teachers in predominantly black schools with materials to acquaint young blacks with their past.

New Threats to Democracy

The Rise of Special-Interest Groups If the health of democracy was directly challenged by the abuse of racial minorities, it was more subtly threatened in the 1920s by what one historian has called the "gildification" of American life, the rise and spread of highly organized special-interest groups. America had never lacked people guided by self-interest, but in the new society individuals seemed ever more lost and insecure, and counted for less and less except as they merged their own interests in those of some organization, institution, or group. When this happened, of course, the values of the group became those of the individual.

The Americans had a long tradition of organizing voluntarily for causes and purposes of all kinds. But in the past these had largely been designed to further the public interest: the public school movement, for example, or abolitionism. The public welfare, not self-interest, had been the motivating factor. It had been assumed that if the public interest were furthered, the individual would benefit. Now the reverse seemed to be true, and if the interests of one's group were served, then the public interest would be furthered—a proposition of dubious merit, but one that lay behind the famous remark made in the 1950s that what was good for General Motors was good for the country.

By the twenties this proposition, gathering strength as America had become more industrialized, urbanized, and specialized, found full expression, and raised serious problems for a democratic society with which we are still struggling. For in such circumstances it becomes difficult to identify what constitutes the public interest, much less to gain any support for it once it has been identified.

Examples of this rise in power and prestige of the special-interest group can be noted in many areas of American society. Such groups became especially prominent in business and industry. General organizations such as the United States Chamber of Commerce and the National Association of Manufacturers had active roles in speaking for general business interests by the 1920s, but the incredibly rapid rise of trade associations—organizations of businesses with interests in common in manufacturing and retailing—illustrates this trend more clearly. At the beginning of the decade there were only a dozen of these; by the end, almost two thousand. In agriculture also the trend gained strength. By 1921 the American Farm Bureau Federation had consolidated the numerous local farm bureaus established in the Progressive era and presumably spoke for farmers in general. But scores of other farm organizations from wheat growers to milk producers had also come into being, dedicated to their particular interest and theirs alone. The labor movement itself, though weakened in the decade, had under the influence of the American Federation of Labor taken the line that labor organization should disassociate itself from any ventures not tied directly to labor's own interests. Even in the professions, which idealized their organizations as advancing standards and ethics, doctors, lawyers, engineers, educators, and others principally sought economic security and protection for their members. The American Medical Association is a clear case in point.

In social groups the trend was also evident. Among ethnic, racial, and religious groups it served as a form of protection in the face of the white, Protestant, Anglo-Saxon, hundred-percent Americanism on the prowl during this decade. But numerous immigrant groups sought to emphasize their separateness in American society. Catholics, under the inspiration of the National Catholic Welfare Council, sought to reverse their past commitment to integration by promoting the parochial school movement and creating organizations such as the Catholic Boy Scouts, Catholic Daughters of America, and others. To a lesser degree, Jews moved in the same direction.

It is important to recognize that in a complex society, special interests served many useful purposes, from giving individuals a sense of meaning in their lives to gaining support for worthwhile programs that would have been neglected without the force of numbers and organization. But granting that, the furor of competing groups made it easy to lose any clear view of the public interest, and often problems were solved in the way that antagonized the fewest groups, and meaningless compromises were reached in the attempt to satisfy everybody. The concept that in a democracy there are certain fundamental ideas shared by all tended to be blurred and lost where people found it difficult to see beyond their own concerns.

Government and the Corporate Interest   The danger that always exists when government is too closely allied with business interests took on a new seriousness in the 1920s if for no other reason than that both had far more power than ever before. Enormously expanded wealth gave business unprecedented economic power, and government after the experience of World War I knew that it had a muscle that made its activities in the Civil War and the Progressive era seem puny by comparison. When these two forces worked in concert, serious problems arose.

The experience of the Progressive era had suggested that an aggressive government in the hands of the people could use its authority to keep business interests from abusing their power. It apparently occurred to only a few that if governmental authority fell into the wrong hands an alliance inimical to the public interest would be in the making. In World War I the government had used existing powers and acquired new ones to mobilize and direct the economy in wartime. Consolidation had been the goal, not competition, and the government had encouraged and promoted standardization of products, market-sharing, price-fixing, and industrial cooperation, many of which practices were continued after the war to the profit of business and with the encouragement of government. Large-scale business combinations continued. No attempt was made to enforce the antitrust laws in any significant way. The Supreme Court, for example, refused to challenge the United States Steel Corporation under the antitrust laws, although it did maintain that unions were subject to such laws.

Federal regulatory agencies, originally designed as a restraining influence on aggressive business interests, now in a more conservative decade became staffed with people who worked in close cooperation with business interests. The chairman of the Federal Reserve System in the 1930s, looking back on that agency's activities in the twenties, noted that "Private interests, acting through the Reserve banks, had made the System an effective instrument by which private interests alone could be served." A variety of federal agencies, such as the Interstate Commerce Commission and the Federal Trade Commission, seemed to become adjuncts of business enterprise. In promoting high tariffs to maintain high prices for certain manufactured goods, in tax policies favoring corporations, in the use of the Commerce and State Departments to promote American business interests abroad, a disturbing alliance was evident between the power of government and the power of business.

Government and Private Morality: Prohibition   It is possible to argue that in the twenties government as an arbiter of private morality posed problems for democracy, assuming as it did a role once handled more expeditiously by family and church. Because the twenties were by and large wide open in literature and the arts, including the new art of the cinema, and because there are always people who worry about everybody's morals but their own, there was bound to be some kind of censorial action. The censorship of books and motion pictures tended to be a local or state matter, although the federal courts and laws did nothing to restrain Boston and other communities notorious for their desire to keep the minds of their citizens pure and clean. Since the 1920s this problem has drawn the attention of the highest court in the land, and in a society of easy mass communication, the question of freedom and morality in such matters has become one of greater and greater complexity.

The major attempt of government in the twenties to dictate private morality and behavior centered on Prohibition. To the more single-minded, drink seemed to be linked to the corruptions of city politics, to immigration, to organized vice, the decline in religion, and even to family problems as evidenced in the rising divorce rate. But while tensions and contrasts between country and city no doubt made things worse, drink was by no means unknown in rural America. In part the trouble came, as often with large and complex problems, from the attempt to find a single simple solution. A variety of factors combined to put the Eighteenth Amendment into effect in 1920, including the modern mass propaganda methods of the Anti-Saloon League and other reform organizations, the influence of rural-dominated

Federal agents smash kegs as the Eighteenth Amendment takes effect.

state legislatures, and the wartime pressure to concentrate grain in the stomach instead of the liver. As an attempt to prevent Americans from drinking it failed, although it did change their drinking habits. Their consumption of alcohol was reduced, and there was a shift from hard liquor to beer and wine. Prohibition did not create organized crime in America, but it made crime a big business and gave it the funds to expand and move into other enterprises. Furthermore, this attempt to legislate an essentially personal matter encouraged people to break the law, a serious challenge to any society. The humorist Will Rogers noted the absurdity of the situation: "If you think this country ain't dry, just watch 'em vote; if you think this country ain't wet, just watch 'em drink." The hypocrisy and corruption that Prohibition engendered contributed strongly to the opinion that it is easier to defy a disagreeable law than to change it. The Americans, of course, got around to changing the law after fourteen years of violating it, but they did not entirely absorb the lesson, and the heritage of that failure has carried over to our time.

The Problem of Power   Yet in the long run the most serious threat to democracy, as became obvious in the 1920s, was simply the existence of a powerful governmental apparatus more and more involved in the lives and interests of its citizens. World War I had shown the power that the state could exercise over the lives of its citizens. If some of this was set aside in the twenties, and the rest was used to promote favored business interests, nevertheless it was obvious that the foundations had been laid for a bureaucracy not directly accountable to the people. If this was not in the 1920s an oppressive fact of life, it was an accepted one, and congressmen and senators were spending more and more of their time not on the wisdom of this or that legislation, but on guiding troubled constituents through the bureaucratic maze. This was a new problem for democracy: the citizen lost in the catalogues of the state. But its full dimensions were not clear until the crises of later decades.

What was clear in the twenties was the continued growth of big business, whose power did pose problems for democracy. Before the decade ended, the supercorporation had become dominant in manufacturing, railroads, communications, public utilities, and finance, and was moving into the retail trade. Consolidation was the order of the day. Thousands of small corporations disappeared into larger ones. Between 1919 and 1929 over eight thousand manufacturing and mining businesses vanished as independent concerns. In a single two-year period 1,940 public utility companies were absorbed into larger enterprises. Chain-store units increased to 160,000 by 1929, acquiring a larger and larger share of the retail trade in food, drugs, clothing, and general merchandise. By 1929 one percent of the banks controlled forty-six percent of the banking assets of the country. By 1929 the two hundred largest corporations possessed almost one-half of the total wealth of American corporations, two-fifths of the total business wealth, and one-fifth of the total national wealth.

The holding company became the chief technique for controlling economic power. Ninety-four of the largest ninety-seven industrial corporations in 1928 were holding companies. In public utilities, ten holding companies controlled seventy-two percent of the electric power. Moreover, the stock structure of the modern corporation with its millions of stockholders—some twenty million by 1930—brought about a final divorce between ownership and control. Control was exercised by corporation executives, who may or may not have owned stock in the companies they directed. Without popular control, by stockholders or anyone else, business executives made the key decisions affecting the economic welfare of millions of people. Whose interests they served is shown by the statistics. Worker income rose eleven percent in the decade, corporate profits sixty-two percent, and dividends sixty-five percent.

Broad prosperity and wide choice in new products and conveniences kept people from questioning corporate power. The unions were weak, falling from a membership of 5.1 million in 1920 to 3.6 million in 1923, while corporations did everything to reduce the dissatisfaction of workers and to draw them into the system. Factories were safer and physically more attractive, with cafeterias serving cheap, well-balanced meals. Companies sponsored athletic teams, provided free legal and medical services, set up group insurance plans and stock-purchase plans, had trained supervisors who knew worker problems, and formed company unions to keep workers organized but under company control. The growth of corporate power in the twenties was quiet but immense.

Conclusion

Whenever a new order takes over and change is everywhere, contrast is legion. The 1920s were such a time. There was foot-dragging if not outright repression, and there were great bursts of creativity. Optimism abounded, but so did doubt. By 1929 the Americans had created a new world, but they didn't quite know what to do with it. A handful of thoughtful men— John Dewey, Charles A. Beard, the authors of *Recent Social Trends*, and others—saw more clearly than most the nature of the problem, and held that to stay humane we somehow had to infuse the traditional values into the social control that a machine age required. This call for a new application of reason and compassion to human affairs was an important legacy of the twenties, and the half-century since has been marked by repeated attempts to respond to that call.

Profile: CHARLES A. LINDBERGH

Born February 4, 1902, Lindbergh electrified the twenties with the first nonstop solo flight across the Atlantic in May 1927. His dramatic achievement brought him worldwide fame, fortune, and such a personal distaste for publicity that he became one of the most private persons in America. Yet publicity pursued him, arising from personal tragedy and later from political controversy. The kidnap-murder in 1932 of his infant son, whose killer was finally brought to justice and executed in 1936, kept Lindbergh's name in the news for years. This was followed by several more years of intense publicity surrounding his controversial views on the international crisis leading to World War II and his opposition to American involvement in the war. After America entered the war Lindbergh so successfully achieved the privacy he had long desired that few were aware of his major war service as a consultant to the Ford Motor Company and the United Aircraft Corporation, including a tour of duty in the Pacific where he flew fifty combat missions, a unique achievement for a civilian. In his later years up to his death, Lindbergh emerged as a major public figure in the worldwide conservation and ecology movements.

The hinge upon which Lindbergh's life swung was his dramatic 33½ hour flight in The Spirit of St. Louis from Roosevelt Field, Long Island, to Le Bourget Aérodrome, Paris, on May 20–21, 1927. The flight not only made him a folk hero, but the public reaction to it revealed the central concerns of the American people in the 1920s as did no other event.

John Ward's study has shown that the public response to the flight revealed how Americans felt about modern society, their frustrations and their aspirations, their fears and their confidence. The reaction was twofold. Lindbergh was praised for qualities traditionally associated with the frontier past: self-reliance, courage, and independence. He was hailed as a pioneer on a new frontier, conquering nature on his own. He became "the lone eagle" of the skies, the "lineal descendant" of Daniel Boone and Davy Crockett. Outlook magazine said he was "the heir of all that we like to think is best in America. He is the stuff out of which have been made the pioneers that opened up the wilderness." And significantly, it added that "his are the qualities which we, as a people, must nourish."

Clearly, in the America of the 1920s many felt they lacked the old virtues. The journalist Joseph K. Hart wrote that "in the response that the world—especially the world of great cities—has made to the performance of this midwestern boy, we can read of the homesickness of the human soul, immured in city canyons and routine tasks, for the freer world of youth, for the open spaces of the pioneer, for the joy of battling with nature and clean storms once more on the frontiers of the earth."

Yet the public also saw in Lindbergh's flight the exact opposite of all this: the triumph of the machine age, for the plane in which he flew bespoke not the past but the future. While not denying Lindbergh's personal role, The New York Times went on to point out the obvious, that "without an airplane he could not have flown at all." What Lindbergh meant by the name he gave his plane, The Spirit of St. Louis, conjectured the Times, "is really the spirt of America. The mechanical genius, which is discerned in Henry Ford as well as in Charles A. Lindbergh, is in the very atmosphere of [the] country."

When President Coolidge pinned the Distinguished Flying Cross on Lindbergh, he noted that the plane—"this silent partner"—"represented American genius and industry." And one magazine typically called the flight "a triumph of mechanical engineering," and went on to observe that "it is not to be forgotten that this era is the work not so much of brave aviators as of engineers, who have through patient and protracted effort been steadily improving the construction of airplanes." Lindbergh himself continually gave the credit to his silent partner. He told newsmen in Paris that "You fellows have not said enough about that wonderful motor," and again and again he declared that the flight "represented American industry."

In this aspect of the public reaction, Lindbergh's remarkable accomplishment seemed to be a symbol of America's dramatic march into the world of science, technology, and industrial development at its most exhilarating.

In Lindbergh and his flight the Americans had for a moment the best of two worlds, the past and the future. How can you harmonize this vision of the free and independent individual with the disciplined demands and organization of an industrial society? America is still struggling with that question.

Chapter 9
THE DEPRESSION AND THE NEW DEAL

The Spirit of the Times
ECONOMIC DISASTER

The stock market crash in the autumn of 1929 led off the greatest economic disaster in the nation's history, and radically altered the lives of millions of Americans. For the great depression which followed was a tragedy of lost jobs, lost income, lost homes, lost careers, lost hopes, abrupt changes in standards of living. It is the story of people in hunger and want, often worrying where their next meal was coming from, worrying whether their children had adequate clothing, worrying about the electricity being cut off, worrying about the mortgage payment when there was no money to meet it. The anxiety, misery, and despair cannot be adequately told, but we can gain some idea of what the depression meant by a few glimpses into the early thirties when the catastrophe was at its peak.

The job market was calamitous. By 1932 Chicago had 660,000 unemployed, New York City over 1 million. The desperate search for jobs found men trying to get jury duty for the pittance it paid per diem and turning up on the streets as shoeshine boys, necktie and toy salesmen, or hawkers of vegetables trundling handcarts. In 1931, when the Soviet Union advertised in the United States for 6,000 skilled workers, their New York office received over 100,000 applications from 38 states. When Birmingham, Alabama, advertised for 750 men at 20 cents an hour to do pick-and-shovel labor on a local relief project, over 12,000 applied. The desperate and near-hopeless search for jobs was the same everywhere.

It is impossible to estimate how many, in losing their jobs, also lost their savings, their homes, and other property, but the number was substantial. Throughout the nation, on the fringe of cities and towns, dispossessed families built shacks out of packing crates, boxes, sheets of old metal, chicken wire, and anything to keep the weather out, calling these communities "Hooverville" in honor of that President's refusal to grant public relief. People slept in empty

A Hooverville rising out of the rubble of a vacant city lot. The largest of these communities was in St. Louis, where more than a thousand people huddled in their shacks. Most cities had at least one Hooverville, however small.

freight cars, shutdown factories, abandoned buildings, subways, caves, and parks. The Commissioner of Public Welfare in Chicago found several hundred unemployed women sleeping in the city's parks at night. The New York Times reported that police had found a woman and her sixteen-year-old daughter in the woods near Danbury, Connecticut, "huddled beneath a strip of canvas stretched from a boulder to the ground. Rain was dripping from the improvised shelter, which had no sides." They had been living there for days, subsisting on wild berries and apples. Iowa farmer Johannes Schmidt lost his farm, home, livestock, and equipment, and after filing for bankruptcy he and his family had only a wagon, an old team of horses, two cows, five hogs, a few pieces of furniture, and no place to go.

Thousands of single men and women, and even families, wandered aimlessly about the country, often traveling illegally in railroad boxcars. By 1932 an estimated one to two million were on the road, living on handouts from relief missions or by begging. Many a small-town household knew that when they heard a freight train stop in town within a few minutes someone would be knocking at the door and asking for food. One Midwesterner, recalling those days, wrote to a friend, "I can't remember how many fried-egg sandwiches I made as an eleven-year-old and handed out to those be-deviled people who showed up on our back porch, to say nothing of what my mother cooked for them if they came when she was home."

Ironically in a nation of vast agricultural abundance, food itself became a problem. Millions went hungry while tons of food were wasted or destroyed. A witness testifying before a Congressional committee reported that while he had seen women picking scraps from the refuse piles of Seattle's main market, in lower Oregon thousands of bushels of apples rotted in the orchards because the price was so low they were not worth harvesting. He had seen men, he reported, fighting over meat scraps in the garbage cans of Chicago, while a sheep-raiser he knew in the West had killed his entire flock and dumped the bodies down a canyon because he could not afford to feed them or ship them to market. People prowled in garbage dumps, picked up leavings and spoiled vegetables in market places, stood in line in charity soup kitchens. Testifying before a Congressional committee in 1933, Karl de Schweinitz of the Community Council of Philadelphia flipped through his file of cases of families who were making meals out of very little:

> One woman said she borrowed 50 cents from a friend and bought stale bread for 3½ cents a loaf, and that is all they had for 11 days except for one or two meals. . . . Here is a family of a pregnant mother and three children. They had only two meals a day and managed by having breakfast about 11 o'clock in the morning and then advancing the time of their evening meal. Breakfast consisted of cocoa and bread and butter; the evening meal of canned soup. One woman went along the docks and picked up vegetables that fell from wagons. Sometimes the fish vendors gave her fish at the end of the day. On two different occasions this family was without food for a day and a half. . . . Here is another family which for two days had nothing to eat but bread, and during most of the rest of the time they had only two meals a day. Their meals consisted of bread and coffee for breakfast and bread and raw or cooked carrots for dinner.

A newspaper reporter told the mayor of Youngstown, Ohio, that he could not believe what his neighbors were subsisting on. "The mother mixes a little flour and water and cooks it in a frying pan. That is their regular meal."

While there were few recorded deaths from starvation, the meagerness of food contributed to malnutrition and diseases such as rickets and pellagra, especially among deprived children. The New York City Health Department reported that twenty percent of the city's school children were suffering from some degree of malnutrition. Similar studies elsewhere revealed the same conditions. Some children got their only meal of the day at school. In 1931 Chicago schoolteachers were contributing from their salaries to provide lunches for some eleven thousand children. Multiplied many times over, such cases give some notion of the effects of the depression.

The Great Depression

The Day the Roof Fell In   On October 29, 1929, the stock market, which had been behaving peculiarly for weeks, collapsed completely, and with that began the collapse of the American economy and the social catastrophe known as the Great Depression. All the fundamental elements of modern American society remained, but it was as though everything had suddenly been pulled inside out. There was no sudden mass destruction or magical disappearance of the economic instruments of society. The resources of land and water remained. Factories and machinery did not disappear into the mists. Workers to operate the machines still existed. Talent to direct operations of production and distribution did not vanish. The need for goods remained. But the system ceased to work.

Oct 29 Dies Irae, *a lithograph by James Rosenberg, captures the devastating effect wrought on Wall Street by the shock of economic collapse.*

Behind the collapse lay the experiences and attitudes of the 1920s and before. After twenty years of saving democracy, first at home and then abroad, the American people were inclined to sit back and enjoy the benefits. And the great boom of the twenties seemed to provide the opportunity to do so. There was less and less interest, therefore, in the direction of public affairs and more in the material satisfaction of private needs. There seemed to be no necessity to keep a close eye and a tight rein on the business operations of the country that were producing so much for so many. The specific economic causes of the depression lay in the blunders made in the operation of the economy, and the blame for that must be laid at the door of the business leadership of the country.

This business leadership, whose influence was reflected in governmental economic policies as well as in private economic decisions, permitted an overexpansion of production in major industries, encouraged a maldistribution of income, and allowed the banking system to become irresponsible. By 1929 the overexpanded automobile industry—upon which so much of the prosperity of the twenties rested—had to cut back production, thus affecting the producers of steel, glass, rubber, lead, and other products. When this happened investment capital did not pour into any other industry to take up the slack. Moreover, the boom of the twenties had brought huge profits that were not sufficiently shared with workers, farmers, or the public in general through wage increases and lowered prices. So neither workers nor farmers had enough purchasing power to sustain the new high-production levels of industry. Installment buying only temporarily disguised the limited ability to buy. With profits so high, many corporations had been able to finance their own growth, pay high dividends, and still have money left over. The urge to speculate on the stock market then became overwhelming. Banks had helped to promote and finance speculation, and themselves became deeply involved in market operations, acquiring assets that were later to be of little value. Corporations and banks as well as individuals bought huge quantities of stocks on margin, paying only a fraction of the cost in cash and borrowing the rest against the value of the stock itself. This system yielded large profits as long as prices rose, but when they fell the loans were called, and buyers either had to pay the difference or forfeit their investments.

All these weaknesses formed the basis for the crash on Wall Street. And when that occurred in October 1929, not only many investors were ruined, but also banks holding securities and loans. More than 1,300 banks failed in 1930; over 3,700 in the next two years. Business confidence and morale was broken, and disaster followed as the economy shriveled over the next three years. People with capital held back from investment. Production was cut in view of decreased purchasing power. Production cuts meant fewer hours worked, or fewer workers, or both. That further reduced purchasing power and resulted in additional cuts in production. And so it went, with each step downward making conditions worse.

The extent of the collapse was appalling. The gross national product, the total of all goods and services produced in the country, fell from $104 billion in 1929 to $74.2 billion in 1933. The national income, the total earnings of all labor and property, collapsed from $87.8 billion in 1929 to $40.2 billion in 1933. New capital investment was only $1 billion in 1932, a tenth of what it had been in 1929. Exports declined from $5.2 billion to $1.6 billion; imports from $4.4 billion to $1.3 billion. Farm prices, which were bad anyway in 1929, fell 61 percent. Cotton was selling for 5 cents a pound, wheat was under 40 cents a bushel, and corn 31 cents. Farm income fell from $13 billion to $5.5 billion. American industry by 1932 was operating at one-half its 1929 capacity, the total amount paid out in wages was down almost 60 percent, and dividends were down 57 percent. Finally, and most frightening of all, was the amount of unemployment. We shall never know the exact numbers out of work, but in the worst year, 1933, at least 13 million were unemployed, more than one-fourth the total work force of the nation. Today there is grave concern if the rate is more than 5 percent.

The Reaction: Violence   The desperation bred by this widespread distress could be seen in the violence with which many responded. Across the country there were major disturbances as people sought their own answers to the seeming indifference to their fate. Private, state, and local relief touched no more than a quarter of the distressed, and the federal government was rendered inactive by President Hoover's conviction that relief for individuals was not a matter of federal concern, that government aid would sap the moral fiber and independence of the people—though for some curious reason assistance to corporations did not seem to weaken their moral fiber and independence.

In these circumstances, little wonder that many people decided to take matters into their own hands. In Minneapolis in February of 1931, for example, a typical unemployment demonstration saw several hundred men and women storming a grocery and meat market and stripping its shelves of food. It took a hundred policemen to bring the protest under control. Far more serious was the clash between police and unemployed auto workers at the Ford plant in Dearborn, Michigan, which turned into a pitched but unequal battle. Rocks were no match for bullets, and four workers were killed and several wounded. The dead lay in state for two days under a red banner with the inscription "Ford Gave Bullets for Bread."

Equally dramatic was the march to Washington in the summer of 1932 by some fifteen thousand veterans of World War I, many with their families, who encamped in shacks and tents on Anacostia Flats and settled in to lobby for the passage of a bonus bill. Although orderly and disciplined, their presence in Washington alarmed the government. When Congress adjourned without passing the bill, many veterans had no place else to go and remained in Washington. District police, attempting to clear some from abandoned buildings on Pennsylvania Avenue, panicked, opened fire, killed two and wounded others. A frightened government then ordered General Douglas MacArthur, Army Chief of Staff, to clear the camp on Anacostia Flats. Using cavalry, infantry, and tanks, MacArthur drove the unarmed veterans and their families out with tear gas and bayonets and burned the camp. MacArthur issued a statement to the effect that he had saved the country from a revolution, but most of the country took the view of the Washington *News:* "What a pitiful spectacle is that of the great American Government, mightiest in the world, chasing unarmed men, women, and children with Army tanks. . . . If the Army must be called out to make war on unarmed citizens, this is no longer America."

Major protest also came from American farmers, traditionally conservative. Angry and outraged farmers banded together to protect their farms from mortgage foreclosures. They threatened judges and drove off sheriffs, and failing that stood ominously with pitchforks and shotguns at foreclosure auctions, discouraging any bidding except by the former owner who often got his farm back for a fraction of its value. In the summer of 1932, farmers in the Middle West organized the National Farm Holiday Association, an attempt to raise farm prices by preventing food from reaching the cities until prices increased. The Association warned:

> We have issued an ultimatum to the other groups of society. If you continue to confiscate our property and demand that we feed your stomachs and clothe your bodies, we will refuse. We don't ask people to make implements, cloth, or houses at the price of degradation, bankruptcy, dissolution, and despair.

Soldiers disperse the veterans of the "bonus army" with tear gas and bayonets from their encampment at Anacostia Flats.

At Sioux City, Iowa, the Milk Producers Association joined forces with the Holiday Association and blocked all roads into the city with spiked telegraph poles, logs, and wagons. Highway 20 got the name of Bunker Hill 20 as the scene of the worst clashes between law-enforcement officers and farmers.

Although the word revolution was bandied about, it was never a serious threat. But events clearly indicated the desperation in the country, and revealed how painful were the wounds of economic collapse. The depth of despair was exposed in testimony before the California State Unemployment Commission by an eighty-year-old man who told how in the past he had gone through hard times but had always been able to recover by homesteading, mining, or getting a job in railroad construction. But now, he declared with bitter humor, "There isn't an acre of decent land to be had for homesteading. There isn't a railroad to be built anywhere. There isn't a chance for a new factory. . . . Years ago Horace Greeley made a statement, Young man, go West and grow up with the country. Were he living today, he would make the statement, Go West, young man, and drown yourself in the Pacific Ocean."

The New Deal

On March 4, 1933, Franklin D. Roosevelt's first Inauguration Day and Herbert Hoover's last day in the White House, the outgoing President declared, "We are at the end of our string." A few hours later the new President flatly rejected such despair and jolted the nation into action:

> This great nation will endure as it has endured, will revive and will prosper. So, first of all, let me assert my firm belief that the only thing we have to fear is fear itself—nameless, unreasoning, unjustified terror which paralyzes needed efforts to convert retreat into advance. . . . We do not distrust the future. . . . The people of the United States have not failed. In their need they have . . . asked for discipline and direction under leadership. They have made me the present instrument of their wishes. In the spirit of the gift I take it.

So began the New Deal and the era of Franklin D. Roosevelt. Next day the new President declared a nationwide bank holiday, presented emergency bank-reform legislation to Congress on March 9, and within just a little over three months had enacted all the major enabling legislation for the New Deal, which fell into the three general categories of relief, recovery, and reform.

Relief   The need was immediate and great. Further delay was unthinkable, even to the few Republicans still in Washington, and there was no time for making intricate long-range plans or philosophical justifications beyond simple humanitarianism. As Harry Hopkins, director of relief, remarked with considerable annoyance when presented with complicated economic schemes for dealing with unemployment in the long run, "People don't eat in the long run. They eat now."

Relief for the distressed was therefore a major program of the New Deal, especially in the early years, but also throughout the decade. The first goal was to get money into the hands of those who did not have any and who were helpless to earn it on their own.

The major channels for this aid included first the Federal Emergency Relief Administration, which passed funds directly to the states for relief, then the Civil Works Administration, the Public Works Administration, and most ambitious of all, the Works Progress Administration. During the brief existence of the CWA in 1933–1934 some four million people were put to work, directly employed by the federal govenment in repairing and building roads, schools, airports, and sewer systems as well as such activities as painting murals on the walls of post offices throughout the country. The PWA, in its six years from 1933 to 1939, was involved in the construction of thousands of public buildings and other projects—schools, post offices, courthouses, bridges, and dams—totaling some four million hours of work. The WPA, created in 1935, lasted until 1943. In its eight years it spent over $11 billion and employed some 8.5 million persons. It too promoted a vast program of public works—schools, hospitals, airports, streets, highways. On

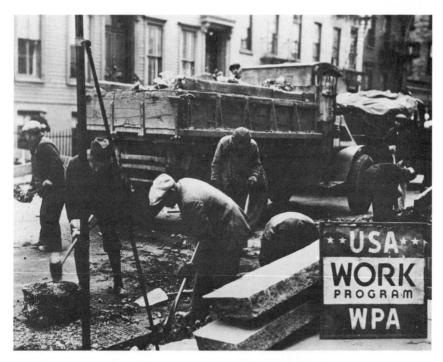

A WPA work program. The light construction work of street widening was typical of the projects that kept people employed and sustained morale, but were not intended to have a substantial effect on economic recovery.

the logical assumption, as Roosevelt noted, that artists and writers have to eat just like everybody else, the WPA also provided work for America's unemployed artistic community. The Music Project gave rise to 122 symphony orchestras and 250 music teaching centers—and uncovered a neglected treasure of folk music. The Federal Theater Project provided jobs for the thousands of actors, actresses, directors, stagehands, and crews who produced plays that had an eventual total audience of 25 million. The Federal Writers' Project put over 6,000 novelists, poets, journalists, scholars, and students of varying literary competence to work turning out over a thousand books, guidebooks, and pamphlets, as well as collecting vast bodies of valuable material on local, state, and regional history and culture that might otherwise have been lost. The Federal Art Project provided painters and sculptors with the opportunity to see their work in schools, hospitals, libraries, and other public buildings, and offered tens of thousands of citizens the opportunity to take free art lessons.

There were other relief measures as well. The Civilian Conservation Corps was created in 1933 to provide jobs for young men between the ages of 18 and 25, and by 1940 when it ended some 2,225,000 young men had worked on a multitude of soil conservation and reforestation projects to the benefit of the American landscape as well as their families, to whom most of their small paychecks were sent directly. Moreover, the National Youth Administration created part-time jobs for over 2 million high-school and college students who did clerical tasks, worked in libraries and laboratories, and assisted faculty members in various projects. An equal number of out-of-school young people were also assisted under the NYA.

All these relief measures helped immeasurably in providing work, in supplying at least a minimum of income and security, and in boosting morale. At a time when private, local, and state agencies lacked the resources to do so, the billions of dollars poured into the economy by the federal government provided relief for millions. And it provided not just direct financial assistance, but psychological relief as well: an easing of tension, a release from fear. A former businessman laying sewer pipe on a government-sponsored relief project spoke for millions when he said:

> I hate to think what would have happened if this work hadn't come along. The last of my savings had run out. I'd sold or hocked everything I had. And my kids were hungry. I stood in front of the window of the bake-shop down the street and wondered just how long it would be before I got desperate enough to pick up a rock and heave it through that window and grab some bread to take home.

There was much wrong with the government's relief programs. Some were of indifferent value, many workers loafed on the job, and some programs were used for partisan political purposes. More significantly, by no means all of the unemployed were reached by these programs. Though billions of dollars were spent, far more were needed, and Roosevelt was too cautious to engage in the kind of massive deficit spending demanded by the situation. When Hopkins, for example, spent over a billion dollars in less than five months under the Civil Works Administration, Roosevelt abolished the agency. Moreover, the wages paid on relief programs were hardly impressive. The young men in the Civilian Conservation Corps received $30 a month, of which $25 went directly to their families. At the end of the decade the average monthly wage for NYA high-school students was $4.74, for college students $12.68, and for graduate students $21.72. The average monthly wage in 1936 under the WPA was $52.14. Yet even this helped: those who got it spent it immediately because of their need, and thus helped stimulate the economy in general, worthwhile and needed public construction and other work was accomplished, skills and talents were developed and preserved, and even those unemployed who did not share directly in the benefits saw such programs as a hopeful sign that the government cared and was trying to do something, so that morale and confidence were greatly improved.

Aid to Distressed Groups Besides programs for direct relief of the unemployed, the New Deal was concerned with helping others who suffered unnecessarily under the impact of the depression and whose position in

American society made them defenseless not only in the face of disaster but also in the day-to-day workings of an economy where the power and decision making so deeply affecting their lives lay in hands other than their own.

The Farmers   The farming community, which had been suffering even before the depression struck, was one of the hardest hit. Farmers were not easily organized, and lacked political force in an urban-industrial society. Two problems were crucial, the loss of their farms through mortgage foreclosures, and prices for farm commodities so low that farmers often could not meet costs, much less make a profit. The New Deal sought to solve both problems. Through the Farm Credit Administration it refinanced one-fifth of the total farm mortgage indebtedness, and through the Farm Bankruptcy Act of 1934, later revised in 1936, it permitted a farmer who had lost his farm to buy it back at a price fixed by a federal district court at one percent interest. In the effort to raise the prices of farm products the New Deal in the first Agricultural Adjustment Act of 1933 and the second AAA of 1938 limited production through acreage controls and marketing quotas, purchased and stored surpluses, lent money to farmers and held their crops as collateral until prices rose and farmers could buy them back and sell on a higher market, and subsidized farm exports. By 1935 farm income had increased from $4.5 billion to $6.9 billion and farm mortgage indebtedness had decreased. But the program, while it helped the efficient, did not help many poor farmers. The acreage taken out of production by landlords deprived many farm tenants and sharecroppers of what little livelihood they had, and thus increased their distress. The money which landlords and owners received for limiting production they often invested in equipment that further reduced the need for farm labor and left additional agricultural laborers, tenant farmers, and sharecroppers in want. The average cash income per person among tenant farmers in the lower Mississippi delta, for example, was $38 a year.

The New Deal did experiment with aid to poor farmers through the Resettlement Admininstration, which bought marginal farm land and moved its occupants to better land. Some nine million acres of marginal land were ultimately taken out of cultivation. Far more significant in the long run was the Rural Electrification Act of 1935, which aided farmers in establishing power facilities through cooperatives or in purchasing electric power from private companies. Its achievements were momentous. At the beginning of the decade only one farm in ten had electricity; twenty years later only one in ten did not. This program not only made possible a rise in the comforts and conveniences of modern living for most farmers, but provided a basis for the expansion of technology on the farm. But none of the New Deal's farm programs halted the trend away from the small family farm and toward the same concentration in agriculture as had already taken place in industry.

Labor   Labor was another group whose members had little capacity to protect themselves and little control over the key economic decisions affecting their lives. In union, and in unions, lay strength; but organized labor was

*Migrants seeking work in the California pea fields. When their own land
or the land of their landlords failed them they abandoned both the land and
what belongings they could not fit into a dilapidated truck or car and
headed across the country. When they finally reached California, they
encountered others like themselves, housing inadequate for decent living,
wages that plummeted because there were so many seeking them, and hatred
because they were poor and because they were homeless.*

weakened in the 1920s, and the depression undermined the union movement even more. By 1933, membership had declined to 2,317,000 in the AFL,
and there were perhaps an additional 650,000 members in unaffiliated
unions.

The New Deal gave a strong boost to union organization, though workers
themselves bore the brunt of the battle to achieve recognition. But Section 7a
of the National Industrial Recovery Act of 1933 had recognized the right of
workers to organize and bargain collectively—the first time that right had
been written into federal law—and with that stimulus trade unions increased
their membership to 3,890,000 by 1935. But employers often bypassed the
intent of the law by forming company unions, which had about 2.5 million
members by 1935, and by using large sums of money and numerous illegal
tactics to prevent unions from being organized. When the Supreme Court
declared the NIRA unconstitutional, a new law with strong enforcement
provisions in it, the Wagner Labor Relations Act, was passed in 1935.

Coming when the industrial union—the organization of workers by industries instead of by trades or skills—was just gaining momentum, the
Wagner Act provided the legal backing for the explosive growth of industrial

unions under the Congress of Industrial Organization, led by John L. Lewis of the United Mine Workers. The key industries organized by the CIO were the automobile industry and the steel industry. Using the sitdown strike as their weapon, the auto workers—who had a mere 30,000 members and no contracts in the fall of 1936—exploded to 400,000 members and contracts with 381 companies by the fall of 1937. Most of the steel industry was organized in 1937, and other basic industries followed. By the time the United States entered World War II, the CIO had about 5 million members, the AFL which had also expanded had approximately 4.5 million, and independent union membership had grown to a million. In eight years union membership had expanded three and a half times. Unions still did not comprise a majority of workers by any means, but they did become a powerful new force backed by law, guaranteeing that henceforth labor would have a voice in those economic decisions that affected its welfare.

The New Deal also aided labor in the Walsh–Healy Government Contracts Act of 1936 and in the Wages and Hours Act of 1938. The latter initially set a minimum wage of 25 cents an hour, a maximum work week of 44 hours, time and a half for overtime, and forbade the employment of children under 16, and under 18 in industries specified as dangerous. Although the law excluded various categories of workers, including agricultural laborers, its immediate effect was to raise wages for over 350,000 people and to reduce work hours for about 1 million. Within two years about 1 million workers had higher wages and over 3 million gained a shorter work week. Since the passage of the law it has been over the years amended many times to raise the minimum wage and to cover more and more workers.

Social Security   The Social Security Act of 1935 also reflected the humanitarian concern of the New Deal for the defenseless. Pensions for the aged had been proposed in the Progressive era, and a number of states had adopted such programs although most were inadequate. But the need was great. The very nature of an urban-industrial society made it difficult to take care of older people in the homes of their children as had been done in rural America in the past. The Social Security Act now established a federal program financed by a payroll tax on both employees and employers. But the program failed to cover a number of groups, and payments were based on earnings, so that those needing support the most received the least. But the commitment was made, and the program was steadily expanded in subsequent years, providing a secure if minimum underpinning in the lives of the aged. The Act also provided for a joint federal–state program of unemployment compensation to tide over those who lost their jobs until they could find others. Finally, it established a joint program with the states for aiding other defenseless groups, such as dependent poor children and the physically handicapped.

In other ways as well the New Deal sought to aid those who through no fault of their own found themselves victimized in a complex modern society. For the ordinary citizen, for example, bank deposits were guaranteed, mortgage protection was provided, and low-cost housing was made available.

About twenty percent of all urban private homes were refinanced by the Home Owners Loan Corporation, the Federal Housing Administration in a three-year period loaned $500 million for home-improvement projects, and a program of support for low-cost public housing for people of low income was set in motion.

These are all major examples of the basic humanitarian concern of the New Deal in coping with the problems of the depression. This concern sprang from the assumption that in a modern society in which so many individuals are lost in the mass, society is responsible through government for the protection of individuals and the promotion of their welfare in those areas of life where they cannot do so on their own as single separate individuals. Abraham Lincoln had said, "The legitimate object of Government is to do for a community of people whatever they need to have done but cannot do at all or cannot do so well for themselves in their separate or individual capacities." Three times in public addresses in the 1930s Roosevelt quoted this statement of Lincoln's to define the essential motivation of the New Deal. On one of these occasions he declared that the minimum to which the American people were entitled were "These three great objectives—the security of the home, the security of livelihood, and the security of social insurance. . . ." As the drama of the depression clearly demonstrated, the power to assure these securities was no longer within the capacity of the ordinary citizen.

Business   The stock market crash and the economic collapse that followed made it clear that a freewheeling private enterprise system had a great potential for disaster. To make the system work again and to change the mechanism in order to prevent such failures in the future were major objectives of the New Deal.

The attempt to aid business began with the effort to provide some rational planning in production and prices through the National Industrial Recovery Act. In some highly competitive fields such as textiles, prices were absurdly low; in others, such as automobiles, production was cut while prices stayed up. The aim was to allow companies in the various industries to band together and write codes of fair practices that would set rational goals of production and establish fair prices without conflicting with the antitrust laws. Although such planning had a precedent in the experiences of World War I, the Act was declared unconstitutional. But by then it had already failed, partly because the New Deal did not inject enough purchasing power into the economy to increase consumption beyond the bare necessities, and partly through poor administration. Moreover, business was willing to accept aid but not the obligations that went with it, such as observing the provisions of the Act respecting the rights of labor. Big business, which to the distress of small businessmen dominated the writing of the codes, also tried to cheat by delaying the codes while increasing production under low wages, hoping to profit by anticipated higher prices before higher minimum wages went into effect. Even so, the Act promoted a temporary revival and contributed to the general atmosphere of confidence that something was being done.

Provisions of the Act pleasing to business interests were continued in the various state fair-trade laws, which were given federal sanction in the Miller–Tydings Act of 1937. This act allowed manufacturers to control the prices of their products through jobbers, wholesalers, and retailers without fear of violating the antitrust laws.

Major direct aid for business came from the Reconstruction Finance Corporation, which had been set up during the Hoover administration to make loans to business on the grounds that benefits to business would eventually trickle down to ordinary citizens. The New Deal greatly expanded the RFC's activities, and by 1941 it had loaned almost $16 billion, principally to banks, insurance companies, railroads, and other corporations.

Another major aid to business came through government contracts for the multitude of public projects sponsored by the various relief programs, which injected billions into the economy and enabled countless businesses to survive. But business was its own worst enemy in terms of recovery. Confidence had been gravely shaken by the depression, and business leaders were extremely cautious and unimaginative. Their thinking by and large remained rooted in the doctrines of the past. They were fearful of the mounting federal debt, they were suspicious of government encouragement to organized labor, they hated the new taxes and regulatory agencies, they came to detest Roosevelt, and freely predicted that the New Deal would bring federal bankruptcy and the collapse of society. Many businessmen hesitated to put capital into plant development or to engage in large-scale spending for expansion, aggravating the problems of the depression, including their own.

Economic Regulation The New Deal also undertook to alter the mechanism of the economic system. The Glass–Steagall Banking Act of 1933 restricted bank credit available for speculation, forced commercial banks to separate completely from investment companies, and gave the Federal Reserve Banks greatly increased power over member banks. The Banking Act of 1935 gave the Federal Reserve Board extensive powers over the banking system, centralizing control in Washington for the first time. Of great importance was the Securities Exchange Act of 1934, which established a Securities Exchange Commission and gave it the power to regulate the issuance of all new stocks and the exchange of all securities traded, including the authority to set margin requirements and the power to enforce full disclosure of the financial condition of companies issuing stocks. The Revenue Act of 1934 closed a series of loopholes, which had permitted men such as J. P. Morgan to avoid paying income taxes. In addition, in 1935 inheritance taxes were increased, a progressive income tax was imposed on incomes over $50,000, and a graduated tax was set up on the net income of corporations. In the same year, the Public Utilities Holding Company Act forbade the use of the holding company beyond the first level, correcting a device that had been flagrantly abused.

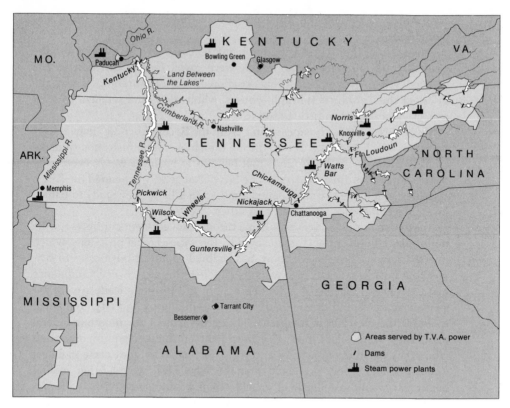

THE TENNESSEE VALLEY AUTHORITY

The New Deal's monetary policies in 1933 and 1934—taking the United States in effect off the gold standard, devaluing the dollar, and establishing a silver-purchase plan—were designed to raise prices, but failed to do so. But they made it clear that hereafter the federal government, not the Wall Street bankers, would play the deciding role in managing the money system and stabilizing the currency.

The TVA   One of the striking creations of the New Deal was the Tennessee Valley Authority, a project that in a sense encompassed the whole range of New Deal purpose, since it not only gave relief to one of the poorest regions in the country, but showed that national social planning worked. TVA sought to rehabilitate an entire region, comprising all or part of seven states, under authorization of the federal government but having its own administrative authority. TVA built dams, power stations, and transmission lines; it sold fertilizer and electricity; it engaged in extensive flood control, reforestation, soil conservation, and river navigation improvement; it encouraged activities from malaria control to recreation; it promoted industry and provided a competitive challenge to private utility companies which cut power rates; and it led to new practices under which private companies found to their surprise they could still make a profit. It was an extraordinary experiment in social planning that rehabilitated a region and raised the standard of living for millions. Though Roosevelt wished to see the concept of the TVA duplicated elsewhere in the nation, Congress did not respond to his suggestion.

Successes and Failures of the New Deal   Although it may not appear in the telling, the flurry of the famous Hundred Days after Roosevelt took office, the passage of all those laws creating one new agency after another, brought people an incredible sense of hope and excitement. "It was one of the most joyous periods in my life," wrote one man looking back on it all. "We came alive, we were eager." Many people felt that they were engaged in the most important and creative events since the Revolution. Certainly the New Deal did shift the direction of the republic to a new point on the compass, and its accomplishments were very great. It nursed the private enterprise system back from the brink of death, even though the patient had to be dragged protesting into the intensive care unit. It gave help to desperate millions and carried them through a time of crisis with their faith in the country intact, and revived their hopes for the future. It strengthened the role of the working class by improving the position of organized labor. And through a series of regulatory measures it greatly reduced the opportunities for the profit motive to degenerate into sheer selfishness, greed, and exploitation. The pressure it put on the business community forced businessmen to become more socially conscious. Significantly, none of the vital New Deal legislation reflecting these accomplishments has been reversed; indeed all has been strengthened and expanded: Social Security, coverage under the Wagner Act, TVA, the Securities and Exchange Commission, and others.

What the New Deal did *not* do is as important as what it did. It did not solve the problem of the depression. Things were better at the end of the decade than at the beginning, but there were still seven or eight million unemployed—about fifteen percent of the labor force—and industry was not operating at full capacity. The New Deal failed to act on a number of crucial social issues, including national health insurance and racial discrimination. It failed to halt the apparently inevitable trend toward economic concentration. Indeed, big business got bigger. It failed to institute large-scale social planning. Conservatives might applaud these failures, but others regarded them as missed opportunities.

The failures can be accounted for in a number of ways. The urgency of the economic crisis naturally focused attention on that problem and left little effort for broader, long-range issues. The magnitude of the crisis was unprecedented, and the New Deal had to feel its way, improvising, trying one measure and then another. No one really knew what would work and what would not. By the latter part of the decade, moreover, things had improved enough so that a conservative coalition developed that put the brakes on New Deal experiments.

The New Deal attempted to ease the fear and restore the lost faith of those crushed by the Depression.

No assessment of the New Deal can ignore its impact abroad. The depression was worldwide but it was worse in the United States than elsewhere. More than half the decline in world industrial production took place in the United States, and the unemployment rate was higher here than in any other country. What took place in the United States in response to the depression was therefore of great interest to others.

Roosevelt was willing to see what Europe had to offer in the way of ideas and programs, and had his aides study European experiences. And what they learned was put to work where it seemed applicable. The securities legislation, for example, was drawn in part from Belgian, German, and particularly British models.

But in general the reverse was true, and the New Deal came to be imitated elsewhere—in France, Belgium, Canada, Mexico, and other countries. Visitors came to the United States from around the world to study such experiments as the shelterbelt tree-planting program in the Midwest, and especially TVA, which became a model for regional development programs throughout the world. The humane approach of the New Deal, in contrast to the drastic austerity approach in Australia and Britain, was greatly admired, as was its success in defusing demagogic and fascist threats such as those of Huey Long, Father Coughlin, the Knights of the White Camelia, and the German-American Bund. Many abroad listened to Roosevelt's radio broadcasts and wished their own governments had such leadership.

Amid all the criticisms of the New Deal, and with due recognition of its follies and blunders, it is still possible to say that it provided an example of democratic resilience that inspired other peoples across the world. In Britain, H. G. Wells summed up this reaction when he said, "America is still what, in the school geographies of my childhood, used to be called so hopefully the New World."

Social Effects of the Depression

All aspects of society and culture were affected in some way or to some degree by the depression. You did not have to be a Marxist to realize how pervasive was the influence of economic forces on human lives and institutions. The evidence was all around you in the 1930s. There were sharp declines in the birth rate, the marriage rate, and even in the divorce rate. Hundreds of thousands of young men and women postponed marriage, and those married postponed additions to the family until better times returned. The economic pinch helped to break down further the barriers to birth control. In the mid-thirties two-thirds of the American people declared in a poll that birth-control information should be made available to all married couples. Partly for these reasons the population growth rate fell from 16.1 percent in the 1920s to 7.2 percent in 1940, and population increased only from 122,775,000 to 131,700,000 in the decade. The rate of increase would have been even smaller except that the death rate also declined, due to advances in medical treatment. Another factor in the smaller population growth was that fewer immigrants entered the country, some 348,289 in the 1930s—the smallest number since the 1820s. The average age increased, and the percentage of the population over 65 rose from 5.4 in 1930 to 6.9 in 1940.

The divorce rate also declined sharply in the early worst years of the depression, from 1.66 per thousand in 1929 to 1.28 in 1932. The latter figure does not take into account the "poor man's divorce"—desertion. There were many of these. "My husband went North about three months ago," declared one California woman in 1932. "For five weeks we have had no word from him. . . . Don't know where he is or what he is up to." But the long-time trend was up, and by 1940 the divorce rate was up to 2 per thousand, a new high.

The impact of the depression upon family cohesiveness and stability varied greatly. Families with strong ties were drawn together, while weaker ones were split and destroyed. Poverty, unemployment, loss of home, overcrowding, the social disgrace of unemployment, and loss of status put enormous strain on many families, and normal behavior and relationships often broke down. Drinking increased, especially among working and lower middle-class males. Prostitution occurred among married women seeking ways to increase the family income. Families who lost their homes or were evicted sometimes sent their children to live with relatives or friends. Some families that doubled up with relatives experienced the tension that comes from overcrowding and the loss of privacy. Ill health became a burden, and inadequate diet made people of all ages more susceptible to illness. The rate of illness in families with a per-capita income of less than $150 was 40 percent higher than for those with per-capita incomes of $425 or more. Families of the unemployed had 60 percent more illness than those of the full-time employed. Working women were under pressure to give up their jobs to unemployed males, and some labor unions proposed this as national policy.

No one who lived through the depression wanted to go through such an experience again, and it shaped their attitudes for years if not for life. The depression also contributed to family problems of later years, for those who grew up then acquired a concern for security, for possessions, which their children in more affluent times found hard to understand, thus widening the normal gap between generations. And parents who later showered their children with material goods and satisfied their every desire were in a way compensating for the lack of material security in their own childhood.

The traditional migration of families seeking economic betterment was not halted by the depression. There was a temporary movement back to the land from the city, but the countryside was as depressed as the city. Despite the stabilization or slight decline in the populations of some cities, the long-term trend toward urbanization continued. Some of the most depressed rural states lost population: Vermont, North and South Dakota, Nebraska, Kansas, and Oklahoma. States such as Florida, Arizona, and especially California grew dramatically. Significantly, these were states with more alluring climates than most: apparently it was easier to be miserable in the sunshine. Tens of thousands of refugees from the dust bowl of the Great Plains, where farms had been destroyed by drought and wind, flocked to California where they helped to make up much of the migrant labor force in that major agricultural state.

Minorities

The Blacks   Black Americans continued their move out of the South to Northern cities, but only half as many went as in the 1920s. More would certainly have moved North if they had had the means to do so. The likelihood of jobs in the North was slight, but at least the possibility of getting on relief was greater. In the South, even the most menial jobs were taken over by desperate whites. Some New Deal programs helped the blacks. There were over a million on the WPA rolls at the end of the decade, a third of all federally funded public housing apartments were occupied by blacks, both the NYA and the CCC accepted blacks equally in their programs. Other programs worsened a bad situation. The NRA codes in some industries provided lower minimum wages for blacks than whites, and in others some employers fired blacks rather than pay them equal wages. Since so many sharecroppers and tenant farmers were black, they were hard hit by the acreage restrictions of the AAA, which prompted landlords to take land out of cultivation.

Significant progress came indirectly from the New Deal's support of organized labor under the Wagner Act. This was particularly true in the case of

The dust bowl. Humanity's hold on the land was loosened.

the CIO and its drive to organize workers in the steel, automobile, rubber, electrical, and other industries that had large numbers of black workers. In hard-fought battles with employers for union recognition and contracts, the solidarity of as large a number of workers as possible was essential, so the new industrial unions of the CIO abolished discrimination in union membership. The result was that black workers joined with white workers in these unions, and "democracy with a union card" came to have real meaning.

In Roosevelt and the New Deal, black Americans found for the first time a national administration cordial to them. Mrs. Roosevelt especially promoted the cause of racial equality and in her syndicated newspaper column gave sympathetic accounts of problems facing black Americans. When New Dealers expressed their concern for "the common people," they meant blacks as well as whites. Blacks such as Clark Foreman and Robert Weaver held relatively important government positions, and a significant number of black professionals entered government service. Discrimination practices in the federal government were modified or removed.

In response, blacks in droves deserted the Republican party and supported the New Deal, bringing about an historic shift in their political allegiance. Yet the New Deal left much undone in civil rights. It is possible that under

This barren Southern Ute Indian reservation reflects the devastating poverty uncovered by the Meriam Report.

the impetus of the economic crisis and the power that flowed into the hands of the federal government major steps could have been taken to reduce discrimination. But important developments did take place, helping to condition politicians, government officials, and the public for the further progress later.

The Indians   If blacks did not see a significant change in status under the New Deal, Indians did. The general prosperity of the twenties had passed Indians by, the urban environment offered them no escape valve, nor had technology and science improved their condition as human beings. By the 1920s the Indian death rate exceeded the birth rate; severalty and the Dawes Act had only provided opportunities to whites to strip the Indians of their land by the millions of acres; traditions and customs had become lost or so distorted that some tribes were reduced to borrowing them from others in their determination to remain Indian.

A reform movement had come into being in the twenties headed by John Collier of the American Indian Defense Association and backed by the Indian Rights Association, the Indian Welfare Division of the General Federation of Women's Clubs, and other groups. The first special council of the all-Pueblo Union took place since the revolt in 1680 against the Spanish, followed by a tour of major cities by Pueblos. Public attention had been drawn to the Indian problem by these events and by denouncement of the Indian Bureau, corruption under the Dawes Act, and the deplorable economic, social, and cultural condition of most Indian tribes. Magazine articles with such titles as "Our Treatment of the Indians," "Red Tragedies," and "The Red Slaves of Oklahoma" had informed the American public of the extent of the disaster. The result was an independent survey backed by the government and Rockefeller money which published its findings in 1928 as the Meriam Report, named after its director, Dr. Lewis Meriam. Although the report did not repudiate the severalty program, for the first time it was admitted that it had been a mistake to try to "Americanize" the Indians and destroy their culture. The United States Senate began to investigate the problem, appropriations were increased, personnel policies in the Indian Bureau were improved, and the Board of Indian Commissioners finally admitted the failure of the severalty program.

But it was not until the election of Roosevelt, after three years of depression had worsened the condition of Indians, if that were possible, that a major change in attitude and policy took place. With the appointment as Indian Commissioner of John Collier, an outstanding social scientist long familiar with Indian affairs and for ten years an officer of the American Indian Defense Association, genuine reform became possible. In January 1934 a conference in Washington attended by representatives from all the national organizations interested in Indian affairs repudiated the severalty policy of breaking up Indian land and called for community land ownership and control. Collier proposed that allotted lands be consolidated for tribal use, that cooperative Indian groups receive financial aid and instruction in land use, that boarding schools be abandoned and day schools be used for adult as well as child education. He pushed for self-government among Indian societies and urged that more Indians be brought into the Indian Service.

The result was the Wheeler–Howard Indian Reorganization Act of 1934. Collier's basic assumption about the Indian had always been that "Clan instinct, clan operation of assets, is inherent in him. The tribal Indian remains the self-reliant and self-supporting Indian." In essence, this was the opportunity the Wheeler–Howard Act offered the Indian tribes. It made possible tribal constitutions and tribal business corporations for economic development. It repealed the allotment acts, continued the trust period indefinitely, and provided that unsold lands remaining after allotment be returned to the tribes. It made possible the purchase of new lands and created a revolving loan fund for Indian agricultural and industrial projects. It further provided for improved educational facilities and student loan funds.

Some Indians who had achieved successful integration opposed the Act. But over a hundred tribes organized under tribal constitutions and over two hundred chartered business corporations. Not all these efforts were successful—a painful consequence of the neglect which left many Indians lacking the knowledge and experience to undertake such ventures. And though past policies restricting the practice of ancient rituals, ceremonies, and crafts were now abolished, many traditions had been forgotten or only half-remembered and could not be resurrected.

Although much remained to be done, considerable improvement took place in tribes that accepted the provisions of the new law. Dry lands were irrigated and wet ones drained, eroded soil was repaired, trees were planted, roads constructed, crops and herds improved. Collier estimated that in the twenty years following the passage of the Wheeler–Howard Act Indian beef production went up 2300 percent and Indian farm productivity 400 percent. Improvements in medical and health services brought about a decline in the death rate, and the downward trend of the Indian population was reversed. Unfortunately World War II was to see the Indian Affairs budget cut, and the postwar period saw new attitudes emerge which gutted the intent of the Wheeler–Howard Act.

Science and Technology

Despite the economic situation, applied industrial research intensified during the thirties, and its results helped to sustain some major corporations. The number of industrial research laboratories doubled, and by 1940 they employed some 60,000 scientists. Their labors brought forth a multitude of new products. DuPont developed cellophane and duprene, a synthetic rubber. Plastics and synthetics of all kinds were produced from such varied sources as soybeans and coal. A major new product was nylon, introduced at the end of the decade and successfully used in such things as stockings and toothbrushes. Other important achievements were plywood, Plexiglas, Lucite, and greatly strengthened steels. The process of cracking heavy oils after extracting gas and gasoline was developed, and increased the supply of fuel for consumer use and provided the raw materials for lacquers, plastics, and synthetic rubber. The first commercially practical photoelectric cell came into use at the beginning of the decade and proved invaluable in making industrial work more accurate and refined. In 1937 the coaxial cable was put into commercial use, by means of which 240 conversations could be carried simultaneously on a single wire, a great advance in communications technology. Frozen foods had been developed in the twenties, were introduced commercially in the thirties, and by the end of the decade were selling 200 million pounds a year.

Improvements in machinery and industrial processes also continued apace. Technology and mechanization also steadily extended their role in American agriculture. By 1940, the number of farm trucks had increased sixteen percent and tractors seventy percent. The mechanical cotton picker, corn picker, and harvester–combine were developed and displaced much agricultural labor, thereby aggravating the depression in rural America. By the end of the thirties, greater agricultural productivity was possible although the number of farmers and farm workers had declined.

Advances also occurred in medicine and health. Vitamins A and B were synthesized in 1936, the use of the B_2 complex in curing pellagra was discovered, and in 1937 vitamin K was isolated. By 1939 vitamins were the second largest-selling item in drug stores, a \$500-million business. The food industry responded to the new knowledge by enriching the vitamin content of many products, and changes in eating habits and cooking methods were influenced by public knowledge of the role of vitamins in health. Initially developed abroad, the first of the miracle drugs, the sulfas, were made available in 1936, and had dramatic results on such infections as pneumonia. By 1940 a vaccine against typhus was produced on a large scale, bringing another deadly disease under control. New surgical techniques were developed, including those making possible the removal of an entire lung to check cancer. Studies of the electric waves of the brain led to new ways of diagnosing epilepsy, locating brain tumors, and treating some mental illnesses through shock treatments.

In pure research there was progress in spite of reduced support from accustomed sources. University budgets were cut, government funds became limited, and private foundations with shrinking capital funds were forced to cut back their contributions almost seventy-five percent. Nevertheless the decade produced such brilliant achievements that the United States moved into a clear position of leadership in astronomy, nuclear physics, radiation, biochemistry, and physiological chemistry. In 1930 the Lowell Observatory in Arizona discovered a new planet in the solar system, Pluto. And the work done at the Mount Wilson Observatory by Edwin Hubble and Melton Humason in measuring the velocity of recession of nebulae provided a new means of cosmic measurement and laid the basis for the theory of an expanding universe. The decade also saw the probing into the nucleus of the atom with the development of the atom smasher, the most significant work being done by Ernest Lawrence of the University of California, who built the first practical cyclotron in 1932.

The depression had its impact upon scientists in prompting them to think about the relationship between their work and the welfare of society. In 1937 the American Association for the Advancement of Science proposed a long-term study of this problem, and Nobel Prize-winner Harold Urey declared that the ultimate goal of scientists was "to abolish drudgery, discomfort, and want from men's lives, and bring them pleasure, leisure, and beauty." Critics, however, continued to argue that science and technology had acquired a kind of momentum and life of their own, unchecked by human values and ill-coordinated with human needs. The evidence could be seen on every side. These problems were to be posed in ever more serious terms in later years.

Education and Learning

The depression had three major effects upon education: financial cutbacks seriously hampered both programs and effective teaching; more students remained in high school and went to college in view of the grim prospects facing them on the outside; and theories were proposed and experiments tried reflecting the varied response of educational leaders to the crisis.

One disadvantage of not having a national school system became apparent in the early worst years of the depression. Local school boards, faced with diminishing revenues, started to cut salaries and programs, and in some instances to close schools. Since the burden could not, under the American local system of education, be shared equally, the poorer districts and states were harder hit than others. In Georgia 1,318 schools were closed in 1933. In a number of districts in many states the academic year was cut by one to six months. Teachers saw their already modest salaries plummet. Many districts in Iowa paid only the minimum required by law—$40 a month. Other states established maximum salaries which were below $100 a month. Chicago teachers were not paid at all for a year. And school districts cut costs further by firing teachers and reducing staff.

The New Deal provided considerable aid in keeping schools open, constructing school buildings, giving aid to needy students through the NYA, and providing for adult education and the employment of fired teachers through the Emergency Educational Act. But Congress refused to fund a massive program of federal aid to education. The consequences of all this were visible in the Census of 1940, which uncovered some ten million illiterates and disclosed that approximately three million children weren't attending school at all.

On the other hand the trend toward secondary education for everyone was given a sharp boost by the depression. Not only was there little economic reason for leaving high school before graduation, but it quickly became apparent that if one were to have a chance at a job at all a high-school diploma would be an advantage. There was an increase in vocational programs, aided by federal funds under the Smith–Hughes Act.

Although higher education lost enrollment early in the depression, enrollments began to increase by mid-decade, and by 1940 almost 1.5 million students were in colleges and universities, a new high in actual numbers and in percentage of the college-age population. Here, too, limited prospects for jobs kept many in college. State colleges and universities because of their low tuitions got most of the needy, who were further aided by NYA and other governmental funds.

Although college life was not grim by any means, the atmosphere was certainly more serious than it had been in the twenties, a seriousness reflected in the increased interest in economics, sociology, political science, and history. Students were also far more politically active than ever before, forming clubs and study groups. The result was that far more graduates moved into the world of government service. If business no longer offered jobs and prestige, government took up the slack. Public service tended to satisfy the idealism of youth as well as their natural desire to eat, and government benefited at all levels. Professors, especially in the social sciences, acquired a new status, even if their finances did not improve. Students turned to them in increasing numbers, and so did government, seeking their expertise to meet the economic and social problems created by the depression.

John Maynard Keynes, whose book,
The General Theory of
Employment, Interest and
Money *influenced the formation of
Roosevelt's economic policies.*

The depression stimulated ideas for drastic change in the educational system. George S. Counts of Teachers College, Columbia University, saw public education as a major force for social change. He believed that the emphasis on individualism in a highly interdependent society was damaging, and urged that education should be oriented to a collectivistic society. He suggested that wiping out inequalities in education between races and economic classes would further the larger cause of democratic reform.

Quite the opposite kind of proposal came from Robert M. Hutchins, the youthful president of the University of Chicago, who denounced the elective system and the vocational aspects of higher education, and argued that in the great literature of the world was to be found a body of ideas and values that should provide the main area of intellectual exploration for students. Hutchins altered the undergraduate curriculum at Chicago to conform to his ideas, but few other institutions followed his lead. The influence of the Chicago program, however, was apparent in the popularity of the Great Books program across the country and in the emphasis in many colleges on a core of general education courses in the humanities and arts.

Scholarship in general also was influenced by the times. Economists, stimulated by the theories of the brilliant Englishman John Maynard Keynes, focused on social control of the economy. Sociologists turned to community and regional studies. Anthropologists explored the nature of race, concluding that cultural differences between races were not of biological origin. Interest in past social, cultural, and intellectual developments spread, taking historians beyond their older concern with political, economic, and military history. The trend in scholarship toward greater specialization continued, and even led to an interdisciplinary tendency, designed to help social scientists communicate with one another. In this a major achievement was the fifteen-volume *Encyclopedia of the Social Sciences*.

Conclusion

At few times in their history had Americans been so conscious of the present, their thoughts so occupied by immediate circumstances. The events of the depression made life for many a day-to-day affair with little thought of the future except for the hope that things would not get worse. In the past only war had so dominated human affairs. The grim pressure of the Great Depression seemed in a way to have erected barriers isolating the Americans from the past and the future. At the same time, in the search for solutions to economic disaster, the Americans gradually acquired through the momentum of the New Deal a confidence that the future would be better, and in the rise of a new interest in the achievements of the past they gained reassurance that they possessed the strength to meet and conquer disaster.

Profile: FRANKLIN D. ROOSEVELT

Those who lead their people in times of crisis do not usually enjoy unanimity of judgment, either then or afterward. Franklin D. Roosevelt, President of the United States from 1933 to 1945, is a major case in point. One of the extraordinary leaders of the twentieth century, the only four-term president in the nation's history, director of the country's destiny in two great crises, depression and war, his stature is not in doubt.

But dispute raged in his lifetime, and still continues, over what kind of leader and what kind of man he was. Worshiped by millions, he was detested by many. In the thirty years since his death there has been no more unanimity among scholars and historians than there was among general citizens in his own day, though all agree that he had a profound effect upon his time. The critics, then and now, have struck from all angles, some saying that he was too conservative and changed nothing significantly, others that he was a dangerous radical who threatened if he did not actually overthrow basic American institutions. He has been called shallow and deficient in learning, cautious and vacillating, limited and narrow. It has been argued that his only concern was to stay in power. H. L. Mencken said he would come out for cannibalism if he thought it would win votes. Some complained that he had no real interest in the poor and the dispossessed beyond the customary charitable stance of the rich toward the unfortunate. Economists have criticized his economic views, political scientists his political judgments and his administrative skills, and moralists his preference for expediency over principle.

Walter Lippmann's famous remark of 1932—which came back to haunt him a thousand times—that Roosevelt was "a pleasant man who, without any important qualifications for the job, would very much like to be President," was not far off the mark, judging by his career up to that time. A mediocre educational record, a mediocre lawyer, a New York state legislator, an Assistant Secretary of the Navy, an unsuccessful candidate for Vice-President, a mediocre businessman, a good governor of New York, a relative of former President Theodore Roosevelt, and a great stamp-collector. Not exactly inspiring. But as a later president observed, there is no training-ground, no apprenticeship for the presidency of the United States. Great presidents have always been men who have risen above their own limitations, including their own past.

Intellectually, perhaps Roosevelt's greatest accomplishment was to chart and follow a middle course. Ogden Mills, Hoover's Secretary of the Treasury, had defined the general conservative view when he said that "We can have a free country or a socialistic one. We cannot have both. Our economic system cannot be half free and half socialistic. There is no middle ground between governing and being governed, between absolute sovereignty and liberty, between tyranny and freedom." The New Republic drew the line at the other end of the spectrum: "Either the nation must put up with the confusions and miseries of an essentially unregulated capitalism, or it must prepare to supercede capitalism with socialism. There is no longer a feasible middle course." But Roosevelt saw things differently. In the campaign of 1932, with his knack for the homely metaphor, he put the matter this way:

> Say that civilization is a tree which, as it grows, continually produces rot and dead wood. The radical says: "Cut it down." The conservative says: "Don't touch it." The liberal compromises: "Let's prune, so that we lose neither the old trunk nor the new branches." This campaign is waged to teach the country to march upon its appointed course, the way of change, in an orderly march, avoiding alike the revolution of radicalism and the revolution of conservatism.

The extreme positions of both conservatives and radicals left a gap in the lines so wide that Roosevelt was able to march an army of New Deal legislation through it. The middle ground was there, as wide as the Great Plains, and the New Deal took it with ease.

In drafting and administering his program Roosevelt drew on the advice and assistance of many groups, businessmen, bankers, labor and farm leaders, and politicians. But he regarded as especially valuable the college professors he attracted to Washington. Progressive governor Robert LaFollette of Wisconsin had used the faculty of the state university in carrying out his reforms, and pragmatic philosopher John Dewey argued that putting intellectuals to work in government would benefit both the intellectual community and society at large. As Governor of New York Roosevelt had made use of academic intellectuals, and he greatly extended the practice as president. He quickly drew sharp criticism from conservative businessmen for this practice, who spoke derisively of "the Brain Trust" and "the professors." The chief criticism was that these men were impractical theorizers who had never "hustled up a payroll" or run a business, and would starve if turned out to make a living in "the real world." In the Senate debate over the confirmation of Rexford G. Tugwell, Columbia University economist, as Undersecretary of Agriculture, Senator Ellison ("Cotton Ed") Smith of South Carolina declared that he wanted in the post "a graduate of God's University, the great outdoors." Roosevelt's own view was that "While there is a certain amount of comment about the use of brains in the national government, it seems to me a pretty good practice—a practice which will continue—this practice of calling on trained people for tasks that require trained people."

Personally, Roosevelt possessed a capacity to inspire hope when all seemed lost, to instill confidence that even in the face of disaster things would go well, to suggest that people could indeed control their own destinies even when everything seemed to indicate that they were helpless victims of events. At his Inaugural he told the nation: "The only thing we have to fear is fear itself." In the campaign he had indicated his willingness to experiment, to institute change to get things going again in the face of the most devastating economic collapse the nation had ever experienced:

> The country needs, and unless I mistake its temper, the country demands bold persistent experimentation. It is common sense to take a method and try it. If it fails, admit it publicly and try another. But above all, try something. The millions who are in want will not stand by silently forever while the things to satisfy their needs are within easy reach.

The day he took office, March 4, 1933, the very day the nation's banking system collapsed, he infected everyone with his optimism, his confidence, his willingness to experiment. As observers noted, in a single day the White House was "full of people who oozed confidence." By late spring of 1933 Washington had become a "breezy, sophisticated and metropolitan center," thronged with bright and intelligent people who came to serve the nation and were "seething with excitement." The sense of things being done spread throughout the country, and the White House was flooded with letters reflecting the hopes and gratitude of Americans. The staff required to handle the mail from citizens expanded from one to fifty.

Somehow Roosevelt managed to establish, with his confidence, buoyancy, and optimism, a tie between himself and the people that seemed open, warm, and intimate. He made brilliant use of informal press conferences, public announcements and activities, and radio "fireside chats," to assure the people that he personally cared about them and was doing everything in his power to help. His pragmatic approach struck a responsive chord in the minds of people who saw that the nation was faced with a situation which called for new methods: "Yesterday's answers," he declared, "are inadequate for today's problems—just as the solutions of today will not fill the needs of tomorrow. Eternal truths will be neither true nor eternal unless they have a fresh meaning for every new social situation." And his candor about the difficulty of finding the right solutions was as reassuring as it was refreshing: "I have no expectation," he quipped in a radio talk, "of making a hit every time I come to bat."

His confidence that something could be done without turning to the extremes of fascism and communism had an immense impact abroad on those seeking a rational way out of a worldwide depression. The English economist, John Maynard Keynes, in an open letter to Roosevelt at the end of 1933, declared:

> You have made yourself the trustee for those in every country who seek to mend the evils of our condition by reasoned experiment within the framework of the existing social system. If you fail, rational choice will be gravely prejudiced throughout the world, leaving orthodoxy and revolution to fight it out. But, if you succeed, new and bolder methods will be tried everywhere, and we may date the first chapter of a new economic era from your accession to office.

Gradually the feeling spread among ordinary people throughout the world that he was on their side, and he became, quite without their knowing why, a major hero to them in their own countries. For those long down-and-out, he became a symbol of hope that the future would somehow be better than the past. The Italian painter, writer, and doctor, Carlo Levi, who was banished by Mussolini in 1935 to a remote primitive village in southern Italy, wrote that in almost every single house in the village there were two pictures, and only two—one of the Madonna of Viggiano, and the other of President Roosevelt. And as late as the 1950s you could find in the huts of poverty-striken Bolivian miners a picture of Roosevelt torn from some newspaper or from the pages of a magazine, worn and tattered but still nailed to the wall.

When war came, a crisis far greater than depression, he inspired a similar confidence, an equal hope among those beset by the horrors of aggression. The English historian and philosopher, Isaiah Berlin, ten years after Roosevelt's death looked back on his effect outside the United States and wrote: "As the skies of Europe grew darker, in particular after war broke out, he seemed to the poor and the unhappy in Europe a kind of benevolent demigod who alone could and would save them in the end. His moral authority, the degree of confidence which he inspired outside his own country . . . has no parallel."

Chapter 10
WORLD WAR II

The Spirit of the Times
THOSE WHO FOUGHT

In World War II 291,000 Americans died in battle, and over 670,000 were wounded. Not much compared to the 6,115,000 Russians killed and the 14,000,000 wounded. In fact, fewer Americans were killed in the war than Yugoslavs. Not a great number, either, compared to the 16,112,000 Americans, men and women, who served at one time or another in the armed forces during the war. Still, a million casualties is large enough, and an indication of the terrible price of war regardless of the cause.

The main concerns of most fighting men were survival and going home, and many talked openly or thought secretly of the "easy" wound that would take them out of it all. Most adjusted to the violence that defines the nature of war, because to question that violence created guilt or cynicism and despair, states of mind that do not contribute much to survival. The character of modern war, moreover, tended to make killing largely impersonal. Few in combat ever met the enemy face to face. Death came from the skies, from shelling, from guns at great distances.

Few who went through the experience would want to do it again, but many who did tended, in looking back on it, to dismiss the misery and the horror and to take some pride in having been in it. The comedian Mort Sahl, in a wry comment on humanity's inclination to violence, remarked that in their reminiscences veterans forgot the bad and remembered only the good—the shooting, the killing, the burnings, the rapes.

Regardless of their attitude, what American fighting men accomplished was considerable. In Europe they shared the battle with Britain and Russia and with guerrilla and underground forces in the occupied countries. They began fighting in North Africa in late 1942, swept on to Sicily, and invaded Italy in 1943. With the British they broke the Nazi hold on Western Europe by invading France in June 1944. While the Chinese held down numerous Japanese troops on the Asian mainland, Americans carried the brunt of the island and sea battles against the Japanese in the Pacific, beginning with the invasion of the Solomon Islands in August 1942 and continuing through the battle for Okinawa in April 1945. The ferocity of island fighting against an enemy whose code did not recognize surrender was perhaps the greatest of the war, although those troops who fought at Cassino or at Stalingrad would dispute such a claim.

Members of the infantry stalk down a rubble-strewn alley in an Italian town. Allied troops invaded Sicily swiftly in 1943 but what was expected to be an equally effective landing on the mainland and subsequent Italian surrender became instead a bitter, nearly year-long campaign.

When it was all over, American soldiers, sailors, marines, and airmen breathed a collective sigh of relief and turned toward home. Most would carry scars, visible and invisible, for the rest of their lives, and few would ever be able to forget the experience. The sense of relief that it had ended was tempered by the painful sense of the irretrievable loss of those who never came back. One young man who had gone overseas with three comrades later recounted his sense of loss after a terrible battle in which one of their number had been killed. Weeks after the battle the surviving three were safely in rest camp, and then

> Late one afternoon our baggage ... caught up with us. Someone had two bottles of whiskey in his trunk and in the midst of unpacking we began to drink. The binge lasted several hours, and ended with our smashing up what little furniture we had managed to scrounge, hurling books, clothes, and equipment all over the tent, and fighting one another with staves drawn from the ends of our cots as though we were medieval ascetics scourging the devil from our bodies. Suddenly we realized one of us was missing. ... He had died trying to get his men across the airstrip. I had tried at least twenty times to write his widow and had torn up every letter. Now all the injustice in a world of death in the midst of life suddenly seemed focused on his absence, and all the frustration in the world at man's inability to solve the mystery seemed concentrated in us. And so we staggered and crawled out into the night to get him back.

> The rain was heavy and the night was very dark. We could not even see the heavens we were calling out to. But we wept, we cried out, and there on our knees in the muck and mud, our tears lost in the rain, we pleaded for him to come back. But he never came.

The appalling destruction and waste of human life and resources which victory required, imposed on friend and foe alike, is captured vividly by Eric Lambert in his novel of the desert campaigns, The Twenty Thousand Thieves, as he describes the scene at the end of the Battle of El Alamein where Rommel was defeated by the British:

> Below them stretched nothing but death and destruction to the very horizon. Shattered trucks, burnt and contorted tanks, blackened and tangled heaps of wreckage not to be recognized; they scattered the landscape as thickly as stars in the sky. Like dead stalks in the sand, rifles were thrust upward—a denuded forest. And each meant a man who had been maimed or killed. Inside each wrecked tank a putrid blackening paste on the walls was what an armor-piercing shell had left of the men who had manned it. Over the miles of wire hung at intervals the bodies of men, like a ghastly and infinite tableau. In dug-outs, pits and trenches the dead lay tangled and piled. Here and there from a heap of dead a hand reached forth as if in supplication, or a pair of eyes stared up accusingly—and would stare so until they rotted in the skull. Here was a body with the limbs torn from it or without a head; and somewhere else a head lay on its own. Ripped-apart bellies with the viscera swelling outward like some great sea-anemone; a throat impaled by the long shard of a shell. These were the details of the scene repeated again and again in every corner of the desert landscape; a great rubbish-heap of metal and human flesh. So the victors sat, gazing across the gigantic desolation.

Such were the realities of war.

The Road to War

As if the Great Depression was not causing enough anxiety, international troubles steadily multiplied during the 1930s and added to the world's worries. In the Far East a Japan increasingly controlled by militarists moved outward from that island kingdom to invade Manchuria in 1931 and China in 1937. Hitler, who had come to power in Germany in 1933, reoccupied the Rhineland, and Mussolini, with visions of the Caesars dancing in his head, sent his forces into Ethiopia. In 1937 both Germany and Italy tested troops and equipment in aid of the fascist revolt of General Franco in the Spanish Civil War. The pace of aggression stepped up in 1938. By the end of that year Japan controlled the coastal cities of China and its principal railroad lines. Hitler occupied Austria and bluffed France and Britain into acceding to his demand for the German Sudetenland of Czechoslovakia. In the spring of 1939 Hitler took over all of Czechoslovakia, and Mussolini, not to be outdone, marched into Albania. Germany moved against Poland in the late summer of 1939, Britain and France were committed to the defense of Poland, and World War II began.

In the spring of 1940 Hitler's forces overran Denmark and Norway, seized Belgium and Holland, smashed the French, and forced British evacuation of the Continent at Dunkirk. In the Far East Japan moved into French Indochina in 1940, and in 1941 completed its takeover with the consent of the Vichy government in France. The Dutch East Indies, British Malaya, and even the Philippines seemed threatened by Japanese expansion in the fall of 1941.

This march of events from 1931 to 1941 presented America with a serious decision. Despite some favorable impressions of Italy and Germany under Mussolini and Hitler—which emphasized their presumed efficiency and organization—Americans as a whole found fascism and nazism repugnant, and were alarmed by the aggressive moves of both nations in Europe and by those of militaristic Japan in the Far East. Yet the Americans were unwilling to intervene in any of the crises that marked this progression of events. Various and compelling factors shaped their unwillingness.

Forces for Noninvolvement Those traditional elements in American opinion that had always emphasized noninvolvement revived and gained strength. The decadent Europe that the Founding Fathers had warned was a threat to American virtue was called to mind and its abominations defined in twentieth-century terms. Conservative political spokesmen such as Herbert Hoover, who could never abandon the belief that Europe was the cause of the American depression and hence his own woes, denounced Europe's "sinister demands for power" and condemned the immorality of the failure of European nations to pay their World War I debts to the United States. Hoover consistently urged that America remain aloof from the contamination of European politics: "When we take sides in their controversies . . . we are playing power politics at the European chess table." The conservative *Saturday Evening Post,* certain that the New Deal itself was an example of Europe's pernicious influence on America, declared that "our destiny is unique," and that it could not be fulfilled by involvement in Europe's troubles. Not only conservatives took this view. Certain New Dealers also saw Europe as a threat, believing that both right- and left-wing critics of the New Deal got their ideas from Europe. Liberal writer Stuart Chase wrote that in Europe, "where the poor devils have never got together since the fall of Rome," problems and troubles were numerous and destructive. But quite the contrary was the case with America: "Fortunate above all others, unified above all others, stronger than any others, in a sense we have civilization in our keeping. The responsibility is passing from the Old World to the New."

The depression gave added weight to these views. Many believed that to get involved elsewhere would detract from our capacity to solve this main problem. The historian Charles A. Beard, whose views were influential—as his frequent appearances in testimony before Congressional committees indicate—wrote that far from getting involved in affairs abroad "We should concentrate our attention on tilling our own garden." And Henry A. Wallace, Secretary of Agriculture, was skeptical of even searching for expanded markets overseas, regarding that as an undesirable form of involvement when we needed to increase consumption at home.

By the 1930s most Americans had concluded that the dangers of involvement overseas were amply documented by U.S. participation in World War I, which seventy percent in a Gallup poll now regarded as an error in judgment on our part. The investigations of the Nye Committee of the United States Senate into the World War I profits of bankers and munitions-makers suggested that perhaps we had been drawn into that conflict by the selfish economic motives of these business interests. The implication was obvious that if there was talk of American involvement in European troubles again, it would stem from the same dubious sources.

Conservative opposition to Roosevelt and the New Deal also fed into the general sentiment toward noninvolvement. Many conservatives, especially after 1936, believed that Roosevelt might well use war to consolidate his hold on the country, and argued, not without some logic, that war would result in far greater regimentation of life and the economy than that produced by the New Deal, which they already saw as menacing the freedom of economic enterprise. Senator Vandenberg declared that in another war "we would get such a regimentation of our own lives and livelihoods, twenty minutes after we entered the war, that the Bill of Rights would need a gas mask, and individual liberty of action would soon become a mocking memory."

Also nourishing the stream of noninvolvement opinion was a rising sense of disillusionment with war among young people, especially college students. A number of young men took the Oxford Peace Pledge never to fight in war, and one group created the Veterans of Future Wars, proposing that they be paid their pensions and bonuses in advance of any conflict.

The extent of such feeling could be measured by the success of antiwar plays, including Sidney Howard's *The Ghost of Yankee Doodle*, Robert Sherwood's *Idiot's Delight*, Paul Green's *Johnny Johnson*, and Irwin Shaw's *Bury the Dead*. It was also revealed in a Gallup poll in 1935 in which seventy-five percent of the American people supported the idea of a national referendum on any decision to go to war rather than leaving the matter up to Congress. The attempt to write that suggestion into the Constitution as an amendment failed only when Roosevelt exerted enormous pressure on the House of Representatives, where the measure was defeated by a mere twenty-one votes. But the power of opinion against involvement was officially expressed in the Neutrality Acts of 1935, 1936, and 1937 which were designed to prevent the sale of munitions and other commodities to belligerents on either side in any war. When Roosevelt, alarmed by events developing elsewhere in the world, gave his famous "Quarantine the Aggressors" speech in Chicago in 1937, public reaction was highly unfavorable and the President was denounced in newspapers across the country. After war broke out in Europe in 1939, opinion favoring noninvolvement took solid shape in the establishment of the America First Committee whose most renowned spokesman was Charles A. Lindbergh, the famed "Lone Eagle" of the skies.

The strength of this opinion both in and out of government determined American foreign policy throughout the thirties. Predictions of what might have happened are by and large pointless. Nevertheless, it is worth noting that *if* the Americans had been more aware of the world and their position in it as a consequence of their own industrial and technological achievements, and had therefore acted with vigor in the crises of the 1930s, things might have turned out differently. But American failure to play a forceful role in part encouraged the Axis powers and discouraged such countries as Britain and France from taking strong positions against them. Hitler might have

Antiwar sentiment is reflected in this May Day parade by Communists in 1934. In the thirties groups on both the right and left agreed that the United States should not involve itself in Europe's war.

been confined to Germany and Mussolini to Italy, and the course of world events greatly changed, in the face of a forceful American policy. If Britain and France are to be blamed for appeasing and retreating before Hitler and Mussolini in the thirties, the United States must bear a share of that blame.

Forces Favoring Involvement   Against noninvolvement was a group of Americans both in and out of government who were internationalist in outlook, believed that the United States had responsibilities in world affairs, were concerned about the rising tide of aggression abroad, and once war broke out in 1939 began to argue the necessity of active American involvement in Europe.

For in spite of a crippling depression, the United States was still the major economic power in the world and had many important economic ties abroad. Her industrial machine used, and in some instances depended on, imported raw materials. The Export-Import Bank, first established to finance proposed exports to the newly recognized Soviet Union, by 1938 was making loans to underdeveloped countries to help create new markets for American goods. In addition, the Reciprocal Trade Agreements Act of 1934 sought to expand American trade abroad, and by 1939 twenty-one such agreements had been negotiated, resulting in a more rapid increase in American exports than in those of any other nation and an increase in the relative share of the United States in world markets. American investments abroad also increased in the 1930s, and by the end of the decade totaled $17 billion.

Furthermore, America had strong social ties to many countries, particularly in Europe. The most basic of these were the family ties of millions of American immigrants with their home countries. These Americans were intensely interested in their ancestral homelands, and when Hitler began to march, their concern was deep. Moreover, the prosperous 1920s had seen tens of thousands of Americans each year visit Europe, where they acquired a more intimate appreciation of their heritage than ever before.

These economic and social ties were reinforced by cultural and intellectual associations with Europe. Ideas do not recognize national boundaries, and there had always been currents flowing between America and the rest of the world, especially Europe. In the cultural and intellectual sense there did exist, as Walter Lippmann emphasized again and again, an Atlantic Community, dramatized by the flow of refugees to America, especially intellectuals in the arts and sciences, including Thomas Mann, the great German novelist, and Albert Einstein, the most famous European scientist. The existence of this international community—probably the most significant body of cosmopolitan opinion since the Enlightenment in the eighteenth century—contributed to the rising concern over developments in Europe.

Finally, modern techniques of warfare left any nation open to the aggressive ambitions of any other. No one saw this reality more clearly than Roosevelt. No one recognized more clearly that there was a community of interest among nations menaced by the totalitarian and militaristic powers. From late 1936 on, Roosevelt became increasingly worried about the threat to world peace by Germany, Italy, and Japan.

Roosevelt was also aware of the strong American opinion against involvement. But he threw the power and prestige of his office into the effort to change that opinion. By the time war broke out in Europe in 1939, he had become convinced that the United States must do everything it could to prevent a victory by the Axis powers. After the fall of France in 1940 he reportedly told William Bullitt, the American ambassador to France:

> Bill, if my neighbor's house catches fire and I know that fire will spread to my house unless it is put out, and I am watering the grass in my back yard, and I don't pass my garden hose over the fence to my neighbor, I am a fool. How do you think the country and the Congress would react if I should put aid to the British in the form of lending them my garden hose?

In a series of moves Roosevelt passed the garden hose over the fence and gradually brought about a change in public opinion. Immediately after war broke out in Europe in 1939 he secured an amendment to the Neutrality Act permitting belligerents to acquire American goods in American ports on a "cash and carry" basis, a move obviously designed to favor Britain. In September 1940 the Destroyer-Bases Deal was signed which provided for the United States to give Britain fifty reconditioned destroyers in return for ninety-nine year leases for naval and air bases in British possessions in the Western Hemisphere—an executive act of dubious legality. The Selective Service Act was passed in the same month.

By the end of 1940, after the fall of France, Denmark, Norway, Holland, and Belgium, Germany held all Western Europe, and Britain was in desperate straits. To carry on the struggle virtually alone, her needs were immense. In late December, Roosevelt took the matter to the American people via radio, proposing that the United States become "the great arsenal of democracy" by supplying those nations attacked by the Axis powers with all the war equipment possible. The public response was highly favorable, and the result was the Lend-Lease Act of March 1941. The need to protect the goods shipped to Britain led to the U.S. Navy escorting convoys to Iceland, which American marines occupied in July 1941, at which point the British Navy took over. American naval air and sea vessels on patrol also notified British warships of the presence of enemy submarines. By September and October 1941 an undeclared shooting war existed in the Atlantic between Americans and Germans. In November all pretense was gone: the Neutrality Act was repealed; American ships were traveling in combat zones; American merchant ships were being armed: the Navy was shooting at enemy vessels on sight; and Lend-Lease goods were not only flowing to Britain but Lend-Lease aid had been extended to Russia as well after the Nazi invasion in June 1941. The garden hose had indeed been passed, and the faucet had been turned wide open.

Over the Brink: Pearl Harbor American public opinion had shifted drastically, but involvement still stopped short of outright war. A public-opinion poll showed in November 1941 that only thirty-five percent of the American people would have voted for war had a national referendum been held on the issue. It remained for the Japanese to make clear to Americans the position the United States occupied in the reality of world affairs.

When Japan seized the Chinese island of Hainan in the South China Sea in February 1939, it became obvious that ambition and economic need were directing Japan south into an area rich in resources: French Indochina, the Dutch East Indies, the Philippines. The only major obstacle to Japanese expansion was the United States, which had consistently opposed Japan's presence in China, but had even more reason for opposing Japanese moves outward into the Pacific. For the United States was no peripheral Pacific nation. It was entrenched in the Philippines, Hawaii, and other Pacific islands, and it drew upon Southeast Asia for rich natural resources such as oil, rubber, and tin. The United States was also the major supplier of the raw materials required by Japan's own war machine.

The Japanese took French Indochina in 1940, concluded a pact with Germany and Italy in September of the same year, and signed a neutrality agreement with Russia in April 1941. The German attack on Russia two months later eliminated any Japanese fears of Russia. The threat was visible if not certain, and the American response was strong economic pressure, particularly control of and embargoes on the shipment of oil, scrap iron, and steel. By the summer of 1941, Roosevelt had frozen Japanese funds in the United States, which in essence prevented Japan from buying or selling here, had closed the Panama Canal to Japanese ships, and had called up the Philippine militia. For the militarists in Japan there was only one course of action now available. The United States stood squarely in the path of Japan's ambitions. So there should be no more nibbling at the edges of the Pacific, but a blow straight at the main obstacle. By the time the United States had recovered, the objective would have been gained and could perhaps be held. This view prevailed. On December 7, 1941—a date Roosevelt said would live in infamy—a Japanese air and naval task force struck at Pearl Harbor and crippled a significant portion of the dozing American fleet. Germany and Italy declared war on the United States four days later, and the nation suddenly found itself engaged in global war.

Events had finally forced Americans to see that in a world bound together by industrialism and technology, there was no such thing as noninvolvement for a major power. The Japanese had known even if the Americans had not, that no country with expansive ambitions could ignore in its calculations the leading industrial and technological power in the world. The Americans learned this the hard way at Pearl Harbor on December 7, 1941. The Japanese were to learn it the hard way also, at Hiroshima on August 6, 1945. In the years between, the lives of both peoples were greatly changed by the impact of total war.

Global Conflict

For the first six months after Pearl Harbor the war looked grim for America and her allies in every theater of operations. In the Pacific the Japanese could scarcely believe their good fortune. In quick succession they took the Philippines, Guam, and Wake from the Americans and put a small force in the Aleutian Islands off Alaska. Sinking the pride of the British Navy, the *Prince of Wales* and the *Repulse,* and driving back in defeat an outgunned Asiatic Fleet of American, British, and Dutch ships, the Japanese took Malaya, Hong Kong, Burma, and most of the Solomon and the Gilbert and Ellice Islands from the British, as well as Thailand, the Dutch East Indies, and the northern half of New Guinea. Such an unexpectedly easy conquest was heady brew and gave Japan what one of its admirals was ruefully to call "victory disease." Japan stood dominant in Asia and the Pacific, and posed a major threat to India and Australia.

On the other side of the world, the situation was equally disastrous. Hitler already dominated Europe, and his armies had penetrated deep into Russia, as far as the outskirts of Leningrad and Moscow, and were turning south to the Caucasus and Stalingrad. The Germans in Africa under the brilliant General Erwin Rommel appeared to be on the verge of seizing Egypt and the Suez Canal. In the Atlantic Hitler's deadly U-boat fleet threatened to seal off shipping from the New World to the Old, sinking over eight million tons of

A Liberty ship slips into the water at the Baltimore-Fairfield shipyard.

allied ships in 1942, more than were being built. Many attacks took place only a few miles off the American coast. The only bright spots in Europe were Royal Air Force control of the air over Britain, and the unbelievable Russian resistance which stopped the Germans within sight of Russia's two great cities. In the Pacific, encouragement came in the Battle of the Coral Sea in May and the Battle of Midway in June 1942, in which Japanese invasion forces heading for Port Moresby and Midway Island were turned back in naval invasions countered entirely by aircraft.

In response to this bleak situation, the American and British leaders made a key decision: they would concentrate their efforts against Hitler as the greater menace. Whatever its correctness militarily, this decision gave second place to that area of the world where European rule over native peoples had long prevailed. This decision wiped out in the East the last remnants of white prestige, already dissipated by Japanese conquest, and guaranteed that colonialism would not be acceptable once victory was secured. Although in the long run resource allocations were carefully balanced between the major theaters of war, most commanders and troops in the Pacific felt they were second in priority in men, supplies, and equipment.

The European Theater The decision to concentrate on the defeat of Germany called for further decisions—how and where to strike at Hitler.

One decision was dictated by circumstances. The Atlantic had to be dominated by the Allies or all other decisions would be pointless. A massive and rapid shipbuilding program was undertaken in Allied and neutral countries. The United States alone built 270 Liberty Ships, 531 Victory ships, and hundreds of tankers and other vessels. The time needed to build a Liberty ship dropped from 355 days in 1941 to 56 by the end of 1942. The coordination of land- and ship-based planes plus well-equipped destroyers with new methods of tracking and sinking submarines combined with extensive shipbuilding to fill the Atlantic with convoys to Britain and Russia. By the middle of 1943 there was an average of 673 merchant ships in escorted convoys at sea every day in the American half of the Atlantic, plus additional unescorted ships and troop convoys. By the end of 1943 the U-boat was under control, though a weapon to be reckoned with until the end of the war. Control of the Atlantic made possible an unending flow of supplies to Europe. Russia, for example, received over 7,000 tanks and 400,000 trucks.

The Russians needed supplies, but even more they wanted relief from the pressure of German armies. This could come only with a major allied landing in Europe, a second front. The Anglo-American decision was to postpone the invasion until it was possible to land an overwhelming force in France. In the meantime the Germans could be weakened in other ways. In 1942 the Allies began a heavy bombardment of German cities, industry, and transportation, designed to weaken the enemy's war production and morale and to force Germany to direct resources to air defense. This continued at increased tempo until the end of the war. Despite heavy civilian casualties, including those from the horrifying fire-bombing of Dresden, neither morale nor production slackened. In fact, Germany was producing more in 1944 than before. Only in transportation was she weakened, as air attacks were mounted on railroads, ports, bridges, roads, canals, and oil refineries and storage tanks.

On the ground, the American, British, and other Allied forces struck first in North Africa, landing in November 1942. In October 1942 the British defeated Rommel at El Alamein. Then with Montgomery's British Eighth Army moving from the east in Egypt, and the American forces under General Omar Bradley pushing forward from the west, the Germans were squeezed into a trap in Tunisia. The German army in Africa surrendered in May 1943.

Two months later the allies crossed the Mediterranean to invade and seize Sicily, a conquest completed within a few weeks. Mussolini was then forced out of office by the King, and Italy sued for peace. Argument over terms delayed a landing and allowed the Germans to move into Italy in force. On September 9, 1943, the day Italy surrendered, the Allies invaded the ancient land of the Romans. German resistance plus the mountainous terrain held up the advance and dragged on the war in Italy far beyond what had been anticipated.

By the summer of 1944 the Allies were prepared to land over a million and a half men in France, where one-quarter of all Hitler's forces were stationed behind what they considered to be impregnable defense. Although fully

*One of the soldiers in the first wave edges his way through the surf to
Omaha Beach on D-Day. Of the forty-mile strip of Normandy coast
chosen for the invasion, Omaha Beach was the most difficult to take.
The American troops lacked air support and the German fortifications,
from underwater mines to concrete pillboxes on the beach, were nearly
overwhelming. But both the American and the British assaults, further to
the east, were ultimately successful, and Allied troops, vehicles, and supplies
poured into France.*

aware of the coming invasion, the Germans were deceived and then confused by the choice of Normandy for the landing. Led by General Eisenhower, an armada of 600 warships, 4,000 landing craft, and 176,000 assault
troops landed at five beaches on the Normandy coast. Though initial German
resistance was fierce, within a few weeks over one million troops were ashore
and advancing. In August an American army landed in southern France and
drove north and west to link up with the Normandy forces. By this time, the
Russians in the east had crushed the Germans at Stalingrad and begun their
offensive to drive the Germans back into their homeland. The outcome was
now inevitable—the total defeat of Hitler's Germany—though the war was to
continue for almost a year.

The Pacific Theater   The main drive against the Japanese was by island-
hopping through the Pacific, taking the key islands and bypassing the rest.

General MacArthur lands on Leyte Island. MacArthur had led the original defense of the Philippines until Roosevelt ordered him to Australia in March of 1942. His successful reinvasion was a personal victory for him, and when the Japanese surrendered in Tokyo Bay in September of 1945, it was MacArthur himself who accepted that surrender.

One drive, under the command of the brilliant but egocentric General Douglas MacArthur, drove up from Australia through New Guinea to the Philippines. The other, under the equally brilliant but easygoing Admiral Chester W. Nimitz, went through the islands of the Central Pacific. The initial task of retaking the Solomons in order to protect Australia was accomplished between August 1942 and February 1943 in bloody land, sea, and air battles.

MacArthur then led his forces along the New Guinea coast and in October 1944 landed his army on the island of Leyte in the Philippines. Two great naval-air battles, the Battle of the Philippine Sea in June 1944 at the time of the Saipan Campaign and the Battle for Leyte Gulf in October 1944, destroyed Japanese air and sea power and crippled their efforts to halt MacArthur's invasion. MacArthur's forces captured Manila in February 1945.

In the Central Pacific a series of invasions gave the Americans control of key islands, including the devastating three-day battle at Tarawa in the Gilbert Islands, the seizure of the Marshalls, and most importantly the capture of Saipan, Tinian, and Guam in the Marianas. This brought Japan within range of American land-based planes which began to bomb and burn Japanese cities with deadly results. The seizure of Iwo Jima and the large island of Okinawa by March and June of 1945, although it cost American forces heavily, made it clear that the end was in sight. Casualties running as high as a million men were forecast for the projected invasion of Japan itself.

This prediction was not made idly, for island fighting had proved to be bitter, bloody, and costly, since the Japanese usually fought to the death. The *kamikazes*—or suicide pilots—who rained death on the American fleet off Okinawa, were evidence that the Japanese civilians as well as military men would fanatically defend their homeland. But the dropping of two atomic bombs in August 1945 on the Japanese cities of Hiroshima and Nagasaki made invasion unnecessary. This new and unspeakable wholesale death from the skies, together with Russia's declaration of war, was too much for even the Japanese, who surrendered rather than endure more.

Soldiers Abroad In World War II Americans served around the globe. Never had so many been abroad and in so many places. They were in China, Burma, the Indian subcontinent, and the islands of the Pacific; they were on duty in Central and South America; they fought in Africa and in Europe; they sailed in ships on every sea and ocean; they flew in the skies over all the lands and waters of the globe.

And they carried in their persons the society and culture from which they came: war proved to be one of the most successful carriers of the American image around the world. Everywhere the Americans went they took with them material comfort, money, machines, and knowhow. Even in Western societies they demonstrated that machines were better for doing the work of the world than back-breaking labor. In backward societies the impact was immense. For it brought to primitive peoples a realization of what modern technology and industrialism can do. From the South Pacific to the south of Italy, from the bulldozer to penicillin, people and their aspirations would never be the same again. In England, wartime austerity may have created a certain resentment at the careless display of wealth and the comforts Americans enjoyed, but among the underprivileged and backward peoples there was only admiration and desire for some of the same. Margaret Mead summed up the reactions of the Manus Islanders in the Pacific to their exposure to the Americans: "The Americans believe in having work done by machines so that men can live to old age instead of dying worn out while they are still young." That was a reaction shared around the world.

But there was more to it than this. The American soldier abroad may often have offended by flaunting his money, he may have been naive about other cultures and societies, and he may have been guilty of the violence common in soldiers on soils not their own. But he was also something expressed in one of Bill Mauldin's wartime cartoons—Willie the ragged, unshaven soldier, handing food to an emaciated urchin: title, "The Prince and the Pauper." With all that may be said against him, the American fighting man abroad carried with him the generous concern for ordinary people that had traditionally been our finest export. As the Manus Islanders described it, "The Americans treated us like individuals, like brothers. . . . From Americans we learned that human beings are irreplaceable and unexpendable, while all material things are replaceable and so expendable."

Bill Mauldin's famous cartoon.

The Prince and the Pauper.

Unintentionally the Americans brought many others to think about themselves, their society and culture, their position in the world and relations with other peoples. The intense curiosity of Americans, who were always asking questions, forced many to reassess the basis for their own national pride. To the Americans, wrote one Australian, "we owe an awakening objectivity of vision. The Americans asked innumerable questions that we were unable to answer, either from lack of knowledge or because we were unable to articulate ideas we had been content to express to each other with a vague, 'You know what I mean—.' The Americans did *not* know. We had to inform ourselves, to find our tongues and speak with precision, or feel ashamed. This happened in varying degrees in all sections of the community."

Finally, as they marched to victory the Americans with their easygoing ways, in such sharp contrast to the disciplined regimentation of the enemy, created a general aura of goodwill toward the United States such as no other nation enjoyed.

A Nation at War

Industrial Mobilization Modern war requires the fullest use of economic resources, which means all-out direction, planning, and control. Only the federal government had the authority and the power to achieve these goals, and a multitude of agencies sprang into being to coordinate and direct the mobilization and use of America's economic resources, industrial and agricultural. The government allocated all basic raw materials, controlled prices, profits, wages, and the activities of labor unions, directed war production, determined what civilian goods could be produced, rationed consumer goods from gasoline to meat, imposed high corporation and personal income taxes as well as excise taxes on communications, transportation, amusements, and luxuries, and created whole new industries for the production of scarce items such as synthetic rubber.

Control was essential, but government did not challenge the basic assumptions of private ownership and profit. No industry was nationalized. Even in the new industry of synthetic rubber, the fifty-one plants were leased to private business interests. Secretary of War Henry L. Stimson had noted earlier, "If you are going to try to go to war, or prepare for war, in a capitalist country, you have got to let business make money out of the process or business won't work." Faced with the need to convert production, expand facilities, and build new plants, many businessmen feared what this would do to them economically. They feared a commitment to a single buyer, the government, whose requirements could easily change, and leave them at war's end with facilities for which there would be no use. The government allayed these fears by underwriting the costs of expansion through tax write-offs, by guaranteeing profits through cost-plus-fixed-fee contracts, and by granting immunity from the antitrust laws to firms pooling resources. The government ultimately approved some six hundred such cooperative and profitable arrangements in the interests of efficient war production.

Likewise there was no basic challenge to labor. A national service law that would let government put any citizen in any job it saw fit—which organized labor fiercely opposed—was never passed. There were necessary controls that kept workers from shifting jobs as they pleased, but no one was ever directed by the government to change from one job to another, and employers were not compelled to hire workers at the government's direction.

The results of economic mobilization were startling beyond belief. Production almost doubled between 1939 and 1945. America produced 300,000 airplanes, 12,000 naval and merchant ships, 64,000 landing craft, 86,000 tanks, millions of rifles and machine guns. These armaments, other instruments of war ranging from radar equipment to flame-throwers, and thousands of items from K-rations to flight jackets, made the American armed forces the best equipped in the world, and strengthened our allies.

The labor force expanded to over 53 million, including millions of women, and approximately one million elderly people who came out of retirement. Manufacturers converted to war production with astonishing speed: Detroit switched from automobiles to tanks, trucks, and weapons; model train manufacturers made bomb fuses. New plants were built and existing ones expanded so fast that construction was greater from 1942 to 1945 than in the fifteen years before the war. By 1943 the railroads were carrying twice as much freight and three times as many passengers as in 1940. The Gross National Product rose from $88.6 billion in 1939 to $199.2 billion in the peak year of 1944. About half of all this went for the war, the other half to maintain the civilian economy—a classic case of providing both guns and butter.

But it all cost money. Between 1941 and 1945 the federal government spent over $320 billion, most of it for the war effort—a sum twice as great as the government had spent in its entire history from 1789 to 1940. Although about 40 percent of the cost was raised by taxation, the rest was borrowed, resulting in an increase in the federal debt from $49 billion in 1941 to $260 billion by 1945.

Research and Development   Recalling the experience of World War I, the government created in June 1940 a National Defense Research Committee, reorganized a year later as the Office of Scientific Research and Development. One of the main tasks of the Office was to mobilize talent by preventing the drafting of scientists and controlling the competition of industry for scientific talent. The other principal task was the assignment of projects. The basic source of talent lay in the nation's universities and colleges, which prompted the decision to let most scientific work for the war effort take place there. Many institutions specialized in certain problems and projects. Thus the California Institute of Technology concentrated on rocket development, while Princeton worked on ballistics.

The achievements of this effort were massive. Radar, for example, had a multitude of uses, serving as a ground warning system as well as aiding pilots to land under conditions of poor visibility. The navigational aid known as LORAN (Long Range Aid to Navigation) permitted ships and planes to locate their own positions accurately by means of special charts and radio signals without giving themselves away to the enemy. Rocket propulsion produced the bazooka, an infantry weapon used against heavy armor and fortifications. The development of the radio proximity fuse proved of enormous value against the V-1 German rocket and against enemy aircraft.

Medical men developed techniques of using blood plasma, created Atabrine as a substitute for quinine in the fight against malaria, and developed such antibiotic drugs as penicillin, which had been discovered in 1929, into a valuable tool to fight infection in wounds as well as in certain types of pneumonia.

The most dramatic achievement was the atomic bomb. Earlier study of atomic energy had made it clear that atomic fission could be turned into a weapon of terrifying proportions. This work had been international in character and, fearful that the enemy might turn to such a task, Enrico Fermi and Albert Einstein urged the government to undertake the creation of an atomic weapon before the enemy did. After Pearl Harbor work intensified as scientists at the University of California, Columbia, the University of Chicago and elsewhere worked to achieve the separation process that was the key to an atomic chain reaction. Success came at the University of Chicago on December 2, 1942. This was the crucial step, but as Dr. H. D. Smyth of Princeton later recorded: "The technological gap between producing a controlled chain reaction and using it as a large-scale power source or an explosive is comparable to the gap between the discovery of fire and the manufacture of a steam locomotive." Yet the gap was closed in a little over two and a half

Hiroshima after the atomic bomb was dropped from the B-29 Enola Gay, *killing approximately seventy thousand, and wounding over one hundred thousand.*

years, and involved the marshaling of scientific talent from not only the United States but from Britain and Canada, and the expenditure of over two billion dollars. The secrecy of the project created problems in getting appropriations from a Congress reluctant to approve vast sums without knowing what they were being spent for. Eventually key Congressional leaders were let in on the secret and got the necessary appropriations through, killing any calls for investigation. On July 16, 1945, in an isolated section of New Mexico, a giant mushroom cloud rose from the desert floor, and a new era for humanity had begun.

The scientific and technological achievements of the war were the indispensable base upon which victory rested. They also laid the basis for a very different kind of world after the war, opening wide the door to a new scientific and technological age. Society was to benefit in peacetime from many of these achievements, but others—from DDT to atomic energy—posed new problems and raised questions about the fate of humanity that are still unanswered. Moreover, the success of the government's support and use of scientific talent altered the role of science. Both science and government now had appetites whetted by their association with one another. Scientists became accustomed to having vast sums available, and government became accustomed to having scientists work on projects related to the national interest. Once an independent community for the pursuit of knowledge, science was now wedded to government support and therefore control.

Repercussions of War

It is one of the tragic ironies of history that as individuals have gained knowledge and experience, which ought to make them more humane and civilized, they have also acquired greater skill in warfare and have waged war on an ever-increasing scale. Modern total war is all-encompassing: no institution, no body of ideas, no set of values, no individual remains quite unaffected. War on the scale of World War II forces the entire society to gear its time, energy, and resources to the effort. Its impact is incalculable. The United States did not have to endure, as other nations did, the direct ravages of fighting. No armies raged across its land, no bombers pulverized its cities, no deprivations affected the health and sanity of its people. Yet the war affected American society deeply and in many ways.

Wartime Prosperity   No country ever engaged in total war and did so well by itself as a consequence. The war effort accomplished what the New Deal had been unable to do: it not only wiped out the depression, but it brought prosperity to America on a scale never experienced before. By any standard, the economic life of the American people was immensely improved.

Unemployment literally disappeared. In 1940 there were still 8.5 million unemployed. By 1943 the unemployed constituted only 1.9 percent of the labor force; by 1944 only 1.2 percent. Virtually anyone wanting a job had one. Worker income rose from $65 billion in 1941 to $123 billion in 1945. Average gross weekly wages increased from $25.20 in 1940 to $43.39 in 1945. Those of workers in manufacturing industries rose by 86 percent. In both instances, these figures were far higher than the 29 percent rise in the cost of living. Many family incomes increased more than these statistics suggest through the added earnings of millions of working wives. Income was also augmented by the serviceman's family allotment. Congress ultimately provided a $50 monthly allotment for wives based on a $22 deduction in a serviceman's pay plus $30 for the first child and $20 for each additional child.

America's agricultural community also prospered, although there was a 17 percent decline in the farm population as the inefficient small farm disappeared and agricultural workers were drafted or moved to better jobs in urban areas. There was less acreage under the plow than in 1932, but production increased with greater mechanization, the extended use of fertilizers and hybrid seed, and the exceptionally good weather of the war years. High yields meant that by 1944 food consumption by civilians was the highest in the nation's history, even though one-quarter of the American agricultural food output went to the armed forces and our allies. As farm prices doubled and production increased, net farm income increased four-fold. Farmers by war's end had not only reduced their mortgages by some $2 billion, but had also managed to save approximately $11 billion.

Business, of course, also did well during the war years. It is true that some firms could not adapt to war production, were unable to share in government contracts, and so collapsed. Many retail businesses suffered from shortages, rationing, or the disappearance of their product when their suppliers converted to war production. Over half a million small businesses failed during the war. But the industrial boom saw corporation profits after taxes almost doubled to $10.8 billion in 1944. Big business especially profited. Two-thirds of all government contracts went to the one hundred largest corporations, which also profited by receiving two-thirds of all government research money. The top ten corporations received 30 percent of all government contracts. Big business also profited by the consolidation of its position of economic dominance in American life during the war years. In short, big business grew bigger in such key industries as iron and steel, petroleum, coal, rubber, electrical products, and others heavily involved in defense contracts. In 1939 corporations with more than 10,000 workers employed 13 percent of the workers in manufacturing industries; by 1944 they employed over 31 percent of such workers.

Scientific and technical specialists of all kinds also enjoyed improved economic status as government, university centers, and industrial laboratories competed for their services. Professionals such as chemists, physicists, engineers, language experts, economists, and scores of other highly trained people discovered that war required such talents in profusion.

Despite difficulties and problems, the government succeeded in controlling this growth and the prosperity it produced. Rationing, price and rent controls, and wage guidelines all helped to curb inflation. But taxation was also a major weapon. The ordinary corporation tax was raised to a maximum of 40 percent and an excess profits tax of 90 percent was imposed, although a portion of that was refundable when plants converted to peacetime production after the war. High excise taxes were imposed on many goods and services. Personal income taxes were paid by only four million Americans in 1939, but after the Revenue Act of 1942 over fifty million paid income taxes, a process made easier by the institution of the withholding system in 1943.

The war naturally made a number of people millionaires, and the rich did well as always. But the share of disposable income received by the top 1 percent of the population declined from 11.5 percent to 6.7 percent, which indicated a broadened sharing of income. The rich may have received more in actual amount in the general prosperity but then so did everybody else. The rich clearly were able to live extremely well during the war despite taxes and other controls. Those without too many scruples could always buy even scarce items at high prices on the black market, and they could dine at clubs and hotels whose ties with wholesalers got them quality food not always available in normal retail markets.

But it is clear that income distribution was more democratic than it had been in the 1920s and 1930s. The average family income doubled during the war, and the sharp increases in real income for skilled workers and salaried workers brought about a dramatic expansion of the American middle class and laid the basis for the affluent society of the postwar period.

By 1943 and 1944, the war—much like a gigantic public works project—had put the American people to work, expanded industrial facilities, and prompted a seemingly limitless production of goods, although much was geared to the wasteful ends of destruction. The scene was one of bustling, almost feverish activity. In spite of shortages, Americans were living better than ever before: an almost ideal economic condition, certainly a far cry from what had been predicted. As late as 1942, many social scientists had painted grim pictures of widespread destitution and suffering, and even Roosevelt's closest advisor, Harry Hopkins, had believed that the standard of living would sink to the lowest levels of the depression in the early thirties. But none of this happened. By the end of the war, it is true, many people had gotten about as much out of the family car as was possible, clothes and furniture were wearing out, and appliances were on their last legs. But there was also some $250 billion in liquid wealth waiting to be spent, including $65 billion in war bonds, savings from long hours of work often at overtime rates, service allotments saved by wives and mothers, accumulated pay unspent by servicemen overseas, earnings in banks and savings companies, stock dividends and business profits. It was the most profitable war in American history—in anybody's history, as far as economic benefits were concerned.

Effects of War on Government   Total war also affected the role and status of government itself. It grew immensely in power and size. Since the federal government was the only agency with the authority and apparatus to organize America for such a war, to direct the economy, create a military machine, and control civilian life for purposes of war, it inevitably grew in size. Agencies, bureaus, departments, offices, and committees proliferated. Civilian employees increased from around a million at the beginning of the war to over 3.5 million at the end.

Congress was not hesitant about making its own suggestions, and challenged Roosevelt on occasion. For example, even after the President came out for it in 1944, the Congress successfully resisted a national service law, which would have permitted government to assign any citizen to a job as it deemed necessary. Over the President's veto Congress passed the Smith–Connally bill restricting strikes and punishing those promoting them. Nevertheless, the real power centered in the executive branch. The President told Congress shortly after Pearl Harbor: "I cannot tell what powers may have to be exercised in order to win the war." But it quickly became apparent that a great deal of power would be necessary. The war thus accelerated the trend toward a powerful federal government and particularly a powerful President. Congress was not a directing but an authorizing agency. The power to authorize was powerful indeed, but it was the President as overall director who was in the best position to suggest what needed to be authorized. And he generally got his way. Although many specific powers granted during the war were dropped or relaxed afterwards, America had grown accustomed to the idea of a powerful Presidency, and there was in the postwar world no lessening of the office.

Effects on Politics   The war also affected political developments and attitudes. One consequence was a swing to conservatism. This could be noted in a number of ways. There was no time, for example, during the war for attempts at reform or a revival of the New Deal. Roosevelt himself remarked, perhaps with some relief, that Dr. Win-the-War had taken over from Dr. New-Deal. This became apparent in the 1942 Congressional elections when numerous New Dealers went down to defeat in both the House and Senate. Republicans and anti-New Deal Democrats, principally Southerners, joined forces to dominate the Congress. A similar move marked state and local elections. Administrative Washington also changed in the direction of conservatism. Big business, largely excluded from the councils of government in the 1930s, made a triumphant re-entry when its managerial talents were needed for the war effort. Big businessmen were put in key positions. Donald Nelson of Sears Roebuck became head of the War Productions Board. *Business Week* greeted this movement with approval: "The management men who have gone to Washington during the war should be the opening wedge for the participation of management men in peacetime government."

The political environment was also subtly altered during and after the war by military men in high places. American military men had never constituted a distinct class, and were subordinate to civil authorities—a matter they had never questioned. Nevertheless, the military mind was a technical one little concerned with social issues and ideas, and naturally emphasized the value of regimentation, hierarchy, and conformity. Now this influence was felt in matters far beyond strategy and tactics. Military recommendations influenced contracts granted for war goods, the decision to evacuate the Japanese-Americans from the West Coast and to impose military rule on the Hawaiian Islands, and the decision to drop the atomic bomb on Japan rather than arrange a test explosion viewed by Japanese observers as scientists proposed.

Effects on the Social Fabric   The social impact of war was greater than its economic and political effects, significant as those were. It had a profound influence on social institutions, relationships, and patterns of behavior. It served as a unifying element in American life; it bound people together in a common cause and seemed to give life a high purpose. After Pearl Harbor, the uncertainty over uninvolvement in the war disappeared overnight. Secretary of War Stimson probably spoke for a great many when he remarked: "My first feeling was of relief that the indecision was over and that a crisis had come in a way which would unite all our people."

The civilian population was swept up in a fever of patriotic concern. Though many initially believed there was danger of air raids, even of invasion, "the cheerful side of this," one civilian defense advocate proclaimed, "is that this war offers us stay-at-homes a greater chance for real service than any war in the past." So, by the millions, the American people rushed to do their bit. They were air-raid wardens, firefighters, auxiliary police, nurses' aides. Over 600,000 citizens belonged to the Ground Observer Corps, including many youths, women, and even the blind, who spent long hours in observation posts. Seven million ultimately were involved in civilian defense. Millions more in the Civilian Voluntary Services were devoted to such varied activities as planting victory gardens, running salvage campaigns, public speaking on governmental policies, serving as block leaders to inform neighbors of government programs, participating in carpools, and providing pre-induction counseling for draftees. Children under fifteen were organized into a Junior Service Corps whose members sold war stamps, collected waste paper, gathered books to be sent to servicemen, participated in war bond and metal collection drives, and scores of other activities. Established youth organizations such as the Boy Scouts and Girl Scouts contributed their time and effort as well.

In many families, grandparents, mothers, and children lived together when a young husband went off to war: 1.5 million people were living "doubled up" by the end of hostilities. Often economic worries dissolved in the general prosperity. But there were also many strains as war altered the normal pattern of life. Long separation of husbands and wives, fathers and children, sorely tested the emotional stability of women left to carry on alone and of children whose memory of their fathers often became blurred and characterized by fantasy. Some wives, especially those without children, broke in various ways: they developed distressing physical symptoms, came to resent their husbands for their absence and blamed them for troubles at home. They forgot what their husbands looked like, or in their loneliness turned to drink or infidelity. A woman wrote: "We must learn to wait. To endure the slow trickle of time from hour to hour, from day to day, for weeks in anguish and suspense. And then wait for some message, a letter sent from far off—a small scrap that tells something of how he was—some time ago when it was sent. We must have a life that's endless fear and doubt."

For the men who came home even in the best of circumstances, there were differences. People change just by the passage of time, to say nothing of their experiences. Most families made the adjustment, but for others it was too much and marriages dissolved. The divorce rate rose sharply during the war, from 16 per 100 marriages on 1940 to 27 per 100 in 1944—and then it exploded after the war to approximately 50 per 100. Yet difficult as marriage seemed in wartime, there was a sharp rise in the marriage rate at the beginning of the war. It fell off in 1943 and 1944, then rose again in 1945.

Women at Work Part of the instability of many families during the war stemmed from the increase in the number of women working, especially

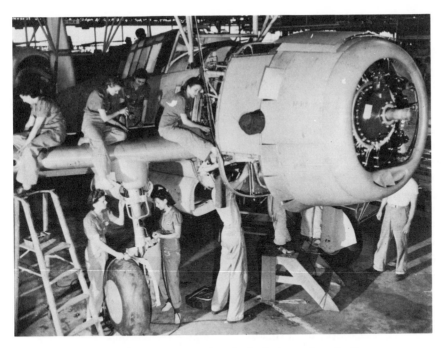

*A team of women workers prepares a plane in final stages of production.
Although women were a considerable force in the war production effort,
often performing difficult and heavy tasks, traditional attitudes about
women and work did not change. When veterans returned at the end of the
war, women returned to the home.*

those who had small children. Women constituted 36 percent of the work
force by the end of the war, up from 25.5 percent in 1940, and they took on
every conceivable kind of job. They worked in coke plants, blast furnaces,
rolling mills, shipyards, and airplane factories. They were riveters, welders,
hydraulic press operators, crane operators, shell loaders. They became bus
drivers, train conductors, section hands, barbers, taxi drivers, ferry command pilots. Government policy in late 1942 required that women be given
equal pay for equal work. Although this resulted in a rise in wages for
women, on the average they still made about 40 percent less than men in
most manufacturing jobs. Many smaller firms evaded the law in various
ways, and in large firms the lack of seniority kept many women in the lower
pay brackets. During the war women proved their capacity for any kind of
work, but within a year after the end of the war over two million had
disappeared from the labor force. Older views of women's role were reas-
serted. Yet unquestionably most women enjoyed working, liked the income
it provided and the freedom it gave to participate in society outside the
home.

The most serious effect of women working was on children they could not
care for and whom society also neglected. Many working mothers were able

to leave their children in the care of grandparents or other relatives, friends, or neighbors. But in many war-impacted centers, the population consisted largely of people new to the area, housing was inadequate, relatives and friends were far away, and neighbors were unfamiliar and often also working. Under such conditions neglect of children often became commonplace. No one knows how many children were locked in cars in parking lots, left in all-night or all-day theaters seeing the same movie over and over again, locked in houses, or simply turned loose to wander aimlessly. A Detroit survey estimates that about twelve percent of the children of working parents were so treated. The manager of a Muncie, Indiana movie theater reported that there were always fifty to sixty children left waiting after midnight for parents coming off the late shift to pick them up. The effect of this on young children was perhaps best put by one little girl who told a social worker: "I'll tell you a secret. When my mother is away and I don't know where she is I cry. She says she's at work but I don't know where she is and I get scared."

Day-care centers were part of the aid planned for war-impacted areas, but only some 3,000 such projects were actually instituted and affected only 100,000 children. Moreover, in such areas school facilities were totally inadequate, and many school-age children were on half-day programs. With teachers also in short supply, the schools had problems enough without attempting to keep track of students, and the absentee rate was high.

Related to the problem of children on the loose was the extraordinary increase in juvenile delinquency, although inadequate schools were hardly its main cause. Juvenile arrests increased twenty percent in 1943, and in some cities by a much higher figure. Such statistics have to be viewed with caution, of course—police definitions of what constituted criminal behavior on the part of the young varied widely from community to community. Nevertheless there was a striking increase in theft, vandalism, destruction, and violence by boys under eighteen, and an even greater increase in violent crimes as well as in "sex delinquency," such as prostitution, by young girls. No one explanation for this is satisfactory—the absence of parental supervision, inadequate housing and limited school facilities, the lack of normal recreational activity, the atmosphere of war itself in which so many values seemed suspended for the duration, all probably played a part. But one thing is clear. None of these problems pressing on the American family in wartime was new, although they were almost certainly accentuated during the war.

Americans on the Move   A chief characteristic of American society had always been its mobility, or more specifically, internal migration toward opportunity. Some 15.3 million civilians moved during the war years, from country to city, from South to North, and from East to West; and many moved in opposite directions as well. Millions of men entering the service were stationed in camps across the country, and families often accompanied them from one camp to another until the day of embarkation. Buses and trains were always crowded. One traveler reported the scene at a Mobile, Alabama bus terminal:

> . . . a milling crowd; soldiers, sailors, stout women with bundled up babies, lanky backwoodsmen with hats tipped over their brows and a cheek full of chewing tobacco, hatless young men in light colored sports shirts open at the neck, countrymen with creased red necks and well-washed overalls, cigar-smoking men in business suits in pastel shades, girls in bright dresses with carefully curled hair piled upon their heads and high-heeled shoes and bloodred fingernails, withered nutbrown old people with glasses, carrying ruptured suitcases, broadshouldered men in oilstained khaki with shiny brown helmets on their heads, negroes in flappy jackets and pegtop pants and little felt hats with turned-up brims, teen-age boys in jockey hats, here and there a flustered negro woman dragging behind her a string of white-eyed children . . .

Southern whites migrated to the shipyards and oil fields in the Gulf states and to the Hampton Roads–Newport News–Norfolk complex as well as to the manufacturing centers in Illinois, Indiana, and especially Michigan. Southern blacks moved to the factories of the Middle West and to the shipyards on the West Coast. Workers from the Northern plains took off for the airplane factories on the West Coast. And so it went. The heaviest migration was to the West Coast. California gained two million in population from 1940 to 1945. Here was where opportunity lay. More than half of all wartime shipping construction and nearly half of all airplane manufacturing took place on the Pacific coast. California alone had by 1944 received almost ten percent of all war contracts.

Housing Such a sudden mass movement created problems for families and communities alike. Good-sized towns and cities experienced abrupt population increases; small towns turned into centers of war production or found themselves dominated by military installations that had moved in next door; new communities suddenly appeared in the middle of nowhere as war plants replaced orchards and croplands. Most migrants ended up not in cities but on their outskirts, in temporary housing ranging from government-built communities to trailer camps to shack and tent settlements. Many such projects were outside the jurisdiction of cities and towns, which often lacked the facilities to provide them with decent living conditions. Schools were overcrowded, law-enforcement agencies were overburdened and testy, hospitals were jammed and doctors overworked, streets and roads crumbled under the impact of increased traffic, water supplies were inadequate and often tainted, sanitation was a menace with limited sewage lines and cesspools improperly placed, fire was a constant hazard.

And everywhere houses were packed with people like cattle in freight cars. In a house in Willow Run five war workers slept in the basement, a family of five lived on the first floor, four men occupied the second floor, nine men slept in the garage, and four families parked their trailers in the yard. Sometimes people had to sleep in shifts. In the Los Angeles area, a social worker found a twelve-year old girl sitting alone in a corner in a beer hall late at night and asked what she was doing there. The girl replied: "I'm just waiting for 12 o'clock. My bed isn't empty until then." In Leesville, Louisiana, which suddenly found a military camp on its doorstep, a reporter discovered young service wives, some with babies and small children, living in a grim nest of sheds, converted chicken coops, and rundown barns. They slept three to a bed, had a single shower and toilet for thirty-five people, and a room and bed partitioned off where wives could meet with their husbands.

Private companies constructed over one million housing units, mostly with federally insured mortgage money, and the National Housing Agency built over 830,000 units. But at best, such housing provided for some seven million migrants. Millions more were on their own. The Lanham Act of 1940, designed to aid war-impacted communities in the form of day-care centers, hospitals, sewer systems, garbage incinerators, fire-prevention equipment, law-enforcement funds, recreational centers, and other facilities, had spent only $343 million by September 1944. Though the money was provided to states on a matching-funds basis and thus involved double the sum indicated, political influence governed much of the distribution, red tape meant endless delays, and many communities opposed application for funds on the ground that it would encourage migrants to stay after the war or would threaten private economic interests.

Such attitudes indicate marked social tension between oldtime residents and migrant families. Many a resident in an established community resented what seemed to be an invasion that poured into a community, upset its routine and pattern of living, strained its resources, and ruined what had once been an attractive town. San Diego, once a sleepy coastal town with one aircraft factory that had six employees, suddenly found it had fifty thousand aircraft workers. The town's entire character was altered. A longtime resident of one war-impacted area spoke for many across the country in similar situations: "Before the bomber plant was built, everything was perfect here. Everybody knew everybody else and all were happy and contented. Then came that bomber plant and this influx of riffraff. . . . You can't be sure of these people." One migrant told a reporter: "Folks in houses think trailer people are vermin." A newcomer to one community said that when she tried to go to church, "nobody ever spoke to me or looked at me." Many migrants were from rural, even backcountry regions, had never been away from home before, and were unfamiliar with cities. They were the ones who often had to live under the worst conditions, and they were frequently homesick and lonely. At Willow Run Village a class of children was instructed to sing the state anthem, "Michigan, My Michigan." They refused. It was *my* Kentucky, *my* Tennessee maybe, but not *my* Michigan. Home is where the heart is.

Minority Groups

Black Americans: A New Mood The war was a watershed in American race relations. The status of blacks as the 1940s opened was hardly attractive. Economic insecurity and humiliation were widespread. Twenty percent of the black work force was unemployed, and those working were excluded from almost all positions above menial labor. Among the 100,000 aircraft workers there were only 240 blacks in 1940, and North American Aviation flatly declared in 1941 that "The Negro will be considered only as janitors and in other similar capacities." In key industries such as the rubber industry, less than three percent of the work force was black. Two-thirds of all black workers were domestics, unskilled agricultural and industrial workers, or worked in service industries. Trade unions of the AFL downgraded and limited black membership, or even excluded blacks. The industrial unions of the CIO publicly supported equal rights, but still had trouble getting locals to give blacks fair treatment.

Despite Mrs. Roosevelt's public views supporting equal rights and the President's general sympathy, there was limited opportunity for blacks in government, there was no administrative challenge to segregation in the South or anywhere else, and when the decade began the Supreme Court still supported such devices of political discrimination as the white primary, which existed in eight Southern states. Blacks were refused enlistment in the Marines and the Air Corps, they could join the Navy only as messboys, and in the Army they were strictly segregated. Southerners supported the view of blacks stated in the Memphis *Cotton-Trade Journal:* "Anyone who hears Delta Negroes singing at their work, who sees them dancing in the street, who listens to their rich laughter, knows that the Southern Negro is not mistreated. He has a care-free, child-like mentality, and looks to the white man to solve his problems and to take care of him."

Little wonder that when after 1939 the United States edged closer to involvement in the war black Americans took a dim view of any argument that the war was to defend democracy, and were opposed to any repetition of the World War I experience when, at the urging of leaders such as Du Bois, they set aside their grievances in the interests of national unity. Not this time. On the contrary, black leaders believed that World War II should not be used to divert them from the drive for equality, and indeed that the war offered an opportunity for mass pressure toward improvement. Although a handful of blacks in the Northern ghettos argued that a Japanese victory would help "liberate the dark races," almost all accepted the view of the NAACP that "If Hitler wins, every single right we now possess and for which we have struggled here in America for three centuries will be instantaneously wiped out." But this did not mean that black Americans should sit passively during the war. The mood, in fact, was for protest and pressure. After Pearl Harbor the black attitude was that this was a two-front war—one for democracy abroad and the other for democracy at home.

Behind this commitment lay concerted pressure on government by the March on Washington Movement. Influenced by mass meetings held over the past year, A. Philip Randolph of the Brotherhood of Sleeping Car Porters and a strong proponent of militancy called for a "thundering march" on Washington on July 1, 1941, "to shake up white America." He argued that "The Administration leaders in Washington will never give the Negro justice until they see masses—ten, twenty, fifty thousand Negroes on the White House lawn!" Fearful of such a march and willing to go as far as he could

A black artillery unit sets up a howitzer in France.

without losing political and business support for his policies, Roosevelt met with a delegation of black leaders and on June 25, 1941, signed Executive Order 8802, which required that discrimination in hiring be eliminated in government agencies, job-training programs, and factories with defense contracts. The order also established a Fair Employment Practices Committee to police the ruling. Roosevelt refused other requests, including an end to segregation in the armed forces. The march was called off, and the black press interpreted the order as a victory and as proof that militancy paid off.

Although the March on Washington Movement tailed off it gave added impetus to the rising strength of traditional organizations such as the NAACP, whose membership rose from 50,000 in 1940 to almost 450,000 in 1946. It also helped lay the groundwork for the Congress of Racial Equality, which stressed nonviolent direct action, and in 1943 instituted the technique of the sit-in to eliminate segregation.

Even though liberals tended to favor equality and to oppose segregation, most Americans urged that war was not the time to institute such profound social changes as the abolition of segregation.

Nevertheless the national mood, to say nothing of the war situation, was changing and with this came gradual changes in the status and condition of blacks. In 1944 the Supreme Court abolished the white primary. In 1942 the Navy agreed to accept blacks for general labor service, and after May 1944 began experiments at integration. By fall of that year integration had been instituted on 25 ships. The Army lowered its literacy requirements, established a special unit to raise the educational level of deprived blacks, and by the fall of 1944 had 700,000 black soldiers in service, including 7,800 officers. In 1944 the Army began an attempt to integrate training facilities. Black troops were increasingly sent overseas, 22 units were engaged in combat, and through some 2,500 black volunteers in the Battle of the Bulge integration got its first test on the battlefield.

Important economic improvements and changes also took place, chiefly stemming from the need for labor. By the end of the war blacks comprised eight percent of all war workers. The number of skilled black workers doubled, and gains among the semi-skilled were even greater. Jobs in urban areas in the South, North, and West opened up new opportunities for hundreds of thousands of blacks, including women. The federal government also contributed to job improvement opportunities, employing more than 200,000 blacks by the end of the war and opening up higher classified positions to blacks. The government also outlawed wage differentials based on race, reversed the policy of the United States Employment Service of specifying race on job requests, and refused to certify unions that excluded minorities. The Fair Employment Practices Committee was not the success blacks hoped it would be, since it lacked authority and often interest, and was frequently defied. But it successfully resolved about one-third of the eight thousand complaints it heard.

True, the war period was marked by incidents of racial tension and trouble. Riots occurred at a number of army bases and several broke out in major cities, the most deadly in Detroit in June of 1943. There the influx of black war workers created tensions over jobs and housing. The police were unable to control the situation, and federal troops had to be used. Twenty-five blacks and nineteen whites were killed and hundreds were injured before the wave of violence was subdued. Fortunately, such disturbances were not common.

In general the war brought a new temper and attitude on the part of blacks to push more aggressively for an equal role in society. It also brought a significant advance economically and politically, and produced cracks in the wall of white policy and white attitude.

Civil Rights   In the general area of civil rights the record was exceptionally good except in one major instance. Religious conscientious objectors were assigned duty in civilian work camps, on farms, in mental hospitals, or in military medical service. Much of the work was unpleasant, and living conditions were sometimes degrading. But only those convicted of actual draft violations received prison sentences, most being Jehovah's Witnesses denied classification as ministers. The hysterical reaction against conscientious objectors that had occurred during World War I was avoided. And the same was true for Americans of German and Italian descent and citizens of enemy countries. Many of the aliens were German refugees, and were required to register with the government and to relinquish any guns, cameras, and shortwave radios. But suspicion of such people was at a minimum. One German refugee teaching in a Midwestern university in a small town hurried to turn in his camera to the sheriff's office as required. The sheriff casually said he saw no point to this, but the professor insisted that he must turn it in as required. "Well, Alex," said the sheriff, "all right, I'll take it, but if you need it for anything just drop by and pick it up."

Things were not so easy for the Japanese-Americans on the West Coast, and indeed the violation of their rights was perhaps the most serious episode of its kind in American history. All Americans of Japanese descent, citizen and noncitizen alike, were forcibly removed from their homes and imprisoned in "relocation centers" in the interior of the country. Eventually all but some eighteen thousand were released, but few returned to their homes. Military rule was also imposed on the Hawaiian Islands because of the large Japanese population there. No case of espionage or sabotage by a Japanese-American ever occurred, but the Supreme Court upheld the constitutionality of both actions. An unjustified panic by the West Coast public as well as by military commanders was responsible for this treatment of a group of Americans who had long been discriminated against anyway, and whose economic loss alone in forced sales and abandoned property was very heavy.

Conclusion

The war ended in April 1945 in Europe and in August 1945 in the Pacific. The Americans had entered the conflict with no high-flown ideals about "saving the world for democracy." They had been that route before. Their attitude was to get the job done as quickly as possible. Yet they had the conviction that their cause was right, that Hitler and what he stood for was wrong and must be destroyed, that Japanese militarism must be defeated and not allowed to rise again. And they had a general hope that something better for the world would come after victory had been achieved. But they had no illusions that some brave new world would come about by magic. They were, as one observer called them, "the disillusioned and deadpan defenders of freedom."

The war shook up the world, and it served as a major agent of change in American life. It profoundly altered the American economy—not only from depression to prosperity, but in many other ways as well. Labor unions emerged as a more powerful element in the economic structure and opposition to them by the business community virtually disappeared. The great corporations were more powerful than ever before, and businessmen enjoyed new prestige and influence. The role of government was greater than even during the New Deal, and there was a new and widespread recognition that it must henceforth play a determining role in the guidance of the economy. This led to a new emphasis on the government's role in society in

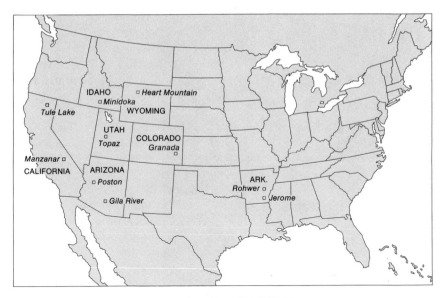

JAPANESE-AMERICAN "RELOCATION CENTERS"

general. People had come to look to Washington for leadership in solving problems, and the federal government would thereafter play a large role in social issues it had been little involved in before.

The war also accelerated social change. More women worked outside the home, giving a new impetus to the demand for social and economic equality. The hard shell of discrimination and racial prejudice was cracked, opening a new era in the struggle for equal rights. The awesome power of science and technology became more apparent than ever before, raising both hopes for a better life and fears that science might lead to an end of all human life on earth if not properly controlled. The war made Americans far more aware of the rest of the world, and opened the door to American involvement in the affairs of the world on a grand scale. The acceptance of world leadership marked a departure from older American ideas of their role in the world, and was to raise problems in the postwar world that few anticipated.

Profile: FREDERICK C. BURTON

He came off the farm and out of small-town America, as many did. Born in 1919, killed in action in Europe in 1945, his life was a brief parenthesis between the end of World War I and the end of World War II.

He was no storybook hero—he led no gallant charges, won no banks of ribbons. He made no contributions to global strategy, concocted no ingenious schemes to confound the enemy, engaged in no planning for the grand alliance. Unknown except to his family and friends, his name never appeared in newspapers across the country—the only time he even came close was in a column by war correspondent Ernie Pyle who forgot to get his name, so he became simply the anonymous young lieutenant who brought the body of Captain Waskow down off a mountainside in Italy, said "I'm sorry," and walked away in the dark. There were a lot like Fred Burton. They just did their jobs.

He detested war—"a monumental stupidity"—but thought this one necessary and his duty. He was different from most because he felt strongly enough about it to cross the border in 1941 and join the Royal Canadian Air Force. After Pearl Harbor he secured his release and came back to the States to become an officer in the infantry. He served in Italy—at Anzio, San Pietro, Monte Cassino, where he confided to his diary that "I am not as confident of my personal immunity as I used to be." Sensitive to art, architecture, and the beauty of the Italian countryside, and later to the equal charms of France—things he had only read about before—all he really wanted was to go home and raise horses. In this he was the universal soldier—"We merely want to finish it so that we can go home."

War by its very nature threatens the humanity of those engaged in it, and after five months in Italy this threat had become very real to Fred. He told his diary: "I am strangely devoid of feeling. I find no joy in living, no hope in the future. . . . I feel detached from the human race—quite by myself in an uninhabited world." Most soldiers spend endless time trying to reassure themselves that there is another world out there where people are not killing one another, where decency and affection prevail, where life not death is the goal. Like so many others, Fred was obsessed with the need to keep in contact with that world, as though it would disappear if he failed to do so, as though his own innate humanity would melt away if he did not. He wrote letters constantly, complained and worried if none came in return, continually asked what the folks at home were doing, all of them—his mother, father, brother, sisters, grandparents, cousins, uncles and aunts, friends. The most ordinary details pleased and reassured him that somewhere all was well. And he sought signs of that world even where he was—"not far from nowhere." An entry in his diary noted that "there's a thrush in these woods which sings in the moonlight—the day was too short for him."

But it wasn't easy. "I am lonely without knowing for whom I long," he confided to his diary. For a time he thought he did know. After a leave in Rome he wrote to a friend: "There are few people of whom I would rather write than the Tuscan beauty, Eva. She is rare among women. Chances are now I'll never see her again. . . . She understands much of this world and its troubles and her observations and judgments are honest and sincere. . . . She lives near the Piazza del Popolo. It's only a little way down to the Piazza del Espana, where the flower vendors cluster on the steps. Shelley's house is there at the corner, overlooking the square and its flowers. Keats came here too." She talked and she listened, she laughed, she lived where the flower vendors are and reminded him of the poets Shelley and Keats—all the things one never associates with war but is afraid of losing because war has no use for them.

Near the end he grew very depressed—it all seemed so endless. But he transferred his concern about himself—though "I have no fears of death"—to others. To a friend who had been wounded in the Pacific and was now back in the States in hospital, he wrote: "I am sustained by the thought of you and that you are safe in the States. Do not come back into all this."

For his own part, he moved toward an uneasy compromise with fate: "There is one thing a man can be sure of. Death is inevitable. Why attempt to delude oneself into attempting to sidestep the inevitable. Relax and enjoy being alive. The leaves will fall again another autumn." And he started to write about his plans after the war in terms of if he came home, not when. To a friend he wrote: "Oh, to hell with the war. . . . I rather expect to get killed. . . . So what—it won't be a stranger when it comes. The thing that makes it easiest, however, is a certain dullness which has come over me. I simply do not care about anything as keenly as I used to."

He was sensitive and intelligent, qualities war always tends to put a strain on. But he had a certain tough-mindedness as well, an adherence to duty, that helped him to survive as long as he did and to serve better than most. His commanding general wrote him a letter of commendation and he was awarded the Bronze Star, but there is nothing to suggest that he attached any significance to either.

The last entry in his diary, dated December 28, 1944, three weeks before he was killed while leading a night patrol, reads:

> Well, it was Christmas in Strasbourg, city of slim, delicate church spires. It was a good Christmas, considering. I was pinch-hitting for Lt. Burdette and was busy. The weather was cold, but we were in buildings and kept quite warm. The Rhine river is not very wide there—only a pistol shot across.

Chapter 11
THE POLITICAL AND ECONOMIC LIFE OF CONTEMPORARY AMERICA

The Spirit of the Times
THINGS AND PEOPLE

It will be recalled that the French observer, de Tocqueville, wrote in the 1830s that the American "grows accustomed to change, and ends by regarding it as the natural state of man. He feels the need of it, more, he loves it; for the instability instead of meaning disaster to him, seems to give birth only to miracles all about him." If de Tocqueville could have spent time in America in the decades after World War II, the 1830s would have seemed a placid untouched mountain lake by comparison, as change swept the country and the inconsequential became the momentous, science fiction turned into science fact, the unexpected emerged as anticipated, the uncommon became the commonplace, and the absurd was now the acceptable.

Air-conditioned home and electric toothbrush ... frozen dinners and McDonald's drive-ins ... the Drinking Man's Diet and Adele Davis ... tranquilizers and heart transplants ... one hundred million television sets and pornographic movies ... a million foreign visitors and ten million Americans abroad ... shopping malls and retirement villages ... the pill and the bug ... the ballpoint pen and rockets to Mars ... giant conglomerates and transistor radios ... polyester suits and eight-lane expressways ... gay liberation and styrofoam ... the jet plane and the mobile home ... teenyboppers and black mayors ... sensitivity sessions and bumper stickers ... Black Power and flying saucers ... organic food and filter-tipped cigarettes ... computers and the twenty million dollar movie fiasco ... marijuana and programmed learning ... strontium 90 and the low-fat diet ... black revolution and sexual freedom ... think tanks and perfumed toilet paper ... aerosol cans

and Medicare ... stereophonic sound and instant replays ... terramycin and nuclear plants ... systems analysis and astronauts. ...

Six percent of the world population consuming forty percent of world resources
... political corruption at the highest levels ... imbalances in nature and an energy
crisis. ...

Are the disasters of change outnumbering its miracles? Is a reassessment in
order, by a generation grown up in a time of change, and a product of it?

Progress and Doubt

The most striking changes in the postwar world were, broadly speaking,
economic—significant because economic change so often affects social, political, and cultural habits and institutions, ideas, and values. Anxieties that
peace would lessen or wipe out the prosperity created by the war turned out
to be unwarranted, and the United States embarked upon unparalleled expansion, so great that it widened the gap between the wealthiest nation and
the rest of the world.

Economic Growth For almost thirty years unchecked economic expansion argued that unlimited growth was a permanent fact of life. There were
minor recessions in 1949, 1953, 1954, 1958, 1970, and 1971, but they had no
real effect on either growth or attitudes toward the inevitability of growth.
The statistics measuring this growth were staggering. The Gross National
Product doubled about every decade, rising from $211 billion in 1945 to $419
billion in 1956, and to over a trillion dollars by 1971. By 1970 the American
GNP constituted two-thirds of the world's production of goods and services.
In 1950 there were some 40 million automobiles in the United States; by
1970 there were 100 million. In 1945 the Bell System had approximately 25
million telephones; by 1971 it had over 100 million. Coal production was
lower in 1970 than in 1945. This did not mean a decrease in production of
fuel, rather a shift in the kind of fuel, for crude oil production doubled and
that of natural gas increased five times. Other expansion was comparable.
From 1945 to 1971, the output of electric energy expanded sevenfold, and in
addition new sources of energy appeared, especially nuclear power. By the
1970s, sixteen nuclear plants were in operation, fifty-four were under construction, and thirty-six more were in the planning stage. Steel production
doubled from 1945 to 1970 while aluminum production increased sevenfold.
Construction also reflected the extent of growth. Total annual expenditures
for construction, public and private, rose from $5.6 billion in 1945 to $89.2
billion by 1970. Durable consumer goods—cars, homes, furniture, and appliances—rose in annual sales from $55.2 billion in 1952 to $132 billion by
1971. Sales of nondurable consumer goods—drugstore products, liquor, gasoline, groceries, and meals in restaurants—rose from $108.8 billion in 1952 to
$246 billion in 1970. Supporting this vast economic growth was an expanded
work force which rose from 52.8 million in 1945 to 85 million in 1973.

*Las Vegas, Nevada—the product of postwar growth and the frantic
search for the things that would make America happy.*

All this represented a scale of growth inconceivable before World War II,
producing equally unimaginable prosperity. Even the prosperity of the war
years seemed slight by comparison. Hence the economist John Kenneth
Galbraith's apt phrase, "the affluent society." The average family income
was $2,400 in 1945 and $10,000 by the 1970s. Total wages and salaries were
$123 billion in 1945, and had expanded to $596 billion by 1970. Although the
consumer price index doubled in the same period, the gain was still extraordinary. Most Americans simply assumed that increasing affluence was here
to stay, and relied on credit buying through installment purchases and the
extensive use of a new technique, the credit card. Consumer credit thus rose
from $8.3 billion in 1946 to $122.5 billion by 1970.

Most Americans shared in the general prosperity. The well-to-do naturally saw their wealth increase, even though they received a smaller share of
total income. By 1970 the highest paid 5 percent of the population was
receiving between 21 and 23 percent of the national income, and the poorest
20 percent saw their dollar income climb significantly, but it continued to
receive only about 5 percent of the national income. Big business, of course,
profited enormously. In the first six months of 1973 alone General Motors,
the giant of American industry, had sales of $20 billion and profits after taxes
of $1.75 billion. Workers, too, did well. Those in manufacturing industries

saw their average earnings increase from $54.92 per week in 1949 to $133.39 in 1970, while workers in nonmanufacturing industries had their weekly earnings increase from $62.77 to $181.40 in the same period. Farm income also expanded, from $12 billion in 1945 to $16.5 billion in 1970, although agriculture's share of the national income decreased from some 15 percent to 2.1 percent. But the drop in the farm population and the reduction in the number of farms were so drastic from 1945 to 1970 that there was a significant gain for individual farmers. Overall, then, America's economic growth was astounding, and general prosperity equally so.

The Causes of Expansion   But to note this growth and prosperity is not to explain it. Why did it all happen? One prime cause was technological. The electronic computer revolutionized the operations of business, industry, education, government, and technology itself, as in the space program. By the 1970s the third generation of computers had come into being, sophisticated marvels capable of millions of calculations per second, and of storing, retrieving, and analyzing vast quantities of information. They could thus direct, control, and correct a multiplicity of operations, and even made possible the automated factory—which led the economist Galbraith to remark wryly that were it not for the hideousness of many of the products, we would be hard put to know that human beings were involved at all.

Other innovations included the laser, the transistor, the semiconductor, and miniaturization, which made possible the integrated circuit—so small that as many as twenty thousand components could be assembled on a unit less than one-quarter inch square. Chemical fertilizers, insecticides, weed control and growth elements, and complicated farm machinery transformed agriculture and secured a productivity as great as that of industry.

Billions were devoted to research and development, which now absorbed over three percent of the Gross National Product. And an almost obsessive faith was revealed in the frantic haste from discovery to application to widespread use—a haste that helps account not only for the dizzy pace of change but for the difficulties of absorbing all these changes.

Among other causes of economic growth was the role of government. World War II had proved what the New Deal had failed to prove, that government spending and taxation could stimulate economic growth. In a variety of ways the federal government helped underwrite expansion, though it was still war or the threat of war that provided the greatest stimulus. The Marshall Plan for the reconstruction of Western Europe spent over $22 billion dollars. Since most of this was for American goods and services, it helped stimulate the American economy. More government billions went as aid to veterans for housing, education, insurance, and pensions. There was the Cold War with Russia, and the associated small hot wars in Korea and Vietnam, each costing at its peak almost $30 billion a year. And the conviction that Russia posed a threat to world peace unless confronted with an overwhelming counterforce saw a massive defense budget become a part of American life. The billions spent yearly—over $80 billion requested even after the American withdrawal from Vietnam—supported large segments of American industry, including aircraft factories, shipyards, electronics manufacturing, weapons producers, and many others.

From 1945 to the early 1970s some $140 billion in military, economic, and technical aid flowed out to countries round the globe. Such sums, averaging $5 billion a year, strengthened the American economy, which supplied most of the goods and services, including military hardware. Government also spent vastly increased sums for education and welfare, while tax cuts in the 1950s under President Eisenhower and in the 1960s under President Johnson released further sums for consumer buying. The government also supplied most of the billions spent on research and development, including $24 billion on the space program which put men on the moon in 1969. The aerospace and related industries relied entirely on government support. In these years the federal government purchased about twenty percent of all that was produced.

Other causes of expansion included developments in the world of business itself. Because of advantages inherent in size, the great corporations grew even larger, until they played the dominant role in the economy. By 1970 there were 115 manufacturing companies with annual sales of over a billion dollars each. In that year American Telephone and Telegraph had assets of $50 billion. By the middle of the 1960s General Motors, Standard Oil of New Jersey, and the Ford Motor Company had a combined gross income larger than that of all the farms in the United States. Corporate growth was stimulated by a new form of supercorporation, the conglomerate. The earlier trusts had been combinations of businesses of one kind, such as oil or steel. The conglomerate was composed of many kinds of businesses under one corporate roof. The LTV Corporation of Dallas in 1973 owned among other things the sixth largest steel producer in the country (Jones and Laughlin), the Plaza International-Regency Hyatt Hotel of Acapulco, Steamboat Village (a ski resort in Colorado), Wilson and Company (the third-largest meat producer), and LTV Aerospace Corporation, manufacturers of the A-7 attack airplane for the Army and Navy. In that year LTV was the twentieth-largest corporation with over $4 billion in sales.

The great corporations could operate with unprecedented efficiency. They controlled the capital to mobilize technical, scientific, and management specialists, and thus had the resources for long-range planning as well as the capacity to take risks and absorb losses from mistakes (such as the Edsel fiasco of the Ford Motor Company). With rare exceptions they controlled their own prices and markets. All these advantages made for still greater growth not only for themselves but for the economy.

Finally, postwar economic expansion rested on the population which grew from 145 million in 1945 to over 205 million by the 1970 Census, making a steadily expanding body of consumers. By 1946 the American people had lived with fifteen years of economic deprivation, first in the depression and then in the war, and they longed for material things. By the end of the war there were consumer assets of $250 billion, and people saw no need to let these savings sit idle. Money is for spending, so they set out on the biggest buying spree in history. It is easy to say that all this was grossly materialistic, that many were conned by the allurements of advertising to purchase things they did not need or even really want. But people are activated by many motives. Privation had left many with a deep urge for material security—for their own homes, and for the things that make homes comfortable. Once the basic needs for food, clothing, and shelter have been satisfied, other elements in the human psyche come into action, and can easily be played upon. People want things that give them a sense of independence, like the automobile. They want conveniences like power lawnmowers and electric mixers. They want esthetic satisfaction, from fine wines and chinaware to smooth lawns and luxuriant shrubbery. They want enjoyment in their leisure time, a second home in the mountains, a motor boat, camping equipment. These desires, too, are self-generating. What at first seems a luxury shortly becomes a necessity. Convenience brings the desire for more convenience. And so comes into being an expanding economy, based on the demand for more and ever more goods and services. Jobs abound, incomes rise, production increases. And ever-increasing production and consumption come to seem only normal.

Trouble in Paradise   But by the 1960s flaws had appeared in the vista of endless growth and dangers in the assumptions that underlay it. And by the 1970s genuine crisis threatened.

In the flush of unprecedented economic triumph, few had time to notice that not all Americans were sharing in the prosperity. In 1960 22 percent of Americans, or approximately 40 million men, women, and children, were still living in poverty, which was defined as less than $4,000 a year for a family of four. In 1962 *The Other America*, by Michael Harrington, called public attention to the problem. Till then the poor had not attracted general attention because they were no longer a single definable class as, for instance, the immigrants had been. The new poor included large numbers of the elderly, young people unable to find jobs in a specialized economy, slum and ghetto residents, Appalachian families and others in deprived regions, the mentally, physically, or socially handicapped. The percentage of poor blacks was twice that of whites.

There were major efforts to deal with poverty. The Economic Opportunity Act of 1964 promoted a series of programs ranging from the Job Corps and Head Start to community action programs and loans to small businesses in poverty areas. Billions were spent on such programs, and although by the 1970s they had helped, it was obvious that they were not the major success many had hoped. Other efforts included expanded social security and welfare payments, medical aid for the aged, and efforts by many businesses to train and employ those previously ignored. By 1970 these efforts and a still-expanding economy had reduced the definable poor by one-half, yet there were still over 20 million who were poor by definition and millions more not far above the line.

But poverty was not the only flaw in the system. Wealth was not being put to the best use. Too much was devoted to personal and private use. Although the great majority of Americans enjoyed the material good life, it cost more than just the price of the goods which made it possible. By gearing the economy so heavily to personal consumption, less wealth was available to improve the quality of life in the broader social arena which affected the personal lives of all Americans directly or indirectly. In consequence, by the 1960s a whole set of problems had begun to get out of hand. For example, the nation had faced before a crime problem of major proportions, notably after the Civil War and during Prohibition. But never had the problem been so great in all categories of crime as now. Fifty percent of arrests were of persons under twenty-four, many of them blacks—suggesting that society was neglecting both the young and its largest racial minority. Many Americans assumed that this was simply a problem of "law and order" which could be solved by beefing up the police and strengthening the courts. But the problem was greater than that. Part of the answer lay in enormously expanded public education, job training, recreation, and housing. Large sums were spent on these things by the 1960s, but never enough, and they too often benefited those who needed them least.

Similarly with health. Billions were poured into medical research, by now the best in the world. But there was no national health insurance program, and greatly increased medical personnel and hospital and clinical facilities never got a fair share of the national wealth. The ironic consequence was a nation that could accomplish one heart transplant after another but was behind Yugoslavia and fifteen other countries in its capacity to save the lives of newborn infants.

Other problems involved the decay of cities. Through the Model Cities program, housing development, and other programs, the government attempted to promote urban renewal and eliminate urban blight, but the results were disappointing. A handful of cities, such as Philadelphia, Boston, and New Haven managed to rebuild central areas, but the total effect was negligible. It was estimated that it would take at least $5 billion to make Los Angeles reasonably livable. Expenditures on private satisfactions clogged streets and highways with automobiles while public transportation languished. Passenger trains nearly disappeared, bus and subway service deteriorated, while some $33 billion in public funds went to construct a vast interstate highway system to satisfy private and certain business interests. The attempted revival of railroad passenger service in the early seventies through government support of the Amtrak system was little more than a token effort. All these were penalties paid for imbalance in the division of wealth between private and public uses.

There were other flaws in the economic achievement, one at the heart of the system. While most Americans took pleasure in consuming, few seemed to get satisfaction from producing. *Work in America,* a 1972 special task force report to the Secretary of Health, Education, and Welfare, pointed out that large numbers were dissatisfied with their jobs, "even . . . such traditionally privileged groups as the nation's 4.5 million middle managers." The report

New York City, 1966. Scenes like this one became commonplace across the nation as air pollution increased, seriously threatening the health of urban dwellers and steadily destroying the quality of life.

noted that satisfaction with one's work related directly to longevity, and queried spending great sums for medical research on diseases resulting from the frustrations of the work system while spending little to alter the working conditions that bring on those very illnesses, such as hypertension and heart disease. By the seventies dissatisfaction with the work system had produced strong opposition, especially in younger industrial workers, who used sabotage, vandalism, absenteeism, and strikes to protest the dehumanization of the work process.

What was needed was flexibility in the work system and freedom from rigid control. Experiments in plants abroad, notably in Sweden, as well as in some in the United States, indicated that increased productivity, lower costs, improved quality, and most importantly high morale were possible under a system of "industrial democracy," in which work operations were decentralized, specialization was reduced, and the work process was controlled by the workers themselves.

By the late 1960s some manufacturers were experimenting with a new work environment. In the Topeka, Kansas pet-food factory of General Foods, workers divided themselves into teams, learned all the jobs on their team, and then moved from one job to another. They made decisions in scheduling, design, hiring, and firing. The technology of the plant was geared to the workers, not the other way around. One of the more advanced experiments took place in a Proctor and Gamble plant in Lima, Ohio, where workers had almost complete control of plant operations, including the setting of pay scales. These experiments touched only a fraction of America's industrial establishments, but they seemed to point to a reorganized work system emphasizing the worker as a human being and thus reducing alienation and dissatisfaction.

From Waste to Conservation   Another flaw in the system was the waste inherent in commitment to unlimited growth and the assumption of unlimited resources. Products were designed to be tossed aside in a no-deposit, no-return economy that threw away more than most countries produced. Beer cans and plastic bottles littered the countryside. Automobile "graveyards" were stacked high with iron cadavers. Appliances, from toasters to dishwashers to television sets, seemed built to disintegrate in a specified time. Basic features were not changed, only external styling in yearly models which outmoded and devalued those of the previous year. Too much economic growth was based on planned obsolescence, calculated waste.

Created wealth in the form of goods was not only wasted by built-in obsolescence, but expanding production hastened the exhaustion of natural resources such as iron ore, oil, and copper. Unlimited and uncontrolled industrial growth also began to destroy the basic resources of our environment: the air, the water, the land itself. Thousands of acres of rich farm land disappeared daily in California as cities and factories expanded indiscriminately into adjacent agricultural areas. Industrial plants and automobiles daily poured millions of tons of pollutants into the air, while factories and mines polluted rivers, streams, and lakes.

Though for years conservationists had warned against the waste of resources and the destruction of the natural environment, there was no widespread concern about such matters until the late 1960s and early 1970s. Private conservation organizations then sprang up by the score, colleges and universities offered courses on "ecology," and politicians discovered the issue. Moved to action by a nationwide concern, Congress passed legislation establishing standards for clean air and water and set deadlines for automobile manufacturers, industrial plants, and other polluters. An Environmental Protection Agency was established and given sweeping authority to enforce such regulations. Business people, union leaders, and local public officials were frequently in opposition, arguing that strict enforcement would cost too much, would wipe out businesses, and would destroy jobs. Recession in the mid-seventies gave an unfortunate weight to their arguments.

The Energy Crisis   The energy crisis which began in 1973, predicted twenty years earlier but generally ignored, compounded the environmental

Robert F. Kennedy and John F. Kennedy conferring during the Cuban missile crisis. The President's response of blockade and mobilization to the presence of Soviet missiles in Cuba resulted in Khrushchev's agreement to remove the missiles and turn back the Soviet ships heading towards Cuba.

problem. The drive for energy forced a relaxation of environmental legislation and threatened to halt the broad workings of the Environmental Policy Act. Congress approved the Alaska pipeline and put aside legislation regulating strip mining. Offshore oil prospecting and drilling was opened up and prospecting allowed even in wildlife refuge areas. Plants were given permission to use high-sulphur coal, which was a plentiful if dirty fuel.

But the energy crisis also dramatically argued that America must give up her high-producing, high-consuming, wasteful ways. It revealed the vanity of a materialistic lifestyle, the arrogance of six percent of the world's population consuming forty percent of the world's resources, the vulnerability of a nation now dependent upon others for so much of its raw materials, and the weakness of a society trusting private entrepreneurs to operate in the public interest. Although it was expected that the United States would find solutions to the energy problem by the 1980s, probably including solar energy and engines run by hydrogen, it was also certain that the United States was by the mid-1970s entering upon a new economic era. Henceforth the economy would be, if not austere, at least less materialistically oriented, and society would be more inclined to direct its resources to public rather than purely private ends.

Political Developments

Congress and the President   Dramatic changes in economic life were not paralleled by equally dramatic changes in American political life—one reason, argued some, why America found itself in both economic and political difficulties by the 1970s.

The Great Wall of China rises behind Richard Nixon, the symbol of what he considered to be one of his greatest triumphs—the re-establishment of relations with the People's Republic of China.

In the postwar era Americans registered their political commitments in various ways. The Democratic party dominated the Congress completely, losing control only during the years 1946–1948 and 1952–1954. Since the Republicans were clearly the party of conservatism, this seemed to suggest a more liberal turn of mind for voters. Yet in fact, the Congress was dominated by a coalition of Republicans and conservative Democrats (mostly Southern). In a sense, this alliance was not far from reflecting the sentiments of most Americans of voting age who tended to regard themselves as moderate or conservative in their views on most subjects. Under such circumstances Congress was unlikely to pass legislation involving significant changes in American society unless the pressure of momentous events required it. Hence the flurry of civil rights legislation in the 1960s in response to the civil rights movement of blacks.

Despite Democratic dominance in Congress, the Americans in the postwar period gave the edge to Republican presidents, sixteen years to fifteen from 1945 to 1976. The feisty Harry Truman, who had become President on the death of Roosevelt, won election in 1948 in one of the great political upsets in American history. A traditional liberal, he sought greater opportunities for the common people and sponsored aid to nations ravaged

Richard Nixon makes his farewell speech to his staff on the day he stepped down from the presidency in 1974.

by the war. But he also set the character of the policy of containment of the Soviet Union that helped fuel the Cold War, and in domestic affairs he lacked the capacity to rally the Congress to support of his programs.

His successor, Dwight D. Eisenhower, the enormously popular military hero of World War II, believed, in his own words, in "progressive moderation," tending to be more liberal in social matters and conservative in economic ones. Eisenhower believed in caution and avoiding controversy—which disturbed those who wanted action on a variety of fronts—but he could be decisive in important matters. It was he who sent federal troops to Little Rock, Arkansas, to enforce school desegregation, and he who flatly refused to get American troops involved in saving Indochina for the French in 1954 despite the advice of associates to do so.

When John F. Kennedy was elected President in 1960 over Richard Nixon in an incredibly close election, many observers believed that a new era was about to dawn. Kennedy was young, forty-three, vigorous, intelligent, and witty. He drew extremely talented people into government, gave high recognition to intellectuals, writers, and artists (the poet Robert Frost spoke at his inauguration), and instilled in the country a feeling of hope for better things. He had a cool head in a crisis, as his handling of the Cuban missile crisis demonstrated. His attempts to persuade a resistant Congress to adopt his liberal proposals were cut off by his assassination on November 22, 1963.

The politician's politician, Lyndon B. Johnson succeeded to the presidency. Johnson, riding on the wave of sympathy from Kennedy's death, but also utilizing his own unusual abilities, got through Congress a series of important laws designed to create what he called The Great Society, including the civil rights acts of the decade. Johnson's downfall came not in domestic affairs, but in foreign affairs. His expanding commitment to American involvement in Vietnam created the most tumultuous reaction in American life since the slavery issue before the Civil War. By 1968 he recognized that he would have to put aside his desire for re-election.

Richard Nixon, who succeeded Johnson, won in an election almost as close as the one he had lost eight years before. Nixon's greatest achievements lay in foreign affairs where he reopened contact with the People's Republic of China and formally instituted the policy of detente with Russia. Despite his argument in 1968 that he would end the war in Vietnam, a settlement was not reached until January 1973. In November 1972 Nixon had won an overwhelming re-election victory. But his road to victory was also the road to the most devastating political collapse of any major American political figure. This was the Watergate scandal, which revealed that the President and his chief aides had not only engaged in illegal political espionage against their political opponents and others, but that the President had lied repeatedly to the American public in his attempts to avoid being linked to the series of disclosures made about illegal and unethical activities. Forced to resign, or face impeachment and conviction, Nixon retired to his San Clemente home in California and turned the reins of government over to Gerald R. Ford whose political immortality is assured by his being the only nonelected Vice President and President in American history.

The final analysis of Nixon is still a long way off, but he does seem to represent at least one aspect of American life. He was the ultimate manufactured man in an industrial-business-mass communications society—promoted, packaged, advertised, and sold like many other products in the United States. As such his human qualities seemed obscured by the image created for the public. At any rate, he left office apparently without feelings of guilt or remorse.

The Public Reacts   There were striking shifts in the political moods and views of the American people in the postwar era, some of which suggested that the people were ahead of their leaders in recognizing the need for change.

One of the sharpest of popular reactions was a decline in traditional respect for established leadership and political processes, and a loss of confidence in political institutions and government itself. The two issues most reflecting this were the civil rights movement and the Vietnam war. In both cases perturbed Americans took to mass action in the streets—sometimes passive, sometimes violent—when established leadership failed to take the initiative and established institutions seemed to be bogged down in inertia. The effectiveness of such pressure in the Vietnam war issue was cancelled out by the almost ten years it took to produce the change intended. In the case of civil rights, such pressure was only partially successful in producing change. In both instances, too, emotionalism predominated over reason and divisiveness was an ugly social byproduct. Both these experiences, however, gave other groups the incentive to adopt the same tactics—as in white opposition to school busing in the North, for example, and even in the conservation movement. Regardless of outcome, such activities revealed a loss of faith in established political institutions and leaders. Not until the 1974 congressional elections when a new class of freshmen was elected—younger men and women, black and white, all believing in change—did it seem apparent that Americans were prepared to revive their faith in the regular elective process as a means of getting things done.

There were other shifts in mood as well. On the one hand, more and more people became distrustful of the role of special and powerful interest groups in politics and government, especially those representing big business but in many instances big labor as well. In 1972 illegal business contributions to Nixon's campaign provided the final incident for public outrage. On the other hand, the public itself moved to exert its influence through its own organization. The rise of a "people's lobby" in the form of the organization Common Cause, and the multitude of groups organized by consumer advocate Ralph Nader provided new means of not only expressing public opinion but exerting political and legal pressure for change as well.

The Constant Struggle: Race and Identity

After World War II there were powerful political challenges to established institutions, practices, and attitudes that had traditionally set racial and cultural minorities outside the mainstream of American life. These challenges arose from the discriminations suffered by America's black minority of almost 25 million, by the nation's 9 million Puerto Rican, Chicano, and other Spanish-American people, and by the Indian population, which totaled some 700,000 in the census of 1970.

The Black Revolution A survey made during World War II revealed that only eleven percent of the black population believed that the war would lead to improvement in their lives. Nevertheless a new and powerful sense of black solidarity and identity was created during the war years, and as large numbers migrated out of the South more and more whites became aware of the problems of race relations. In the first few years after the war a pattern of change began to emerge. Segregation was abolished in the armed forces. Political activity by blacks increased, and 3.5 million voted in the 1948 election. The poll tax was eliminated in several Southern states. A small number of blacks entered political life in the South and gained local office.

Constitutional challenges led to their admission to graduate and professional schools in eight of the Southern states by 1950, and to the University of Maryland as undergraduates. Over 120,000 blacks were in institutions of higher learning throughout the country. Educational expenditures for black schools in the South's segregated system increased sharply. The Red Cross abandoned its policy of segregation of blood donations. Over 150 public-housing authorities across the nation adopted a policy of nonsegregation. The black professional and business class was increasing in numbers and respect. Over 1.5 million blacks were in labor unions. And then in 1954 the Supreme Court in its historic decision of *Brown* vs. *The Board of Education of Topeka,* struck down the institution of segregation in education, concluding that "in the field of public education the doctrine of separate but equal has no place. Separate educational facilities are inherently unequal." If this were so, then segregation in any other area of society was unequal. Even though it did not change the established pattern of school segregation overnight, and indeed produced strong resistance, this decision began a new era. In the next twenty years the struggle for equal rights reached a new intensity, became organized, and made real progress toward abolishing white discrimination, eliminating racial prejudice, and drawing blacks into full participation in American life.

A variety of agencies came together in this movement. Political and governmental forces shifted from support of discrimination to opposition. The Supreme Court, in decision after decision, struck down segregation in many aspects of life. Congress passed a series of civil rights acts in 1957, 1960, 1964, and 1965. The weight of the presidency was brought to bear in the historic decision of Dwight D. Eisenhower to use federal troops to enforce desegregation in the schools of Little Rock, Arkansas, and in the multitude of suits filed by the Justice Department to enforce the new laws. Both Democrats and Republicans became officially committed to equal rights in their party platforms.

More broadly, the increased tempo of urban-industrial development brought blacks in increasing numbers into the main arena of American life and gave them opportunities for protest as well as for advancement. International events also gave impetus to the movement for equal rights. As a world leader of democracy, the United States was impelled to support the nationalistic aspirations of nonwhite peoples trying to break out of colonial systems everywhere. The absurdity of being champions abroad and oppressors at home became apparent to many white Americans. In fact, the rising movement for equal rights aroused the deep concern of many. Those worried about the fate of democracy came more and more to believe that it could not long survive unless all citizens participated equally in society. President Kennedy in 1963 posed this issue bluntly:

> We are confronted primarily with a moral issue. It is as old as the Scriptures and is as clear as the American Constitution. The heart of the issue is whether all Americans are to be afforded equal rights and equal opportunities, whether we are going to treat our fellow Americans as we want to be treated. If an American, because his skin is dark, cannot eat lunch in a restaurant open to

The raised clenched fist became a symbol of black power, black solidarity, and black pride as the attitudes of blacks towards their rights and their roles in American society changed dramatically in the postwar years.

the public, if he cannot send his children to the best public school available, if, in short, he cannot enjoy the full and free life which all of us want, then who among us would be content to have the color of his skin changed and stand in his place? Who among us would then be content with the counsels of patience and delay?

But the most important force in the movement was the blacks themselves, not just the intellectuals and the elite, but the masses of the population. It was this which made it accurate to call the movement "The Black Revolution" and to predict its ultimate fulfillment. This drive passed through three major phases. First, under the leadership of Martin Luther King, Jr., it relied upon nonviolent, passive resistance in the form of boycotts, sit-ins, demonstrations, marches, and strikes. Even conservative organizations such as the NAACP joined in. In the 1960s violent white resistance by bombings, beatings, murder, and assassination by disreputable Klans and White Citizens' Councils, as well as mob violence and the brutal use of police authority and power, resulted in a new approach among blacks, particularly the young, who proclaimed the doctrine of Black Power and the use of force and violence. Shootouts with police, murder and assassination, and riots in major cities dramatized the urgency of the problem, for as the journalist I. F. Stone noted: "The cry of 'black power' is less a program than an incantation to deal with the crippling effects of white supremacy. . . . It is not practical politics; it is psychological therapy." The separatism implicit in the call for black power and the violence explicit in its approach solved no problems, but it did proclaim the desperate view of their plight felt by most blacks. Indeed, a survey indicated that a huge majority, seventy-two percent, believed they had been pushed around long enough and were now prepared, as one of them said, "to go for broke." And twenty-five percent believed that only by fighting could they obtain their freedom.

Black power made its point and gave way to the third phase of the black revolution, in operation by the 1970s—the drive to work through the existing political and social system. Champions of black power such as Bobby Seale of the Black Panthers moved into the political arena and, joining forces with concerned whites, began rebuilding a sense of community in America at large. The successes of the black revolution by the middle of the 1970s were striking, even though a long road yet lay ahead. By the end of 1973, for example, there were black mayors in eighty-three communities, including the metropolis of Los Angeles. Seventeen blacks sat in Congress. Blacks sat on the Supreme Court, federal appeals courts, district courts, the Customs Court, and the Court of Military Appeals. There were 200 black state legislators and 2,400 others holding public office, half of them in the South. More blacks moved into higher income brackets. More graduated from high schools and the number in colleges and universities increased sharply. More blacks moved into white-collar jobs and to the suburbs.

But impressive as these gains were, much remained to be done. The number of elected black officials constituted only one-half of one percent of all those in the nation, even though blacks numbered twelve percent of the population. Thirty percent were now making more than $10,000 a year, but almost a third were still below the poverty level of $4,275. Sixty-five percent of those in their twenties were high school graduates, but sixty-three percent still attended predominantly black schools. Thirty-three percent of all employed blacks were in white-collar jobs, but the unemployment rate among blacks was twice that of whites.

Almost all black leaders agreed that progress had been made, but a concerted effort on the educational, economic, and legal front was still needed to close the visible gaps. But the question no longer was whether it would be done, but how soon.

The Spanish-Speaking Minority   The achievements of the black revolution were far greater than those of the Spanish-speaking population, particularly the Puerto Rican ghetto-dwellers of New York City and the Mexican-Americans in the West and Southwest, and of the native American Indians. Numbers had something to do with this, since these groups were small by comparison. But other factors kept the spirit of militancy down among these groups and held back effectively organized protest.

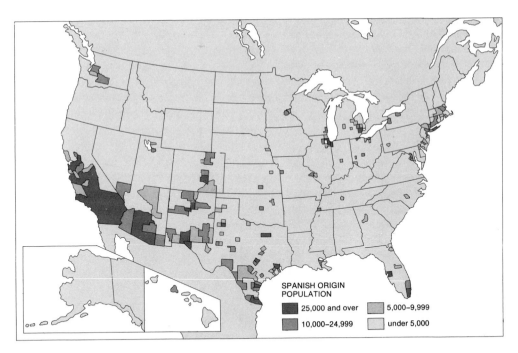

CENTERS OF SPANISH-ORIGIN POPULATION

Among these differences it was important that little of the discrimination against the Spanish-speaking peoples in the West and Southwest was part and parcel of the law. Rather, discriminatory practices in housing and jobs, as well as their rural and farm-labor background, kept many Mexican-Americans in a constant state of economic deprivation. By the 1960s they were eighty percent urban, in California, Arizona, New Mexico, Texas, and Colorado, a circumstance that did not necessarily lead to improvement.

In addition, most Spanish-speaking people were recent immigrants. The Cubans concentrated in Florida after 1960; the Puerto Ricans came mainly after World War II and centered in New York City. And though Mexican immigration began as early as 1910, most of it came during and after World War II. All these peoples had a powerful sense of cultural identity fresh in mind, a pride in their cultural past, a strong desire to preserve it as a bulwark against the outside world, and in the family a powerful institution through which that identity could be maintained and preserved. The distinct differences in their backgrounds—from Cuba, from Puerto Rico, from Mexico—hampered rather than aided any sense of common identity and mission, and limited opportunities for large-scale organization among them.

Although they wanted organization strong enough to eliminate discrimination and create opportunities for improvement, particularly among the young, the chief goal seemed to be preserving cultural identity, a goal enhanced by the concentration of Mexican-Americans in the barrios of Los

Chicanos who filled the ranks of vegetable pickers in the Southwest gained recognition as a union from the AFL-CIO in 1972, after nearly nine years of labor activity as the United Farm Workers Organizing Committee. Leader César Chavez used strikes and secondary boycotts of lettuce, grapes, and wine effectively in his efforts to establish the farm workers as a force to be dealt with in the farming community.

Angeles, for example, although such enclaves hampered social and economic opportunities in American society at large. The emphasis on cultural identity was revealed in their demands for their own representatives in state legislatures and other public offices, for recognition of Spanish as an equal language in schools, courts, and elsewhere, and for ethnic studies based on their own heritage. Political and economic power was sought by Mexican-Americans through such organizations as the Raza Unida party in Texas and the MAPA in California, and César Chavez sought political power through his United Farm Workers Union. Some protests by the young in the cities became minor riots, but most of the young seemed to seek educational opportunity as a base for future leadership and power.

The American Indian The fate of the American Indian remained precarious. Two new policies threatened Indian cultural if not indeed physical survival: termination and relocation. The Hoover Commission in 1949 had recommended the transfer of social programs for Indians from federal to state governments. This policy was endorsed by the Commissioner of Indian Affairs in 1950, and under the Eisenhower administration a series of termination laws was passed to get, as one senator put it, the government out of the Indian business. Essentially the termination laws were another means of depriving Indians of their lands. The first Indians to whom these laws were applied were the Menominees of Wisconsin and the Klamaths of Oregon, both of whom owned valuable timber lands. About 10,000 Indians had their ties with the federal government cut off at the height of termination in the 1950s, and some 500,000 acres of Indian land passed into non-Indian hands. Protest brought the process to a halt by the end of the fifties, and in 1970 President Nixon formally cancelled the policy of termination with the strong assertion that no decisions regarding Indian welfare would be made in the future without agreement by the Indians. Paralleling termination was a program of relocation designed to get Indians off the reservation and into the mainstream of American life. Although this was presumably a voluntary program, many Indians unprepared for life outside the reservation were pressured by Indian agents to accept relocation to urban areas where they lived in the worst poverty, suffered job discrimination, and were not allowed welfare benefits. By 1960 some 20,000 Indians had been steered with great reluctance into relocation. One Hopi woman described why they agreed: "We're like wheat. The wind blows, we bend over. It blows the other way, we bend that way. All we know is you better do what they want. You can't stand up when there's wind."

The Census Bureau recognized over 700,000 Indians in 1970, although this figure included those whose identification because of intermarriage with whites was only one-quarter or perhaps even only one-eighth Indian ancestry. Many of these had made their way in American society at large and were unidentifiable as Indian unless pride prompted them, as it did many, to proclaim their ancestral ties. Only about 460,000 Indians lived on or near reservations. Of these only fifty percent of the employable had jobs. The average family income was approximately $1,500 a year, and eighty percent of all reservation Indians had income below the poverty level. Standards of education and health were low, despite the assumption in 1955 of responsibility for Indian health and medical problems by the Public Health Service. By 1971 total federal support for Indian affairs had reached $626 million annually, half to the Bureau of Indian Affairs and half to the Department of Health, Education, and Welfare. Administrative costs were high, and less help reached the average Indian family than was needed. But the postwar trend to turn over the administration of the Indian budget to Indian tribal corporations and their elected and paid officials eased this problem somewhat.

The potential of Indian economic development remained low. Only 635,000 acres out of nearly 56 million acres of Indian land were actually cultivated or used by Indians. The remainder was unused or leased to non-Indians. Aided by the Indian Business Development Fund, a new program established by the Bureau of Indian Affairs, more and more Indians began to

ORIGINAL INDIAN TRIBES AND PRESENT-DAY RESERVATIONS

start new businesses or expand existing ones, businesses often related to tourism, such as the Sierra Blanca Ski Area in southern New Mexico operated by the Mescalero Apaches. By 1970 195 industrial plants employing 6,000 Indians were located on or near reservations. In addition, Indian economic life was stimulated by judgments awarded in federal courts since 1946 for lands unjustly seized, totaling some $400 million. But none of this produced any significant rise in economic status.

The postwar era did see important changes in the legal status of Indian social and political life. The last of the states to give Indians the right to vote in non-Indian elections—Arizona and New Mexico—did so in 1948. Liquor prohibition laws were repealed in 1953. The Indian Civil Rights Act of 1968 extended the benefits of the Bill of Rights to reservation Indians and required Indian consent before states could assume law-and-order jurisdiction in reservations.

These developments combined with the basically unimproved economic situation and further fed by the revival of the drive for Indian cultural identity—a drive long underway but now spurred by the strong urge of young Indians to associate themselves with their rich and heroic past—together produced a call in the late 1960s and early 1970s for Red Power similar to that for Black Power. Young Indians dramatized this demand with an invasion of Alcatraz Island in San Francisco Bay in 1968 and with the gun battle with federal agents at Wounded Knee, South Dakota, in 1973. But the handicap of numbers, the disastrous loss of culture through decades of neglect, and intratribal struggles for authority weakened and confused the demand for Red Power. In the 1970s the fate of the American Indian was tragically uncertain, and the future was not encouraging.

America and the World

The impact of the United States on the rest of the world was very great in the postwar years, and this fact affected traditional images of America nearly everywhere.

Economic Impact   Our most obvious impact was economic. This took two principal forms: government and private aid abroad for relief, reconstruction, and development, and the rapid flow of private American capital investment and business knowhow overseas. The United States emerged from the war as the wealthiest nation on earth. Alone of all countries it possessed the resources to rebuild shattered economies and lay the foundations for new economies. What occurred, therefore, was an outward flow from the United States of economic resources, both public and private, unequaled in all history.

Total American governmental aid from 1945 to 1971 was approximately $140 billion, and was funneled abroad either directly or through various international agencies. The initial $8 billion for relief in wartorn countries in

1945 and 1946 went primarily through the United Nations. Over a third of all government aid in those years was for military assistance, a reflection of the Cold War with the Soviet Union. But such aid had its own economic effect on the countries involved by helping to free their economies from military expenditures; thus military aid constituted a form of indirect economic aid.

Private American aid both direct and indirect sought to improve the lives of the distressed and the deprived. In the early years, most private aid was direct relief; later it was concentrated on education, health, medicine, self-help, technical assistance in developing basic skills in agriculture and industry, and research to improve crops and animal husbandry. In the first ten years over $6 billion in private funds and assistance flowed overseas, sixty percent of it directly to friends and relatives of Americans, and the rest from secular and religious agencies and institutions. After 1956 most private philanthropic aid was dispersed through agencies and institutions. By 1960 assistance from Protestant, Catholic, and Jewish agencies as well as from various nonsectarian institutions such as CARE and Project HOPE was averaging $300 million a year. Various foundations—Rockefeller, Ford, and Kellogg, for example—also channeled funds abroad for economic, technical, educational, and medical assistance.

Relief immediately after the war fed and clothed millions, provided basic health assistance, and aided millions of refugees to resettle or rejoin their families. From 1948 to 1952 the Marshall Plan helped restore both industrial and agricultural production in Western Europe above prewar levels. And long-range development aid from 1952 to 1965 helped numerous economies attain greater efficiency, mass production, technological innovation, and consumer-orientation. Many underdeveloped countries saw improvement in education and health, transportation and communication, and industrial growth.

Accompanying this flow of aid was a dramatic rise in private American investment. The 1950s alone saw some $30 billion in American capital go overseas. By the 1970s the market value of American investment was approximately $100 billion, and constituted one of the four largest economies in the world. Though spread out in a hundred countries, the major part of it was concentrated in Europe, Canada, and Latin America. Paralleling the flow of capital was that of American business managers, their staffs, and their methods.

Great as its benefits were, certain aspects of this extension of America into the rest of the world caused serious problems and created unfavorable views of the United States. Few who benefited directly were ungrateful, but gratitude was often tempered. Most American economic aid went to the Western and developed nations, leaving undeveloped countries feeling not just neglected but deliberately discriminated against, especially since most of the undeveloped world was nonwhite. This view was reinforced by the nature of American investment in the undeveloped world. For American capital was concentrated on the development and exploitation of natural resources, and this made the Americans look like the new imperialists, exploiting the natural wealth of undeveloped countries, often in collaboration with local ruling castes who did not share the profits of development with their own people. This was often true in the Near East, Africa, the Orient, and Latin America, where American investment intensified a type of economic exploitation that went back to the beginning of this century and had long been resented. Furthermore, the frequent reluctance of American firms to open their operations to local investors, or to hire local staff except as manual or clerical labor, strengthened the fear that the United States was embarked on a form of colonialism as unpleasant and degrading as that of former European masters.

Even in the Western developed nations American economic influence was resented. By the 1970s American investment in Canada totaled over $23 billion, enough to control much of Canada's industrial life. This naturally aroused fears of American domination and rubbed raw the nerves of Canadian national pride. Rising French resentment against the United States, evident from the 1960s on, stemmed in part from the role of American capital, which dominated, among others, the French computer industry.

Finally, the United States was resented because it tied economic aid to support of the American position in the Cold War. Alignment with the United States in the containment of communism, and willingness to take a strong stand against communism in their own countries, became the passport to economic assistance from the United States. It was this policy which gave South Vietnam more economic aid than all of Africa, and almost as much as Latin America. Many developing nations, such as India, which believed their basic interest lay in detachment from the Cold War, strongly resented such forced association with American policy.

Political Impact Equally significant was the political impact the United States had on the rest of the world. A dramatic example of this influence, stemming from the American role as the architect of victory in the Pacific, was the occupation of Japan, during which the United States sought to remold an autocratic country into a democracy. In less time than it took the Founding Fathers, the American authorities turned out a new constitution, introduced political and social equality, reorganized the educational system, and sought to create in Japan a model democracy based on the American pattern. It was a remarkable venture and surprisingly successful, though real problems arose from the attempt to impose outside institutions upon an ancient culture with its own traditions, habits, values, and beliefs. As one Japanese gently remarked, "Some roses of the West, when transported to the East, lose their fragrance." In Germany, where the Americans shared the occupation, a similar influence did not prevail. But for Western Europe as a whole, the example of American federalism offered at the least a precedent for a United States of Europe. The ties of economic unity achieved by the European Common Market perhaps foreshadowed a politically united Europe.

But the chief political impact came from the continuing influence of the American revolutionary past, and from strong opposition to the apparent

Roy M. Cohn, Senator Joseph McCarthy, and G. David Schine at the Army-McCarthy hearings. The climate of cold war following World War II led to a period in the nation's history characterized by a pervasive fear of Communist infiltration in all levels of government and public life. Seizing the Communist issue as his own crusade was Sen. Joseph McCarthy, who from his powerful position on a Senate investigations committee made sensational accusations without proof that destroyed careers and reputations but that never uncovered any actual Communists. McCarthy's flamboyant style captured the imagination of the American people, to whom he had given a tangible "enemy." But by 1954 the voices of those who saw him as a demagogue were finally heard when McCarthy's abuses were exposed by the nationally televised Army-McCarthy hearings.

threat of expanding communist influence. In the chaos that followed the war old empires crumbled, social systems weakened, old values wasted away, old convictions perished. Into this vacuum moved the energies of emergent nationalism and revolution. Around the globe colonial peoples shook the chains that bound them to European masters, and in established nations despairing people tried to overthrow the regimes which were the cause of their despair. One of the great revolutions of history swept Asia and Africa, and to a lesser extent Latin America.

Out of its own past the United States had much to offer people engaged in such vital enterprises, as the new nationalists and revolutionists were well aware. The wave of independence and the revolutionary movements of the time rested more than we knew on the historic American example. From the days of the American Revolution and the rise of the republic, America had traditionally been the great example of a people seeking to shake off colonialism and embark upon their own destiny. The United States had been the first such nation brought into being in the modern world, created by its own people and faced with the problem of finding its own character. More than sixty new nations emerged after World War II, and many of them on the American pattern of emerging from the breakup of old empires. Like us before them, they depended on the support of their own people and took pride in their own distinctive characteristics and independence of judgment in determining their own affairs. In one country after another these revolutionaries invoked the American precedent. Sukarno proclaimed Indonesian indebtedness to the American example in the revolt against the Dutch; Castro in Cuba quoted extensively from the Declaration of Independence to justify his revolution from the Sierra Maestra; Cypriot rebels distributed throughout the world a pamphlet closely comparing the American Revolution with their own conflict against the British Empire; a young African leader described America as "my second home;" and in the jungles of Indochina Ho Chi Minh issued a Vietnamese Declaration of Independence closely modeled on the American.

But the image of the American past was in conflict with the present American fear of expanding communism and Communist Russia. Shaken by what it saw as threats to world order and stability, and fearful of communist influence, the United States assumed aggressive leadership in rallying other countries in opposition to these threats. Its weapons were the development of the most powerful armed forces in the world, military and economic aid to those nations joining in the struggle, and military alliances and compacts from NATO to SEATO, all designed to contain Soviet and communist influence.

The political impact of these actions was momentous. They placed eminent countries, such as Britain and France, in the uncomfortable position of seeming to depend on the United States. They offset the influence of America's revolutionary past and created a new image of America. By defining membership in the Free World in terms of anti-communism or anti-Sovietism, the United States frequently found itself supporting and maintaining reactionary regimes around the globe. By placing stability and order ahead of social and political democracy, the Americans placed themselves across the path of the most significant movement of the twentieth century and found themselves for the first time a defender of the status quo, a far cry from their traditional role as champions of freedom and self-determination. Out of this came an image of the United States as a self-centered nation willing to sacrifice democracy for a world stability designed to guarantee American security at the expense of nearly everyone else.

The application of containment found expression in the Truman Doctrine of 1947 providing military and economic aid to Greece and Turkey to prevent their fall to communist influence, in the Berlin Airlift of 1948 to maintain western access to a Berlin isolated by Soviet blockade, in the establishment of the North Atlantic Treaty Organization in 1949 to bind the Western

Dwight D. Eisenhower in Korea. In his election campaign against Adlai Stevenson in 1952, Eisenhower pledged that if elected, "I shall go to Korea," to bring the war to an "early and honorable end." There was considerable partisan dissension over the handling of the Korean conflict: Truman saw the war as one of containment, checking Soviet aggression before it developed into a third world war; the Republicans, prompted by the accusations of MacArthur, felt that Truman's failure to recognize that aggression earlier and deal with it decisively was a policy of appeasement. It remained a small war, without victory, and the armistice negotiations begun in July 1951 continued for two years while the killing continued as well.

nations together in a mutual defense pact, in the defense of South Korea against North Korea in a bloody war which dragged on from 1950 to 1953, and in numerous other activities around the globe.

The Vietnam war marked the bloody climax of the American policy of containment—large-scale military involvement in what was essentially a civil war. The cost was high: 50,000 American dead and 300,000 casualties, a small country half-destroyed, millions of its people killed, maimed, or homeless, its life and culture perhaps damaged beyond repair, the American democratic image distorted in the eyes of many peoples in the world and a seriously divided and embittered people at home. The cost was not only high, but by 1968 the American people and their leaders by and large recognized it was too high. Rising protest against the war forced President Johnson's withdrawal from political life at the end of his term. Yet it took until 1973 before President Nixon was able to effect a settlement that resulted in

John Gunther Dean, the last U.S. ambassador to Cambodia, evacuates Phnom Penh with the American flag in his right hand. The American presence in Southeast Asia, a bitter, bloody issue for over twenty years, finally ended in April 1975.

the withdrawal of American troops, and two more years before the complete collapse of South Vietnam ended all American economic and political involvement in Vietnam.

The American withdrawal and the victory of the Viet Cong and North Vietnam in South Vietnam began an era of reappraisal of the American role in the world. One thing was obvious: the American people no longer had the desire to engage in military ventures around the globe in the cause of "containing" communism. Indeed, one of the ironies of the Vietnam war as part of the policy of containment was that at the same time America was gradually improving relations with the Soviet Union. Cultural and intellectual exchanges, rising trade, and negotiations in the SALT talks to control the proliferation of nuclear weapons and reduce the arms race all added up to reduced hostilities and tensions and the rise of new attitudes on the part of the major powers toward one another. Khrushchev's earlier call for peaceful coexistence led to the detente begun in Nixon's administration. Moreover, the beginning of a new and friendlier relationship with China was also a repudiation of containment. Visits by many different Americans—from politicians to scientists—opened the eyes of many to a country of remarkable achievements even if its methods of organizing life and society had little appeal to most Americans. But clearly the majority of Americans were now in the mood for a new foreign policy—one that did not deny either American national interest or American responsibility in world affairs, but that at the same time was no longer geared to attempting to direct and control the affairs of the rest of the world. Sharing of responsibility and cooperation in dealing with the serious problems of the world would, in the future, have to be the cornerstones of American foreign policy.

At the end of World War II the United States possessed a great reservoir of goodwill, admiration, and respect. Its potential for promoting the betterment of the human condition was large. But by and large America did not take full advantage of the opportunity. In the last quarter of the twentieth century the opportunity remained, though the problems were far greater than before—poverty, illiteracy, limited food supplies, preservation of the natural world and its resources, social injustice, population control, national hatreds, peace—not one of which could be solved by force.

Having cleansed themselves of corruption in the highest office in the land, having reopened ties with a China once regarded as a deadly enemy, and having inaugurated a new era of detente with the Soviet Union—perhaps the decks were cleared for America's best qualities to come into play, and cooperation for the good of all would prevail in the world.

Perhaps this was too much to ask, but as the Americans entered the last quarter of the twentieth century, it was time to recall the words of President John F. Kennedy in 1963, five months before his death: "If we cannot end now our differences, at least we can help make the world safe for diversity. For, in the last analysis, our most basic common link is that we all inhabit this small planet. We all breathe the same air. We all cherish our children's future. And we are all mortal."

Profile: MARTIN LUTHER KING JR.

Born January 15, 1929 in Atlanta, Georgia, he died from an assassin's bullet on a Memphis, Tennessee motel balcony on April 4, 1968, destroyed by the violence he condemned. Grandson of a man born into slavery, son of an Atlanta pastor, leader of the local NAACP, and member of the Atlanta Voters League, Martin Luther King Jr. learned from both that humiliation and degradation were evil and should not be endured.

Intelligent, sensitive, and alert, he marched rapidly up the ladder, skipped grades in school, attended Morehouse College in Atlanta, Crozer Theological Seminary in Pennsylvania, and took a Ph.D. in philosophy from Boston College in 1954. Booker T. Washington's program, he later wrote, "had too little freedom in its present and too little promise in its future." W.E.B. DuBois was closer to the mark on the necessity of protest, but his concept of an advanced intellectual black elite who would lead the masses to the promised land ignored, in essence, the humanity of the masses. Reading Gandhi in college at a time when India's independence seemed to prove that passive nonviolent resistance worked, King found virtue in this method, which Thoreau had proposed in Civil Disobedience a century before. Deeply religious, King drew strength from the teaching of Jesus that love was superior to hate in every way.

King went to Montgomery, Alabama, in September 1954 as pastor of the Dexter Avenue Baptist Church. Over a year later, he was at the heart of the Montgomery bus boycott, and his course was henceforth fixed. When Rosa Parks entered a Montgomery bus on December 1, 1955, and refused out of sheer weariness to sit in the black section, the idea of a mass protest took shape in a black boycott of city buses which lasted 382 days. King became head of the Montgomery Improvement System, whose very title described his approach: blacks must rely on "persuasion, not coercion," he declared. The guiding emotion must be love, not hate. The goal, he told Montgomery blacks, was not "to defeat or humiliate the opponent, but to win his friendship and understanding." Though King's own home was bombed, there was no violence by blacks, and he proved that "nonviolent resistance does resist." Practical victory came in November 1956 when the Supreme Court declared unconstitutional Alabama laws requiring segregation on public buses.

It was a small victory in a large war. Yet it was of utmost significance. As King noted, it produced "a new sense of dignity and destiny among blacks," who had acted together and proved their worth as a community.

For the next seven years King was their guiding spirit and the acknowledged leader of the movement. In the sit-in movement, the Freedom Rides, the "liberation" movement in Birmingham, in marches and demonstrations across the country, King's approach was put to the test, and despite frequent brutal suppression and various failures it seemed to be working. The conscience of the nation was touched by what it saw on television; the President proposed national legislation; cities began programs to desegregate public facilities. The peak of influence came in the great March on Washington in August 1963, when on the steps of the Lincoln Memorial King told a peaceful throng of over 200,000, "I have a dream"—a dream of coming justice, when all Americans could join in brotherhood and sing "Free at last! Free at last! Thank God Almighty, we are free at last!"

But the movement began to sweep beyond King's control. His successes and failures alike inspired a new militancy dissatisfied with nonviolent resistance. To the young especially, dignity and pride were not to be found in humble submission but in fighting back. A new militancy moved in to take over the movement: the Black Muslims and Malcolm X, Stokely Carmichael of SNCC and Floyd McKissick of CORE, H. Rap Brown and the Black Panthers of Huey Newton and Bobby Seale. Preaching black nationalism or violence or both, they injected a sense of rage that showed at the very least that anger and hate are as powerful as love. Even King recognized that "certain elements . . . will respond with violence if the people of the nation do not recognize the desperate plight of the Negro. . . . The brutality they are experiencing as a result of their quest for equality may call for retaliation." Harlem exploded in 1964, Watts in 1965, and the summer of 1967 saw forty-one riots in thirty-nine communities across the country.

There was violence on the other side as well, and the word "Peace" in the Nobel Peace Prize which King received in 1964 had lost the meaning he had given it. He had written that "Violence ends by defeating itself. It creates bitterness in the survivors and brutality in the destroyers." And he was right. Yet this violence he deplored made him its victim too, and his death produced further violence as blacks in rage and frustration rioted in 130 cities, including the nation's capital.

King had ignited the torch of freedom, and it turned into a firebrand burning in the city night. This was not what he had intended. But firebrands burn out, and perhaps his very death hastened the process. At any rate, militant power wasted away, to be replaced by political power, and the movement for black equality moved onto a new level where there was hope of realizing his dream through processes open to black and white alike, working together. If this were the case, then he had been more than right, and the violence that destroyed him was itself destroyed by the sacrifice. As he had said, "If you are cut down in a movement that is designed to save the soul of a nation, then no other death could be more redemptive." If in dying he had made possible the redemption of the nation, he had indeed accomplished his mission.

Chapter 12
SOCIAL AND CULTURAL LIFE IN CONTEMPORARY AMERICA

The Spirit of the Times
BEWILDERMENT

"Wonders are many, but none, none is more wondrous than man." So, we may recall, wrote Sophocles twenty-five hundred years ago in praise of the most remarkable of living creatures. Human achievement since then has, in many ways, documented Sophocles' observation. And the Americans, in their history, have seemed to give special emphasis to the thought. In less than four centuries they rocketed to preeminence in the world in scientific and industrial development, in material benefits and prosperity, in education and learning, in political experimentation with democratic institutions.

But Sophocles had also thoughtfully warned that wise though humanity's plans are, "artful beyond all dreaming, they carry . . . both to evil and to good." Thirty years after the end of history's greatest war, the Americans had cause to listen to this warning voice from the beginning of civilization. Scientific and technological achievements were two-edged swords—not only productive but destructive as well. Atomic energy could provide electricity and also blow up the world. Industrial expansion could improve life enormously, but the greedy use of the natural resources which made that possible could denude the earth of the basis of a decent life for everyone. The industrial process itself could, as it created a materially better life, make that life physically impossible and stunted through pollution of air, earth, and water. Wealth and power had proved equally uncertain in their application and consequences—beating back the tyranny of Hitler, but also ruining a small country in Southeast Asia. Praise for the one, condemnation by the world

America began its celebration of the nation's bicentennial with a recreation of the battle at the old North Bridge in Concord. President Ford addresses the crowd, the statue of the Minuteman rising behind him, as present-day Minutemen line the bridge and Secret Service men flank the President.

for the other. Social and political democracy had been broadly applied, encompassing a majority of Americans and demonstrating the virtues of freedom, but had proved an illusion when withheld from a nonwhite minority.

In learning and education the Americans had clearly demonstrated the enormous intellectual capacity of certain individuals, but the pileup of unsolved problems suggested that modern society was so complex that its management might well be beyond the collective intelligence of its members. The willingness of Americans to embrace change in all aspects of life, and their capacity to absorb it and turn it to advantage, had brought quick enjoyment of the benefits of science and industrialism, but had also left social institutions and values stumbling in the rear. Every aspect of modern life—science, technology, industrialism, learning, literature, and the arts—demonstrated, for example, the interdependence of the modern world, but Americans still clung to the narrow parochialism of political nationalism and the equally narrow parochialism of political ethnicity.

Little wonder, then, that one of the dominant characteristics of contemporary Americans has been bewilderment at what they have wrought. Few would deny, as the nation began to celebrate rather unenthusiastically its two hundredth birthday, that there was in the air a certain confusion not only about the past and the present but the future as well.

Part of the explanation is that not just America but the whole world is passing through one of those great transitional periods of history, a condition that is certain to continue for at least another thirty years and perhaps longer. Such periods are inevitably marked by confusion and bewilderment as older institutions, ideas, values, behavior patterns, and relationships come under stress, weaken, and crumble—some never to recover—and new ones struggle to emerge—some to survive, others to falter and disappear.

Human beings tend to want at least <u>some</u> certainties, some solid values, some permanence about them to reassure them that their lives have purpose and meaning, that there is a continuity to human affairs. They want some sort of anchor to windward. But in times of transition, especially those marked by rapid change and upheaval, this desire is difficult to fulfill.

There is no "answer" to this. There is only hope that the Americans and their fellow human beings around the globe have the capacity not just to endure but to cope with this world in transition with intelligence, goodwill, and imagination, so that the new age will be a more satisfying one than we have at present.

Shifts in Population

One of the substantial changes affecting the quality of life that occurred in the postwar period was that in population. Since the end of World War II the American population had grown by some 60 million from 1945 to over 205 million by 1970. And the population became increasingly urban, though the definition of urban now meant, in Census Bureau language, a Standard Metropolitan Statistical Area—that is, not just an incorporated city of 50,000 or more, but its adjacent suburban and unincorporated areas. By this definition, 75 percent of the population was urban by 1970, and there was no sign of reversing this trend. Over 150 million Americans lived in an urban environment, on 1.5 percent of the nation's land mass. Most of this growth was in the suburbs, where more Americans now live than in either the central cities or the country—over 76 million of them. In 1950 35 percent of the population lived in central cities and 27 percent in suburbs. By 1970 the ratio was reversed, with 31 percent in the central cities and 37 percent in suburbs. In the 1960s alone the SMSA population increased by about 20 million, of which 16 million was in the suburbs. Most large cities lost population. While the New York Metropolitan Statistical Area, for example, grew in numbers, its Manhattan Island core lost population and by 1970 had only half what it had in 1920. Population was also more densely concentrated than ever before, much of it along large bodies of water. By 1970 more than half the population lived in eight states—California, Illinois, Michigan, New Jersey, New York, Ohio, Pennsylvania, and Texas—and because of the location of the SMSAs in those states, most people were within easy driving distance of the Atlantic or the Pacific ocean, one of the Great Lakes, or the Gulf of Mexico. The state with the highest population density in the 1970 census was New Jersey with 953.1 per square mile, whereas Alaska had a density of only 0.5 per square mile. The density for the United States as a whole was 58.

A significant feature of urban population growth was the decline in the number of whites living in the central cities and the increase in the number of blacks. Whereas only 20 percent of all metropolitan blacks lived outside the central city, more than half the whites did. Thus even though there were more blacks in the suburbs, the suburban movement was mainly white. Some 40 percent of the whites lived in the suburbs by 1970, but only 16

The urbanization of the American landscape. The aerial photo above, taken in 1950, shows the well-defined city of Santa Clara in the upper right corner surrounded by orchard lands and scattered farms along the roads leading from the city.

percent of the blacks, and blacks constituted only 4.8 percent of the suburban population. This was less than half the percentage of blacks in the American population.

Every major region had an increase in population, but the rate of growth was fastest in the Far West and the South, especially after 1960. Although black emigration kept the South more or less static in population up to 1960, after that the South experienced a remarkable rate of growth. In fact by 1970 the sixteen Southern states had the largest population of any region in the country, some 62 million people, and still had 53 percent of the black population in spite of migration to other regions. These figures revealed a new South. Out of the 21 new Standard Metropolitan Statistical Areas recognized by the Census Bureau between 1970 and 1972, eleven were in the South, and

This photo of approximately the same area in the Santa Clara Valley as that on the left indicates the effects of twenty years of growth. By 1970 the boundaries of the city are obliterated and the orchard lands have become a sprawl of housing developments.

in that region more people lived in central cities—over 18.6 million—than in any other part of the country.

The rural population in America had remained constant for over 50 years at about 53 million. Those actually living on farms, however, declined in number as the national population rose. In 1950 they numbered some 23 million. Ten years later they had dropped to 16 million, and by 1969 to below 10 million. Yet the farm population remained one of the most efficient work forces in the nation. In 1950 the average farm worker produced enough food to sustain 15.5 people. By 1969 the figure was 47 and still rising.

After World War II immigration became a less significant element in the population than ever before. Although the immigration law of 1965 abolished the national-origins quota system and thus allowed Asians as well as

Eastern and Southern Europeans equal access to the United States, the total flow since 1945 has averaged only about 300,000 a year. These figures do not include Puerto Ricans, who were not legally classified as foreign and whose numbers rose steadily. Even so, the census of 1970 counted only 11 million of foreign birth, or 4.6 percent of the population, a figure not quite half what it had been in 1940. Of these, 4.3 million were in two states, California and New York. A census survey at the end of the 1960s revealed that only about one-third of all Americans were conscious of their ethnic origins, and of these more than two-thirds identified themselves as English, German, or Irish, that is of the old immigration.

Changing Life Styles

In these years the number of men in the population decreased from 98.6 per hundred women in 1950 to 94.8 per hundred in 1970. The percentage of older people increased, and among them women outnumbered men by a considerable margin. Both these developments subtly affected the pattern of life.

Marriage and Divorce   Until 1960 the average age of first marriages for women had been slowly dropping, but thereafter the trend reversed. In 1960 72 percent of women between 20 and 24 had been married, whereas by 1970 only 64 percent had been. The average age of bearing a first child began to rise after 1960, paralleling the rise in age of marriage. Statistics reflecting dissatisfaction with marriage took a startling upward turn. The divorce rate after World War II, when there were many hasty and ill-considered marriages, was the highest in history. In the first two years after the war there were over a million divorces. The number dropped sharply in the 1950s, but rose again through the 1960s, and had nearly doubled to 800,000 in 1972. At the same time there were more late marriages, and by 1970 nearly half the women under 35 were still single. Among these however were many living with men they later married. Yet marriage did not seem to be a dying institution. In 1970 83 percent of women between 16 and 70 had been married. And in 1971 the Bureau of the Census showed that there were not only 48,125,000 married couples in America, but that a third of these had been married 25 years or more.

A Declining Birthrate   At the same time the birthrate had been going down steadily. The fertility rate—the number of children per thousand women between the child-bearing ages of 15 and 44—sank to 75.8 per thousand in 1936, the lowest level till then in U.S. history. After World War II the rate rose sharply to 122.9 in 1957. But by 1972 it had dropped to 73.4, the lowest ever. In that year there were 2 percent more women of child-bearing age than in 1971, but 9 percent fewer births. In fact, by the end of 1972, the rate was below that required to replace the population. The decline noted in the 1970 census was not confined to any region, age group, class, or race, and reflected the rising concern over population growth, the availability of "the pill" and other contraceptive devices, and the feminist movement. If it continued, this decline in the birthrate was certain to have a profound influence on society at large. The decline between 1960 and 1970, for example, resulted in a drop of 15 percent in the number of children under five years of age—the greatest drop in the nation's history and one which would have many effects: on school budgets, the teaching profession, the manufacture of goods for children, and probably the crime rate, to say nothing of family habits, relationships, and ways of living which differ with family size.

Women's Liberation   An important factor in this development was the rise in the number of working women. It was ironic that even as "the work ethic" came under question as never before, women were moving into the work force in increasing numbers. By 1960 34 percent of American women over 14 had jobs. By 1970, this percentage had risen to 43. Significantly, this included more married women. By 1960 31 percent of all married women were working; by 1970 over 41 percent, and a third of those had children under 18.

Promoters of women's rights were justly worried about not just the opportunity to work, but about equal job opportunities with men and equal pay. A wry explanation of why women seemed unable to get ahead was advanced by Smith College Dean Marjorie Hope Nicolson, who, in a delightful dig at the male ego, remarked: "The fundamental reason that women do not achieve so greatly in the professions as do the men is that women have no wives." At any rate, traditional discrimination did not disappear, and in some respects got worse. For example, while the median income for full-time male workers in 1971 was $9,630, for women it was only $5,700, a more discriminatory ratio than that in 1955. Moreover, only a handful of women were in medicine, law, engineering, and corporate management.

But there were signs of change by the 1970s. Seven times as many women were earning over $10,000 a year in 1969 as in 1959. Government pressure through the Civil Rights Act of 1965 and its affirmative action program resulted in the admission of more women to schools of law and medicine, and similar pressure improved somewhat the hiring of women Ph.D.s in colleges and universities, though unfortunately this move occurred at a time of declining enrollments. An equal rights amendment to the Constitution was passed by Congress, and its ratification seemed certain sooner or later.

The drives for economic and professional opportunity were related to but did not necessarily stem from the dissatisfaction—indeed alienation—apparent in the 1960s. By then a new element had been added to the situation, the desire for an identity beyond but not necessarily separate from women's traditional roles. While some feminists argued that only careers outside the home could give women their full potential as individuals, others argued that

Betty Friedan addresses a rally in support of the Equal Rights Amendment. Her book The Feminine Mystique *(1963) verbalized the frustrations of American women and made her a spokeswoman for the liberation movement. In 1966 she founded the National Organization for Women, and one of its goals was the passage of the Equal Rights Amendment, which feminist groups have been advocating since the twenties. The amendment passed the House in 1971 and the Senate in 1972 and has now gone to the states for ratification. Basically, it states: "equality of rights under the law shall not be denied or abridged by the United States or by any state on account of sex."*

full development was possible without a career if family life were restructured for equal participation by both partners in family duties and with a recognition that family duties were equal in value to other creative human endeavor.

The dissatisfaction was not limited to middle- and upper-class women with education. Working-class wives also were dissatisfied. Almost a third of those surveyed in eight metropolitan areas in 1973 indicated that if they had it to do over again they would not choose homemaking as a career.

The chief obstacle to women's liberation was not discrimination in its more obvious forms. This was an issue open to political and economic solution. The real obstacle lay in traditional attitudes toward women common to most American males, suggested by black leader Stokely Carmichael's famous remark, "the position of women in our movement should be prone." Until the American male could be brought to share in household and family duties and responsibilities, to see that these were honorable labor, that wives were not menials and were capable of outside endeavors if they wished, the prospects for American women to play out their individual destinies as naturally as men were not encouraging.

Children and Youth   Never in the nation's history had so much time and thought been devoted to understanding the young. Children were analyzed exhaustively for the benefit of parents and educators. One journal, which appeared in the 1970s, was devoted to a study of childhood throughout history. The most popular book of advice to parents—and fortunately also the one most marked by common sense—was that by Dr. Benjamin Spock, whose sound counsel enabled millions of parents to survive the vicissitudes of having children. Others included Haim Ginott whose book, *Between Parent and Child,* was the basis for Thomas Gordon's popular program, *Parent Effectiveness Training.* Every branch of psychology contributed to the study of children, and educators, scientists, and technologists joined in programs using computers and programmed learning to explore the capacity to learn early and rapidly. The concern for children also uncovered the unstudied phenomenon of child abuse, which affected up to 500,000 children a year and ranged across social, economic, and ethnic lines. So serious was the problem that in 1973 the federal government appropriated funds for programs designed to identify, intervene, and treat the abused child and his family. A model Child Abuse Reporting law was drafted as a guide for states.

The children of the postwar era were the first to be exposed to television from birth. Psychologists, educators, and parents could not agree on the nature of that influence. Many found it wholly negative, even though they used it as a pacifier. Many children in the first sixteen years of their lives spent more time before the television set than in the classroom, and in their first five years television competed with parents as a major influence. Whether television or parents did more in establishing the values children absorbed was a matter of dispute, but its influence was undeniable. Many feared its stress on violence, commercialism, and materialism, to say nothing of its unfailing reflection of the commonplace.

But television did provide a broader view of the world, and it did provide information of a kind on an infinity of subjects. It would be idle to claim that it had no influence on the young; the difficulty lay in determining its extent, and whether it was good or bad.

Buffeted as it was by the winds of change, the American family seemed to many observers to be doomed. But it was hard to judge the changes. Someone once remarked that the family resembled that other major American institution, the automobile—its external style varied on large models and small from year to year to meet the dictates of fashion and commerce, but its inner workings, except for technical refinements, remained unchanged from the original. And if the family seemed only to stumble along, perhaps you could say of it what Winston Churchill once said of democracy, that it was an impossible system under which to live except when you considered the alternatives.

Religion Strives for Influence

World War II continued to prove that religion cannot do much to control the darker side of human behavior. After the greatest war in history—marked by unprecedented death and bloodshed and concluded by the use of a weapon whose power threatened all life on earth—some might have hoped for a demonstration that there was something to the principles preached by the great religions, an indication that the churches, the instrument of faith, would become powerful institutions in guiding and shaping people's lives. But this was not the case in America or anywhere else in the world.

Statistics on church attendance and membership showed a steady rise, more rapid than population growth up to 1960, but not thereafter. By 1973 church and synagogue membership in America was over 130 million—the Roman Catholics leading with 48.2 million, followed by the Baptists with 27.3 million, the Methodists with 13 million, the Lutherans with 8.8 million, and the Jews with 5.6 million.

Thus on the surface the Americans in the 1950s seemed to place great stock in religion. President Eisenhower announced every Saturday that he planned to attend church on Sunday, and every Monday the newspapers reported that he had done so. He also opened cabinet meetings with prayer. Congress, apparently worried that for over a century and a half the nation had been out from under the shelter of the Lord, decreed that henceforth Americans were to pledge allegiance to "one nation, under God." It was also decreed that the word PRAY would be used to cancel stamps on all letters passing through the mails—though given the growing inefficiency of the postal system perhaps this was not so much in gratitude as in hope. Many ministers continued to emphasize social activities, particularly for the young, but these more and more ran into competition from television, sports, and activities organized by secular institutions such as schools and recreational districts.

All this was quite inconsequential. Of real significance were developments that began to affect religious thinking and the churches in the 1950s and exploded in the 1960s. A number of theologians, adopting the views of the German Karl Barth that God was above and beyond man and concerned only with man's soul, not his society, rejected the doctrine of the social gospel which had drawn the American churches into the arena of social reform. The American theologian Reinhold Niebuhr did not turn his back on the social gospel but placed it in a different perspective with his contention that individuals must recognize their limitations, that they had no monopoly on goodness and wisdom, and what they could achieve was limited. Older concepts of God and faith were also challenged by Paul Tillich, who sought to redefine God in terms of the modern individual's anxieties about the meaning of life, and by those who declared that God was dead and the humanism of Jesus was what mattered.

The Catholic Church was affected by the Second Vatican Council, convened by Pope John XXIII from 1962 to 1965. Among the changes it produced was the use of modern national languages in the mass instead of the traditional Latin, and alterations in the ritual that gave closer involvement in the experience. A number of priests, responding to Pope John's call for more human warmth, compassion, and openness, used folk singers, guitarists, and lay readers of the gospel. Many welcomed relaxation of the old rigidity, but

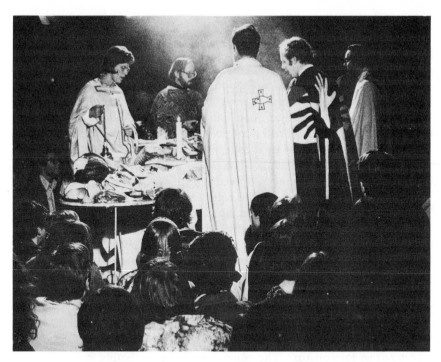

*The Catholic Church made considerable changes in the way Mass could be
celebrated—changes that appealed especially to the young. The altar has
been moved to the center of the congregation and is piled high with loaves of
bread replacing the traditional host.*

others wondered if turning the services into a folk festival was any improvement. New versions of the Bible were authorized, presumably easier to
read than the Douay, perhaps improving clarity but losing the majesty
of the language. Nuns abandoned cumbersome habits for more comfortable
and attractive dress, and some priests took to sport shirts and motorcycles.
But the Catholic Church remained stubbornly opposed to birth control, a
married clergy, and other matters of concern to the laity.

Both Protestant and Catholic churches were deeply affected by the civil
rights and anti-Vietnam war movements of the 1960s. Many ministers and
priests marched in civil rights demonstrations and joined in the antiwar
movement, some so fervently that they ended in jail. A few were able to lead
their congregations in protest, but most ended with controversy and dissension. It was an uneasy time for the church. Many people, especially the
young, tired of internal struggles in the churches and unsympathetic with
high-flown theological doctrines, returned to a simple and fundamental,
perhaps primitive, approach which concentrated on the Bible, and became
known as the Jesus Freaks. Others turned their backs on Christianity and
drifted toward Zen and other Eastern cults.

The Education Explosion

Since World War II more people have gone to schools and colleges in America than ever before; 10 million were registered in colleges and universities by 1974. Enrollments and graduations soared at all levels. Typical of the trend, the number of doctorates rose from 6,400 in 1950 to 37,700 in 1973. By then half the population had finished high school, and of those under 30, 66 percent of blacks had done so and 80 percent of all persons in that age bracket. By 1970, in a total college population of over 6.3 million, 727,000 were blacks, or 9 percent, a figure close to their percentage in the total population. Much of this increase occurred after 1964, when there was a 211 percent rise in black enrollment in colleges.

If more and more were being formally educated, the country was also spending more on education, both in terms of total expenditures and cost per student. In the 1949–1950 school year, expenditures for public schools exceeded $5.8 billion. By 1959–1960 expenditures were running $15.6 billion, and by 1972–1973 they were over $52 billion. More money was also spent per student, the average rising from $259 in 1949–1950 to $1,232 in 1972–1973.

Government in Education   The postwar period was notable for the expanded role of the federal government in education. The government had always provided aid to education, as in the land grants of the Northwest Ordinance of 1787 and the Morrill Act of 1862. But after World War II government aid became immense. After the Elementary and Secondary Education Act of 1965, federal contributions to public education rose into the billions. By the 1971–1972 school year the federal contribution to elementary and secondary education was over $3.3 billion a year, and that to higher education had reached $4.4 billion. Beginning with the GI Bill which provided billions to educate veterans, the government became committed to support of a wide variety of educational programs on all levels. These included such diverse things as school milk programs, aid to school districts in areas affected by federal agencies (such as military bases), assistance to strengthen offerings in science, math, and foreign languages which arose out of the Sputnik crisis of 1958, student loans and fellowships, and direct aid to colleges and universities facing financial disaster. Through its support of research in major universities, some of whose graduate budgets heavily depended on such grants, government became crucial and sometimes controversial. While such grants often funded research otherwise impossible, they sometimes dictated its nature. Defense-related research contracts came under heavy criticism by the 1960s. But in most ways government aid tended to broaden and improve education at every level.

Most Americans were willing to support education on such a scale because it seemed to pay off economically, as the Census Bureau showed. In 1971 the median income for white males with eight years of schooling was $5,566, and for blacks $4,726. For whites with a high-school degree it was

A student lies dead, one of four slain at Kent State University. Within days, two more students were killed at Jackson State University in Mississippi by state police. The deaths stunned the nation, and in reaction students throughout the country struck and closed hundreds of schools.

$9,263; for blacks $6,579. For those with one or more years of college, median white male income was $11,990, and black income $8,627. In addition, the great expansion in higher education involved large numbers of students whose parents were not college graduates and whose incomes were middle- or lower-class. Three-fifths of white college students came from such families and three-quarters of black students. If the relationship between education and income held, then education could play the central role in the economic advancement not only of blacks but of poorer whites as well. Another motive for education was that as the economy became more sophisticated, society had less use for the unskilled and more use for the skilled.

The Student Protest Movement   But whatever the motives and however grand the expansion, education came under heavy criticism. Many argued that the system was grinding out trained but docile people who accepted the established order without question. Others argued that mass admissions inevitably lowered standards. Some criticized the emphasis on scientific and technological training at the expense of the arts, humanities, and social sciences. By the 1960s students themselves joined the criticism, principally in the colleges and universities, although some high schools were not spared either. The student protest was not confined to learned arguments. Students relied not only upon words and occasionally vulgar ones at that, but on action as well—to the great discomfiture of their elders and the astonishment of their teachers.

Much student complaint was directed against the seeming indifference of a vast mass educational system. Opening the doors wide was fine as it created opportunity, but efficiency and cost dictated not small institutions but large state systems like those of New York, California, and Wisconsin, which had 233,000, 186,000, and 105,000 students respectively. The result was large campuses of 30,000 and more students. Few students could feel comfortable in such institutions, and many felt lost. The whole experience seemed mechanized and impersonal—everything that learning should not be. Protest was not directed merely at the educational system but at the impersonality of a highly organized, bureaucratized, impersonal society. From the beginning in 1964 in the Free Speech Movement on the Berkeley campus of the University of California to the shooting of Kent State students by Ohio National Guardsmen in the spring of 1970, the nation's colleges were rocked by upheaval, disruption, and demonstration. In the single spring semester of 1968 there were 221 demonstrations on 101 campuses. Feeding this protest was student concern over such social issues as civil rights, poverty, the draft, and especially the Vietnam war.

The student protest movement involved only a handful of revolutionaries and never engulfed the majority of students beyond rhetoric. But many secretly or openly sympathized with the movement. By 1972, however, the movement had dissipated its energies. Fiery issues such as the Vietnam war and the draft had been defused by the Nixon administration. Tough stands were taken by university and public officials, some of whom proved willing to rely on police authority to maintain order and control. Skillful moves were made by administrators to bring students into some kind of participation, even if only token, in university decision making. Many students reacted against the violence which began to mark the actions of both sides. A new generation of students arrived on the campuses, the job market for graduates tightened, and there appeared new issues of vital concern such as ecology, which could not be dealt with by demonstrations but required patient political work and the accumulation of knowledge. All these developments helped end the brief but turbulent era of student protest. The campuses entered a new period of calm, but the protest movement had made its point.

Universities and colleges did indeed try to provide a more personal atmosphere through such experiments as cluster colleges within large institutions as well as a return to smaller classes. Interdisciplinary programs bringing to bear a variety of disciplines upon major problems were established, as in the development at Stanford University of a new undergraduate program in human biology designed to train experts to cope with overpopulation, urban sprawl, pollution, and conservation. University administrations also adopted

*The culmination of the American space program was the moon landing.
Science answered the challenges of space exploration with the paraphernalia
of that voyage, from the astronaut's life-supporting backpack to the Lunar
Roving Vehicle. But it is indicative of our age that when the astronauts
lifted off from the moon, they left more than the footprints visible in the
foreground.*

more liberal attitudes toward student behavior on the assumption that the
private social lives and habits of their students were none of the university's
business. While by the mid-1970s the campuses seemed placid in comparison to the 1960s, and the interests of students centered on their own personal
lives and careers much as in the 1950s, there was a quiet ferment at work in
American higher education, a ferment soundly based in knowledge, focused
on broad concerns such as overpopulation and conservation, and oriented
toward realistic political action.

The Growth of Knowledge   Knowledge expanded rapidly after World
War II. New medical knowledge included open-heart surgery, organ transplants, the use of radioactive isotopes against cancer, vaccines to prevent
polio, mumps, and German measles, and the extensive use of new drugs
such as aureomycin and terramycin to combat infections. Indeed the rise of
chemotherapy, the use of drugs to fight illness, was a vital part of the expansion of medical knowledge. From 1966 to 1973 alone, fifty-six new drugs

significant in the treatment of disease were uncovered. Extensive research suggested that one possible cause of cancer lay in viruses, which if true opened the way to the eventual control of this dread disease by drugs, and the laborious search for such drugs went on year after year in laboratories all over the country. The relatively new science of genetics leaped forward with work on the chromosomal constituent DNA, discovered by the American James B. Watson and the Englishman Francis Crick. The gene itself was isolated in 1969. Geneticists were now predicting the control of disease, intelligence, and even creativity through genetic engineering.

The space program extended knowledge in a variety of fields and opened the door to understanding the nature of the universe itself. The great expansion of knowledge in the postwar world was underlined by the awarding of seventy-six Nobel Prizes in physiology and medicine, chemistry, and physics to Americans in the years from 1945 to 1972. The expansion of knowledge in the biological and physical sciences was paralleled by research in the social and behavioral sciences—in history, economics, sociology, anthropology, and psychology, the latter gaining most attention as psychologists probed all aspects of human behavior and motivation in the attempt to understand the anxieties and tensions plaguing modern people.

Knowledge is now so international in character, so interdependent in its development, that it is difficult to identify specific advances as originating in any one society. But America had tens of thousands of scholars and scientists at work, it poured far greater sums into the expansion of knowledge than any other nation, and it had more advanced and extensive facilities for research and study. As a result, great numbers of scholars and students from around the world came to the United States every year. The country had become one of the world's great centers of research, learning, and study.

The Growth of Culture

Just as everything else grew in the postwar era, so the paraphernalia of culture could be measured by the statistics of growth. By 1973 there were forty-three major art museums in America's principal cities, plus hundreds of galleries and museums on campuses and in smaller cities across the country. There were sixty-three opera companies, twenty-eight major symphony orchestras, seventy-eight metropolitan orchestras, and scores of community, college, and university symphony orchestras. The nation had thirty-nine professional resident and repertory theaters in addition to the commercial theater of Broadway and off-Broadway in New York City, and the road companies on tour. Few colleges or universities were without their theater season, and scores of towns and cities had their own community theaters. Attendance ran into the tens of millions yearly for concerts, operas, plays, and art exhibits. The growth of music appreciation could be seen in total record sales which were approximately $250 million in 1950, $500 million in 1960, and over $1.7 billion in 1971. Publishers were bringing out over 37,000 new book titles a year by 1971, in addition to ever-expanding sales of existing titles. Culture had become a major industry in America, and only an expanding and wealthy society could devote so much attention to it. Some of the arts, like architecture, were stimulated by a direct tie to economic growth; witness the vast enclosed shopping mall and the high-rise glass and steel building. Conscious, too, of the aesthetic appeal of painting and sculpture to enhance their image as well as their buildings, corporations became patrons of the arts, and at least two hundred of them acquired their own collections of paintings. Many American families as well willingly spent money on the works of contemporary artists. Art appreciation, painting, and sculpture classes reached new heights of popularity in the universities and colleges by the 1970s, and the sale of art materials boomed accordingly. The long-playing record and the tape recorder revolutionized musical taste and the commercial sale of music. Television's major networks reported in 1973 a record $213.4 million in profits before taxes.

By 1970 over 96 percent of all American homes had at least one television set. Although television entertainment was mainly on the lighter side, it provided excellent news coverage, taking Americans to the moon with the astronauts, to Peking with President Nixon. It also had the capacity to lay bare America's uglier moments, as in its coverage of the Army–McCarthy hearings in 1954 and the Watergate scandal in 1973 and 1974. Television also covered sports with technical skill, and presented fine drama and superb musical events. Television had an allure for young and old, and its impact on the movies was shattering. Attendance at the movies collapsed from a high of 80 million a week in 1953 to 18 million twenty years later. As a result the motion picture industry changed drastically. Independent producers became the rule as the old studios sold out, closed, or went into the production of television shows. The disbanding of the great studios moved much motion picture making "out on location," which increased the realistic flavor of films. Other improvements made the fewer motion pictures produced technically superior to those of Hollywood's days of glory. Hollywood dominance of motion pictures disappeared, and Italian, French, and English producers frequently surpassed Americans in making high-quality pictures. Indeed the foreign film, rarely seen in America before the war, became a staple in the American market.

Radio, supposed to be wiped out by television, flourished as television expanded. But its format changed completely. The network programs of comedy, drama, soap opera, and other entertainment went to TV, and radio concentrated on music interspersed with capsule news programs. FM radio made its appearance, frequently specializing in particular types of music. Publishing was struck by the paperback revolution, but hardcover books were more numerous than ever.

New ideas and attitudes affected cultural as they did other aspects of American life. Blacks were treated in a more realistic fashion in American films, as opposed to the shuffling, humming caricature of the 1930s and 1940s. Black writers such as Ralph Ellison, James Baldwin, and LeRoi Jones acquired recognition and stature. Problems of social degradation, poverty, drug abuse, and violence may have received more than their share of exposure. The

Elegy to the Spanish Republic, 54 *by Robert Motherwell (1957–1961).*

contention, in fact, that violence was a part of American life extended even into the sacred realm of the Western film, as in *The Wild Bunch*, a film of blood and brutality inconceivable before 1960. In books, motion pictures, and even television, scenes of nudity and sex earlier unimaginable were routine, and themes never before openly discussed got public treatment. Television not only explored such subjects as abortion in documentaries, but introduced the subject as a theme on one of its most popular series, *Maude*.

Literature, the Arts, and Music   Although American literature gained international recognition in the postwar era with three Nobel Prize winners, all three were older writers whose reputations had been made between the two great wars—Faulkner, Hemingway, and Steinbeck. Many new younger writers appeared on the scene, each momentarily promising to maintain the high levels achieved by the giants of an earlier period. Norman Mailer, author of *The Naked and The Dead*, perhaps the best of the many war novels but hardly the equal of Hemingway's *A Farewell to Arms* on World War I, offered promise of becoming a new major writer in America. In some respects Mailer fulfilled that promise—for his skill grew and was rarely equaled by any of his contemporaries—but he turned to a kind of personal journalism on a variety of contemporary subjects from the moonshot to boxing that left unused his larger imaginative talents. Joseph Heller, in *Catch-22*, a brilliant, searing, comic denunciation of war, also gave promise but up to 1976 his total output amounted to only two books. J.D. Salinger, especially in *The Catcher in the Rye*, particularly captured the fancy of the young concerned about their identity in an increasingly complicated and confused world. Scores of other writers, including the productive and brilliant Saul Bellow, black writers James Baldwin and Ralph Ellison (whose *The Invisible Man* was hailed by critics as the most important novel in twenty years), Philip Roth, Bernard Malamud, John Hersey, Nelson Algren, John Updike, Kurt Vonnegut, Jr., and many others made the American literary scene a fruitful and exciting one.

Alienation and doubt about American culture characterized almost all serious writing. In this sense, American writers in the postwar era were victims of the times much as most of their characters were. Their range was for the most part limited to the crushed, manipulated, defeated, and helpless. Any exaltation of the human spirit (beyond the capacity simply to endure) which implied that living might after all be worthwhile, was rare, or if dealt with at all slipped off in the hands of the less able and unimaginative into sheer sentimentality. Moreover, in a time of broad social turmoil and change no major writer seemed to have any conception that good might ultimately come from such change, and few had any conviction about those enduring human values which might make that possible. Their pessimism was a contrast to that of the American people as a whole.

Art similarly was affected, victimized by the world it deplored in the sense that it allowed that world to define the form and content of much of the new painting and sculpture. Although the Americans in the postwar era for the first time finally freed themselves from dependence upon Europe and became the initiators rather than the imitators in art, the nature of the achievement was largely technical. The main trend was toward nonrepresentational art, although painters such as Andrew Wyeth and Richard Diebenkorn sought to emphasize a new realism. But abstract expressionism was the explosive postwar American contribution to art. A contribution as original as jazz had been in music, abstract expressionism came out of the experiments of Robert Motherwell, Jackson Pollock, Willem de Kooning, and Arshile Gorky. Pollock and de Kooning particularly became the recognized leaders in the movement. The possibilities inherent in new forms of painting which were opened up by the success of abstract expressionism, led to "op" art in which color and shape became ends in themselves.

The striking thing about these trends was the disappearance of human figures. Geometric shapes, optics, all the forms dictated by science and technology dominated many canvases. Representing an intellectual and emotional rejection of much of a mass industrial society, such painters were unable any more than the writers to go beyond rejection and hence were tied down in their imaginations and ideas by the very elements they deplored. Just as with many writers, however, their amazing skill and versatility provided an aesthetic satisfaction that made the art world an exciting and fascinating one for viewers and artists alike. Grizzled Thomas Hart Benton, the John Steinbeck of the canvas, dismissed these new trends as nonsense and died in his eighties painting as he always had.

Developments in popular music were as startling as those in art, and broader in their impact since they reached such a vast audience in American youth. The music of swing and jazz with their often sentimental lyrics gave way early in the 1950s to rock and roll, characterized by a driving beat which dominated melody and lyrics. Modified by the sixties into folk-rock, a significant portion of such music not only expressed a general feeling of alienation held by the young, but also became the vehicle for the counterculture of protest against Establishment policies on civil rights, war, drugs, and other matters of concern. The music of such popular singers as Elvis Presley, the Rolling Stones, Simon and Garfunkel, and Bob Dylan was often characterized by new melodic touches and penetrating lyrics.

Bob Dylan particularly was a dominant influence, leading almost every new trend since he started his career in the early sixties. Writing most of his own songs, Dylan moved from folk songs to social protest, his "Blowin' in the Wind" becoming, as one cultural historian has noted, "the spiritual anthem of the civil rights and antiwar movements." His "The Times They Are A-Changin' " was a declaration of revolutionary change on the way. By the end of the decade, however, Dylan had, after periods of withdrawal and experimentation, returned to songs that concentrated on those things making for the satisfactory personal life, giving up social protest, the drug scene, and youthful alienation. In this he reflected the new spirit of the young in the decade of the seventies.

Profile: THE AMERICAN

Born July 4, 1776. Shortly thereafter the French immigrant and observer, Hector St. John De Crèvecoeur, in his Letters from an American Farmer (1782) posed this question about the new arrival: "What, then, is the American, this new man?" Americans have been asking this question repeatedly for the past two hundred years, for few people have been as self-conscious about themselves and their identity as we have. As John Kouwenhoven once pointed out, while Henry James once wrote a novel called The American, no Russian has ever written one called The Russian nor has any Englishman ever written one titled The Englishman.

The question raised by Crèvecoeur was and still is a legitimate one. It is rather dangerous to attempt a portrait of a people as diverse and varied in their composition as the Americans and complicated still further by the fact that they share a common characteristic with the rest of the human race in being naturally divided into men and women. Nevertheless, some generalizations are worth making for the purpose of better understanding so long as this warning is kept in mind. Particularly so if one believes that the Americans are facing a difficult future. Knowing something about our character might provide a clue to our chances.

The American of the past—and we are here talking about the white male who has dominated the course of the last two hundred years—has rarely been humble or self-effacing. On the contrary, superior, assertive, boastful, arrogant, self-centered, and looking-out-for-number-one would describe him better. He has, in fact, been guilty of the same grand arrogance possessed by Professor Henry Higgins in "My Fair Lady," who wondered aloud why everyone couldn't be "like me." Only recently have American blacks and women taken him up on this challenge. These qualities have not endeared the American to others. They have led him into all kinds of unpleasant behavior to say the least. The record is clear on that.

But the Americans in general have also displayed notably attractive qualities of character. Self-centered in many ways because both their economic and political beliefs have emphasized the virtues of individualism and going one's own way, they have often neglected the obvious and allowed things to get out of hand. But at the same time they have also justified Jefferson's contention that "whenever things get so far wrong as to attract their notice, they may be relied on to set them to right." In the last thirty years the Americans have had their notice dramatically called to a number of things gone dreadfully wrong—political corruption, poverty, pollution, racial discrimination. American society has been in upheaval and turmoil in the last three decades not because the Americans have gotten nastier in character, but because more and more of them have been unwilling to tolerate wrongdoing and seek to change the circumstances of social, political, and economic life in order to prevent it. The disclosures of Watergate, for example, prompted the Americans to turn against the man they had just overwhelmingly re-elected, to remove him from office, and to begin changing the rules of political behavior. In short, instead of ignoring such problems—a fault of many other societies—the Americans have sought to solve them, though the complexity and long neglect of some will require continued and expanded efforts. But the process is underway.

In the face of such problems and in spite of their own bewilderment at the rapid pace of change in the country, the Americans still retain another attractive quality—their confidence and optimism about their ability to meet whatever fate throws at them. A recent Gallup poll, for example, showed that three-quarters of the American people maintained a deep faith in the United States and were confident in regard to the future. Such optimism does not spring from a willingness to neglect or tolerate problems, but from the conviction that they are open to solution if resources, energy, and imagination are devoted to the task.

Moreover, the Americans remain an essentially compassionate people. There are plenty of examples of the opposite in the present as well as the past, but few people have been as humane and generous in their concern for others as the Americans, and they have always admired most the leaders who exhibited this quality. No people in history equaled the generosity the Americans displayed after World War II in their public and private aid to those abroad suffering the ravages of war. No people support so extensively private philanthropic endeavors at home, from medical research to educational scholarships. Few respond personally so promptly when disaster strikes their fellows. A family burned out of its home by fire gets food, clothing, and shelter from its neighbors. Volunteers search for lost hikers, rally to dig out a child who has fallen into an abandoned well, and send their quarters and dollars to the family of a police officer killed in the line of duty.

The Americans also remain idealists, even though they have too often seen achievement fall short of their ideals. For most Americans still maintain a faith in the basic purposes for which the Republic was founded. As that perceptive journalist, Bill Moyers, has written: the Founding Fathers made an agreement with respect to justice and the common good, and the American people "in their heart know they cannot abandon it."

Finally, the American remains what Crévecoeur said of him: "The American is a new man, who acts upon new principles; he must therefore entertain new ideas, and form new opinions." In the face of trying times, this may well be the American's most useful asset. He, she, they will need it in the decades ahead.

Selected Reading

General Works

The following general works survey different aspects of American development and should be referred to for their pertinent references throughout chapters one to twelve.

The most comprehensive study of American cultural and intellectual life and institutions is Merle Curti, *The Growth of American Thought* (Harper & Row, New York, 1964) which also contains a superb bibliography current to the last revised edition. Stow Persons, *American Minds* (Holt, Rinehart, & Winston, New York, 1958) concentrates on certain intellectual themes with great illumination. Harvey Wish, *Society and Thought in America* (2 vols., David McKay, New York, 1962) looks at social and intellectual life in great detail. Daniel Boorstin's three volumes on *The Americans* (Vintage, New York, 1959, 1965, 1973) are exciting and original works. Extremely thoughtful essays by important scholars compose *Paths of American Thought* (Houghton Mifflin, Boston, 1963) edited by Morton White and Arthur M. Schlesinger, Jr. Stephen B. Oates, *Portrait of America* (2 vols., Houghton Mifflin, Boston, 1973) is an excellent anthology of historical essays. Carl Degler, *Out of Our Past* (Harper & Row, New York, 1959), is a superior general interpretation.

The best general sources for brief biographies of Americans are the multivolume older *Dictionary of American Biography* (Scribner's, New York, 1936), the *Encyclopaedia Britannica* 15th edition (Encyclopaedia Britannica, Inc., Chicago, 1974), and the one-volume *Encyclopedia of American Biography* (Harper & Row, New York, 1974) edited by John Garraty. Roderick Nash has written a biographical history of the United States, *From These Beginnings* (Harper & Row, New York, 1973), in which he shows what can be done with this approach in the study of a limited number of key Americans.

The Comparative Approach to American History (Basic Books, New York, 1968), edited by C. Vann Woodward, demonstrates the importance of viewing American experience in relation to that of other peoples. The two-volume *The Underside of American History* (Harcourt Brace Jovanovich, New York, 1971), edited by Thomas R. Frazier, reminds us of the unhappy side of America's past. G. D. Lillibridge's essay, "The American Impact Abroad: Past and Present," in *The American Scholar,* Winter 1965–1966, outlines the theme of American influence abroad. Also see Lillibridge, ed., *The American Image* (Heath, Lexington, Mass., 1968) and Michael Kraus, ed., *The North Atlantic Civilization* (Van Nostrand, Princeton, N.J., 1957). Gerald Stearn has edited *Broken Image* (Random House, New York, 1972) which establishes a grimmer side to this theme.

Other books on particular subjects include Ronald W. Hogeland, ed., *Women and Womanhood in America* (Heath, Lexington, Mass., 1973) and Edith

H. Altbach, *Women in America* (Heath, Lexington, Mass., 1974) on the neglected sex. Carl Wittke, *We Who Built America* (Prentice-Hall, Englewood Cliffs, N.J., 1964) and Maldwyn Jones, *American Immigration* (University of Chicago Press, Chicago, 1960) survey the immigrant experience. Norman F. Cantor and Michael S. Werthman, eds., *The History of Popular Culture Since 1815* (Macmillan, New York, 1968), which leaps back and forth across the Atlantic, and Russel B. Nye, *The Unembarrassed Muse: The Popular Arts in America* (Dial, New York, 1970) explore this subject. Hans Kohn studies *American Nationalism* (Macmillan, New York, 1957) and Ross M. Robertson surveys the *History of the American Economy* (Harcourt Brace Jovanovich, New York, 1960). Richard Chase surveys *The American Novel and its Tradition* (Doubleday, Garden City, N.Y., 1957) and Robert E. Spiller exhaustively examines *The Literary History of the United States* (Macmillan, New York, 1964) in three volumes. William T. Hagan sums up the story of the *American Indians* (University of Chicago Press, Chicago, 1961), Oliver W. Larkin looks at *Art and Life in America* (Holt, Rinehart, & Winston, New York, 1962), and R. Freeman Butts and Lawrence A. Cremin examine the *History of Education in American Culture* (Holt, Rinehart & Winston, New York, 1953). John Hope Franklin gives a general history of blacks in *From Slavery to Freedom* (Knopf, New York, 1956).

The great majority of these books and those subsequently listed are in paperback.

Chapter 1

For biography, see Fawn M. Brodie, *Thaddeus Stevens: Scourge of the South* (Norton, New York, 1959). For a general treatment of Reconstruction see Randall and Donald, *The Civil War and Reconstruction*. Also Kenneth Stampp, *The Era of Reconstruction* (Knopf, New York, 1965) and John Hope Franklin, *Reconstruction After the Civil War* (University of Chicago Press, Chicago, 1961).

Chapter 2

For biography, see Louis R. Harlan, *Booker T. Washington: The Making of a Black Leader* (Oxford University Press, New York, 1972). On the fate of the black, see C. Vann Woodward, *The Strange Career of Jim Crow* (Oxford University Press, New York, 1955), R. W. Logan, *The Betrayal of the Negro* (Macmillan, New York, 1968), and David Reimers, ed., *The Black Man in America Since Reconstruction* (Crowell, New York, 1970).

Chapter 3

See the pertinent chapters in Jones, *American Immigration* and Wittke, *We Who Built America*. Also the extensive detail in Wish, *Society and Thought in America*. Oscar Handlin analyzes the immigrant as *The Uprooted* (Little, Brown, Boston, 1951), and John Higham the hostile reaction to the immigrant in *Strangers in the Land* (Rutgers University Press, New Brunswick, N.J.,

1955). See also Philip Taylor, *The Distant Magnet* (Harper & Row, New York, 1971) on the lure of America, and F. J. Brown and J. S. Roucek, *One America* (Prentice-Hall, New York, 1945).

Chapter 4

On biography, see Nannie T. Alderson and Helena Huntington Smith, *A Bride Goes West* (University of Nebraska Press, Lincoln, 1942). Excellent general coverage is found in Billington, *Westward Expansion* (Macmillan, New York, 1974). For more specific information see Rodman W. Paul, *Mining Frontiers of the Far West* (Holt, Rinehart & Winston, New York, 1962), Walter Webb, *The Great Plains* (Ginn, Boston, 1931), R. R. Dykstra, *The Cattle Towns* (Knopf, New York, 1968), Ernest S. Osgood, *The Day of the Cattleman* (University of Minnesota Press, St. Paul, 1929), Joe B. Frantz and Julian Ernest Choate, Jr., *The American Cowboy: The Myth and the Reality* (University of Oklahoma Press, Norman, 1955), Everett Dick, *The Sod-House Frontier 1854–1890* (Appleton-Century, New York, 1937), and Fred A. Shannon, *The Farmer's Last Frontier* (Farrar & Rinehart, New York, 1945). See pertinent chapters in Hagan, *American Indians* (University of Chicago Press, Chicago, 1961), Francis Paul Prucha, ed., *The Indian in American History* (Holt, Rinehart & Winston, New York, 1971), and Wilcomb E. Washburn, ed., *The Indian and the White Man,* (Doubleday, Garden City, N.Y., 1964).

Chapter 5

On biography see Joseph Frazier Wall, *Andrew Carnegie* (Oxford University Press, New York, 1970) and Carnegie's *Autobiography* (Houghton Mifflin, Boston, 1920). On business ideas and motivation, see Edward C. Kirkland, *Dream and Thought in the Business Community* (Franklin Watts, New York, 1956). On industrial development see Thomas C. Cochran and William Miller, *The Age of Enterprise* (Harper & Row, New York, 1961), Samuel P. Hays, *The Response to Industrialism* (University of Chicago Press, Chicago, 1957), Edward C. Kirkland, *Industry Comes of Age* (Quadrangle, New York, 1967). See also Ray Ginger, *The Age of Excess* (Macmillan, New York, 1965). On the city, Blake McKelvey, *The Urbanization of America 1860–1915* (Rutgers University Press, New Brunswick, N.J., 1963) and Alexander B. Callow, ed., *American Urban History* (Oxford University Press, New York, 1969). A wealth of interesting detail is in Lloyd Morris, *Incredible New York* (Random House, New York, 1951). For labor, see Henry Pelling, *American Labor* (University of Chicago Press, Chicago, 1960). See also Bremner, *From the Depths,* on poverty.

Chapter 6

For biography see Justin Kaplan, *Mister Clemens and Mark Twain* (Simon and Schuster, New York, 1966). For general coverage of culture and intellectual life, see pertinent chapters in Curti and Wish. For women and family life, the pertinent material in Hogeland, *Women and Womanhood in America,* Friedman and Shade, *Our American Sisters*, Riegel, *American Women*, William L. O'Neill, *Everyone was Brave* (Quadrangle, New York, 1969). On education see Lawrence A. Cremin, *The Transformation of the School* (Knopf, New York, 1961) and L. R. Veysey, *The Emergence of the American University* (University of Chicago Press, Chicago, 1965). For a specific history, see Merle Curti and Vernon Carstensen, *The University of Wisconsin 1848–1925* (2 vols., University of Wisconsin Press, Madison, 1949). For the clash between science and religion, see Paul Carter, *The Spiritual Crisis of the Gilded Age* (Northern Illinois University Press, DeKalb, 1971). See also Henry Steele Commager, *American Mind: An Interpretation of American Thought and Character Since the 1800s* (Yale University Press, New Haven, Conn., 1950).

Chapter 7

A balanced account of Wilson is Arthur C. Walworth, *Woodrow Wilson* (2 vols., Longman's Green, New York, 1958). On Progressivism, see the pertinent chapters in Richard Hofstadter, *The Age of Reform* (Knopf, New York, 1960) and Eric Goldman, *Rendezvous with Destiny* (Random House, New York, 1956). Also George Mowry, *The Era of Theodore Roosevelt and the Birth of Modern America 1902–1912* (Harper & Row, New York, 1958), Gabriel Kolko, *Triumph of Conservatism: A Reinterpretation of American History 1900–1916* (Free Press, New York, 1967), and R. H. Wiebe, *Businessmen and Reform: A Study of the Progressive Movement* (Harvard University Press, Cambridge, 1962). On World War I, Ross Gregory, *The Origins of American Intervention in the First World War* (Norton, New York, 1971), Daniel M. Smith, *The Great Departure—1914–1920* (Wiley, New York, 1965), H. C. Peterson and G. C. Fite, *Opponents of War 1917–1918* (University of Washington Press, Seattle, 1957), Allen Churchill, *Over Here* (Dodd Mead, New York, 1968), Charles Genthe, *American War Narratives 1917–1918* (David Lewis, New York, 1969), and Arthur S. Link, ed., *The Impact of World War I* (Harper & Row, New York, 1969). On both Progressivism and war, see pertinent chapters in Curti.

Chapter 8

For biography see Kenneth S. Davis, *The Hero: Charles A. Lindbergh and the American Dream* (Doubleday, New York, 1959) and the stimulating essay by John W. Ward, "The Meaning of Lindbergh's Flight," in *The American Quarterly*, vol. 10 (1958). For a general survey, see George Soule, *Prosperity Decade: From War to Depression 1917–1929* (Harper & Row, New York, 1947), William E. Leuchtenburg, *The Perils of Prosperity 1914–1932* (University of Chicago Press, Chicago, 1958), and Arthur M. Schlesinger, Jr., *The Crisis of the Old Order* (Houghton Mifflin, Boston, 1957). A survey of the automobile, the movies, and radio is found in Lloyd Morris, *Not So Long Ago* (Random House, New York, 1949). See also Alfred D. Chandler, Jr., ed., *Giant Enterprise: Ford, General Motors, and the Automobile Industry* (Harcourt, Brace & World, New York, 1964), Daniel M. Smith, *War and Depression* (Forum Press, St. Louis, 1972), and J. W. Prothro, *The Dollar Decade: Business Ideas in the 1920s*

(Greenwood, New York, 1954). For labor, the first part of Irving Bernstein, *The Lean Years* (Houghton Mifflin, Boston, 1966). On the changing role of women, William Henry Chafe, *The American Woman: Her Changing Social, Economic, and Political Roles 1920–1970* (Oxford University Press, New York, 1972). For extensive coverage of social history, see Frederick Lewis Allen, *Only Yesterday* (Harper & Row, New York, 1931). John Kenneth Galbraith explores *The Great Crash, 1929* (Houghton Mifflin, Boston, 1961), and Frederick J. Hoffman analyzes the impact of the decade on literature in *The Twenties* (Free Press, New York, 1955).

Chapter 9

The best biography of Roosevelt is James M. Burns, *The Lion and the Fox* (Harcourt Brace Jovanovich, New York, 1956) and *Roosevelt: The Soldier of Freedom* (Harcourt Brace Jovanovich, New York, 1970). More about his personal life is found in Joseph Lash, *Eleanor and Franklin* (Norton, New York, 1971). Surveys on the depression are Dixon Wecter, *The Age of the Great Depression* (Franklin Watts, New York, 1948) and Broadus Mitchell, *Depression Decade* (Harper & Row, New York, 1947). See also William E. Leuchtenburg, *Franklin D. Roosevelt and the New Deal* (Harper & Row, New York, 1963), Otis L. Graham, Jr., *An Encore for Reform: The Old Progressives and the New Deal* (Oxford University Press, New York, 1967), and Thomas C. Cochran, *The Great Depression and World War II* (Scott, Foresman, Glenview, Ill., 1968). For workers, see the last part of Irving Bernstein, *Lean Years*, and his *Turbulent Years* (Houghton Mifflin, Boston, 1971). For effects of the depression, see Bernard Sternsher, ed., *Hitting Home: The Great Depression in Town and Country* (Quadrangle, Chicago, 1970), Caroline Bird, *The Invisible Scar* (David McKay, New York, 1966), and Studs Terkel, *Hard Times* (Pantheon, New York, 1970). See also Robert Bindiner, *Just Around the Corner: A Highly Selective History of the Thirties* (Harper & Row, New York, 1967) for life in the decade. On women see Chafe, *The American Woman*. On blacks, Raymond Wolters, *Negroes and the Great Depression* (Greenwood, New York, 1970).

Chapter 10

For the effect of war on those who fought, see Desmond Flowers and James Reeves, eds., *The Taste of Courage: The War 1939–1945* (Harper & Row, New York, 1960) and J. Glenn Gray's moving *The Warriors: Reflections on Men in Battle* (Harper & Row, New York, 1959). Examples of the fighting are covered in Don Congdon, ed., *Combat: World War Two, European Theater* (vol. 1, Dell, New York, 1958) and Robert Sherrod, *Tarawa: The Story of a Battle* (Admiral Nimitz Foundation, Fredericksburg, Tex., 1944). The best general account of the war is A. Russell Buchanan, *The United States and World War II* (2 vols., Harper & Row, New York, 1964). Arnold A. Offner deals with *America and the Origins of World War II 1933–1941* (Houghton Mifflin, Boston, 1971). Social history is found in Richard R. Lingeman, *Don't You Know There's a War On?* (Warner Paperback Library, New York, 1971), Richard Polenberg, *War and*

Society: The United States 1941–1945 (Lippincott, Philadelphia, 1972), and his edited volume *America at War: The Home Front 1941–1945* (Prentice-Hall, Englewood Cliffs, N.J., 1968). See also Chester Eisinger, ed., *The 1940s: Profile of a Nation in Crisis* (Doubleday & Co., Garden City, N.Y., 1969). For the role of women, see Chafe, *The American Woman.* James P. Baxter tells of the organization of science for war in *Scientists Against Time* (M.I.T. Press, Cambridge, Mass., 1946). Roger Daniels recounts the fate of the Japanese-Americans in *Concentration Camps USA: Japanese Americans and World War II* (Holt, Rinehart & Winston, New York, 1971).

Chapter 11

For biography see David L. Lewis, *King: A Critical Biography* (Praeger, New York, 1970). Eric Goldman, *Crucial Decade—And After* (Random House, New York, 1960) and John Brooks, *The Great Leap: The Past Twenty-five Years in America* (Harper & Row, New York, 1966) survey the postwar period. Max Lerner comprehensively looks at modern American life in *America as a Civilization* (Simon and Schuster, New York, 1957). E. S. Woytinsky, *Profile of the United States Economy: A Society of Growth and Change* (Praeger, New York, 1967) and John Kenneth Galbraith in *The Affluent Society* (Houghton Mifflin, Boston, 1958) and *The New Industrial State* (Houghton Mifflin, Boston, 1967) analyze economic development and change. The editors of *Fortune* examine both *America in the Sixties: The Economy and the Society* (Harper & Row, New York, 1960) and *The Exploding Metropolis* (Doubleday & Co., Garden City, New York, 1958). Peter F. Drucker, *The Age of Discontinuity: Guidelines to Our Changing Society* (Harper & Row, New York, 1968), Andrew Hacker, *The End of the American Era* (Atheneum, New York, 1970), and Michael Harrington, *The Accidental Century* (Macmillan, New York, 1966) give different reactions to postwar America. Harrington also called attention to poverty in *The Other America* (Penguin, New York, 1963). Stan Steiner, *The New Indians* (Harper & Row, New York, 1968) and Alvin M. Josephy, Jr., *Red Power* (McGraw-Hill, New York, 1971) look at the fate of the Indian. Louis E. Lomax analyzed *The Negro Revolt* (Harper & Row, New York, 1962). See also Manuel P. Servin, *An Awakened Minority: The Mexican-Americans* (Glencoe, Riverside, N.J., 1970). America on the international scene is dealt with in Walter LaFeber, *America, Russia, and the Cold War, 1945–1966* (Wiley, New York, 1967) and J. William Fulbright, *The Arrogance of Power* (Random House, New York, 1966).

Chapter 12

Max Lerner comprehensively looks at modern American life in *America as a Civilization* (Simon and Schuster, New York, 1957). On the relationship which developed between government and science, see Daniel S. Greenberg, *The Politics of Pure Science* (New American Library, New York, 1967). Books on special topics include Report of a Special Task Force to the Secretary of HEW, *Work in America* (M.I.T. Press, Cambridge, Mass., 1973), Ramsey Clark, *Crime in America* (Simon and Schuster, New York, 1970), and E. C.

Higbee, *Farms and Farmers in an Urban Age* (Kraus Reprint Co., Millwood, N.Y., 1963). On the environmental crisis see R. Buckminster Fuller, *Approaching the Benign Environment* (Macmillan, New York, 1970), Harold W. Helfrich, Jr., ed., *The Environmental Crisis* (Yale University Press, New Haven, Conn., 1970), and Sheldon Novick and Dorothy Cottrell, eds., *Our World in Peril: An Environment Review* (Fawcett, New York, 1971). Curti thoughtfully analyzes the postwar period as a time of moral and intellectual crisis in America.

The Declaration of Independence

When in the Course of human events, it becomes necessary for one people to dissolve the political bands which have connected them with another, and to assume among the Powers of the earth, the separate and equal station to which the Laws of Nature and of Nature's God entitle them, a decent respect to the opinions of mankind requires that they should declare the causes which impel them to the separation.

We hold these truths to be self-evident, that all men are created equal, that they are endowed by their Creator with certain unalienable Rights, that among these are Life, Liberty and the pursuit of Happiness. That to secure these rights, Governments are instituted among Men, deriving their just powers from the consent of the governed, That whenever any Form of Government becomes destructive of these ends, it is the Right of the People to alter or to abolish it, and to institute new Government, laying its foundation on such principles and organizing its powers in such form, as to them shall seem most likely to effect their Safety and Happiness. Prudence, indeed, will dictate that Governments long established should not be changed for light and transient causes; and accordingly all experience hath shown, that mankind are more disposed to suffer, while evils are sufferable, than to right themselves by abolishing the forms to which they are accustomed. But when a long train of abuses and usurpations, pursuing invariably the same Object evinces a design to reduce them under absolute Despotism, it is their right, it is their duty, to throw off such Government, and to provide new Guards for their future security.—Such has been the patient sufferance of these Colonies; and such is now the necessity which constrains them to alter their former Systems of Government. The history of the present King of Great Britain is a history of repeated injuries and usurpations, all having in direct object the establishment of an absolute Tyranny over these States. To prove this, let Facts be submitted to a candid world.

He has refused his Assent to Laws, the most wholesome and necessary for the public good.

He has forbidden his Governors to pass Laws of immediate and pressing importance, unless suspended in their operation till his Assent should be obtained; and when so suspended, he has utterly neglected to attend to them.

He has refused to pass other Laws for the accommodation of large districts of people, unless those people would relinquish the right of Representation in the Legislature, a right inestimable to them and formidable to tyrants only.

He has called together legislative bodies at places unusual, uncomfortable, and distant from the despository of their Public Records, for the sole purpose of fatiguing them into compliance with his measures.

He has dissolved Representative Houses repeatedly, for opposing with manly firmness his invasions on the rights of the people.

He has refused for a long time, after such dissolutions, to cause others to be elected; whereby the Legislative Powers, incapable of Annihilation, have returned to the People at large for their exercise; the State remaining in the mean time exposed to all the dangers of invasion from without, and convulsions within.

He has endeavoured to prevent the population of these States; for that purpose obstructing the Laws of Naturalization of Foreigners; refusing to pass others to encourage their migration hither, and raising the conditions of new Appropriations of Lands.

He has obstructed the Administration of Justice, by refusing his Assent to Laws for establishing Judiciary Powers.

He has made Judges dependent on his Will alone, for the tenure of their offices, and the amount and payment of their salaries.

He has erected a multitide of New Offices, and sent hither swarms of Officers to harass our People, and eat out their substance.

He has kept among us, in times of peace, Standing Armies without the Consent of our legislature.

He has affected to render the Military independent of and superior to the Civil Power.

He has combined with others to subject us to a jurisdiction foreign to our constitution, and unacknowledged by our laws; giving his Assent to their acts of pretended legislation:

For quartering large bodies of armed troops among us:

For protecting them, by a mock Trial, from Punishment for any Murders which they should commit on the Inhabitants of these States:

For cutting off our Trade with all parts of the world:

For imposing taxes on us without our Consent:

For depriving us in many cases, of the benefits of Trial by Jury:

For transporting us beyond Seas to be tried for pretended offences:

For abolishing the free System of English Laws in a neighbouring Province, establishing therein an Arbitrary government, and enlarging its Boundaries so as to render it at once an example and fit instrument for introducing the same absolute rule into these Colonies:

For taking away our Charters, abolishing our most valuable Laws, and altering fundamentally the Forms of our Governments:

For suspending our own Legislature, and declaring themselves invested with Power to legislate for us in all cases whatsoever.

He has abdicated Government here, by declaring us out of his Protection and waging War against us.

He has plundered our seas, ravaged our Coasts, burnt our towns, and destroyed the lives of our people.

He is at this time transporting large armies of foreign mercenaries to compleat the works of death, desolation and tyranny, already begun with circumstances of Cruelty & perfidy scarcely paralleled in the most barbarous ages, and totally unworthy the Head of a civilized nation.

He has constrained our fellow Citizens taken Captive on the high Seas to bear Arms against their Country, to become the executioners of their friends and Brethren, or to fall themselves by their Hands.

He has excited domestic insurrections amongst us, and has endeavoured to bring on the inhabitants of our frontiers, the merciless Indian Savages, whose known rule of warfare, is an undistinguished destruction of all ages, sexes and conditions.

In every stage of these Oppressions We have Petitioned for Redress in the most humble terms: Our repeated Petitions have been answered only by repeated injury. A Prince, whose character is thus marked by every act which may define a Tyrant, is unfit to be the ruler of a free People.

Nor have We been wanting in attention to our British brethren. We have warned them from time to time of attempts by their legislature to extend an unwarrantable jurisdiction over us. We have reminded them of the circumstances of our emigration and settlement here. We have appealed to their native justice and magnanimity, and we have conjured them by the ties of our common kindred to disavow these usurpations, which, would inevitably interrupt our connections and correspondence. They too have been deaf to the voice of justice and of consanguinity. We must, therefore, acquiesce in the necessity, which denounces our Separation, and hold them, as we hold the rest of mankind, Enemies in War, in Peace Friends.

We, therefore, the Representatives of the united States of America, in General Congress, Assembled, appealing to the Supreme Judge of the world for the rectitude of our intentions, do, in the Name, and by Authority of the good People of these Colonies, solemnly publish and declare, That these United Colonies are, and of Right ought to be Free and Independent States; that they are Absolved from all Allegiance to the British Crown, and that all political connection between them and the State of Great Britain, is and ought to be totally dissolved; and that as Free and Independent States, they have full Power to levy War, conclude Peace, contract Alliances, establish Commerce, and to do all other Acts and Things which Independent States may of right do. And for the support of this Declaration, with a firm reliance on the Protection of Divine Providence, we mutually pledge to each other our Lives, our Fortunes and our sacred Honor.

The Constitution of the United States

We the people of the United States, in Order to form a more perfect Union, establish Justice, insure domestic Tranquility, provide for the common defence, promote the general Welfare, and secure the Blessings of Liberty to ourselves and our Posterity, do ordain and establish this CONSTITUTION for the United States of America.

Section 1. All legislative Powers herein granted shall be vested in a Congress of the United States, which shall consist of a Senate and House of Representatives.

Section 2. The House of Representatives shall be composed of Members chosen every second Year by the People of the several States, and the Electors in each State shall have the Qualifications requisite for Electors of the most numerous Branch of the State Legislature.

No Person shall be a Representative who shall not have attained to the Age of twenty-five Years, and been seven Years a Citizen of the United States, and who shall not, when elected, be an Inhabitant of that State in which he shall be chosen.

Representatives and direct Taxes shall be apportioned among the several States which may be included within this Union, according to their respective Numbers, which shall be determined by adding to the whole Number of free Persons, including those bound to Service for a Term of Years, and excluding Indians not taxed, three fifths of all other Persons. The actual Enumeration shall be made within three Years after the first Meeting of the Congress of the United States, and within every subsequent Term of ten Years, in such Manner as they shall by Law direct. The Number of Representatives shall not exceed one for every thirty Thousand, but each State shall have at Least one Representative; and until such enumeration shall be made, the State of New Hampshire shall be entitled to chuse three, Massachusetts eight, Rhode-Island and Providence Plantations one, Connecticut five, New-York six, New Jersey four, Pennsylvania eight, Delaware one, Maryland six, Virginia ten, North Carolina five, South Carolina five, and Georgia three.

When vacancies happen in the Representation from any State, the Executive Authority thereof shall issue Writs of Election to fill such Vacancies.

The House of Representatives shall chuse their Speaker and other Officers; and shall have the sole Power of Impeachment.

Section 3. The Senate of the United States shall be composed of two Senators from each State, chosen by the Legislature thereof, for six Years; and each Senator shall have one Vote.

Immediately after they shall be assembled in Consequence of the first Election, they shall be divided as equally as may be into three Classes. The Seats of the Senators of the first Class shall be vacated at the Expiration of the second Year, of the second Class at the Expiration of the fourth Year, and of the third Class at the Expiration of the sixth Year, so that one-third may be chosen every second Year; and if Vacancies happen by Resignation, or otherwise, during the Recess of the Legislature of any State, the Executive thereof may make temporary Appointments until the next Meeting of the Legislature, which shall then fill such Vacancies.

No Person shall be a Senator who shall not have attained to the Age of thirty Years, and been nine Years a Citizen of the United States, and who shall not, when elected, be an Inhabitant of that State in which he shall be chosen.

The Vice President of the United States shall be President of the Senate, but shall have no vote, unless they be equally divided.

The Senate shall chuse their other Officers, and also a President pro tempore, in the absence of the Vice President, or when he shall exercise the Office of the President of the United States.

The Senate shall have the sole Power to try all Impeachments. When sitting for that purpose, they shall be on Oath or Affirmation. When the President of the United States is tried, the Chief Justice shall preside: And no person shall be convicted without the Concurrence of two thirds of the Members present.

Judgment in Cases of Impeachment shall not extend further than to removal from Office, and disqualification to hold and enjoy any Office of honor, Trust, or Profit under the United States: but the Party convicted shall nevertheless be liable and subject to Indictment, Trial, Judgment, and Punishment, according to Law.

Section 4.   The Times, Places and Manner of holding Elections for Senators and Representatives, shall be prescribed in each state by the Legislature thereof; but the Congress may at any time by Law make or alter such Regulations, except as to the Places of Chusing Senators.

The Congress shall assemble at least once in every Year, and such Meeting shall be on the first Monday in December, unless they shall by Law appoint a different Day.

Section 5.   Each House shall be the Judge of the Elections, Returns and Qualifications of its own Members, and a Majority of each shall constitute a Quorum to do Business; but a smaller number may adjourn from day to day, and may be authorized to compel the Attendance of absent Members, in such Manner, and under such Penalties, as each House may provide.

Each House may determine the Rules of its Proceedings, punish its Members for disorderly Behavior, and, with the Concurrence of two thirds, expel a Member.

Each House shall keep a Journal of its Proceedings, and from time to time publish the same, excepting such Parts as may in their Judgment require Secrecy; and the Yeas and Nays of the Members of either House on any question shall, at the Desire of one fifth of those Present, be entered on the Journal.

Neither House, during the Session of Congress, shall, without the Consent of the other, adjourn for more than three days, nor to any other Place than that in which the two Houses shall be sitting.

Section 6.   The Senators and Representatives shall receive a Compensation for their Services, to be ascertained by Law, and paid out of the Treasury of the United States. They shall in all Cases, except Treason, Felony, and Breach of the Peace, be privileged from Arrest during their Attendance at the Session of their respective Houses, and in going to and returning from the same; and for any Speech or Debate in either House, they shall not be questioned in any other Place.

No Senator or Representative shall, during the Time for which he was elected, be appointed to any civil Office under the Authority of the United States, which shall have been created, or the Emoluments whereof shall have been increased, during such time; and no Person holding any Office under the United States shall be a Member of either House during his continuance in Office.

Section 7.   All Bills for raising Revenue shall originate in the House of Representatives; but the Senate may propose or concur with Amendments as on other bills.

Every Bill which shall have passed the House of Representatives and the Senate, shall, before it become a Law, be presented to the President of the United States; If he approve he shall sign it, but if not he shall return it, with his Objections, to that House in which it shall have originated, who shall enter the Objections at large on their Journal, and proceed to reconsider it. If after such Consideration two thirds of that House shall agree to pass the bill, it shall be sent, together with the objections, to the other House, by which it shall likewise be reconsidered, and if approved by two thirds of that House, it shall become a Law. But in all such Cases the Votes of both Houses shall be determined by Yeas and Nays, and the Names of the Persons voting for and against the Bill shall be entered on the Journal of each House respectively. If any Bill shall not be returned by the President within ten Days (Sundays excepted) after it shall have been presented to him, the Same shall be a Law, in like Manner as if he had signed it, unless the Congress by their Adjournment prevent its Return, in which Case it shall not be a Law.

Every Order, Resolution, or vote to which the Concurrence of the Senate and House of Representatives may be necessary (except on a question of Adjournment) shall be presented to the President of the United States; and before the Same shall take Effect, shall be approved by him, or being disapproved by him, shall be repassed by two thirds of the Senate and House of Representatives, according to the Rules and Limitations prescribed in the Case of a Bill.

Section 8. The Congress shall have Power To lay and collect Taxes, Duties, Imposts and Excises, to pay the Debts and provide for the common Defence and general Welfare of the United States; but all Duties, Imposts and Excises shall be uniform throughout the United States.

To borrow money on the credit of the United States;

To regulate Commerce with foreign Nations, and among the several States, and with the Indian Tribes;

To establish an uniform Rule of Naturalization, and uniform Laws on the subject of Bankruptcies throughout the United States;

To coin Money, regulate the Value thereof, and of foreign Coin, and fix the Standard of Weights and Measures;

To provide for the Punishment of counterfeiting the Securities and current Coin of the United States;

To establish Post Offices and post Roads;

To promote the Progress of Science and useful Arts, by securing for limited Times to Authors and Inventors the exclusive Right to their respective Writings and Discoveries;

To constitute Tribunals inferior to the Supreme Court;

To define and punish Piracies and Felonies committed on the high Seas, and Offences against the Law of Nations;

To declare War, grant Letters of Marque and Reprisal, and make Rules concerning Captures on Land and Water;

To raise and support Armies, but no Appropriation of Money to that Use shall be for a longer Term than two Years;

To provide and maintain a Navy;

To make Rules for the Government and Regulation of the land and naval forces;

To provide for calling forth the Militia to execute the Laws of the Union, suppress Insurrections and repel Invasions;

To provide for organizing, arming, and disciplining the Militia, and for governing such Part of them as may be employed in the Service of the United States, reserving to the States respectively, the Appointment of the Officers, and the Authority of training the Militia according to the discipline prescribed by Congress;

To exercise exclusive Legislation in all Cases whatsoever, over such District (not exceeding ten Miles square) as may, by Cession of particular States, and the acceptance of Congress, become the Seat of Government of the United States, and to exercise like Authority over all Places purchased by the Consent of the Legislature of the State in which the Same shall be, for the Erection of Forts, Magazines, Arsenals, dock-Yards, and other needful Buildings;—And

To make all Laws which shall be necessary and proper for carrying into Execution the foregoing Powers, and all other Powers vested by this Constitution in the Government of the United States, or in any Department or Officer thereof.

Section 9. The Migration or Importation of such Persons as any of the States now existing shall think proper to admit, shall not be prohibited by the Congress prior to the Year one thousand eight hundred and eight, but a tax or duty may be imposed on such Importation, not exceeding ten dollars for each Person.

The privilege of the Writ of Habeas Corpus shall not be suspended, unless when in Cases of Rebellion or Invasion the public Safety may require it.

No Bill of Attainder or ex post facto Law shall be passed.

No capitation, or other direct, Tax shall be laid unless in Proportion to the Census or Enumeration herein before directed to be taken.

No Tax or Duty shall be laid on Articles exported from any State.

No Preference shall be given by any Regulation of Revenue to the Ports of one State over those of another: nor shall Vessels bound to, or from, one State, be obliged to enter, clear, or pay Duties in another.

No Money shall be drawn from the Treasury, but in Consequence of Appropriations made by Law; and a regular Statement and Account of the Receipts and Expenditures of all public Money shall be published from time to time.

No Title of Nobility shall be granted by the United States: And no Person holding any Office of Profit or Trust under them, shall, without the Consent of the Congress, accept of any present, Emolument, Office, or Title, of any kind whatever, from any King, Prince, or foreign State.

Section 10.   No state shall enter into any Treaty, Alliance, or Confederation; grant Letters of Marque and Reprisal; coin Money; emit Bills of Credit; make any Thing but gold and silver Coin a Tender in Payment of Debts; pass any Bill of Attainder, ex post facto Law, or Law impairing the Obligation of Contracts, or grant any Title of Nobility.

No State shall, without the Consent of the Congress, lay any Imposts or Duties on Imports or Exports, except what may be absolutely necessary for executing its inspection Laws: and the net Produce of all Duties and Imposts, laid by any State on Imports or Exports, shall be for the Use of the Treasury of the United States; and all such Laws shall be subject to the Revision and Control of the Congress.

No State shall, without the Consent of Congress, lay any duty of Tonnage, keep Troops, or Ships of War in time of Peace, enter into any Agreement or Compact with another State, or with a foreign Power, or engage in War, unless actually invaded, or in such imminent Danger as will not admit of delay.

ARTICLE II

Section 1.   The executive Power shall be vested in a President of the United States of America. He shall hold his Office during the Term of four years, and, together with the Vice-President, chosen for the same Term, be elected, as follows:

Each State shall appoint, in such Manner as the Legislature thereof may direct, a Number of Electors, equal to the whole Number of Senators and Representatives to which the State may be entitled in the Congress; but no Senator or Representative, or Person holding an Office of Trust or Profit under the United States, shall be appointed an Elector.

The Electors shall meet in their respective States, and vote by Ballot for two persons, of whom one at least shall not be an Inhabitant of the same State with themselves. And they shall make a List of all the Persons voted for, and of the Number of Votes for each; which List they shall sign and certify, and transmit sealed to the Seat of the Government of the United States, directed to the President of the Senate. The President of the Senate shall, in the Presence of the Senate and House of Representatives, open all the Certificates, and the Votes shall then be counted. The Person having the greatest Number of Votes shall be the President, if such Number be a Majority of the whole Number of Electors appointed; and if there be more than one who have such Majority, and have an equal Number of Votes, then the House of Representatives shall immediately chuse by Ballot one of them for President; and if no Person have a Majority, then from the five highest on the List the said House shall in like Manner chuse the President. But in chusing the President, the Votes shall be taken by States, the Representation from each State having one Vote; a quorum for this Purpose shall consist of a Member or Members from two-thirds of the States, and a Majority of all the States shall be necessary to a Choice. In every Case, after the Choice of the President, the Person having the greatest Number of Votes of the Electors shall be the Vice President. But if there should remain two or more who have equal votes, the Senate shall chuse from them by Ballot the Vice-President.

The Congress may determine the Time of chusing the Electors, and the Day on which they shall give their Votes; which Day shall be the same throughout the United States.

No person except a natural-born Citizen, or a Citizen of the United States, at the time of the Adoption of this Constitution, shall be eligible to the Office of President; neither shall any Person be eligible to that Office who shall not have attained to the Age of thirty-five years, and been fourteen Years a Resident within the United States.

In Case of the Removal of the President from Office, or of his Death, Resignation, or Inability to discharge the Powers and Duties of the said Office, the same shall devolve on the Vice President, and the Congress may by Law provide for the Case of Removal, Death, Resignation, or Inability, both of the President and Vice President, declaring what Officer shall then act as President, and such Officer shall act accordingly, until the disability be removed, or a President shall be elected.

The President shall, at stated Times, receive for his Services a Compensation, which shall neither be increased nor diminished during the Period for which he shall have been elected, and he shall not receive within that Period any other Emolument from the United States, or any of them.

Before he enter on the execution of his Office, he shall take the following Oath or Affirmation:—"I do solemnly swear (or affirm) that I will faithfully execute the Office of President of the United States, and will, to the best of my Ability, preserve, protect, and defend the Constitution of the United States."

Section 2. The President shall be Commander in Chief of the Army and Navy of the United States, and of the Militia of the several States, when called into the actual Service of the United States; he may require the Opinion, in writing, of the principal Officer in each of the executive Departments, upon any subject relating to the Duties of their respective Offices, and he shall have Power to Grant Reprieves and Pardons for Offences against the United States, except in Cases of Impeachment.

He shall have Power, by and with the Advice and Consent of the Senate, to make Treaties, provided two thirds of the Senators present concur; and he shall nominate, and by and with the Advice and Consent of the Senate, shall appoint Ambassadors, other public Ministers and Consuls, Judges of the supreme Court, and all other Officers of the United States, whose Appointments are not herein otherwise provided for, and which shall be established by Law: but the Congress may by Law vest the Appointment of such inferior Officers, as they think proper, in the President alone, in the Courts of Law, or in the Heads of Departments.

The President shall have Power to fill up all Vacancies that may happen during the Recess of the Senate, by granting Commissions which shall expire at the End of their next Session.

Section 3. He shall from time to time give to the Congress Information of the State of the Union, and recommend to their Consideration such Measures as he shall judge necessary and expedient; he may, on extraordinary occasions, convene both Houses, or either of them, and in Case of Disagreement between them, with respect to the Time of Adjournment, he may adjourn them to such Time as he shall think proper; he shall receive Ambassadors and other public Ministers; he shall take Care that the Laws be faithfully executed, and shall Commission all the Officers of the United States.

Section 4. The President, Vice President and all civil Officers of the United States, shall be removed from Office on Impeachment for, and Conviction of, Treason, Bribery, or other high crimes and Misdemeanors.

ARTICLE III

Section 1.   The judicial Power of the United States, shall be vested in one supreme Court, and in such inferior Courts as the Congress may from time to time ordain and establish. The Judges, both of the supreme and inferior Courts, shall hold their Offices during good Behaviour, and shall, at stated Times, receive for their Services, a Compensation, which shall not be diminished during their Continuance in Office.

Section 2.   The judicial Power shall extend to all Cases, in Law and Equity, arising under this Constitution, the Laws of the United States, and treaties made, or which shall be made, under their Authority;—to all Cases affecting ambassadors, other public ministers and consuls;—to all cases of admiralty and maritime Jurisdiction;—to Controversies to which the United States shall be a Party;—to Controversies between two or more States;—between a State and Citizens of another State;—between Citizens of different States,—between Citizens of the same State claiming Lands under Grants of different States, and between a State, or the Citizens thereof, and foreign States, Citizens or Subjects.

In all Cases affecting Ambassadors, other public Ministers and Consuls, and those in which a State shall be Party, the supreme Court shall have original Jurisdiction. In all the other Cases before mentioned, the supreme Court shall have appellate Jurisdiction, both as to Law and Fact, with such Exceptions, and under such Regulations as the Congress shall make.

The trial of all Crimes, except in Cases of Impeachment, shall be by Jury; and such Trial shall be held in the State where the said Crimes shall have been committed; but when not committed within any State, the Trial shall be at such Place or Places as the Congress may by Law have directed.

Section 3.   Treason against the United States, shall consist only in levying War against them, or in adhering to their Enemies, giving them Aid and Comfort. No Person shall be convicted of Treason unless on the Testimony of two Witnesses to the same overt Act, or on Confession in open Court.

The Congress shall have power to declare the Punishment of Treason, but no Attainder of Treason shall work Corruption of Blood, or Forfeiture except during the Life of the Person attainted.

ARTICLE IV

Section 1.   Full Faith and Credit shall be given in each State to the public Acts, Records, and judicial Proceedings of every other State. And the Congress may by general Laws prescribe the Manner in which such Acts, Records, and Proceedings shall be proved, and the Effect thereof.

Section 2.   The Citizens of each State shall be entitled to all Privileges and Immunities of Citizens in the several States.

A Person charged in any State with Treason, Felony, or other Crime, who shall flee from Justice, and be found in another State, shall on demand of the executive Authority of the State from which he fled, be delivered up, to be removed to the State having Jurisdiction of the crime.

No Person held to Service or Labour in one State, under the Laws thereof, escaping into another, shall, in Consequence of any Law or Regulation therein, be discharged from such Service or Labour, but shall be delivered up on Claim of the Party to whom such Service or Labour may be due.

Section 3.   New States may be admitted by the Congress into this Union; but no new State shall be formed or erected within the Jurisdiction of any other State; nor any State be formed by the Junction of two or more States, or parts of States, without the Consent of the Legislatures of the States concerned as well as of the Congress.

The Congress shall have Power to dispose of and make all needful Rules and Regulations respecting the Territory or other Property belonging to the United States; and nothing in this

Constitution shall be so construed as to Prejudice any Claims of the United States, or of any particular State.

Section 4.   The United States shall guarantee to every State in this Union a Republican Form of Government, and shall protect each of them against Invasion; and on Application of the Legislature, or the Executive (when the Legislature cannot be convened) against domestic Violence.

ARTICLE V

The Congress, whenever two-thirds of both Houses shall deem it necessary, shall propose Amendments to this Constitution, or, on the Application of the Legislatures of two-thirds of the several States, shall call a Convention for proposing Amendments, which, in either Case, shall be valid to all Intents and Purposes, as part of this Constitution, when ratified by the Legislatures of three-fourths of the several States, or by Conventions in three-fourths thereof, as the one or the other Mode of Ratification may be proposed by the Congress; Provided that no Amendment which may be made prior to the Year One thousand eight hundred and eight shall in any Manner affect the first and fourth Clauses in the Ninth Section of the first Article; and that no State, without its Consent, shall be deprived of its equal Suffrage in the Senate.

ARTICLE VI

All Debts contracted and Engagements entered into, before the Adoption of this Constitution, shall be as valid against the United States under this Constitution, as under the Confederation.

This Constitution, and the Laws of the United States which shall be made in Pursuance thereof; and all Treaties made, or which shall be made, under the Authority of the United States, shall be the supreme Law of the Land; and the Judges in every State shall be bound thereby, any Thing in the Constitution or Laws of any State to the Contrary notwithstanding.

The Senators and Representatives before mentioned, and the Members of the several State Legislatures, and all executive and judicial Officers, both of the United States and of the several States, shall be bound by Oath or Affirmation to support this Constitution; but no religious Test shall ever be required as a qualification to any Office or public Trust under the United States.

ARTICLE VII

The Ratification of the Conventions of nine States shall be sufficient for the Establishment of this Constitution between the States so ratifying the same.

Done in Convention by the Unanimous Consent of the States present the Seventeenth Day of September in the Year of our Lord one thousand seven hundred and Eighty seven, and of the Independence of the United States of America the Twelfth. In Witness whereof We have hereunto subscribed our Names.

Articles in Addition to, and Amendment of, the Constitution of the United States of America, Proposed by Congress, and Ratified by the Legislatures of the Several States, Pursuant to the Fifth Article of the Original Constitution.

AMENDMENT I [1791]

Congress shall make no law respecting an establishment of religion, or prohibiting the free exercise thereof; or abridging the freedom of speech, or of the press; or the right of the people peaceably to assemble, and to petition the Government for a redress of grievances.

AMENDMENT II [1791]

A well regulated Militia, being necessary to the security of a free State, the right of the people to keep and bear Arms shall not be infringed.

AMENDMENT III [1791]

No Soldier shall, in time of peace, be quartered in any house, without the consent of the Owner, nor in time of war, but in a manner to be prescribed by law.

AMENDMENT IV [1791]

The right of the people to be secure in their persons, houses, papers, and effects, against unreasonable searches and seizures, shall not be violated, and no Warrants shall issue, but upon probable cause, supported by Oath or affirmation, and particularly describing the place to be searched, and the persons or things to be seized.

AMENDMENT V [1791]

No person shall be held to answer for a capital or otherwise infamous crime, unless on a presentment or indictment of a Grand Jury, except in cases arising in the land or naval forces, or in the Militia, when in actual service in time of War or public danger; nor shall any person be subject for the same offence to be twice put in jeopardy of life or limb; nor shall be compelled in any criminal case to be a witness against himself, nor be deprived of life, liberty, or property, without due process of law; nor shall private property be taken for public use, without just compensation.

AMENDMENT VI [1791]

In all criminal prosecutions, the accused shall enjoy the right to a speedy and public trial, by an impartial jury of the State and district wherein the crime shall have been committed, which district shall have been previously ascertained by law, and to be informed of the nature and cause of the accusation; to be confronted with the witnesses against him; to have compulsory process for obtaining witnesses in his favor, and to have the Assistance of Counsel for his defence.

AMENDMENT VII [1791]

In suits at common law, where the value in controversy shall exceed twenty dollars, the right of trial by jury shall be preserved, and no fact tried by a jury, shall be otherwise reexamined in any Court of the United States, than according to the rules of the common law.

AMENDMENT VIII [1791]

Excessive bail shall not be required, nor excessive fines imposed, nor cruel and unusual punishments inflicted.

AMENDMENT IX [1791]

The enumeration in the Constitution, of certain rights, shall not be construed to deny or disparage others retained by the people.

AMENDMENT X [1791]

The powers not delegated to the United States by the Constitution, nor prohibited by it to the States, are reserved to the States respectively, or to the people.

AMENDMENT XI [1798]

The Judicial power of the United States shall not be construed to extend to any suit in law or equity, commenced or prosecuted against one of the United States by Citizens of another State, or by Citizens or Subjects of any Foreign State.

AMENDMENT XII [1804]

The Electors shall meet in their respective States and vote by ballot for President and

Vice-President, one of whom, at least, shall not be an inhabitant of the same State with themselves; they shall name in their ballots the person voted for as President, and in distinct ballots the person voted for as Vice-President, and they shall make distinct lists of all persons voted for as President, and of all persons voted for as Vice-President, and of the number of votes for each, which list they shall sign and certify, and transmit sealed to the seat of the government of the United States, directed to the President of the Senate;—The President of the Senate shall, in the presence of the Senate and House of Representatives, open all the certificates and the votes shall then be counted;—The person having the greatest number of votes for President, shall be the President, if such number be a majority of the whole number of Electors appointed; and if no person have such majority, then from the persons having the highest numbers not exceeding three on the list of those voted for as President, the House of Representatives shall choose immediately, by ballot, the President. But in choosing the President, the votes shall be taken by states, the representation from each state having one vote; a quorum for this purpose shall consist of a member or members from two-thirds of the states, and a majority of all the states shall be necessary to a choice. And if the House of Representatives shall not choose a President whenever the right of choice shall devolve upon them, before the fourth day of March next following, then the Vice-President shall act as President, as in the case of the death or other constitutional disability of the President.—The person having the greatest number of votes as Vice-President, shall be the Vice-President, if such number be a majority of the whole number of Electors appointed, and if no person have a majority, then from the two highest numbers on the list, the Senate shall choose the Vice-President; a quorum for the purpose shall consist of two-thirds of the whole number of Senators, and a majority of the whole number shall be necessary to a choice. But no person constitutionally ineligible to the office of President shall be eligible to that of Vice-President of the United States.

AMENDMENT XIII [1865]

Section 1.   Neither slavery nor involuntary servitude, except as a punishment for crime whereof the party shall have been duly convicted, shall exist within the United States, or any place subject to their jurisdiction.

Section 2.   Congress shall have power to enforce this article by appropriate legislation.

AMENDMENT XIV [1868]

Section 1.   All persons born or naturalized in the United States, and subject to the jurisdiction thereof, are citizens of the United States and of the State wherein they reside. No State shall make or enforce any law which shall abridge the privileges or immunities of citizens of the United States; nor shall any State deprive any person of life, liberty, or property, without due process of law; nor deny to any person within its jurisdiction the equal protection of the laws.

Section 2.   Representatives shall be apportioned among the several States according to their respective numbers, counting the whole number of persons in each State, excluding Indians not taxed. But when the right to vote at any election for the choice of electors for President and Vice-President of the United States, Representatives in Congress, the Executive and Judicial officers of a State, or the members of the Legislature thereof, is denied to any of the male inhabitants of such State, being twenty-one years of age, and citizens of the United States, or in any way abridged, except for participation in rebellion, or other crime, the basis of representation therein shall be reduced in the proportion which the number of such male citizens shall bear to the whole number of male citizens twenty-one years of age in such State.

Section 3.   No person shall be a Senator or Representative in Congress, or elector of President and Vice-President, or hold any office, civil or military, under the United States, or under any State, who, having previously taken an oath, as a member of Congress, or as an officer of the United States, or as a member of any State legislature, or as an executive or judicial officer of any State, to support the Constitution of the United States, shall have engaged in insurrection or rebellion against the same, or given aid or comfort to the enemies thereof. But Congress may by a vote of two-thirds of each House, remove such disability.

Section 4.   The validity of the public debt of the United States, authorized by law, including debts incurred for payment of pensions and bounties for services in suppressing insurrection or rebellion, shall not be questioned. But neither the United States nor any State shall assume or pay any debt or obligation incurred in aid of insurrection or rebellion against the United States, or any claim for the loss or emancipation of any slave; but all such debts, obligations, and claims shall be held illegal and void.

Section 5.   The Congress shall have the power to enforce, by appropriate legislation, the provisions of this article.

AMENDMENT XV [1870]

Section 1.   The right of citizens of the United States to vote shall not be denied or abridged by the United States or by any State on account of race, color, or previous condition of servitude.

Section 2.   The Congress shall have power to enforce this article by appropriate legislation.

AMENDMENT XVI [1913]

The Congress shall have power to lay and collect taxes on incomes, from whatever source derived, without apportionment among the several States, and without regard to any census or enumeration.

AMENDMENT XVII [1913]

The Senate of the United States shall be composed of two Senators from each State, elected by the people thereof, for six years; and each Senator shall have one vote. The electors in each State shall have the qualifications requisite for electors of the most numerous branch of the State legislatures.

When vacancies happen in the representation of any State in the Senate, the executive authority of such State shall issue writs of election to fill such vacancies: *Provided,* That the legislature of any State may empower the executive thereof to make temporary appointments until the people fill the vacancies by election as the legislature may direct.

This amendment shall not be so construed as to affect the election or term of any Senator chosen before it becomes valid as part of the Constitution.

AMENDMENT XVIII [1919]

Section 1.   After one year from the ratification of this article the manufacture, sale, or transportation of intoxicating liquors within, the importation thereof into, or the exportation thereof from the United States and all territory subject to the jurisdiction thereof for beverage purposes is hereby prohibited.

Section 2.   The Congress and the several States shall have concurrent power to enforce this article by appropriate legislation.

Section 3.   This article shall be inoperative unless it shall have been ratified as an amendment to the Constitution by the legislatures of the several States, as provided in the Constitution, within seven years from the date of the submission hereof to the States by the Congress.

AMENDMENT XIX [1920]

The right of citizens of the United States to vote shall not be denied or abridged by the United States or by any State on account of sex.

Congress shall have power to enforce this article by appropriate legislation.

AMENDMENT XX [1933]

Section 1. The terms of the President and Vice-President shall end at noon on the 20th day of January, and the terms of Senators and Representatives at noon on the 3d day of January, of the years in which such terms would have ended if this article had not been ratified; and the terms of their successors shall then begin.

Section 2. The Congress shall assemble at least once in every year, and such meeting shall begin at noon on the 3d day of January, unless they shall by law appoint a different day.

Section 3. If, at the time fixed for the beginning of the term of the President, the President elect shall have died, the Vice-President elect shall become President. If a President shall not have been chosen before the time fixed for the beginning of his term, or if the President elect shall have failed to qualify, then the Vice-President elect shall act as President until a President shall have qualified; and the Congress may by law provide for the case wherein neither a President elect nor a Vice-President elect shall have qualified, declaring who shall then act as President, or the manner in which one who is to act shall be selected, and such person shall act accordingly until a President or Vice-President shall have qualified.

Section 4. The Congress may by law provide for the case of the death of any of the persons from whom the House of Representatives may choose a President whenever the right of choice shall have devolved upon them, and for the case of the death of any of the persons from whom the Senate may choose a Vice-President whenever the right of choice shall have devolved upon them.

Section 5. Sections 1 and 2 shall take effect on the 15th day of October following the ratification of this article.

Section 6. This article shall be inoperative unless it shall have been ratified as an amendment to the Constitution by the legislatures of three-fourths of the several States within seven years from the date of its submission.

AMENDMENT XXI [1933]

Section 1. The eighteenth article of amendment to the Constitution of the United States is hereby repealed.

Section 2. The transportation or importation into any State, Territory, or possession of the United States for delivery or use therein of intoxicating liquors, in violation of the laws thereof, is hereby prohibited.

Section 3. This article shall be inoperative unless it shall have been ratified as an amendment to the Constitution by conventions in the several States, as provided in the Constitution, within seven years from the date of the submission hereof to the States by the Congress.

AMENDMENT XXII [1951]

No person shall be elected to the office of the President more than twice, and no person who has held the office of President, or acted as President, for more than two years of a term to which some other person was elected President shall be elected to the office of the President more than once.

But this Article shall not apply to any person holding the office of President when this Article was proposed by the Congress, and shall not prevent any person who may be holding the office of President, or acting as President, during the term within which this Article becomes operative from holding the office of President or acting as President during the remainder of such term.

AMENDMENT XXIII [1961]

Section 1. The District constituting the seat of Government of the United States shall appoint in such manner as the Congress may direct:

A number of electors of President and Vice President equal to the whole number of Senators and Representatives in Congress to which the District would be entitled if it were a State, but in no event more than the least populous State; they shall be in addition to those appointed by the States, but they shall be considered, for the purposes of the election of President and Vice President, to be electors appointed by a State; and they shall meet in the District and perform such duties as provided by the twelfth article of amendment.

Section 2. The Congress shall have the power to enforce this article by appropriate legislation.

AMENDMENT XXIV [1964]

Section 1. The right of citizens of the United States to vote in any primary or other election for President or Vice President, for electors for President or Vice President, or for Senator or Representative in Congress, shall not be denied or abridged by the United States or any State by reason of failure to pay any poll tax or other tax.

Section 2. The Congress shall have the power to enforce this article by appropriate legislation.

AMENDMENT XXV [1967]

Section 1. In case of the removal of the President from office or his death or resignation, the Vice President shall become President.

Section 2. Whenever there is a vacancy in the office of the Vice President, the President shall nominate a Vice President who shall take the office upon confirmation by a majority vote of both houses of Congress.

Section 3. Whenever the President transmits to the President pro tempore of the Senate and the Speaker of the House of Representatives his written declaration that he is unable to discharge the powers and duties of his office, and until he transmits to them a written declaration to the contrary, such powers and duties shall be discharged by the Vice President as Acting President.

Section 4. Whenever the Vice President and a majority of either the principal officers of the executive departments, or of such other body as Congress may by law provide, transmit to the President pro tempore of the Senate and the Speaker of the House of Representatives their written declaration that the President is unable to discharge the powers and duties of his office, the Vice President shall immediately assume the powers and duties of the office as Acting President.

Thereafter, when the President transmits to the President pro tempore of the Senate and the Speaker of the House of Representatives his written declaration that no inability exists, he shall resume the powers and duties of his office unless the Vice President and a majority of either the principal officers of the executive departments, or of such other body as Congress may by law provide, transmit within four days to the President pro tempore of the Senate and the Speaker of the House of Representatives their written declaration that the President is unable to discharge the powers and duties of his office. Thereupon Congress shall decide the issue, assembling within 48 hours for that purpose if not in session. If the Congress, within 21 days after receipt of the latter written declaration, or, if Congress is not in session, within 21 days after Congress is required to assemble, determines by two-thirds vote of both houses that the President is unable to discharge the powers and duties of his office, the Vice President shall continue to discharge the same as Acting President; otherwise, the President shall resume the powers and duties of his office.

AMENDMENT XXVI [1971]

Section 1. The right of citizens of the United States, who are eighteen years of age or older, to vote shall not be denied or abridged by the United States or by any State on account of age.

Section 2. The Congress shall have power to enforce this article by appropriate legislation.

Presidential Elections, 1789–1972

Year	Candidates	Party	Popular vote	Electoral vote	Percentage of popular vote
1789	**George Washington**	No party designations		69	
	John Adams			34	
	Minor Candidates			35	
1792	**George Washington**	No party designations		132	
	John Adams			77	
	George Clinton			50	
	Minor Candidates			5	
1796	**John Adams**	Federalist		71	
	Thomas Jefferson	Democratic-Republican		68	
	Thomas Pinckney	Federalist		59	
	Aaron Burr	Democratic-Republican		30	
	Minor Candidates			48	
1800	**Thomas Jefferson**	Democratic-Republican		73	
	Aaron Burr	Democratic-Republican		73	
	John Adams	Federalist		65	
	Charles C. Pinckney	Federalist		64	
	John Jay	Federalist		1	
1804	**Thomas Jefferson**	Democratic-Republican		162	
	Charles C. Pinckney	Federalist		14	
1808	**James Madison**	Democratic-Republican		122	
	Charles C. Pinckney	Federalist		47	
	George Clinton	Democratic-Republican		6	
1812	**James Madison**	Democratic-Republican		128	
	DeWitt Clinton	Federalist		89	
1816	**James Monroe**	Democratic-Republican		183	
	Rufus King	Federalist		34	
1820	**James Monroe**	Democratic-Republican		231	
	John Quincy Adams	Independent Republican		1	
1824	**John Quincy Adams**	Democratic-Republican	108,740	84	30.5
	Andrew Jackson	Democratic-Republican	153,544	99	43.1
	William H. Crawford	Democratic-Republican	46,618	41	13.1
	Henry Clay	Democratic-Republican	47,136	37	13.2
1828	**Andrew Jackson**	Democratic	647,286	178	56.0
	John Quincy Adams	National Republican	508,064	83	44.0
1832	**Andrew Jackson**	Democratic	687,502	219	55.0
	Henry Clay	National Republican	530,189	49	42.4
	William Wirt	Anti-Masonic	33,108	7	2.6
	John Floyd	National Republican		11	

The percentage of the popular vote for any given year may not total 100 percent since candidates who received less than 1 percent of the popular vote have been omitted.

Data from *Historical Statistics of the United States, Colonial Times to 1957* (1961), pp. 682–683, and *The Official Associated Press Almanac 1975*.

Year	Candidates	Party	Popular vote	Electoral vote	Percentage of popular vote
1836	**Martin Van Buren**	Democratic	**765,483**	**170**	**50.9**
	William H. Harrison	Whig		73	
	Hugh L. White	Whig		26	
	Daniel Webster	Whig	739,795	14	49.1
	W. P. Mangum	Whig		11	
1840	**William H. Harrison**	**Whig**	**1,274,624**	**234**	**53.1**
	Martin Van Buren	Democratic	1,127,781	60	46.9
1844	**James K. Polk**	**Democratic**	**1,338,464**	**170**	**49.6**
	Henry Clay	Whig	1,300,097	105	48.1
	James G. Birney	Liberty	62,300		2.3
1848	**Zachary Taylor**	**Whig**	**1,360,967**	**163**	**47.4**
	Lewis Cass	Democratic	1,222,342	127	42.5
	Martin Van Buren	Free Soil	291,263		10.1
1852	**Franklin Pierce**	**Democratic**	**1,601,117**	**254**	**50.9**
	Winfield Scott	Whig	1,385,453	42	44.1
	John P. Hale	Free Soil	155,825		5.0
1856	**James Buchanan**	**Democratic**	**1,832,955**	**174**	**45.3**
	John C. Frémont	Republican	1,339,932	114	33.1
	Millard Fillmore	American	871,731	8	21.6
1860	**Abraham Lincoln**	**Republican**	**1,865,593**	**180**	**39.8**
	Stephen A. Douglas	Democratic	1,382,713	12	29.5
	John C. Breckinridge	Democratic	848,356	72	18.1
	John Bell	Constitutional Union	592,906	39	12.6
1864	**Abraham Lincoln**	**Republican**	**2,206,938**	**212**	**55.0**
	George B. McClellan	Democratic	1,803,787	21	45.0
1868	**Ulysses S. Grant**	**Republican**	**3,013,421**	**214**	**52.7**
	Horatio Seymour	Democratic	2,706,829	80	47.3
1872	**Ulysses S. Grant**	**Republican**	**3,596,745**	**286**	**55.6**
	Horace Greeley	Democratic	2,843,446	66	43.9
1876	**Rutherford B. Hayes**	**Republican**	**4,036,572**	**185**	**48.0**
	Samuel J. Tilden	Democratic	4,284,020	184	51.0
1880	**James A. Garfield**	**Republican**	**4,453,295**	**214**	**48.5**
	Winfield S. Hancock	Democratic	4,414,082	155	48.1
	James B. Weaver	Greenback-Labor	308,578		3.4
1884	**Grover Cleveland**	**Democratic**	**4,879,507**	**219**	**48.5**
	James G. Blaine	Republican	4,850,293	182	48.2
	Benjamin F. Butler	Greenback–Labor	175,370		1.8
	John P. St. John	Prohibition	150,369		1.5
1888	**Benjamin Harrison**	**Republican**	**5,447,129**	**233**	**47.9**
	Grover Cleveland	Democratic	5,537,857	168	48.6
	Clinton B. Fish	Prohibition	249,506		2.2
	Anson J. Streeter	Union Labor	146,935		1.3
1892	**Grover Cleveland**	**Democratic**	**5,555,426**	**277**	**46.1**
	Benjamin Harrison	Republican	5,182,690	145	43.0
	James B. Weaver	People's	1,029,846	22	8.5
	John Bidwell	Prohibition	246,133		2.2

The percentage of the popular vote for any given year may not total 100 percent since candidates who received less than 1 percent of the popular vote have been omitted.

Year	Candidates	Party	Popular vote	Electoral vote	Percentage of popular vote
1896	**William McKinley**	**Republican**	**7,102,246**	**271**	**51.1**
	William J. Bryan	Democratic	6,492,559	176	47.7
1900	**William McKinley**	**Republican**	**7,218,491**	**292**	**51.7**
	William J. Bryan	**Democratic; Populist**	**6,356,734**	**155**	**45.5**
	John C. Wooley	**Prohibition**	**208,914**		**1.5**
1904	**Theodore Roosevelt**	**Republican**	**7,628,461**	**336**	**57.4**
	Alton B. Parker	Democratic	5,084,223	140	37.6
	Eugene V. Debs	Socialist	402,283		3.0
	Silas C. Swallow	Prohibition	258,536		1.9
1908	**William H. Taft**	**Republican**	**7,675,320**	**321**	**51.6**
	William J. Bryan	Democratic	6,412,294	162	43.1
	Eugene V. Debs	Socialist	420,793		2.8
	Eugene W. Chafin	Prohibition	253,840		1.7
1912	**Woodrow Wilson**	**Democratic**	**6,296,547**	**435**	**41.9**
	Theodore Roosevelt	Progressive	4,118,571	88	27.4
	William H. Taft	Republican	3,486,720	8	23.2
	Eugene V. Debs	Socialist	900,672		6.0
	Eugene W. Chafin	Prohibition	206,275		1.4
1916	**Woodrow Wilson**	**Democratic**	**9,127,695**	**277**	**49.4**
	Charles E. Hughes	Republican	8,533,507	254	46.2
	A. L. Benson	Socialist	585,113		3.2
	J. Frank Hanly	Prohibition	220,506		1.2
1920	**Warren G. Harding**	**Republican**	**16,143,407**	**404**	**60.4**
	James M. Cox	Democratic	9,130,328	127	34.2
	Eugene V. Debs	Socialist	919,799		3.4
	P. P. Christensen	Farmer-Labor	265,411		1.0
1924	**Calvin Coolidge**	**Republican**	**15,718,211**	**382**	**54.0**
	John W. Davis	Democratic	8,385,283	136	28.8
	Robert M. La Follette	Progressive	4,831,289	13	16.6
1928	**Herbert C. Hoover**	**Republican**	**21,391,993**	**444**	**58.2**
	Alfred E. Smith	Democratic	15,016,169	87	40.9
1932	**Franklin D. Roosevelt**	**Democratic**	**22,809,638**	**472**	**57.4**
	Herbert C. Hoover	Republican	15,758,901	59	39.7
	Norman Thomas	Socialist	881,951		2.2
1936	**Franklin D. Roosevelt**	**Democratic**	**27,752,869**	**523**	**60.8**
	Alfred M. Landon	Republican	16,674,665	8	36.5
	William Lemke	Union	882,479		1.9
1940	**Franklin D. Roosevelt**	**Democratic**	**27,307,819**	**449**	**54.8**
	Wendell L. Willkie	Republican	22,321,018	82	44.8
1944	**Franklin D. Roosevelt**	**Democratic**	**25,606,585**	**432**	**53.5**
	Thomas E. Dewey	Republican	22,014,745	99	46.0
1948	**Harry S. Truman**	**Democratic**	**24,105,812**	**303**	**49.5**
	Thomas E. Dewey	Republican	21,970,065	189	45.1
	J. Strom Thurmond	States' Rights	1,169,063	39	2.4
	Henry A. Wallace	Progressive	1,157,172		2.4
1952	**Dwight D. Eisenhower**	**Republican**	**33,936,234**	**442**	**55.1**
	Adlai E. Stevenson	Democratic	27,314,992	89	44.4

The percentage of the popular vote for any given year may not total 100 percent since candidates who received less than 1 percent of the popular vote have been omitted.

Year	Candidates	Party	Popular vote	Electoral vote	Percentage of popular vote
1956	**Dwight D. Eisenhower**	**Republican**	**35,590,472**	**457**	**57.6**
	Adlai E. Stevenson	Democratic	26,022,752	73	42.1
1960	**John F. Kennedy**	**Democratic**	**34,227,096**	**303**	**49.9**
	Richard M. Nixon	Republican	34,108,546	219	49.6
1964	**Lyndon B. Johnson**	**Democratic**	**43,126,506**	**486**	**61.1**
	Barry M. Goldwater	Republican	27,176,799	52	38.5
1968	**Richard M. Nixon**	**Republican**	**31,785,480**	**301**	**43.4**
	Hubert H. Humphrey	Democratic	31,275,165	191	42.7
	George C. Wallace	American Independent	9,906,473	46	13.5
1972	**Richard M. Nixon**	**Republican**	**47,167,319**	**521**	**60.7**
	George S. McGovern	Democratic	29,168,509	17	37.5
1974	**Gerald R. Ford**	**Republican**	Appointed as Vice President after Spiro T. Agnew resigned in 1973. Sworn in as President on August 9, 1974, after Richard M. Nixon resigned.		

The percentage of the popular vote for any given year may not total 100 percent since candidates who received less than 1 percent of the popular vote have been omitted.

ART CREDITS

page ii courtesy Union Pacific Railroad Company

pages 2–3 courtesy Union Pacific Railroad Company

Chapter 1
page 5 The New York Historical Society, New York City   page 10 Historical Pictures Service, Chicago   page 12 The Bettmann Archive   page 16 The New York Public Library   page 17 The Bettmann Archive   page 18 Culver Pictures   pages 20, 21 The Bettman Archive

Chapter 2
page 25 Brown Brothers   page 27 Constantine Manos, Magnum, from CRISIS IN AMERICA published by Ridge Press and Holt Rinehart & Winston   page 32 Brown Brothers   page 34 The Bettmann Archive   page 37 Historical Pictures Service, Chicago   page 39 Brown Brothers   page 40 The Bettmann Archive   pages 42, 43 Brown Brothers

Chapter 3
pages 51, 55, 59, 61 Brown Brothers   pages 64, 69 The Bettmann Archive

Chapter 4
page 76 Wide World Photos   page 78 Courtesy of History Division of Los Angeles County Museum of Natural History   page 80 U.S. Signal Corp, National Archives   page 86 Buffalo Bill Historical Center, Cody, Wyo.   page 90 The Bettmann Archive   page 94 Museum of the American Indian, Heye Foundation   pages 97, 101 The Bettmann Archive

Chapter 5
page 104 reproduced from collections in the Library of Congress   page 106 courtesy Union Pacific Railroad Company   page 110 Historical Pictures Service, Chicago   page 111 United Press International   page 113 The Granger Collection   pages 117, 121 Historical Pictures Service, Chicago   page 123 Byron Collection, Museum of the City of New York   pages 126, 127 Brown Brothers   page 129 Wide World Photos

Chapter 6
page 133 Brown Brothers   page 136 United Press International   page 141 The Bettmann Archive   page 148 Brown Brothers   page 153 Wide World Photos   pages 156, 158 The Bettmann Archive   page 159 Museum of Fine Arts, Boston   page 161 United Press International

Chapter 7
page 165 The Granger Collection   page 170 United Press International   pages 174, 179, 182, 186 The Bettmann Archive   pages 187, 190 United Press International   page 192 Historical Pictures Service, Chicago   page 193 Culver Pictures

pages 196–197 Ellis Herwig/Stock, Boston

Chapter 8
pages 199, 203 Brown Brothers   page 201 Redrawn by permission from THE AMERICAN HERITAGE PICTORIAL ATLAS OF UNITED STATES HISTORY, © 1966   pages 210, 212, 213 The Bettmann Archive   page 215 The Metropolitan Museum of Art, The Alfred Stieglitz Collection, 1949   page 218 Brown Brothers   page 221 The Bettmann Archive   page 223 United Press International   page 227 Culver Pictures   page 229 Brown Brothers

Chapter 9
page 232 Brown Brothers   page 234 Philadelphia Museum of Art, The Carl Zigrosser Collection   pages 237, 239 The Bettmann Archive   pages 242, 248 Dorothea Lange, Magnum   page 251 The Bettmann Archive   page 252 Museum of the American Indian, Heye Foundation   pages 257, 258 The Bettmann Archive

Chapter 10
page 263 United Press International   page 267 The Bettmann Archive   page 271 United Press International   page 273 Robert Capa, Magnum, courtesy LIFE Magazine   page 274 Brown Brothers   page 276 from UP-FRONT, drawing copyrighted 1944 by United Features Syndicate,

Inc., reproduced by courtesy of Bill Mauldin   page 279 Brown Brothers   page 285 Wide World Photos   page 290 The Bettmann Archive

Chapter 11
page 298 Burk Uzzle, Magnum   page 303 United Press International   pages 305, 306, 307 Wide World Photos   page 311 Hiroji Kubata, Magnum   page 314 Gerhard E. Gscheidle, Magnum   page 320 Eve Arnold, Magnum   page 322 Brown Brothers   page 323 Ernest Iiaccobucci, New York Times Pictures   page 324 Wide World Photos

Chapter 12
page 328 United Press International   page 330 Air Photo Co., Inc.   page 331 Santa Clara County Transportation Agency   page 334 Jean Claude Lejeune/Stock, Boston   page 337 Cliff Garboden/Stock, Boston   page 339 United Press International   page 341 NASA   page 344 Robert Motherwell, "Elegy to the Spanish Republic, 54" (1957–61), oil on canvas, 70" x 7'6¼" Collection the Museum of Modern Art, New York, given anonymously page 347 Peter Vandai, Editorial Photo Archives

Maps drawn by Dick Sanderson

Index

Abilene, Kansas, 83
Addams, Jane, 172, 219
Advertising, 210
Africa: Empire of, 222; allied landing in, 272; American investment in, 319
Agricultural Adjustment Act, 241
Agriculture, mechanization of, 89–91, 254. *See also* Crops; Farmers
Aiken, Conrad, 211
Airplane industry, 111
Alabama, segregation laws of, 325
Alaska: pipeline, 305; population of, 329
Alcatraz Island, Indian invasion of, 317
Alcohol: American Indians and, 99; and prohibition laws, 226, 227; during Great Depression, 249
Alderson, Nannie Tiffany, profile of, 101–102
Aleutian Islands, 270
Alger, Horatio, Jr., 104
Algren, Nelson, 345
Alienation, 345
Allied Powers, 181. *See also* World War II
Amalgamated Association of Iron and Steel Workers, 170
Amalgamated Clothing Workers, 65
America, *see* United States
America First Committee, 266
American Association for the Advancement of Science, 150, 255
American Council of Learned Societies, 216
American Emigrant Company, 56
American Farm Bureau Federation, 224
American Federation of Labor, 65, 168–169, 225; Jim Crow locals affiliated with, 33
American Historical Association, 74, 145
American Indian Defense Association, 252
American Indians, 177; culture of, 93; adaptability of, 95–97; reservations for, 98–99; population decline of, 99–100; New Deal and, 252; Americanization of, 253; death rate, 254; after World War II, 309; in 1970s, 314–317
Americanization, 74, 98; via classroom, 51; of immigrants, 142; in public schools, 216; of Indians, 253
American Medical Association, 225
American Protective Association, 68
American Telephone and Telegraph Company, 300
Amnesty, for ex-Confederates, 8
Amtrak system, 302
Anaconda Copper Company, 82
Anderson, Sherwood, 211
Anglo-Saxons, 68
Anthropologists, 153, 257, 275
Anti-Saloon League, 226

Antitrust laws, 226; and New Deal, 244. *See also* Business
Antiwar sentiment, 265–267; Vietnam war, 337
Apache Indians, 93; Mescalero, 317
Appalachian families, 301
Appomattox Courthouse, surrender at, 6
Arapaho Indians, 95
Architecture: brownstones, 126; and industrial growth, 158–160; in 1920s, 214; *See also* Dwellings
Argonne Forest, *190*
Arizona, Indians in, 317
Armed forces, racial segregation in, 289, 309. *See also* Military; Soldiers
Armour and Swift Meat Company, 112
Armstrong, Louis, 214
Armstrong, Gen. Samuel C., 44
Army-McCarthy hearings, *320*, 343
Arts: in urban environment, 154–160; of 1970s, 343, 344–346. *See also* Literature
Ashcan School, of painting, 160
Assimilation: forces of, 49–52. *See also* Immigration
Association for Improvement of Condition of Poor in New York, 128
Association for Study of Negro Life History, 224
Astor, William, 122
Astronauts, *341*
Astronomy, 255
Athletics, commercialized, 147. *See also* Sports
Atlanta Compromise speech, of B. T. Washington, 32–34
Atlantic Monthly, 156
Atlantic Ocean, control of, 272
Atomic bomb, 275, 278
Attitudes, 75; racial, 19; urban, 118; toward sex, 139; toward labor, 175; and Great Depression, 250; toward women's work, 285; of black Americans, 291; of 1970s, 343. *See also* Values
Automobile industry, 107, 200; mass production techniques in, *203;* and unions, 243
Automobiles, 125, *199*
Axis powers, 268. *See also* World War II

Bachelor's degrees, *145. See also* Colleges
Baer, George, 103
Balance of trade, 90
Baldwin, James, 343, 345
Baltimore and Ohio Railroad, strike on, 170
Baltimore-Fairfield shipyard, *271*
Banking Act, 245
Banking system: failure of, 234–236; centralization of, 245
Banks, 120; immigrants and, 60